Printed reference material and related sources of information

PRINTED REFERENCE MATERIAL
and related sources of information

THIRD EDITION

EDITED BY
PETER W. LEA

with

Alan Day

THE LIBRARY
ASSOCIATION
LONDON

© this compilation: Peter W. Lea and Alan Day
© the articles: the contributors

Published by
Library Association Publishing Ltd
7 Ridgmount Street
London WC1E 7AE

First edition 1980
Second edition 1984
Third edition 1990

British Library Cataloguing in Publication Data

Lea, Peter W.
    Printed reference material and related information
    sources. – 3rd ed.
    1. Reference books
    I. Title   II. Day, Alan
    011.02

    ISBN 1-85604-018-6 (cased)
    ISBN 0-85365-749-1 (paper)

Typeset in 11/12pt Baskerville by Library Association Publishing Ltd
Printed and made in Great Britain by Bookcraft (Bath) Ltd

To all students, past, present and future,
of the Department of Library and Information Studies,
Manchester Polytechnic.

'No bird soars too high if he soars with his own wings.'
William Blake

Contents

Contents

COMPILED BY SHELAGH M. FISHER
and ANTHONY J. OULTON

Contributors

ANGELA M. ALLOTT BA ALA
Librarian
Science and Technology Library
Sheffield City Libraries

ELIZABETH ANKER
British Official Publications Librarian
University of Warwick

C. PETER AUGER FLA
Information Consultant
Redditch
Worcester

KENNETH G. B. BAKEWELL MA MBIM MIInfSc FLA
Reader
School of Information Science and Technology
Liverpool Polytechnic

ALLAN J. BUNCH BA DMS MBIM ALA
Information Librarian
Cambridgeshire Libraries and Information Service

Contributors

ALAN DAY MA MPhil PhD DipLib FRGS FLA *Editor*

SHELAGH M. FISHER BA MPhil ALA
Senior Lecturer
Department of Library and Information Studies
Manchester Polytechnic

SUSAN FLEETWOOD BA ALA
Head of Business Information Department
City of Birmingham, Public Libraries Department

DENIS J. GROGAN BA FLA
Senior Lecturer
Department of Information and Library Studies
University College of Wales
Aberystwyth

JOHN GURNSEY FLA
Consultant
Bellingdon
Nr Chesham
Buckinghamshire

SUSAN V. HOWARD BA MSc DipLib ALA
Deputy Librarian
Birkbeck College, University of London

PETER W. LEA MLS ALA *Editor*
Senior Lecturer
Department of Library and Information Studies
Manchester Polytechnic

J. DAVID LEE FLA
Consultant
Harrow
Middlesex

BARRIE I. MACDONALD ALA
Librarian
Independent Broadcasting Authority

CHRIS E. MAKEPEACE BA ALA
Local Historian, Library and Information Consultant
Disley
Cheshire

VALERIE NURCOMBE BA ALA
Consultant
Winsford
Cheshire

ANTHONY J. OULTON MA MSc DipSocAnth ALA MIInfSc
Principal Lecturer
Department of Library and Information Studies
Manchester Polytechnic

FRANCES TAIT ALA
Library and Information Manager (West London) BBC
London

ANTHONY HUGH THOMPSON MA PhD FLA
Consultant
Aberystwyth

A. JOHN WALFORD MBE MA PhD FRHistS FLA
Editor, Walford's guide to reference material

KENNETH A. WHITTAKER MA FLA
Principal Lecturer
Department of Library and Information Studies
Manchester Polytechnic

HAZEL WOODWARD BA ALA
Senior Assistant Librarian
Pilkington Library
Loughborough University of Technology

Preface to the First Edition

The third (and final) edition of *Introduction to reference books*, by A. D. Roberts, appeared in 1956. First published in 1948, the book was written because the author considered that existing textbooks on the subject were badly out-of-date. The work was a great success, and I still have on my own shelves a copy of the first edition, which I bought in 1949 when I was a student.

The period since 1956 has been one of great significance in the field of librarianship in general, and in the area of information retrieval and dissemination in particular; it has, in fact, been the period of the 'information explosion', during which a vast amount of reference material has appeared for the first time. Many important and well-established items, which the reference librarian now takes for granted as being an integral part of his stock, had not appeared in print when Roberts produced his final text. Examples which spring to mind include *British technology index*; *Guinness book of records*; *McGraw-Hill encyclopedia of science and technology*; and *Who owns whom*.

A growing awareness of the need for effective library-based information services has resulted in the establishment of many new libraries, particularly in the fields of industry, commerce, and further education. The number of universities has increased and some 30 polytechnics have been created. To deal with the information explosion, many more librarians and information scientists have been needed; extra schools of librarianship have been formed, and larger annual intakes of students accepted. Finally, the Library Association's examinations have been largely replaced by degrees in librarianship, or by postgraduate diplomas in the subject.

In 1976, the Panel of Assessors of the Library Association concluded that there was a demonstrable need for a work which would effectively update Roberts. In producing this work, at their request, I have kept Roberts' framework in mind: due account has been taken, however, of subsequent developments such as online retrieval, and appropriate space has been allocated to conference proceedings, symposia, standard specifications, patents, reports, statistical materials and microforms.

The objective has been to provide, for students and researchers, recently appointed reference staff and practising librarians, working in small information units, with limited stocks, a practical handbook containing:

(a) some general remarks on reference materials, their evaluation and use;
(b) a consideration of the reference process, including general strategies for dealing with reference enquiries;
(c) a series of succinct chapters, each by an authoritative contributor, dealing with the various categories of reference material.

Each chapter normally consists of a short general/historical introduction, followed by brief descriptions and comparative critical evaluations of individual items, including those, where appropriate, in microform. It concludes with citations and references, numbered sequentially, as in the text, and with suggestions for further reading. It will be apparent that some contributors have provided these suggestions in the form of a narrative, while others have preferred to list items alphabetically and to add any necessary notes of explanation. Students should examine both methods and assess their respective merits and disadvantages. The discerning reader will notice that throughout the text there are variations in bibliographical presentation.

Although the British Standards Institution has published recommendations relating to bibliographical references (BS 1629: 1976), the librarian and the researcher will still encounter such variations; the opportunity has therefore been taken to provide examples in these chapters.

A work of this nature and length cannot, and should not, aim to be comprehensive; as its title states, it is intended to be a handbook: therefore it does not deal in depth with the literatures of special subject fields. Instead, it concentrates on categories of reference material. Fortunately, two excellent surveys of the literature are available – Walford's *Guide to reference material*, and Sheehy's *Guide to reference books*. The first edition of the British work by Dr Walford was still in the production stages in 1956; in contrast, the American work now edited by Sheehy was originally issued in 1902, and had respectively as its previous editors Alice Kroeger, Isadore Mudge, and Constance Winchell. The present work is in no way intended to duplicate Walford or Sheehy; wherever possible, students and practising librarians should use it in conjunction with one or both of the guides.

In general, a structured approach has been adopted in the writing of this book. There would be little point in presenting a detailed account of the value and contents of such a generally available work as *Whitaker's almanack*, since all of our readers should have access to it and be able to examine it for themselves. In deciding at what length to write on any particular item or kind of reference material, we have been guided by its relative importance, and by the extent to which it is likely to be available in small, medium or large reference systems; we have also taken into consideration the existence of other satisfactory accounts which the student can read to supplement our own description. Where possible, we have taken a first-rate, easily obtainable example and used this as a criterion against which other examples can be measured.

Finally, I should like to record my grateful thanks to all the contributors, who cheerfully accepted their allotted chapters – and met their deadlines!

May 1979   GAVIN HIGGENS

Preface to the Third Edition

The increasing trend in the availability of reference material from print to a range of other formats is acknowledged by use of an expanded title to this work for the first time. Indeed the momentum is so strong as possibly to justify a complete renaming to reflect this phenomenon. However, for the sake of continuity *Printed reference material* is retained as the working title.

The essential structure of the work also remains unchanged. This was formulated by our predecessor, Gavin Higgens, and his Preface to the First Edition should be consulted for a clear explanation of the genesis and organization of *PRM*.

We would like to thank our contributors both original and new for their sterling efforts in either rewriting or creating new chapters. We are particularly grateful to those who both followed the 'Guidelines to authors' assiduously and delivered their manuscripts on or before the deadline. Such cooperation is much appreciated by harassed editors. We would especially like to thank Elizabeth Anker for accepting a very late commission and delivering the goods on time.

Thanks are also due to the sub-editors of the first chapter, to David Lea for his 'contribution' of which he is very proud and Linda Myers for providing her exemplary keyboard skills.

The Editors would welcome any constructive criticism about

the contents of *PRM*, so that any future editions can provide a service which, in the best possible way, meets the needs of its users.

PETER W. LEA

July 1990

1

Introduction

Peter Lea

Librarians attempting to provide an up-to-date reference service face one inescapable problem: the built-in obsolescence of many of the tools of their trade. Often, publications are wholly or partly out-of-date before they are published, and even more so by the time they appear on library shelves, such is the rate of change in some subject areas. Unfortunately, there is no 'sell-by-date' on information presented in all good faith to library patrons. The unsuspecting enquirer, therefore, may be obtaining inaccurate data which could affect important decision-making. When this is discovered it will, at best, present the information service in an unfavourable light and, at worst, in fee-charging services, may even involve litigation for providing false information.

The reference librarian's task is certainly made no easier when libraries are forced, by economic constraints, into adopting policies whereby some annuals are replaced biennially, or even less frequently, in order to reduce the standing-order burden on limited budgets. Of course, the librarian will endeavour to keep sources as current as possible despite the difficulties, by careful editing, weeding out obsolete or redundant material and allocating funds prudently and wisely, so that new titles may enhance existing stock.

This latest edition of *Printed reference material* is designed to assist librarians in their constant struggle to optimize service with limited resources. As in previous editions, the contributors briefly describe and discuss the corpus of reference material that has appeared since 1984, or has been announced to appear. They also provide a structured evaluation of the main categories of such material, so that students and practising librarians alike will gain the necessary background information to aid selection and use of the sources described. An excellent rationale of *Printed reference material* is presented in the Preface to the First Edition written by Gavin Higgens. He also emphasizes the complementary nature of those stalwarts of the bibliographical world, *Walford's Guide to reference material*,[1] and Sheehy's *Guide to reference books*,[2] both of which are currently under revision.

Alert readers will have noticed that for the first time an expanded title has been used, but *Printed reference material* has been retained for both continuity and goodwill. A case could have been made for the replacement of the word 'Reference' with 'Information' in the main title, reflecting a discernable trend in public libraries during the past ten years where many libraries have discarded the traditional separate reference department staffed by specialists, for the integrated reference and lending information service. Although a commendable desire to improve the quality and effectiveness of the service provided has undoubtedly influenced this development, its direct cause may be more safely attributed to the urgent need to husband funds and to rationalize use of available staff. 'Information' was also a fashionable word of the 1980s and, as often happens, fashion prevails over expediency and sometimes over common sense. This change of emphasis has not been welcomed with total unanimity. Some of the arguments for and against this semantic distinction were summed up by McKee[3] and Duckett[4] in *Refer*, the journal of the Library Association Information Services Group (changed from *Reference*, Special and Information Services Group in 1986!). McKee's well-argued case promoted the use of information technology in libraries as a means of improving communication of information. He used a number of telling phrases which crystallize many of the concerns of the library profession today, referring to the off-putting 'building-based' services; the structural hierarchy creating barriers between staff and patrons and the lack of time spent communicating with patrons. The solution, he claimed, may be in the promotion of a community *information* service which would break down some of these barriers. Duckett responded with an equally well-constructed argument for the retention of the word 'reference' as opposed to 'information', as a term known and preferred by the public. He warned against too much reliance on information technology. Both authors came together in their assertion that there are barriers, both institutional and organizational, between librarians and patrons and that to succeed in communicating effectively these barriers must be overcome.

At the moment it seems probable that the bulk of reference material will appear in traditional printed form for many years to come. However, the editors acknowledge that the dominance of print will be eroded by other formats. No doubt future editions of *PRM* will reflect this inevitable trend but it is unlikely that the current title and sub-title will be reversed in the foreseeable future. Despite a number of predictions to the contrary, printed reference material will continue to appear in abundance, either as new editions or as new titles, when gaps in the market are identified.

There are a number of important changes in this edition, in addition to the inclusion of many new examples of information sources. Most of the chapters have been rewritten, some by their original contributors and others by new authors, most of whom are library practitioners. All are expert in their subject fields. In general, the familiar structure of chapters is retained: the scope, development and evaluation of a particular category of materials is first outlined before a more detailed inspection is made of significant individual titles.

Increasingly, reference works are becoming available in different formats: CD-ROM, microform, online, etc. With this in mind it has been decided to refer to these in the appropriate chapters, e.g. subject encyclopaedias will include print, online and CD-ROM versions for certain titles, thereby reinforcing the message that electronic publishing extends rather than supplants traditional print publishing. As a consequence the chapters 'Online Information-Retrieval Systems' and 'Viewdata Systems' in the previous edition have been replaced by a trenchant overview of electronic publishing with a survey of the directory sources available.

Two other totally new chapters make their appearance: 'Community Information' and 'Audio-Visual Sources'. The former qualifies as an important category of reference material reaching a market which up to a few years ago generally remained oblivious to public library services, simply because the ephemeral nature of much of its documentation failed to attract professional notice. 'Audio-Visual Sources' provides a salutary shock to those so besotted with print that they ignore the benefits of what the wide range of different hardware and software can offer.

To make room for these vital contributions an esteemed chapter from the previous edition regrettably has had to be omitted. However David Lee's 'Printed Visual Sources' remains an authoritative summary of a much neglected area, and can still be consulted as such.

It was decided to retain the chapter on 'Indexes', partly because of its uniqueness, and partly because a good understanding of this feature can allow more efficient use of many of the works dealt with elsewhere in this book. In any case, even in the days of 'glasnost', who would wish to offend an author with the initials K.G.B. before his name?

Periodicals, arguably, have experienced the greatest impact from electronic publishing in the past 30 years. With this in mind, the chapter dealing with this category of material has been completely rewritten with a greater emphasis on alternatives to printed versions.

Other changes to this edition include the merging of the chapters dealing with current and retrospective bibliographies into a single chapter and an extension of the scope of the chapter dealing with newspaper sources into more of a survey of current event sources.

A further important change resulted from one of the more significant developments in reference work during the past ten years, namely the growing emphasis on business and commercial information. Librarians are experiencing an increasing demand for this type of service both from the business community and from the public. A new chapter has been included which reflects this development describing the wide range of sources available to fulfil users' needs.

Two further casualties of the space war have been the chapters in the second edition which, respectively, set the scene and describe the reference process. Initially the editors intended to retain both chapters, but the imposition of an upper word limit required that this edition concern itself solely with materials and sources. There are, after all, a number of excellent works dealing with the fundamentals of the reference process such as Grogan[5] and Katz,[6] which together with Chapter 2 of the second edition of this work[7] provide much useful advice and guidance to the student or tyro reference librarian.

The editors felt, however, that mention must be made of one of the most significant aspects of the reference process prominent in recent professional literature. A number of investigations have been undertaken in the past few years examining the quality of answers given to library patrons during the reference transaction. Interest in this subject began in the 1960s but it seems that only relatively recently has the library profession begun to pay careful attention to the implications of such investigations. Unobtrusive studies, both formal and informal, carried out mainly in public but also in some academic libraries,[8] do not show reference services in a very good light, particularly with regard to the accuracy of answers to enquiries. This is just one area which has come under criticism. McClure and Hernon's[9] extensive list includes such critical comments as:

- staff members answer correctly a low percentage of test questions
- they infrequently engage in referral, either internal or external to the library
- the length of the search process does not increase the likelihood that a correct answer will be received
- the interpersonal communication skills of some library personnel are limited and these people can be abrasive in their dealings with the public
- staff fail to negotiate question

The chance of an enquirer receiving an accurate answer to a

reference question is about 50% and has been shown to be much lower at times.[10] When this percentage is translated into transactional figures the results provide alarming reading. It is estimated by the Library and Information Statistics Unit at Loughborough University of Technology that approximately 40 million enquiries are made each year in the public libraries of England and Wales. If half of the answers to these enquiries are wrong or only partially right, 20 million incorrect answers are being supplied to an unsuspecting public. There is little room for complacency here.

Some libraries have recognized the problem and are attempting to address it in a very positive way. In the United States, Baltimore County Public Library experienced the typically low percentage of correctness of answers in an unobtrusive test of their service. The organization which conducted the research also established two highly important facts from the study. Firstly, that technical factors such as the amount of reference stock available, the size of staff and business of the library did not affect reference performance as much as previously had been thought. Secondly, that communication behaviours, controllable by the librarian, were the main influence on improved reference service. A workshop was designed and a number of librarians were trained in the skills and processes which had been identified. Further unobtrusive tests showed a marked increase in the quality of answers given to library patrons; in one particular branch the percentage of accurate answers rose to 97.5%.[11]

The practice of good non-verbal behaviour was obviously an important feature of the training but the two key elements responsible for the marked increase in the success rate were firstly, verifying the question by paraphrasing or repeating it as understood by the librarian, to ensure that the search was starting from the right premise and secondly, asking a follow-up question at the end of the transaction, using a phrase such as 'Does this completely answer your question?' These simple, yet essential stages of the reference interview had a huge effect on the quality of answers provided. Other factors such as the ability to listen constructively, not jump to conclusions, to develop the ability to ask 'open' and 'closed' questions at appropriate times were also recognized as contributory factors to the success of the transaction. The latter when correctly employed can often elicit useful information from a patron reluctant or unable to offer it too readily. 'Open' questions such as 'Which sections do you wish to use, could you please give me more details, what kind of information . . .?' give rise to a wide range of possible answers, shifting the responsibility to the patron to specify his requirements, and therefore encourage more than a one-word answer. On the other hand, 'closed' questions often encourage one-word answers, thus requiring further questioning to obtain more information. They do have a specific use at appropriate points in the reference interview, to verify choice or possibly conclude the transaction, but provide less opportunity to elaborate than 'open' questions and are therefore used more sparingly.

The Baltimore programme includes nothing which is either new or unique to reference librarians, no matter where they practise. Of much more significance is the structure of the interview and the formalized training programme adopted after the specific behaviours have been identified. There can be no doubt that the sequence of the 'model reference behaviours' correctly employed can have an enormous influence on an area of reference work which desperately needs improvement.

In order to sustain the techniques learned during the training programme which the Baltimore County staff undertook, some form of follow-up process is required. Typically, attendance on courses, workshops or other training functions provides a wealth of useful information and guidance on improved practices. However, once the participant returns to his own workplace the lessons learned may be forgotten and the enthusiasm for improvement rapidly disappear unless some form of reinforcement is applied.

The method proposed by the Baltimore County trainers is the use of 'peer coaching' or 'partnering'.[12] This skills-transfer technique requires partners to work together at the reference desk and, as appropriate, observe each other's activities, handling reference enquiries, and later commenting on performance in a positive and sensitive manner. This practice, developed from the commercial sector, is claimed to have a powerful effect on sustaining a consistent performance of the newly acquired reference behaviours if maintained over a reasonable period of time. Libraries which cannot initiate a formal 'peer coaching' scheme can still benefit from its theoretical basis. A simple expedient such as locating staff at an enquiry desk close enough to observe each other's behaviour, even without the feedback process, can often create a subconscious urge to improve performance and the quality of service. Results of obtrusive tests of reference work consistently show a much higher figure of correctness of answers than those provided when the practice is unobtrusively observed. For the same reason the proximity of a colleague may also improve personal performance of staff.

This introductory chapter began with a statement about the out-of-date nature of much information in reference works, and critics might well point out that 'people in glass houses . . . ', since such is the nature also of books about reference materials. However, to help obviate this problem there are a number of periodicals which should be consulted regularly in order to identify new editions or new titles being published.

Some very useful sources emanate from the United States, in particular from the American Library Association. *Choice*, 1964 – , monthly, reviews all types of books but its largest section covers reference material. It has also expanded to list forthcoming titles on an annual basis. *Choice* is to take over the editorial control of Sheehy's *Guide to reference books*, to which a supplement will be published in 1992, covering 4,500 works which have appeared so far since the end of 1984. A revised 11th edition is planned for 1995.

A very useful annual cumulation of reviews which have appeared in the fortnightly *Booklist*, 1905 – , is in *Reference books bulletin* (formerly *Subscription books bulletin*), 1983/84 – . This work covers English-language sources on all subjects, reviewed by subject specialist librarians. A similar annual listing is *American reference books annual*, 1970 – .

R Q, 1960 – , monthly, contains a section reviewing both new reference sources and databases together with regular, useful articles on reference practice.

In Britain one of the most useful sources which has appeared recently is *Reference reviews*, 1987 – , monthly. This provides invaluable informative reviews of a wide range of reference sources by librarians for librarians and is certainly a very welcome addition to British book-selection tools. The well-established *Aslib book list*, 1943 – , monthly, also includes reference books in its listings of scientific, technical, medical and social science publications. All the books reviewed in this source are coded as to the level of treatment. Reference works are indicated by the letter D following the review. The *Library Association record*, 1899 – , regularly reviews reference books in its Review section and also as short notices in Book Briefs. *Refer*, 1980 – , the twice-yearly journal of the Information Services Group of the Library Association has a very useful feature, 'Reference books you may have missed'. This very readable survey of both well-known and more obscure sources is accompanied by a valuable summary of new government and EEC publications. *British book news*, 1940 – , is a monthly publication from the British Council. This also features symbols which highlight readership levels of many new and forthcoming British books on all subjects. The list of books is annotated and graded and is accompanied by review articles on a range of books in selected subjects.

Walford's *Guide to reference material* is being revised by a team of seven subject experts in a new 5th edition. Volume 1 *Science and technology* appeared at the end of 1989; volume 2 *Social and historical sciences, philosophy and religion* is due in the late Autumn 1990; and volume 3 *Generalities, languages, the arts and literature* will follow in 1991. The present intention is that all volumes will appear triennially thus avoiding recent long delays between editions.

REFERENCES AND CITATIONS

1   Walford, A. J. (ed.), *Walford's guide to reference material*. 4th ed. London: Library Association, 1980 – 87. 3v.
2   Sheehy, E. P. (ed.), *Guide to reference books*. 10th ed. Chicago: American Library Association, 1986.
3   McKee, R., 'Information without communication: the irrelevant library', *Refer: Journal of the ISG*, **5** (1), Spring 1988, 3 – 7.
4   Duckett, R., 'The relevance of libraries and the presumption of IT', *ibid.* **5** (2), Autumn 1988, 8 – 11, 24.

5 Grogan, D. J., *Practical reference work*. London: Bingley, 1979.
   Grogan, D. J., *Grogan's case studies in reference work: 1. Enquiries and the reference process*. London: Bingley, 1987.
6 Katz, W. A., *Introduction to reference work*. Vol. 2, *Reference services and reference processes*. 5th ed. New York: McGraw-Hill, 1987.
7 Higgens, G. L. (ed.), *Printed reference material*. 2nd ed. London: Library Association, 1984. Chap. 2, The reference process.
8 Birbeck, V. P. and Whittaker, K. A., 'Room for improvement', *Public library journal*, **2** (4), July/August 1987, 55 – 61;
   Weech, T. L. and Goldhor, H., 'Obtrusive versus unobtrusive: evaluation of reference service in five Illinois libraries: a pilot study', *Library quarterly*, **52** (4), 1982, 305 – 24;
   Williams, R., 'An unobtrusive test of academic library reference services', *Library and information research news*, **10** (37/38), 1987, 12 – 40.
9 McClure, C. R. and Hernon, P., 'Unobtrusive testing and the role of library management', *Reference librarian*, **18**, Summer 1987, 71 – 85.
10 Lea, P. W. and Jackson, L., 'The exception or the rule?: the quality of reference service in public libraries', *Library Association record*, **90** (10), October 1988, 582 – 5.
11 Isenstein, L., 'On the road to STARdom: reference accuracy training at the Baltimore County Public Library', *Illinois libraries*. January 1991 (in press).
12 Gers, R. and Seward, L. J., 'I heard you say . . . : peer coaching for more effective reference service', *Reference librarian*, **22**, Summer 1988, 245 – 60.

2

Dictionaries

Kenneth A. Whittaker

A dictionary is a book that deals mainly, if not wholly, with words. It is usually a work that is arranged alphabetically, but many dictionaries are arranged in other ways. Not all dictionaries are so called, some preferring to call themselves wordbooks, lexicons, glossaries or thesauri, or possibly some other name.

The term 'wordbook' is self-explanatory, but a comment is called for on the other three. The term 'lexicon' is derived from a classical Greek word, 'lexikon', meaning dictionary, and is most often applied to dictionaries of ancient languages, such as Liddell and Scott's *A Greek-English lexicon*. The term 'glossary' is most commonly used in the subject dictionary area, as with Harrod's *The librarians' glossary*, and such dictionaries usually explain, not merely define, the words they include. The name 'thesaurus' was used by Roget in 1852 when he published his best-selling *Thesaurus of English words and phrases*. It means a storehouse or treasury of knowledge, and has subsequently usually been used to describe dictionaries, which, like Roget's, arrange words in a classified order, and not in the usual alphabetical one. In recent years, the word 'thesaurus' has become better known as the name given, in information retrieval, to a list of the terms to be used in a particular information-retrieval system (especially a computerized system).

SCOPE

Within the limits already laid down, that is, that dictionaries must be to do with words (and phrases), the scope of dictionaries is wider than is often realized. Not only are there dictionaries dealing with virtually every language and subject, there are also dictionaries for special purposes such as rhyming, and dictionaries which aim to aid special groups of people such as crossword addicts. There are also works, which concern themselves with words as literature, rather than with words as language; notably books of quotations, and concordances (these latter do not limit their indexing to the most quotable passages). They have been included in this chapter because they are so closely related to other kinds of wordbooks. There are in addition encyclopaedias that are dictionaries as well, such as the famous French *Petit Larousse illustré*. They thus serve a double purpose. The overall scope of dictionaries will be considered further when they are divided into types, and representative and important titles of each type considered.

DEVELOPMENT

The first step towards the compilation of English-language dictionaries (to which this section on development will limit itself) was taken in Anglo-Saxon times. It resulted from readers of Latin words jotting down explanations in Anglo-Saxon of some of the more difficult Latin words they encountered. The explanations ('glosses' is the name given to them) were actually placed between the lines, or in the margins, of the books being read. Later, monastic scribes began to extract all the 'glosses' from a manuscript, and to make a list of them. These lists were not at first arranged in alphabetical order, but towards the end of the fourteenth century, alphabetical order became the rule.

The first real dictionary of the English language was published in 1604 – Robert Cawdrey's *A table alphabeticall*. The subtitle[1] of this work reveals, however, that its scope was much narrower than that of modern dictionaries, as it read: 'containing and teaching the true writing and understanding of hard usuall English words, borrowed from Hebrew, Greeke, Latine, or French, etc.'

Other early English dictionaries also limited themselves to difficult words, and it was not until 1721 that a dictionary was published that included words in common use. This was Nathaniel Bailey's *Universal etymological dictionary*.

In 1755 the great Dr Samuel Johnson published his *Dictionary of the English language*. The dictionary, as we know it, may be considered to date from this year. Johnson's work was not only influential, but personal, and his character comes out in many of his definitions. My favourite is:[2]

'LUNCH. As much food as one's hand can hold.'

Dr Johnson believed that dictionaries should lay down the words worthy of use, and so he would not have anything to do with slang expressions, for example. Many dictionary compilers since Dr Johnson have also held this view, which is now called the prescriptive one of a dictionary's function. The view that the purpose of a dictionary is to lay down standards of word acceptability and usage has come more and more under attack in recent times, but it is not dead. The alternative view of the function of a dictionary is the descriptive one, that a dictionary should record words as they are being used (and misused), without passing judgment any more than it has to.

The great dictionaries of the nineteenth century, the *American dictionary of the English language*, first produced in 1828, and the work of Noah Webster; and the *New English dictionary on historical principles*, first published in parts between 1884 and 1928 (now known as the *Oxford English dictionary*), took a middle course between the descriptive and prescriptive viewpoints. In its last edition, however (3rd, Merriam-Webster, 1962), Webster's caused considerable controversy by becoming more descriptive in its approach. But while some differences remain in the opinions held today as to the primary function of these dictionaries, there is no dispute over the increasing need for the major dictionaries to be supplemented by more specialized works, such as technical dictionaries and glossaries. And so the twentieth century has seen an ever-swelling number of dictionaries of every size and kind being published, and, of course, being stocked by libraries.

USES

Obviously the uses of a dictionary depend to a large extent on what kind of a dictionary it is, but some general comments are called for, to complement those made later considering the various types of dictionaries. Four broad uses of dictionaries may be distinguished, though there is some overlap between them.

Quick-reference tool

From the librarian's point of view, this is the important use. A dictionary will indicate the pronunciation, spelling and meaning of a word. It may also give further information about the word, such as its origin, what part of speech it is, examples of its use, and words related to it. It may, in addition to giving information about words, give all sorts of other useful quick-reference information, such as tables of weights and measures, and how to address people when writing letters to them. Of course, many dictionaries exist to give rather specialized information about words, such as equivalent words in foreign languages. Probably no other type of quick-reference book is consulted as often as the dictionary, and this type of book will be found not only in libraries, but in homes, schools, offices – and even in pockets.

The librarian will use his collection of dictionaries to answer readers who have enquiries such as 'What is the meaning of serendipity?'; 'When do I use the word "unreadable", and when the word "illegible"?'; 'What is the name given to a person who is afraid of heights?' He may also use his dictionary stock when he has to carry out a literature search, or answer an enquiry on a subject with which he is not familiar. In the latter case he would especially have to do this with enquiries received through the post, as he could not ask the reader for clarification on such occasions.

Sometimes in enquiry work, even though his library has a reasonable stock of dictionaries, the librarian will find that they fail to give him the answer he requires. Before he tries sources of information outside his library, such as ringing up a larger library, he should check various types of books he stocks, which, though not dictionaries, contain information on words. In particular he should check his encyclopaedias (their value as dictionaries has already been mentioned); his standard works (for many, especially those on technical subjects, will be found to contain short subject glossaries); and, if appropriate, the vocabularies in his textbooks relating to foreign-language study.

Language recorder

Those dictionaries which set out to provide a fairly comprehensive picture of the words of language or of a subject, especially when they have been compiled from what has been called the descriptive viewpoint, are obviously effective in providing a basic record, for all time, of the words in use when the dictionary was produced. Such dictionaries, after they have been published for some years, also provide an historical record. An historical record is likewise provided by dictionaries like the *Oxford English dictionary*, which set out to trace the development of each word they include, not limiting themselves to current words and usage.

Language standardizer

Probably all dictionaries, not just those produced from a prescriptive viewpoint, act as language standardizers; certainly the spelling of English words today is much more standard than it was in Shakespeare's day because, now, unlike then, authoritative dictionaries exist. Incidentally, in the newly developing countries of the world, where the language of an area may be being written down for the first time, dictionaries are being published alongside the first newspapers, books, and other writings in that language. The result is that variations in usage, such as different spellings, are being eliminated before they can start.

Aid to language study

The value of dictionaries during the study of foreign languages is accepted, but their value when one's own language is being studied is sometimes overlooked. And dictionaries like the *Oxford English dictionary* are also used as a quarry for research workers as they delve into specialized aspects of language, literature and history.

DICTIONARY-MAKING

Amongst the research workers just mentioned will be found the compilers of dictionaries, for few dictionaries are made without the study of existing ones. The name given to dictionary-making is 'lexicography'. To aid the study of lexicography a Dictionary Research Centre was established at Exeter University in 1984. Originally the compilation of dictionaries was undertaken by one person, or perhaps by a small team of lexicographers. Nowadays, large teams, aided by such devices as the computer, are common. However, there are still today many dictionaries which are small enough to be compiled by a single knowledgeable person.

The steps which the compiler of a dictionary has to take before it is ready for publication usually will be as follows: first he has to bring together a team of helpers; at the same time he will probably consult experts, who will advise him and his team on policies and methods. The second step is the already mentioned consultation of existing dictionaries. Of course, the compiler must stop short of actually copying other dictionaries. The next step is the building-up of a file of information which the compiler thinks will be useful, and which is not easily to be found anywhere else. This file, traditionally assembled in card form but now more probably on a computer or word-processor, is built up gradually from searching all sorts of printed material, and possibly through correspondence. Often an important purpose of the file is to give examples of how words which are to be included in the dictionary have actually been used. The fourth step is to select from the information collected what to place in the dictionary. The material selected for inclusion must then be prepared for the printer and, when set up in type, proof-read. However, dictionaries increasingly, as well as being conventionally printed, are being made available in other formats, especially microform and machine-readable formats such as CD-ROM.

EXAMINING

It has often been said that most people who consult a dictionary never read the instructions it includes on how to use it. Perhaps this is partly because they do not realize the considerable guidance which is to be found in nearly all dictionaries. Students of reference must, however, know not only about the guidance which dictionaries offer their users, but about all their features. The average dictionary comprises the following five features. In the order they are normally found, they are: Preface; Key to abbreviations; Key to pronunciation; Main sequence of words; Supplementary sequences of words. All need to be examined before any dictionary can be used fully and efficiently.

The **Preface** will indicate the scope as well as the aim of the dictionary. If guidance on how the dictionary should be used is not included in the Preface, a separate 'how to use' feature will be found nearby. The **Key to abbreviations** is a self-explanatory feature, as is the **Key to pronunciation**, though a comment about the latter is necessary: there are two main ways of indicating pronunciation, and neither of them is perfect from the dictionary compilers' point of view. One way is to use an accepted phonetic alphabet; this indicates pronunciation in a scholarly fashion, and so is not always easily understood by the layman. The other way is to re-spell words, using the ordinary letters of the alphabet; this method is more understandable, but also more clumsy.

The **Main sequence of words** is occasionally a classified one, as in the already mentioned *Roget's thesaurus*, whilst there are a number of dictionaries which have more than one alphabetical sequence. Translating dictionaries usually have two sequences; rhyming dictionaries are amongst those which normally have more than two, as they commonly arrange their words by the number of rhyming syllables they contain. However, the vast majority of dictionaries are, of course, arranged in a single alphabetical sequence. Two main methods of organizing any alphabetical arrangement exist: they are word by word (e.g. New Zealand before and not after Newfoundland) and letter by letter. Many of the larger general English-language dictionaries use the letter-by-letter scheme probably because it is the more logical. However, some readers find words more easily when they are arranged word by word.

The content of the entries in the main sequence of a dictionary should be examined to see what each includes. It is surprising how much information a general language dictionary, for example, may give in addition to basic information about its words. It may disclose the origin of them; trace their history; show how writers have used them; give related words and phrases, including synonyms and antonyms; and include cross-references. Furthermore, it will usually indicate words not in common use, or not generally acceptable, by giving them a label, e.g. *Dialect*; *Slang*; *American*.

Supplementary sequences of words, where they exist, should be obviously listed on the contents pages of dictionaries, but sometimes they may still be missed. Their purpose may be just to update the main sequence, but more usually it is to deal with special categories of words which do not really belong in the main sequence, such as a list of Christian names and their meaning. As well as supplementary sequences of words, encyclopaedic information, such as the names of the Kings and Queens of England, may be found.

EVALUATING

The examination and evaluation of dictionaries go together, as evaluation cannot take place until a thorough examination has been made. The ability to evaluate a dictionary is essential not only for book selection purposes, but for reference work, as enquirers need to be given answers which are from the best available reference books. The evaluation of dictionaries is obviously related to the evaluation of other quick-reference books, and so this section limits itself to just four criteria which are particularly pertinent to dictionaries. They are (in alphabetical order): Authority; Ease of use; Word coverage; and Word treatment.

Authority. The authority of a dictionary is especially determined by who has compiled it, and who has published it. Information about the compiler, his advisers and his support staff should be displayed prominently near the front of the dictionary. Beware if it is not. However, it is not as easy for the average librarian to judge the precise standing of compilers as it is for him to assess the authority of the publisher because of his knowledge of the book trade. Amongst British dictionary publishers, the Oxford University Press stands supreme, whilst in the United States, the firm of W. & C. Merriam (the publishers of *Webster's new international dictionary*) has a very high reputation. The name Webster is not copyright, and there are poor dictionaries called 'Webster's' published by other American firms. There are several other firms with good reputations, although not all important dictionaries are published by them. Most of these firms will be mentioned when individual dictionaries are considered later in this chapter.

Ease of use. Though dictionaries are seldom really hard to use, they need to be made as easy to use as possible, with each page virtually self-explanatory. However, there needs also to be clear introductory information on the purpose, scope and features of the dictionary, as well as keys to its abbreviations and to its method of showing pronunciation. Dictionaries are easier to use if they have been well designed, with care taken over their legibility and guiding.

Word coverage. It may be possible for subject and special purpose dictionaries to cover their fields reasonably comprehensively without becoming excessively large, but it is impossible for general language and general translating dictionaries to do so. The English language, for example, comprises no less than about half a million words, and so many dictionaries limit their coverage in some way. They may exclude obsolete words; they may exclude words which are used only in specialized subject fields, like medicine; they may exclude words which are used only in a particular locality, for example on Merseyside. However, although most English-language dictionaries are select, providing they have a hundred thousand entries, they are adequate.

Many dictionaries consider that they need to supplement their coverage of words with information about people, places and other encyclopaedia-type material. They are sometimes called encyclopaedic dictionaries. Such dictionaries are useful in the home, where few other reference books exist, but librarians prefer dictionaries which concentrate on word coverage.

A type of word missing from all dictionaries is the newly coined word which has come into use only since the dictionary was published. As librarians often get asked the meaning of new words, it is important that the word coverage of a dictionary is as up-to-date as possible. As some standard dictionaries are reprinted without being brought up to date, librarians often need to supplement their more comprehensive compilations with smaller but more up-to-date dictionaries, and with dictionaries that specialize in new words like the *Longman register of new words*.

An interesting approach to the listing of new words is the American quarterly publication *The Barnhart dictionary companion* which deals with new and changed meanings of existing words as well as with new words.

Two final points on word coverage need to be added. The first is that a few dictionaries, notably the American Thorndike dictionaries, select the words they include on the basis of statistical study of the frequency of use of words. The Thorndike dictionaries, incidentally, are mostly designed for use by children. The second is that the number of words that a dictionary includes can be counted in different ways. Some dictionaries count each of their definitions as separate entries, and so arrive at a coverage total which is really an inflated one. Other dictionaries do not do this, but have a policy of giving derivations separate entries (for example 'glossary' would have its own entry, and not come under 'gloss'). These dictionaries will have less inflated word totals, but they will still be inflated compared with those in dictionaries which include derivations under the basic word-stem.

Word treatment. All dictionaries will set out the information they give about their words in a consistent form and order (which should be explained). It is important to know how any one dictionary treats its words. Does it give their etymology (i.e. origin and history)? Does it give quotations from literature to support its definitions? Does it include illustrations and diagrams to make its definitions clearer? The amount of information given with each word must, then, be noted, as must the arrangement of the dictionary's most basic information, its definitions. With words which have more than one meaning, either the earliest or the most common will usually be given first. The latter arrangement is the better for quick-reference work.

The quality of a dictionary's definitions is dependent on their accuracy and their clarity. Most dictionary definitions today can be considered reasonably accurate, but their clarity may leave something to be desired. To check accuracy, examine how a dictionary defines specialized words with which you are very familiar; to check clarity, do the same, but also compare a few definitions with those for the same words in other dictionaries.

Final questions to be asked about the word treatment of any dictionary under evaluation are: how does it deal with alternative spellings, and how does it treat words derived from other words? Alternative spellings should be indicated in the entry under the form chosen as entry word, and there should be cross-references from alternative forms. Concerning derivations, most good dictionaries seem to deal with these under the appropriate stem-word, though this practice does make them harder to find.

When dictionaries are evaluated, using guidelines such as the ones just laid down, it will probably be found that Dr Johnson's verdict[3] on dictionaries still holds good: 'Dictionaries are like watches; the worst is better than none, and the best cannot be expected to be quite true.'

TYPES AND TITLES

General language dictionaries

So far, dictionaries have been looked at overall; they will now be considered type by type, and the important and representative titles commented upon. For comments on a wider range of titles, Walford's *Guide to reference material*, or Sheehy's *Guide to reference books*, should be consulted. But, of course, consulting books which give information on dictionaries is no substitute for examining the dictionaries themselves.

General language dictionaries are often divided into two types, unabridged (or comprehensive) and abridged (or select). It is the comprehensive dictionary that is of most value generally speaking, and so it receives first attention here. Of course, no dictionary can be fully comprehensive in its coverage of the words of a language, except perhaps one covering a dead language. Even the monumental *Oxford English dictionary* (OED) is not all inclusive as regards specialized subject terms such as scientific ones.

OXFORD ENGLISH DICTIONARY. 2nd ed. 20 vols. Oxford: Clarendon Press, 1989. 20 vols.

By far the most comprehensive and detailed English dictionary, it is in a class of its own. It is a pure dictionary, having no encyclopaedic features; but, as its words are treated so as to reveal their history, and with a great wealth of illustrative quotation, this work is a word-encyclopaedia. It was originally published between 1884 and 1928 with the title *A new English dictionary on historical principles*, and the original set of volumes is still in use in some libraries. This dictionary is remarkable for the quality of its information. However, for quick-reference purposes it cannot be recommended, as its aim is not to give current usage, but to record the development of words. In addition, because it is so large and detailed, it is often hard to find and extract information from it quickly. For quick-reference purposes, one of the abridged versions of this work is more suitable. The *Shorter Oxford English dictionary* is the largest of these abridged versions, and may indeed be classed amongst the comprehensive dictionaries of the English language, as it covers two-thirds of the nearly half million words in the main work, though it gives less information in its entries. The text of the new edition is being made available in machine-readable form (as a CD-ROM) and this will aid research use of the dictionary.

The creation of the *Oxford English dictionary* led to the compilation of other scholarly dictionaries on historical principles, probably the best known being the *Dictionary of American English on historical principles*. However, of the dictionaries on historical principles available for foreign languages, one at least, the German *Deutsches Wörterbuch*, is older than the *Oxford English dictionary*. It took over a hundred years, 1854 – 1960, for this dictionary to complete publication.

The other two important unabridged dictionaries are both compiled in the United States.

WEBSTER'S NEW INTERNATIONAL DICTIONARY OF THE ENGLISH LANGUAGE. 3rd ed. Springfield, Massachusetts: Merriam, 1962.

Unlike the comprehensive dictionaries already mentioned, this one is not on historical principles, but concentrates on current usage. First published in 1828, this dictionary, unlike the *Oxford English dictionary*, has some encyclopaedic features – for example, a section on forms of address. However, the latest edition of Webster's has fewer encyclopaedic features than earlier editions; it also omits many words which were in the previous edition; many libraries still stock the previous one. The current edition of Webster's, though it was criticized when it was published for failing to prescribe correct usage, is of a very high quality, and its usefulness to libraries on this side of the Atlantic is furthered by its indicating British spellings and meanings when they differ from American ones. In 1986 a supplement *12000 words* was published, whilst supplementary words are also included in recent printings of this work.

RANDOM HOUSE DICTIONARY OF THE ENGLISH LANGUAGE. 2nd ed. New York: Random House, 1987.

This is the smallest of the three comprehensive dictionaries, yet it has 2,500 very large pages. It incorporates a number of encyclopaedic features, including an atlas. Its particular virtue, compared with *Webster's*, is its overall up-to-dateness.

The larger abridged dictionaries are normally called desk dictionaries, the smaller ones pocket dictionaries. Most libraries will stock several of the better desk dictionaries that are available. The largest is based on the great *Oxford English dictionary*.

SHORTER OXFORD ENGLISH DICTIONARY. 2 vols. Oxford: Clarendon Press, 1973.

A mine of information, though a little old-fashioned in the way its material is presented.

Two other physically large desk dictionaries of note, both having been recently revised, are:

READER'S DIGEST UNIVERSAL DICTIONARY. London: Reader's Digest Association, and Hodder and Stoughton, 1987.
NEW HAMLYN ENCYCLOPEDIC WORLD DICTIONARY. 2nd ed. London: Hamlyn, 1988.

The first is based on the Reader's Digest *Great illustrated dictionary*. It is a handsome publication whose contents cover nearly 200,000 words. There are also encyclopaedic features, and indeed this and the Hamlyn work have a number of similarities. Both publications now have sufficient quality about them to become established and widely recognized works.

The most popular desk dictionaries are those of more physically modest proportions, yet whose contents may be as wide ranging. The number of words included will usually be over 100,000. There is considerable competition between the publishers of these medium-sized desk dictionaries because they can become best-sellers. The three outstanding titles during the 1980s have been:

CONCISE OXFORD DICTIONARY OF CURRENT ENGLISH. 8th ed. Oxford: Clarendon Press, 1990.
COLLINS ENGLISH DICTIONARY. 2nd ed. London: Collins, 1986.
CHAMBERS ENGLISH DICTIONARY. Edinburgh: Chambers, and Cambridge University Press, 1988.

This last work was known before its last revision as *Chambers twentieth-century dictionary*. Well established under its previous title, this work continues to be a no-nonsense, pure dictionary covering a very wide number of words. The *Concise Oxford* (COD) is also a pure dictionary with a high reputation but it includes fewer entries than the two rivals here discussed. The Collins dictionary is different from the others in having encyclopaedic features. It is probably the easiest to use of the three, and overall is a particularly good buy for home or office use.

The choice of medium-sized desk dictionaries seems continually to increase, and titles such as the *Longman dictionary of the English language* seem likely to prove strong rivals to the three dictionaries already described.

As regards titles published in the United States, as opposed to Britain, there is again a considerable choice. One that can be recommended is *Webster's ninth new collegiate dictionary*.

Many of the general language dictionaries already named, especially the encyclopaedic ones, are capable of being used by older children, but there are a number of dictionaries available specifically designed for children. These include the *Oxford children's dictionary* and *Chambers children's colour dictionary*. As regards the needs of foreigners learning English, several dictionaries exist catering for them especially. Two examples are the *Oxford advanced learner's dictionary of current English* and *Longman's dictionary of contemporary English*.

Turning briefly to dictionaries of foreign languages, it should be noted that though such dictionaries are less frequently found in libraries than are translating dictionaries, they complement translating dictionaries by having more detailed entries. Two examples of high reputation are the French *Lexis: dictionnaire de la langue française,* and the Dutch *Groot woordenboek der Nederlandse taal*, by J. H. Van Dale.

Subject dictionaries

In the last section on general language dictionaries, it was possible to mention many important titles; in this one it will be possible to discuss only a few examples. For information on a larger number of subject dictionaries, bibliographies of dictionaries, such as those described in the last section of this chapter, should be referred to, or alternatively, appropriate subject literature guides consulted.

Subject dictionaries complement general language dictionaries in two main ways. First, they include highly specialized terms not in general dictionaries (this applies especially in the fields of science and technology). Second, they often have more detailed descriptions of word meanings than those in general dictionaries, commenting on and explaining their terms, not just defining them. Some so-called subject dictionaries are encyclopaedias which incorporate definitions of subject terms. Subject dictionaries, such as Haggar's *Dictionary of art terms*, which are entitled dictionaries of terms, will always be found to be genuine dictionaries.

Some subject dictionaries are aimed at the general public, others at students, the remainder at specialist audiences. Dictionaries in this last category especially can be expected to be prepared by an appropriate body, contain very authoritative definitions and be regularly revised. A good example of one is the *Meteorological glossary*, compiled by the Meteorological Office. Other good examples of subject dictionaries are:

Harrod, L. M., THE LIBRARIAN'S GLOSSARY. 6th ed. London: Gower, 1987.

The best known dictionary of librarianship, and a typical subject dictionary – typical in that some of its entries are long, almost encyclopaedic, and also in that it gives only the spelling and meaning of its words, not other common dictionary information like pronunciation. Compare this dictionary with the much smaller *Glossary of documentation terms* (BS 5408: 1976) published by the British Standards Institution, which, of course, sets out not just to record but to prescribe.

CHAMBERS SCIENCE AND TECHNOLOGY DICTIONARY. Edinburgh: Chambers, and Cambridge University Press, 1988.

Another typical subject dictionary, but one covering a broader area of knowledge. A revision of *Chambers dictionary of science and technology*, its brief entries are aimed at the layman as well as at the person with more specialized knowledge. The American *McGraw-Hill dictionary of scientific and technical terms* packs similar contents into its pages and should be compared with the Chambers compilation.

Special purpose dictionaries

Like subject dictionaries, special purpose dictionaries (sometimes called supplementary wordbooks) complement general language dictionaries. They do this in a number of ways, as there are many varieties of them. In the main, they complement by specializing in a class of words which most general dictionaries omit (or are weak on), e.g. dialect; by specializing in one aspect of language, e.g. pronunciation; or by approaching words in some special way, e.g. by their rhyming qualities.

Publications which complement in the first way form a group made up of seven types of dictionary: dictionaries of slang; dialect dictionaries; dictionaries of obsolete words; dictionaries of new words; dictionaries of names; dictionaries of abbreviations; and dictionaries of phrases. Four representative titles in this group are singled out for comment:

Partridge, E., DICTIONARY OF SLANG AND UNCONVENTIONAL ENGLISH. Rev. ed. London: Routledge & Kegan Paul, 1984.

Eric Partridge was a well-known lexicographer, and this is his best known work. An abridged version is available, as a Penguin book, under the title *Dictionary of historical slang*. Australian slang features in Partridge's work, but for American slang the *Dictionary of American slang* by H. Wentworth and S. B. Flexner (New York: Crowell) should be consulted.

Ekwall, E., CONCISE OXFORD DICTIONARY OF ENGLISH PLACE-NAMES. 4th ed. Oxford: Clarendon Press, 1960.

This type of dictionary should not be confused with books, such as gazetteers, which give information on places. It is concerned solely with the history and meaning of place-names. Dictionaries of surnames and Christian names, such as that equally standard work, the *Oxford dictionary of English Christian names*, also exist. (So do ones of eponyms, that is, words like diesel, which originate in a person's name: e.g. C. P. Auger, *Engineering eponyms*, 2nd ed. Library Association, 1975.)

EVERYMAN'S DICTIONARY OF ABBREVIATIONS. Rev. ed. London: Dent, 1986.

This is amongst the better of the many dictionaries of abbreviations available. Libraries should stock several such dictionaries, as they complement one another. Some include signs and symbols; most, as this one, include acronyms, that is, pronounceable words formed from a group of initial letters, e.g. *Anzac* from *Australian-New Zealand Army Corps*.

Brewer, E. C., BREWER'S DICTIONARY OF PHRASE AND FABLE. 14th ed. London: Cassell, 1989.

Some dictionaries specialize in phrases of a particular kind, like clichés, or proverbs, but this one is more general; indeed it is not only a dictionary, but an encyclopaedia of literary and historical information. Brewer's famous work is perhaps the most readable of all dictionaries; certainly it needs to be browsed through; features such as its heading *Dying sayings* might otherwise well be overlooked.

Special purpose dictionaries in the second group, that is, those which deal with a specialized aspect of language, comprise five types of dictionary: dictionaries of pronunciation; dictionaries of spelling; etymological dictionaries; dictionaries of usage; and dictionaries of synonyms and antonyms. Two outstanding titles are chosen for comment:

Fowler, H. W., A DICTIONARY OF MODERN ENGLISH USAGE. 2nd ed. Oxford: Clarendon Press, 1965.

This book will be found in many homes, as well as in libraries. The compiler was a famous lexicographer, and his pronouncements on how to use words are respected. First published in 1926, this dictionary was prepared for its second edition by Sir Ernest Gowers of *Plain words* fame. Its entries include one, on the word 'enquiry', that is especially worth examining. It may also be compared with the entry in a more recent guide to usage, the *Bloomsbury good word guide* published in 1988.

Roget, P. M., THESAURUS OF ENGLISH WORDS AND PHRASES. New ed. London: Longmans, 1987.

Compiled by a doctor after he had retired, and first published in 1852, it is the best known of all dictionaries of synonyms and antonyms, and has been published in a number of versions. Its main sequence is a classified one, because Roget wanted to arrange his entries in the way that would best allow users to find the exact word to fit a thought. Most dictionaries of this kind, though, are alphabetical, as is *Webster's dictionary of synonyms*. Indeed, this work is different from Roget in another way, in that it carefully distinguishes between shades of meaning. Crossword-puzzle enthusiasts find dictionaries of synonyms and antonyms invaluable, though they also use the dictionaries specially designed for them.

The third group of special purpose dictionaries is the one that approaches words in some special way. In fact Roget, because it is classified, approaches words in a special way, and so belongs to this group of dictionaries as well as to the group just dealt with. Most crossword dictionaries belong to this group, as they usually arrange their words by the number of letters in them, whilst reverse-dictionaries also come into it. The reverse-dictionary is of especial interest to the librarian, as it enables enquiries to be answered that would otherwise be very difficult. Indeed, one of the first reverse-dictionaries was published by a library, as a result of the staff having to compile a file of information to help them solve enquiries that demanded words to fit already known meanings (i.e. the opposite of the normal dictionary enquiry). It was *'Isms* compiled by the staff of Sheffield Public Libraries. The most useful reverse dictionary is:

READER'S DIGEST REVERSE DICTIONARY. London: Reader's Digest Association, and Hodder and Stoughton, 1989.
  This attractive publication not only solves questions like 'What is the name for an expert on wine?' (oenologist); it includes tables that bring together the names of things such as philosophies and phobias.

OXFORD-DUDEN PICTORIAL ENGLISH DICTIONARY. Oxford: Oxford University Press, 1981.
  An adaptation of a German work, it shows what objects look like. Its classified approach also allows names of objects to be traced if they are known. It forms part of a series of Oxford-Duden dictionaries, the majority of which are translating dictionaries, like the *Oxford-Duden pictorial Dutch and English dictionary*.

Translating dictionaries

Translating dictionaries, unlike the ones dealt with so far, are not monolingual (or single language); they are either bilingual or multilingual. There are a great number of translating dictionaries published, many of them limited to single subject fields, and so it is usually possible to find one that gives the information needed. It should be pointed out, though, that translating dictionaries do not normally give the meaning of words, just equivalent words in the one or more foreign languages they cover.

As with general language dictionaries, some translating dictionaries are more comprehensive than others. Where a comprehensive and detailed bilingual dictionary exists for a foreign language, it will be found to be of outstanding use to the librarian, as well as to the scholar, the student, and the translator.

Two examples of such dictionaries follow:

HARRAP'S NEW STANDARD FRENCH AND ENGLISH DICTIONARY. 4 vols. London: Harrap, 1972 – 80.

The original version of this dictionary was published in the 1930s; it has been both abridged and supplemented, and is now completely revised. A similar multi-volumed work for Italian is the *Sansoni-Harrap standard Italian and English dictionary*, in four volumes, completed in 1976.

LANGENSCHEIDT'S ENCYCLOPAEDIC DICTIONARY OF THE ENGLISH AND GERMAN LANGUAGES. 4 vols. London: Methuen, 1962 – 75.

The largest completed translating dictionary for German.

Then there are single-volume translating dictionaries, such as those in the series published by Collins. They will answer the majority of reference enquiries and are inexpensive enough to be stocked by most libraries.

It should be noted that the two sequences of bilingual dictionaries are not always of equal length. In a few bilingual dictionaries there is only a single sequence in fact, as in the *Greek-*

English lexicon by H. G. Liddell and R. A. Scott. But this work is still indispensable to students of ancient Greek.

The second type of translating dictionary, the multilingual or polyglot dictionary, is usually concerned with a single subject, and it is particularly common in the fields of science and technology. The arrangement of multilingual dictionaries is not standard, and an examination of a collection of them will reveal interesting differences. Tabular arrangement, alphabetically by the English words, with the equivalent words following in the foreign languages covered, is one method of arrangement. Separate alphabetical indexes for each foreign language represented will be appended, with such an arrangement. It should be noted that directories with multilingual headings or indexes can be used as polyglot dictionaries, and that they are sometimes both more specific and more up-to-date than any relevant dictionary.

Amongst the publishers of multilingual dictionaries are the Dutch firm of Elsevier. An example of the many specialist polyglot works that they issue is *Elsevier's fiscal and customs dictionary*. This particular title deals with the four languages of English, German, French and Dutch.

Translating dictionaries, like monolingual dictionaries of foreign languages, can obviously present problems of use, at least when they deal with languages which the user does not know; for example, the alphabetical arrangement of words in Swedish puts those beginning with å and ö after z. However, problems of use will, over all, probably be less than expected, and when they do arise, handbooks like C. G. Allen's *A manual of European languages for librarians* can be referred to.

Books of quotations

Books of quotations set out to provide quotations on certain subjects, or by certain authors, and to give sources of quotations; through their indexes they enable half-remembered quotations to be traced. They are frequently used by writers and speech-makers, and are also eminently works to be browsed through.

Most libraries need to provide a selection of them, as books of quotations complement rather than duplicate each other. This is partly because they include different quotations, but in addition because they are arranged in a variety of ways. The main methods of arrangement are alphabetical by author and alphabetical by subject. No matter how a book of quotations is arranged, a detailed index to the key-words in its quotations is essential. Books of quotations can be general, like Bartlett's *Familiar quotations*; limited to a single author such as Shakespeare; limited to a single subject, such as religion; or even limited to a single book, such as the Bible.

The three standard books of quotations are:

Bartlett, John, FAMILIAR QUOTATIONS. 15th ed. Boston, Massachusetts: Little Brown, 1980.
OXFORD DICTIONARY OF QUOTATIONS. 3rd ed. Oxford University Press, 1979.
Stevenson, B. E., HOME BOOK OF QUOTATIONS. 10th ed. New York: Dodd Mead, 1967.
(As STEVENSON'S BOOK OF QUOTATIONS. London: Cassell, 1974).

Of these three large works, only the Oxford publication is British in origin. But they complement each other not only in origins and therefore in their selection of quotations but in arrangement. Oxford is alphabetical by author, Stevenson alphabetical by subject and Bartlett has the unusual arrangement of chronological by author. Two smaller works are also worthy of mention, not just because they are recent, but because of the way they form a pair. They are the *Bloomsbury dictionary of quotations* (1989) and the *Bloomsbury thematic dictionary of quotations* (1988).

Sometimes, quotations which cannot be traced in books of quotations will be found elsewhere. Valuable sources are general language dictionaries of the *Oxford English dictionary* type, and dictionaries of phrases. Also of use, of course, are concordances.

Concordances

Concordances index not just the most quotable passages of a famous author, or book, but every sentence; only unimportant words are omitted. Their comprehensiveness is their particular virtue. Nowadays they are produced with the aid of computers and so are less arduous undertakings than they once were. Indeed the compiler of the most famous concordance, Alexander Cruden, was in such a state of mind after he had completed his compilation that he had to be confined in a lunatic asylum at Bethnal Green (from which he managed to escape). Cruden's *Concordance to the Old and New Testaments* has gone through many reprints since it was first published in 1737, though other Bible concordances now exist. Shakespeare is probably the author to have had the most concordances compiled of his work. An outstanding example of these concordances is the *Oxford Shakespeare concordances*, a series of computer-produced titles, which were published by the Oxford University Press between 1969 and 1973.

LIBRARY PROVISION

To aid librarians in their provision of dictionaries a number of bibliographical aids are available, and some are listed at the end of this section. It should also be remembered that general aids to stock selection such as *British book news* and *Reference reviews* should be consulted from a current awareness point of view. However, for specialist dictionaries subject journals will need to be scanned.

Brewer, A. M., DICTIONARIES, ENCYCLOPEDIAS, AND OTHER WORD-RELATED BOOKS. 4th ed. 2 vols. Detroit: Gale, 1987.
Wide-ranging entries; catalogue-type details.

Kister, K. F., BEST DICTIONARIES. Phoenix, Arizona: Oryx. Announced.

Loughridge, B., WHICH DICTIONARY?: A GUIDE TO OVER 100 ENGLISH-LANGUAGE DICTIONARIES. London: Library Association, 1990. Announced.

Sader, M., GENERAL REFERENCE BOOKS FOR ADULTS: AUTHORITATIVE EVALUATIONS OF ENCYCLOPEDIAS, ATLASES AND DICTIONARIES. New York, London: Bowker, 1988. Pt. 4 Dictionaries and word books. 227 – 571.

Walford, J. (ed.), THE WORKING LANGUAGES OF THE EUROPEAN COMMUNITY: a guide to learning resources. London, Library Association, 1990.

WORLD DICTIONARIES IN PRINT, 1983. New York: Bowker, 1983.

Wynar, B. S. (ed.), ARBA GUIDE TO SUBJECT ENCYCLOPEDIAS AND DICTIONARIES. Englewood, Colorado: Libraries Unlimited, 1986. Based on the *American reference books annual.*

REFERENCES AND CITATIONS

1　Cawdrey, R., *A table alphabeticall*. London: I. R. for Edmund Weaver, 1604.
2　Johnson, S., *Johnson's dictionary: a modern selection*. London: Gollancz, 1963, 240.
3　Johnson, S., *Letters of Samuel Johnson*. Oxford: Clarendon Press, 1952, **3**, 206.

SUGGESTIONS FOR FURTHER READING

In addition to the items here mentioned, further reading should include the relevant chapters of textbooks on reference materials and works.

Gray, R. A., 'The *New Oxford English dictionary* and the uses of machine-readable dictionaries', *Reference services review*, **16** (4), 1988, 82 – 95.
This reading can be supplemented by the article 'The *Oxford English dictionary* on compact disc', *British book news*, February 1989.

Grogan, D. J., *Grogan's case studies in reference work: vol. 5, Dictionaries and phrase books*. London: Library Association, 1987.

Hartmann, R. R. K. (ed.), *Lexicography: principles and practice*. New York: Academic Press, 1983.

Kister, K., 'The big dictionaries: hoards and hoards of words', *Wilson library bulletin*, **62** (6), 1988, 38 – 43.

McArthur, T., *Worlds of reference: lexicography, learning and language from the clay tablet to the computer*. Cambridge University Press, 1986.

'Special feature: dictionaries', *Bookseller*, 7 April 1989, 1253 – 62.

Whittaker, K., 'Fame and Dr Roget', *Refer*, **5** (1), 1988, 12 – 13.

3

General Encyclopaedias

A. John Walford

The *Oxford English dictionary* defines 'encyclopaedias' as '1. The circle of knowledge, a general system of instruction'; and '2. A literary work containing extensive information on all branches of knowledge usually arranged in alphabetical order'. The word 'encyclopaedia' did not form the title or part of the title of a compendium in either ancient or medieval times and appears only in the sixteenth century. Written knowledge was treated systematically as far back as the first century AD in Pliny the Elder's *Natural history* in 37 books and 2,493 chapters, with analytical table of contents. The systematic – as opposed to the A – Z – approach continued to flourish in such compilations as Johann Heinrich Alsted's *Encyclopaedia septem tomis distincta* (1630) in 7 volumes, 35 books and 7 classes, treating of 'everything that can be learned by man by his lifetime'.

The earliest alphabetically arranged encyclopaedia in English was the work of John Harris, first secretary of the Royal Society, in 1704. The eighteenth century, in fact, saw the appearance of several important encyclopaedias. More comprehensive than any previous compilation of its kind was Johann Heinrich Zedler's 64-volume *Grosses vollständiges Universal-Lexicon aller Wissenschaften und Kunste* (1730 – 50); Supplement vols. 1 – 4: A – Caq. (1751 – 4). It also broke with tradition by including entries, as from vol. 18, for the lives of illustrious living persons, and is heavily documented. Ephraim Chambers' *Cyclopaedia: or, An universal dictionary of art and sciences* (1728. 2 vols.) is much slighter, excluding historical, biographical, geographical and associated entries, but it did carry numerous cross-references and a prefatory 'analysis of the divisions of knowledge'. Moreover, it achieved a French translation in 1745 and served as an inspiration to Diderot's *Encyclopédie* (1751 – 80). The latter, product of the Age of Enlightenment, was based on a new concept. The text was largely original; it attacked the Church, government and Christianity itself.

The first edition of the *Encyclopaedia Britannica* (1771. 3 vols.) consisted of 45 treatises: that on 'Surgery' ran to 238 pages, with definitions of technical terms arranged A – Z, a compromise between systematic and alphabetical order. The attempt to gather together what is dispersed features in the 'Classified list of articles' contained in the index to the last British edition of the *Britannica* (1910 – 11). This 'circle of knowledge' aspect is amplified in the *Britannica*'s latest Propaedia volume.

So much for the form background. In the twentieth century the span of information has increased and intensified so rapidly in both breadth and depth that the general encyclopaedia cannot provide answers in the detail that it might have done in Zedler's day. Hence the proliferation of multi-volume special or subject encyclopaedias (e.g. *New Grove dictionary of music and musicians* or the *McGraw-Hill encyclopedia of science and technology*, and their progeny).

CRITERIA

In choosing – and using – a modern general encyclopaedia, especially if it is multi-volume, certain points must be borne in mind.

Authority and accuracy

The preface to an encyclopaedia usually lists the names of editors, editorial staff, advisers and contributors. The fact that Louis Shores was, in his day, editor-in-chief of *Collier's encyclopedia* gives it prestige. Some encyclopaedias cite qualifications or present status of contributors, as in the *World book encyclopedia*, or even note their major writings, as in *Collier's*. As a corollary, articles should be signed or initialled.

Authoritativeness can also be linked to the publisher's reputation for scholarly output. Change of publisher in successive editions may not augur well. When the *Encyclopaedia Britannica* passed into American ownership with the 1924 edition, the text was cut. Excisions, marked by 'x' after the original contributor's initials, betrayed use of the editorial scissors, not always judiciously applied. Again, the text of a well-known encyclopaedia may have been adapted as a basis for international coverage in the national encyclopaedia of another country. Thus the Brazilian *Enciclopedia Delta universal* (1980. 15 vols.) is translated and adapted from the *World book encyclopedia*.

Two German encyclopaedias reflect the Roman Catholic viewpoint: *Der grosse Duden* (5th ed. 1955 – 6. 10 vols.) and the shorter *Der neue Herder* (1965 – 70. 7 vols.).

The scope of a general encyclopaedia may go beyond what is commonly accepted. As an example, both the *Enciclopedia universal ilustrada europeo-americana* and the *Grand Larousse encyclopédique* incorporate native-language dictionaries. *Brockhaus Encyclopädie* (17th ed. 1966 – 75) devotes a supplementary volume to a German-language dictionary.

A further embellishment to a general encyclopaedia may be the provision of an atlas-gazetteer volume. Ideally, this should be of large format, unlike that of the encyclopaedia itself. Thus, *Atlas général Larousse* (1973) accompanies *La grande encyclopédie* (1971 – 6. 20 vols.). On the other hand, the atlas volume appended to *Meyers neues Lexikon* is demy octavo size only, matching the text volume; as a result some maps are overcrowded with detail. The 64-page atlas appended to volume 12 of *Everyman's encyclopaedia* is in the nature of an afterthought, since there is no supporting gazetteer or cross-references from the text.

Arrangement

Entries in general encyclopaedias are usually arranged in A – Z order, for quick reference. This leads to fragmentation of related material, partly compensated for by adequate 'see' and 'see also' references, plus a detailed analytical index. *Everyman's encyclopaedia* dispenses with the index, the editor claiming that 'comparatively short articles arranged in alphabetical order, backed by an extensive cross-reference system, are the best solution'. This claim is not wholly substantiated. A further prop to A – Z order, a classified list of articles or outlines for subject study, has already been mentioned.

Systematic arrangement on a grand scale is exemplified in *Encyclopédie de la Pléiade*, with its 50 or more subject volumes, each with its own editor and index, and each revised as necessary. The *Oxford illustrated encyclopaedia* (1985 –), due in 8 volumes, attempts to make the best of both worlds by providing subject volumes with entries in alphabetical order.

Readership

Encyclopaedias normally declare intended level of readership. This raises doubts when the *Academic American encyclopedia* assumes the British title *Macmillan family encyclopedia*. The *Encyclopedia Americana* claims a wide appeal: 'The tens of thousands of articles in the *Americana* serve as a bridge between the world of the specialist and the general reader.' The *World book encyclopedia* is more specific. Its aim is 'to meet the reference and study needs in the elementary school, junior high school, high school . . ., also as a family reference book'. Style should be adapted accordingly, with carefully escalated reading levels, as in *Merit students' encyclopedia*. Nor should junior encyclopaedias be written in a condescending manner. Some contributors to earlier editions of *Children's Britannica* were accused by a *Times literary supplement* reviewer of 'writing down' to their readers.[1] The change seems to have been made, but the result still makes for rather dull reading.

Slant and scope

The rapid growth of scientific and technical research has created problems for multi-volume encyclopaedias that traditionally paid more attention to the arts. The fourth supplement to the *Enciclopedia Italiana*, spanning the years 1961 – 78, highlights developments in technology, such as space stations, in line with recording advances in the humanities and social sciences.

A national slant in an encyclopaedia may express itself in two ways:

(a) The proportion of text, bibliography, illustrations, maps, etc. devoted to the home country and surrounding areas, as well as the proportion of native contributors. Although this type of slant can be turned to account, there are extremes. (Thus the *New book of knowledge* devotes five pages to a US President Hayes and only one to Haydn.)[2]

(b) The bias may be nationalist or ideological in the interpretation of events and achievements (e.g. in one country's role in World War II, or on the question of sovereignty over the Falkland Islands/Malvinas. The ideological slant of *Bolsh'shaya 3* is particularly marked. Thus the article on Stalin omits mention of the atrocities committed during his régime. *Marxism, Communism and Western society: a comparative encyclopedia*, edited by C. D. Kernig (1972 – 83. 8 vols.), however, carries few articles on Marxism or the Marxist viewpoint. 'Critical comparison always seems to favour the Western or capitalist point of view.'[3]

Bibliographies

Multi-volume encyclopaedias usually provide bibliographies of sources and further reading for at least major entries. When articles are monographic in length and sectionalized, it is kinder to the user to sectionalize the bibliographies as well. While *Enciclopedia italiana* does break down its bibliographies in this way, the 1985 *Britannica* groups bibliographies at the end of completed articles (e.g. 'Judaism': 6 columns). *Grand Larousse encyclopédique* collects its bibliographies at the end of each volume concerned, where they are liable to be overlooked. *Collier's encyclopedia* devotes 200 pages of its index volume to about 10,000 references under topics A – Z, and the index itself carries sub-entries to such references. The *World book encyclopedia* has a comparable practice of inserting references or 'for further reading' at appropriate points in its index. *Enciclopedia italiana* articles include in their bibliographies pointers to periodical articles, documents and iconography; the *Britannica*'s lengthy bibliographies are given running commentary.

Visual appeal

This being an age of colour television, general encyclopaedias have not been slow in using colour for illustrations. The *Grand Larousse encyclopédique* and its supplements have 31,458 illustrations, mostly in colour; and the newer *Grand dictionnaire encyclopédique* (1982 – 5. 10 vols.) extends colour to boxed data and similar devices. The size of the illustrations is of some importance. They may be relegated to margins and become decorative rather than functional. The *Britannica*'s Micropaedia, with its three-column page, reproduces many of its illustrations column-width, i.e. double postage-stamp size. Small town plans in encyclopaedias may well fail to name main thoroughfares. Coloured maps of countries, states, etc., accompanied by gazetteers of place-names, are a feature of many American encyclopaedias.

Indexes

The ratio of number of index entries to text words is a useful pointer to the thoroughness of indexing. The *Academic American encyclopaedia/Macmillan family encyclopaedia* has a ratio of about 1:36 (250,000 index entries; 9 million words). The *Britannica*'s ratio is about 1:100, and *Collier's* about 1:50.

When the publishing programme of an encyclopaedia extends over several years, interim cumulating indexes become desirable. Volumes 1 – 5 of the *Enclopaedia of Islam* (1960 – 86: A – Mahi) have an interim index (1988). Such a cumulating index became imperative in the case of the volume-by-volume translation, *Great Soviet encyclopedia* (1973 – 83. 31 vols. and general index).

Typography and format

A magnifying glass should be at hand for deciphering the tiny print used for the indexes, gazetteers, illustration captions and bibliographies in some general encyclopaedias. This applies to the text of *Grand dictionnaire encyclopédique Larousse* and the index volumes of *Joy of knowledge*. The former operates a three-column page, plus margin illustrations, and the reduced type-size is in sharp contrast to the much more ample page, two-column text and sizeable coloured illustrations of *La grande encyclopédie* (1971 – 8), the previous Larousse multi-volume set. The text of *Petit Robert 2* certainly calls for magnification.

The cramming of the contents of an encyclopaedia into a single weighty volume poses problems for the reader at the shelves, as well as creating an eventual binding problem. The *New Columbia encyclopedia* (1975), with over 3,000 pages, weighs 10.5 lbs. Even heavier is the *Random House encyclopedia*, designed as a family reference book, which weighs 11.5 lbs. Perhaps a lectern should be provided in such cases, as part of a package deal? Fortunately for their younger readers, the *Children's Britannica*, *New Caxton encyclopedia*, and *Joy of knowledge* (the English version of *Random House encyclopedia*) are in slim, largish, manageable volumes. Paper quality is another consideration. Junior encyclopaedias require strong paper. The once well-used *New Columbia encyclopedia* has flimsy paper.

Spine lettering needs to be conspicuous, particularly when encyclopaedias are placed on bottom shelves. Insufficient attention is paid by publishers of multi-volume sets to denoting text-coverage on spines sufficiently prominently. The *World book encyclopedia* and *Compton's encyclopedia* both allot one complete letter of the alphabet to each volume, as far as possible. Elsewhere the publisher's urge to provide uniformly paged volumes is paramount.

Currency

There are various devices for keeping encyclopaedias up to date. Annual revision of 10% of the text, where considered necessary, is normal practice for American encyclopaedias. The 30-volume

Americana claims a 15% annual revision, with interpolation of pages to avoid extensive resetting of type. The smaller 21-volume *Academic American encyclopedia*, the newest of these adult sets, offers 20% annual revision. *Compton's encyclopedia* concentrates revision on selected volumes each year. In 1987 the letters E, G, Q, T received extensive revision.[4] There comes a time, however, when complete overhaul becomes necessary. The *New encyclopaedia Britannica* had such overhauls in 1974 and 1985. The advice of Katz to American reference librarians is cautionary: 'When the set is more than five years old it should be discarded'.[5] This does overlook the value of some older sets such as the 1910 – 11 *Encyclopaedia Britannica*, for pre-twentieth-century events, persons, etc.

The practice of issuing yearbooks, ostensibly in order to update encyclopaedias is not wholly satisfactory. At worst these annuals may be little more than lavishly illustrated records of the previous year's noteworthy events, without systematically updating material in the parent work. The *Britannica* and *Collier's* yearbooks are among the best of their kind. Searching through a series of such yearbooks for particular articles can be tedious. The Spanish *Enciclopedia universal ilustrada*, however, has a cumulative index to supplements covering 1934 – 80.

ENGLISH-LANGUAGE ENCYCLOPAEDIAS

The NEW ENCYCLOPAEDIA BRITANNICA of 1985 is a restructuring of the set published in 1975, with its division of the text into Micropaedia ('rapid reference') and Macropaedia ('knowledge in depth'). The 1985 encyclopaedia, in 32 volumes, now includes a two-volume index. It was produced at a cost of $24 million. The new Micropaedia comprises 12 volumes, with 65,000 shortish unsigned articles. Its entries include cross-references to entries in the Macropaedia for more extended treatment of 680 signed, well-documented essays averaging 30,000 words, on countries and selected major persons and subjects. Some Macropaedia articles are of book length, e.g. 'Languages of the world': 225 pages, including 20 columns of grouped bibliography, with commentary, 'Music' (*c*. 200 pages) comprises four separate articles: 'The art of music'; 'The history of Western music'; 'Musical forms and genres'; and 'Musical instruments'. Each of these articles on music lists its constituent section headings, plus an appended bibliography. Whereas the entry on 'China' in the Micropaedia is largely a list of the main Chinese dynasties, that in the Macropaedia covers pages 31 – 255 of volume 16. The 100 selected biographical essays in the Macropaedia are reserved for persons 'who have profoundly influenced world history, culture and thought', e.g. Freud; Jung finds a place in the Micropaedia. In total, the 32-volume *Britannica* has 32,201 pages, 1,300 maps and 14,500 illustrations (8,500 in colour and particularly lavish on aspects of art). Propaedia ('outline of knowledge') has been reshaped to give greater emphasis to the history of mankind. The vital two-volume index exceeds 400,000 entries and sub-entries – a distinct advance on the 1974 edition's reliance on the Micropaedia as an indexing and cross-reference source.

Harvey Einbinder's strictures on the 1985 *Britannica*[6] focus on failure to keep up with the times. He instances over-reliance on material from the 1974 edition, 'without critical scrutiny', and the missed opportunity to update bibliographies – always a key factor in checking whether citations are recent enough. The 58-page article in the Macropaedia on 'The biological sciences' carries no references beyond 1973. Einbinder concedes, nevertheless, that the *Britannica* is the leading general encyclopaedia in the English language.

Apart from pursuing a policy of continuous revision, the *Britannica* has an excellent annual adjunct – the *Britannica book of the year*, an integral part of the whole. The 1989 yearbook comprises a feature article, a chronology of 1988, 'Britannica update', 'The year in review' (people and events), a list of contributors, and 'World data' (numerous statistical tables, with bibliography and list of sources), plus an index.

ENCYCLOPEDIA AMERICANA (Grolier, 1987 ed. 30 vols.) was first published in 1829 – 33, then being largely based on *Brockhaus Konversations-Lexikon* of 1827 – 9. Annual or frequent revisions began in 1936. While the *Americana*'s scope is avowedly international, there is evident concentration on US themes, especially history, persons, places and the individual US states. Canada is also well covered. The *Americana*'s 31 million words place it next to the *Britannica* in size. Its articles, too, can be lengthy, signed, well-documented and sectionalized, with a preliminary list of headings. Its 23,000 illustrations, mostly in black and white, are well placed. Maps, accompanied by gazetteers, cover the states, Canadian provinces and many countries. Each century is given a documented article and chronology ('Nineteenth century': 6 pages). The index musters 353,000 entries, a ratio to text words of 1:90. The result is a well-established, 'no nonsense' encyclopaedia, for adults and sixth-formers. The *Americana annual* (Grolier, 1923 –) helps to update both the *Americana* and *Academic American encyclopedia.*

COLLIER'S ENCYCLOPEDIA (Macmillan Educational, 1987 ed. 24 vols.) was first issued in 1949 – 51. It is easier to consult than the *Britannica* and more attractively produced than the *Americana*. It has fluent narrative style and visual appeal. 'The editors have included the essential content of the curriculum of colleges and secondary schools, as well as the upper grades' (Preface, vol. 1). Where *Collier's* differs from its two rivals is in the grouping of all the bibliographical references in the index volume: over 10,000 numbered and very briefly annotated entries. This robs the articles themselves of their references and sources. The combined 'index to text, bibliographies, illustrations and maps' has 450,000 entries. Volume 1 lists the contributors to the 23,000 signed articles. Continuous revision is the order of the day. *Collier's yearbook*, serving both *Collier's encyclopedia* and *Merit student's encyclopedia*, is one of the better annual reviews of noteworthy events.

ACADEMIC AMERICAN ENCYCLOPEDIA (Grolier, 1987 ed. 21 vols.), reprinted as *Macmillan family encyclopedia*, was first published in 1980. It breaks new ground by being available not only online, but also in disc form – 'Grolier electronic encyclopedia'.[7] It has *c.* 30,000 entries, mostly brief, but often signed, 20,000 illustrations (over 50% in colour), and 1,000 coloured maps. The comprehensive index has a high ratio of 1:45, comparing entries with text words. As a medium-sized multi-volume encyclopaedia, it is attractively produced and fairly up-to-date, striking a good balance between the 'academic' and the 'popular'. Its stated readership – US schools and universities – needs to be borne in mind. The *Americana annual*, also published by Grolier, serves as an annual.

Neither of the two British multi-volume encyclopaedias – *Chambers'* and *Everyman's* – has kept pace with the times. CHAMBERS' ENCYCLOPAEDIA, reprinted by Pergamon Press in 1982, is a patched-up version of the 1967 issue, itself an overhaul of the 1950 edition. *Chambers'* is well organized and was for some years regarded as the standard British publication in its field, but it has failed to stay with its American counterparts. Its latest bibliographical reference on Japan is dated 1939, and the latest on World War II is 1962. The 15-million word text has greater depth of treatment on historical subjects than has the *Macmillan family encyclopedia* (9 million words). The index volume carries a 64-page Bartholomew atlas, a gazetteer, a list of 3,000 contributors and a classified list of articles. *Chambers' encyclopaedia yearbook* (1968 – 73) has subsequently appeared as *A year of your life* (Caxton, and English Educational Programme International Ltd).

EVERYMAN'S ENCYCLOPEDIA (6th ed. Dent, 1978. 12 vols.) first appeared in 1913 – 14. With each edition, at ten-yearly intervals, features have been added. The 6th edition has a larger format and well-placed monochrome illustrations. It is also the easiest to handle of the medium-range sets. The British slant appears in the separate entries given to London, Oxford and Cambridge colleges, to British regiments, and to outline maps of English counties. Longer articles are sectionalized and often briefly documented. On the debit side, entries are not signed, although volume 1 carries a list of 350 contributors. The greatest drawback is the lack of an index. Despite its limits, *Everyman's* has value for desk and home use, as well as public libraries. To compensate for *Everyman's* lack of coloured illustrations, the *New illustrated Everyman's encyclopaedia* (Octopus Books, 1978; Dent, 1986. 2 vols.), first issued in 80 weekly parts, contains some 27,000 of the more important articles from the parent set, 'revised, updated and condensed to their essential elements'. The larger format accommodates *c.* 1,000 illustrations, mostly in colour. An index is still lacking.

THE NEW COLUMBIA ENCYCLOPEDIA (4th ed. New York and London, Columbia University Press, 1975. 3952pp.), first published in 1975, compares in some respects with *Everyman's*. Each has *c*. 10,000 unsigned entries, although *Everyman's* does list contributors. Both have outline maps, some illustrations and a national slant. While *Everyman's* carries 8 million words of text, *New Columbia* provides 6.5 million words in one weighty volume. Both add bibliographies to longer articles, *New Columbia* being more generous in this respect. Neither boasts an index, relying on cross-references. Much has occurred since 1975, but the *New Columbia* is at least partly updated by the *Concise Columbia encyclopedia* (1983), with its 15,000 entries.

THE LONGMAN ENCYCLOPEDIA (editor-in-chief Asa Briggs, 1989) states in its Foreword that the *Concise Columbia encyclopedia* 'was used as an indispensable base', its entries revised and updated and 'thousands of new entries' added. The *Longman encyclopedia* has *c*. 20,000 undocumented entries, with adequate outline maps and monochrome illustrations. Although weighty and lacking references, this *Longman encyclopedia* certainly helps for quick reference.

JUNIOR ENCYCLOPAEDIAS

The first choice for children's libraries is often the *World book encyclopedia* (1987. 24 vols.), first published in 1967. It musters about 3,000 contributors. Illustrations are a feature: 25,000 coloured; 5,000 black-and-white; 2,400 maps. Longer, signed articles have appended 'Study areas' (cross-references; questions; additional sources). Volumes 23 – 4, 'British Isles', claim to cover the region in a geographical, not a political sense. Yet, while these two volumes contain articles on British and Irish counties, the main set carries essays, with maps, on England, Scotland, Wales, Northern Ireland and the Irish Republic. This makes for confusion. Volume 22, 'Research guide/Index' includes more than 200 hours' reading and study guides, apart from 150,000 index entries. This popular junior encyclopaedia is also available in large print, Braille and cassette form, as well as online. Annual continuous revision is supported by a well-planned yearbook.

NEW BOOK OF KNOWLEDGE (Grolier, 1983. 21 vols.) has much to commend it for children aged 7 to 14. There are 7 million words of text and 8,890 articles, mostly signed. Two-thirds of the 23,000 illustrations are in colour – a notable feature. The text shows a pronounced emphasis on things American. There are 83,000 index entries, apart from volume indexes and cross-references. The *New book of knowledge* annual is particularly adapted to the interests of youngsters and has a good index, plus a separate paperback *Home and school reading and study guide*.

MERIT STUDENT'S ENCYCLOPEDIA (Macmillan Educational Corp. 20 vols.) is more closely based on US high-school requirements and assembles *c*. 2,500 contributors. Of the 20,000 illustrations, only 25% are in colour. Lengthy articles have appended 'Books for further reading'. Volume 20 includes a 140,000-entry index. Continuous revision appears to be largely devoted to statistical and basic data. The *Collier's yearbook* serves both *Collier's* and *Merit student's* encyclopaedias.

THE CHILDREN'S BRITANNICA (20 vols.) carries 3 million words in 4,230 articles. It caters for an audience similar to that of *New book of knowledge*, but it lacks its rival's wealth of coloured illustrations, and articles are neither signed nor documented. The American version is entitled *Britannica junior encyclopedia* (15 vols.).

Two junior encyclopaedias that are now out of print deserve a mention. the NEW CAXTON ENCYCLOPAEDIA (1978. 20 vols.) excels for its 15,000 coloured illustrations, but its 13,000 unsigned articles are less adequate and lack notes on further reading. Volume 20 bears the title 'The book of key facts study guide index'. The MITCHELL BEAZLEY BOOK OF KNOWLEDGE (1983. 10 vols.) has eight subject volumes ('Science and the universe' ... 'The modern world'), specializing in two-page spreads that could help with school project-writing. The two-volume 'Fact index' is a type of Micropaedia, with brief biographies, dictionary definitions and marginal illustrations. The American title is *Random House encyclopedia*.

OXFORD ILLUSTRATED ENCYCLOPEDIA (Oxford University Press, in association with Rainbird, 1985 – .) promises eight self-contained volumes. 'The physical world' and 'The natural world' (both 1985) and 'World history' (1988. 2 vols.) have so far appeared. The work acts as a revamped *Oxford junior encyclopedia* (1961, reprinted 1974. 12 vols. and index), and follows a similar

A – Z sequence of entries. The set is designed for school and home, reference and browsing. Volume 8 is to include a general index.

FOREIGN-LANGUAGE ENCYCLOPAEDIAS

'The forefront of encyclopedia progress has passed overseas', concluded the American critic, Einbinder in 1980.[8] He based his impression on two events: (a) the striking visual appeal of *La grande encyclopédie, Encyclopaedia universalis*, and the Dutch *Grote Winkler Prins*; (b) depth of treatment of current topics, and new devices in presenting information. Thus *Grote Winkler Prins in 25 delen* (8th ed. Amsterdam, Elsevier, 1979 – 84), well documented and illustrated, used coloured boxed data and chronological tables in biographical articles. It further appended to each volume a chronology of a particular century's events (e.g. vol. 2: 2nd century AD). *Encyclopaedia universalis* gives prominence in its final volume, 'Symposium', to essays on current concepts and controversial issues. Einbinder contrasts these initiatives with the patching-up process of annual revision and the eye-catching expedient of American encyclopaedia yearbooks. On the other hand, it may be argued that the continental tendency to spread publication of encyclopaedias over a period of years, especially in the German tradition, has its drawbacks.

German

German encyclopaedias have a long history. Although international in scope, they allot more space to Central European matters.

The *Brockhaus* encyclopaedias go back to the 1796 – 1808 edition. The 17th edition of BROCKHAUS ENZYKLOPÄDIE comprises vols. 1 – 20 (the main A – Z sequence); vol. 21: Atlas, with a 100,000 gazetteer of place-names; vols. 22 – 3: Supplement; and vol. 24, an illustrated German-language dictionary. The 18th edition, as *Das grosse Brockhaus*, is in 12 volumes (1977 – 81, with supplements, 1981 – 4). The 19th edition, reverting to the title *Brockhaus Enzyklopädie*, is to be in 24 volumes (1986 –). It has the traditional octavo format, stout binding and smallish type. Volume 8: FRU – GOS (1989) runs to 688 pages, with small coloured illustrations. Helping to bridge the gap until completion of the 19th edition is the compact one-volume *Der Brockhaus in einem Band, neu, von A biz Z* (2nd ed. 1988, 1016pp.). This has 55,000 entries, covering personal and place-names, and is heavily abbreviated. Illustrations, including 3,500 in colour, are normally of column width or relegated to margins. Coloured boxed information is a feature, but less satisfactory is the 16-page coloured atlas, crowded with place-names.

MEYERS ENZYKLOPÄDISCHES LEXIKON (9th ed. Mannheim, Bibliographisches Institut, 1971 – 81. 29 vols.) was first published in 1857 – 60. It includes lengthy articles, many small coloured illustrations and bibliographies. The main sequence (vols. 1 – 25) is followed by a supplement, world atlas, proper-name index and a German-English-French illustrated dictionary, rather like the *Brockhaus*. This Mannheim production is not to be confused with the East German MEYERS NEUES LEXIKON (2nd ed. Leipzig, VEB Bibliographisches Institut, 1972 – 8. 18 vols.). This latter has 120,000 undocumented entries and 24,000 illustrations. It will be recalled that the firm of Meyer openly hailed the coming of National Socialism in the Germany of 1933. The Meyer concern was liquidated in 1946, and the Bibliographisches Institut thereafter operated from two ideologically differing centres – Leipzig and Mannheim.

French

The pride taken by the French in their language, its precision of vocabulary and syntax is reflected both in the variety of French dictionaries and also in the range of French encyclopaedias and encyclopaedic dictionaries.

GRAND DICTIONNAIRE UNIVERSAL DU XIXe SIÈCLE (Larousse, 1865 – 88. 17 vols.) was the first French multi-volume encyclopaedia to be designed for a wide public. It combined a dictionary of words with extensive articles on subjects occasioned by those words, as felt necessary. Although it is still of value as a source of biographical, historical and technical data, as well as anecdotage, its illustrations are scant and its bibliographies slight.

Nevertheless, it created a Larousse house-style, much as did the first *Brockhaus*.

LA GRANDE ENCYCLOPÉDIE (Lamirault, 1880 – 92. 32 vols.) has been compared with the 9th edition of the *Encyclopaedia Britannia* (1875 – 89) for its scholarly signed contributions and valuable bibliographies. This set is rich in biographies, especially of minor personages not mentioned in other encyclopaedias, in the historical aspects of subjects, and as a gazetteer of France as it then was.

LA GRANDE ENCYCLOPÉDIE (Larousse, 1971 – 8. 20 vols. and index. Supplements, 1981, 1985) complements the Lamirault by stressing twentieth-century achievements. Numerous short entries mingle with *c.* 8,000 lengthy signed articles. Much wordage is given to French towns, as opposed to foreign cities. The broad page gives ample setting to the 14,000 illustrations and the index claims 400,000 entries. *Atlas général Larousse* (1976), published separately because of its large format, contains 184 pages of maps, a gazetteer of 54,000 names and a statistics section. *La Grande encyclopédie*'s popularity with a wide section of the public is ascribed by Einbinder to the dearth of public libraries in France and to its value as a working tool for students who need to obtain their baccalauréat as a stepping stone to a career.

The GRAND DICTIONNAIRE ENCYCLOPÉDIQUE LAROUSSE (1982 – 5. 10 vols.) is an updated but condensed version of *La Grande encyclopédie* of 1971 – 8, for quick reference. Its format is less generous, using a three-column page, plus marginal drawings, and smaller illustrations and type. There are 190,000 entries in all. Bibliographies appear at the end of each volume, where they are likely to be overlooked. However, the 2,500 illustrations and 250 maps are all coloured.

ENCYCLOPAEDIA UNIVERSALIS (Paris, 1985 ed. 22 vols.), first published in 1968 – 75, breaks with the Larousse tradition in several ways, and its structure bears comparison with the 1985 *Britannica*. Thus Corpus (18 vols.) forms a sort of Macropaedia and has 80,000 references attached to substantial articles. Thesaurus index (3 vols.) resembles the Micropaedia in its abundance of short entries and congested four-column page in small print. The shortish essays in the Symposium, the final volume, discuss aspects of the contemporary world. Articles in the Corpus are strikingly placed, and definitions are well separated from the extensive commentaries that follow in smaller type. The entry 'Espace (conquête de l')' occupies 32 pages of volume 7; it includes 51 illustrations (32 in colour), numerous tables and cross-references, and 4 columns of bibliography. *Universalia: les événements, les hommes, les problèmes* is the *Encyclopaedia*'s yearbook, and there is a cumulative index covering the 1974 – 85 issues.

PETIT ROBERT 2: DICTIONNAIRE UNIVERSEL DES NOMS PROPRES ALPHABÉTIQUE ET ANALOGIQUE DE LA LANGUE FRANÇAISE (new ed. 1988. 1952pp.) is the fullest of the one-volume French encyclopaedias. It is, in fact, a one-volume version of the five-volume *Dictionnaire universel alphabétique et analogique des noms propres* (1984). *Petit Robert 2* – companion to *Petit Robert 1*, which is a French – French dictionary – has 38,000 entries, 4,200 coloured illustrations and 210 maps. It is superior to the corresponding part of the annual *Petit Larousse illustré*.

The ENCYCLOPÉDIE DE LA PLÉIADE series (Gallimard, 1935 –) comprises about 50 mutually exclusive subject volumes, each with its own editor, contributors and index. Revised editions appear as necessary. Titles range from *Ethnologie régional* (1978) to *Histoire des religions* (1978 – 83. 3 vols.). Individual volumes may run to over 1,000 pages of solid text – for concentrated reading rather than quick reference.

Italian

ENCICLOPEDIA ITALIANA DI SCIENZE, LETTERE ED ARTI (Milan, Istituto Giovanni Trecani; latterly Rome, Istituto della Enciclopedia Italiana, 1929 – 39. 36 vols. *Appendice* 1: 1938; 2: 1939 – 48; 3: 1949 – 60; 4: 1961 – 78 (1979 – 81. 3 vols.) is a major general encyclopaedia. Authoritative, signed and well-documented articles are supported by fine-quality illustrations. The complete set, so far, totals 42,422 pages and 12,400 illustrations (some in colour). Maps are the work of the Touring Club Italiano. Volume 36, the index, includes Appendice 1 and has about 400,000 entries. The humanities and social sciences are particularly well covered in the main sete. 'Inghilterra' has

67 pages on history, language, ethnology and folklore, art, music and literature. Bibliographies are extensive and include periodical articles. The celebrated contribution 'Fascismo' (vol. 14, 847 – 84) includes the section 'Dottrina' by Mussolini, but this does not reflect the general political stance of the encyclopaedia. Supplements 1 – 4 are increasingly international and pay more tribute to scientific and technical achievements. *Enciclopedia del novecento* (Rome, Istituto della Enciclopedia Italiana, 1975 – 89. 8 vols. Vol. 8 has subtitle: Supplemento) updates and complements *Enciclopedia Italiana* in style and coverage.

GRANDE DIZIONARIO ENCICLOPEDICO UTET (3rd ed. Turin, Unione Tipografico-editrice Torinese, 1967 – 79. 20 vols. and Appendice; first published in 1933 – 40) is, like the *Enciclopedia*, well produced. Volume 20 comprises a 200,000-entry index and atlas of 78 maps (by the Istituto Geografico de Agostini), plus 30 pages of historical maps.

Spanish

ENCICLOPEDIA UNIVERSAL ILUSTRADA EUROPEO-AMERICANA (Barcelona, Espasa, 1903 – 33. 80 vols. in 81; 10 vols. of *Apendice*) adds supplements, 1934 – . Known as 'Espasa', it is the largest of the twentieth-century general encyclopaedias and has over one million unsigned entries. 'Espasa' combines the functions of an encyclopaedia, a multi-lingual dictionary (covering French, Italian, English, German, Catalan and Esperanto equivalents of Spanish terms), a gazetteer and biographical sourcebook. Major subjects are treated at length, with extensive bibliographies. Volume 21, 'España', is revised at ten-yearly intervals. Emphasis throughout is on the Iberian peninsula and Latin America. The latest supplement (1987) covers 1983 – 4.

GRAN ENCICLOPEDIA RIALP (Madrid, 1971 – 6. 24 vols.) is more manageable than the 'Espasa'. It carries 15,000 articles by 3,000 contributors worldwide, and its 20,000 pages are particularly strong on the history, geography, literature and arts of Spain and Hispanic America. As a major Spanish general encyclopaedia, it is superior to 'Espasa' pictorially; over half of its 20,000 illustrations are in colour. But its index is insufficiently specific and lacks references to the illustrations. Accompanying the index is an atlas, a gazetteer and a list of contributors.

Portuguese

VERBO: ENCICLOPEDIA LUSO-BRASILIERA DE CULTURA (Lisbon, 1963 – 84. 20 vols., vols. 19 – 20 being supplements) has signed and documented articles, mainly on Portugal and Brazil, but not neglecting other parts of the world. Some of the many small illustrations are in colour. A feature is the use of UDC schedule terms for hundreds of articles.

Russian

Of the earlier Russian encyclopaedias, ENTSIKLOPEDIYA SLO-VAR' (Moscow, Granat, 1910 – 48. 74 parts) is important for coverage of nineteenth-century Russian literature, of the lives of earlier Russian Socialists, and for Lenin's article on Karl Marx in volume 28.

The first BOL'SHAYA SOVETSKAYA ENTSIKLOPEDIYA (Moscow, 1926 – 47. 66 vols.) was conceived on a grand scale, with lengthy signed and documented entries. A second edition followed in 1950 – 8 (51 vols.), plus a two-volume index. An updating yearbook (*Ezhegodnik*) began in 1957. This second edition stressed Soviet economic, industrial and technical achievements. We are now in the Stalin era, and the *Bol'shaya* 2nd edition reflects purges of the theoretical and political errors of the previous set. Publishers delayed until 1957 the issue of volume 40, which contained the article on Stalin (who died in 1953). Volume 50, *USSR*, is a comprehensive work of reference on the Soviet Union, with sections on political structure, economy, history, geography and scientific developments. An English translation, *Information SSR* (Oxford, Pergamon Press) appeared in 1962. Volume 51, a supplement, had many biographical entries – some for persons included for the first time, others for people whose reputations had been rehabilitated. The two-volume index to *Bol'shaya 2* carried 200,000 entries.

The third edition of the *Bol'shaya* (1969 – 78. 30 vols.) has

100,000 entries and represents a more factual approach than the second edition, while maintaining its ideological viewpoint. The US Declaration of Independence is briefly described as the product of a bourgeois revolution; the article on Glasgow concentrates on the strikes that have occurred there. National emphasis is also marked. Thus, 'Azerbaidzhanskaya SSR' occupies columns 716 – 75 of volume 1, with 25 sections, 5 illustrations, 8 tables, 3 maps and half a column of bibliography. Volume 31 includes a list of contributors. While book production shows an improvement (type is clear and paper white instead of greyish), photographs are still of inferior quality.

THE GREAT SOVIET ENCYCLOPEDIA: A TRANSLATION OF THIRD EDITION OF THE BOL'SHAYA SOVETSKAYA ENTSIK-LOPEDIYA (New York, Macmillan, 1973 – 82. 30 vols.) is a volume-for-volume version of the original. Because entries per volume are taken from the Russian, the English translation of headwords, and therefore articles, sets up a different A – Z order. While the *Bol'shaya*'s volume 1 contains entries under the Russian letter 'A', the translation begins with 'Aalen Stage' and ends with 'Zulu War'. Thus, each translated volume has its own A – Z sequence. Interim cumulative indexes to individual articles are finalized by the general index in volume 30. The translation omits all maps and most of the illustrations – a distinct drawback, since the original contained a number of World War II Soviet-front campaign maps, for example. Translation is thorough[9] and the quality of book production sound. This English-language version is certainly to be valued as a consistent statement of the Soviet stance as of 1981.

SOVETSKII ENTSIKLOPEDICHESKII SLOVAR' (1980. 1601pp.) has some 150,000 brief entries in three columns. Over 700 category labels are applied. Illustrations and maps are small, but there are four pages of coloured maps. The article on Lenin runs to 1½ columns, and the appendix carries six tables.

LISTS OF GENERAL ENCYCLOPAEDIAS

One of the fullest listings appears in *British Library general catalogue of printed books, to 1975* (Munich, K. G. Saur, 1978 – 87. 360 vols.), under the form heading 'Encyclopaedias'. (Supplements include further titles of encyclopaedias under their individual names.) The fourth edition of *Dictionaries, encyclopaedias and other word-related books*, edited by A. M. Brewer (Detroit, Gale, 1988. 2 vols. 1333pp.) provides reproductions of Library of Congress printed cards for 35,000 titles. Entries indicate inclusion of bibliographies.

Annotated lists of general encyclopaedias appear in the Totok-Weitzel *Handbuch der bibliographischen Nachschlagewerke* (6th ed. Frankfurt am Main, Klostermann, 1984 – 5. 2 vols., vol. 1, 330 – 69). Also in Sheehy's *Guide to reference books* (10th ed. Chicago, American Library Association, 1986) 134 – 46; and *Walford's guide to reference material* (4th ed. vol.3., 1987) 117 – 31.

BUYERS' GUIDES

A helpful aide-mémoire is *Purchasing an encyclopedia: 12 points to consider* (2nd ed. Chicago, American Library Association, 1988). This 40-page booklet states criteria and reviews 10 sets. The ALA's *Reference books bulletin* is a leading reviewing source. '1988 annual encyclopedia update', fifth in a series, appeared in the 1988/9 *Bulletin*. It enumerates 10 points and notes significant changes in purpose, arrangement, content, style and general quality of 10 sets, with a summary comparative chart. 'Encyclopedia annuals, supplements and year-books: a 1985 overview' (*Reference books bulletin, 1985/86*), has an appended chart analysing eight encyclopaedia yearbooks.

Kister's concise guide to best encyclopedias, by K. P. Kister (Phoenix, Arizona, Oryx Press, 1988) is the latest version of his *Encyclopedia buying guide* (Bowker, 1981) – a critical consumer guide to 12 English-language sets. *The buyer's guide to encyclopedias* (Cheltenham, Simply Creative, 1989, rev. ed.) compares in chart form 13 multi-volume sets, divided between adult and junior titles. 'In depth' reviews of eight of these precedes. The late J. P. Walsh's handy folded chart, *Encyclopedia ratings* (11th ed. 1982) analysed ratings and age-groups for 20 sets, half of these British.

ONLINE ENCYCLOPAEDIAS

Four English-language general encyclopaedias have their text – but not their illustrations – online: *Encyclopaedia Britannica* (via Mead Data Central 1981 – , but not available to libraries);[10] the *World book encyclopedia* (for CompuServe subscribers); *Everyman's encyclopedia* (via DIALOG); and *Academic American encyclopedia* (via BRS, DIALOG, CompuServe, etc.; also available on a CD-ROM disc).

G. Flagg's article, 'Online encyclopedias'[11] discusses disadvantages of cost and the delay in quick retrieval of information, compared with a printed A – Z article text and its detailed index.

One needs to distinguish between updating of an encyclopaedia's files by means of a database and an encyclopaedia available online. Century Hutchinson, for example, has set up its own encyclopaedia database, using BRS Search, in order to update files for the *Hutchinson encyclopedia* (now in its 8th edition) as well as for producing Concise and Pocket versions.[12]

Availability to the general public of an online encyclopaedia, using modern storage and retrieval techniques, is still in its early stages. 'Online encyclopedias: potential for improving access to knowledge and information', by S. P. Harter and K. F. Kister,[13] instances the case of a full-text searching, using the *Academic American encyclopedia* on the BRS search system. The query was 'Who were the leaders of the twentieth-century modernist movement in English-language poetry?' As a result of the BRS search, after several 'false drops', a list of 91 relevant articles was retrieved. The names of W. B. Yeats, William Carlos Williams, Stephen Spender and Ezra Pound met the search conditions. Harter explores the potential of the online encyclopaedia (why not *Whitaker's almanack* online?) in his admirable article, 'Online encyclopedias'.[14]

REFERENCES AND CITATIONS

1 *Times literary supplement*, 3555, 10 April 1970, 412.
2 *The buyer's guide to encyclopedias*. Cheltenham: Simply Creative, 1989, 18.

3 *Wilson library bulletin*, **47** (6), February 1973, 539.
4 *Reference books bulletin*, 1987/8, 10.
5 Katz, W. A., *Introduction to reference work*. 5th ed. New York: McGraw-Hill, 1987, vol.1, 192.
6 Einbinder, H., 'The new Britannica: pro and con', *Library journal*, 1987, 48 – 50.
7 Bendig, M. W., 'The encyclopedia online', *RSR*, **10** (2), Summer 1982, 25 – 6.
8 Einbinder, H., 'Encyclopedias: some foreign and domestic developments', *Wilson library bulletin*, **55** (4), December 1980, 257 – 61.
9 Grimsted, P. K., 'Détente on the shelves?' *Wilson library bulletin*, **48** (10), January 1975, 728.
10 Katz, W. A., *op. cit.*, 203 – 4.
11 Flagg, G., 'Online encyclopedias: are they ready for librarians? Are libraries ready for them?', *American libraries*, March 1983, 134 – 5.
12 *Information world review*, November 1988, 20.
13 Harter, S. P. and Kister, K. F., 'Online encyclopedias: potential for improving access to knowledge and information', *Library journal*, 100, 1 September, 1981, 1600 – 2.
14 Harter, S. P., 'Online encyclopedias', in *Encyclopedia of library and information science*, vol. 38, supplement 3 (1985), 313 – 24, 20 refs.

4

Subject Encyclopaedias

Denis J. Grogan

For many readers the term 'reference book' immediately suggests 'encyclopaedia', inasmuch as they will often turn first to a general encyclopaedia when they seek information. Within a particular subject field, however – say physics or economics or the theatre – a searcher's first step is often much less confident. Yet here too there are available hundreds, even thousands, of subject encyclopaedias, offering in most disciplines an obvious first place to look things up. Typically, they are handy single-volume compilations, often designed for the home or the office-desk or the work-bench. Many are planned as 'one-stop' reference tools, aiming to answer as many queries as possible without having to refer the searcher elsewhere. The student should note that they may not always be described as subject encyclopaedias.

Drabble, M. (ed.), THE OXFORD COMPANION TO ENGLISH LITERATURE. 5th ed. Oxford: Oxford University Press, 1985.

This was the earliest of the now extensive series of Oxford Companions (all of which are actually subject encyclopaedias) and a model of its kind. Though its reputation stands high with academics and literary critics, and its new editor is herself an eminent novelist, critic and literary biographer, it is not designed primarily for specialists. Its original compiler, Sir Paul Harvey, made clear in his preface to the first edition in 1932 that it was for 'ordinary, everyday readers of English literature', and his successor confirms that this is still the intended audience for her much revised edition.

Though over 80 contributors are listed, none of the articles are signed. Scarcely any exceeds half a page, and the majority are much less; with the extensive system of cross-references this enables users very speedily to run their quarry to earth. The emphasis is on primary factual information rather than critical appreciation, and as well as the expected articles on authors, titles and subjects there are brief entries for hundreds of characters from literature, and for many other allusions which contain a proper name: actual celebrities as well as legendary characters, such as John Wesley and Robin Hood; and places real and imaginary such as Grub Street and Xanadu.

For its specific purpose, to 'quickly, easily, and clearly satisfy the immediate curiosity of the common reader', it tries to be self-sufficient: there are no bibliographies to suggest further sources to consult and there is no index.

An important advantage of the single-volume format is the relative ease with which new editions can be produced, compared with the massive investment of time and effort necessary to revise the great multi-volume general encyclopaedias. One noticeable effect of this flexibility is the way in which over the years succeeding editions of some titles have differed markedly from their predecessors, responding to changing needs and demands.

Considine, D. M. (ed.), VAN NOSTRAND'S SCIENTIFIC ENCYCLOPEDIA. 7th ed. 2 vols. New York: Van Nostrand Reinhold, 1989.

From its first publication in 1938 this work steadily acquired a well-deserved reputation as 'the world's most consulted one-volume science reference'. Now an estimated 4 million words from over 200 specialist contributors, its doubling in size from the 2 million words of the fifth (1976) edition has made obligatory the two-volume format which was offered only as an option for purchasers of the sixth edition of 1983. Covering technology and medicine as well as science, and illustrated with over 3,000 photographs, drawings, diagrams and charts, virtually one for each page, it still fulfils its claim to 'obviate the need for you having a multi-volume work in your library, home or office'.

From the fifth edition onwards bibliographies were appended to a number of the major articles. A more radical change was the consolidation of many of the short entries, 'thus yielding more concentrated information in fewer locations', and reducing the number of articles from 16,500 to 7,200 (generally unsigned). The provision of over 8,000 cross-references, increased to 9,500 in the sixth edition, only partly compensated the searcher for this reduction in access via the alphabetical headings. To enhance access to the 6,773 A to Z articles of this seventh edition, the compilers have wisely decided to provide a 109-page alphabetical index as well. Making a virtue out of a necessity, they now claim that this index 'finds few rivals in the realms of technical literature'.

The range of subjects now supplied with weighty encyclopaedias is astonishing. There are, for instance, 1,354 entries in B. S. Wynar (ed.), *ARBA* [American reference books annual] *guide to subject encyclopedias and dictionaries* (Littleton, Colorado: Libraries Unlimited, 1986), which covers only 17 years and is restricted to 'only the most useful sources'. Even experienced librarians are regularly surprised to encounter some of the minutely specialized titles now available, e.g. A. L. Hunting, *Encyclopedia of shampoo ingredients* (Cranford, New Jersey: Micelle, 1983), with 467 pages; K. M. Briggs, *A dictionary of fairies, hobgoblins, brownies, bogies and other supernatural creatures* (London: Allen Lane, 1976), with 481 pages, which is an encyclopaedia despite its title (the American edition (New York: Pantheon, 1977) does indeed call itself *An encyclopedia* . . .).

We now also have a collective index to contents in the shape of J. Ryan (ed.), *First stop: the master index to subject encyclopedias* (Phoenix, Arizona: Oryx, 1989), covering selectively the articles in 430 reference works, mainly subject encyclopaedias but also including some handbooks, dictionaries, yearbooks, etc.

ROLE AND CONTENT

As has often been said, the real task of an encyclopaedia is to provide 'first and essential facts' only: **first**, meaning those obvious details that any enquirer would want to know, and **essential**, in the sense of those intrinsic facts without which it is not possible to perceive the nature of the topic under discussion. Obviously all encyclopaedias have to be selective to some extent, and so it is quite unfair to judge any example solely by the amount of information between its covers: it is no task for an encyclopaedia to attempt to exhaust its topic. There is a more important criterion to apply in assessing whether a work warrants the accolade of 'encyclopaedia': historically and etymologically such works were intended to encompass the whole circle of learning. This of course has not been feasible in a strictly literal sense for generations, but it is scarcely possible to allow the description of 'encyclopaedia' to a work that does not at least aim for **comprehensiveness**. This must not be confused with completeness: a comprehensive work is one with a coverage of its field that is all-embracing, though its depth may vary according to circumstances.

ALEXIS LICHINE'S NEW ENCYCLOPEDIA OF WINES AND SPIRITS. 7th ed. London: Cassell, 1987.

By a wine-grower and former wine merchant, this volume is designed to be world-wide in its coverage and claims that it is 'the most comprehensive, authoritative book in its field'. Most of it is taken up by the 562-page alphabetical sequence of entries, but this is preceded by ten chapters on the history of wine, serving wine, spirit-making, etc., and is followed by 100 pages of appendices covering, for example, containers and measures and a comparative table of spirit strengths. The whole is rounded off by a 250-item bibliography and a 12,000-entry index. It provides a rapid and concise response to queries such as 'What are all the various sizes of champagne bottles called?', 'What is a bumper?', 'How is sake served in Japan?'

Multi-volume encyclopaedias

No library user can remain unaware for long of another quite distinct category of subject encyclopaedia, the great multi-volume compilations found in ever-increasing numbers in the major disciplines, matching in many respects *New Britannica*, *World book*, *Americana* and *Italiana* in the general field.

ENCYCLOPEDIA OF WORLD ART. 15 vols. New York: McGraw-Hill, 1959 – 68. SUPPLEMENT (vol. 16), 1983; SUPPLEMENT (vol. 17), 1987.

Printed in Italy (and simultaneously published in Italian), this is an outstanding example of a work planned as 'a major historical synthesis covering the arts of all periods and countries'. Further lofty aims are to be 'factually complete within the limits of possibility', and to be intelligible to an audience without previous specialized preparation. Understandably, illustrations figure prominently: in addition to thousands of line drawings in the text, a good half of each volume is taken up by half-tone plates.

In facing the dilemma of how to arrange the material the editors found that 'None of the usual plans of classification or exposition can be followed rigidly without doing violence to the autonomy and individuality of one aspect or another of the many-faceted world of art.' They concluded that the best arrangement was 'a series of separate but co-ordinated monographs, presented in alphabetical order without regard to their content'. Detailed access to the thousand or so long articles is provided by a 20,000-entry index volume, and each is supplied with an extensive scholarly bibliography of sources, including both books and periodical articles.

Even though a subject may already be furnished with a standard multi-volume encyclopaedia of this kind, changes in the *nature* of the discipline, apart from simply its growth, may be such as to require from time to time a completely new approach.

Eliade, M. (ed.), THE ENCYCLOPEDIA OF RELIGION. 16 vols. London: Collier Macmillan, 1987.

Believing that 'the "information explosion" of recent decades has demanded a new presentation of available materials', and furthermore that 'a radical change of perspective' is called for, the compilers of this landmark work have set out to provide nothing less than an 'objective description of the totality of human experiences of the sacred'. Compared to the great standard 13-volume set, J. Hastings (ed.), *Encyclopaedia of religion and ethics* (Edinburgh: Clark, 1908 – 26), which was reprinted in 1955 and is still in print in 1990, the new work emphasizes the practical and sociological dimensions as well as the theoretical, and is less Western-based.

It is clearly a scholarly work, articles often extending to several pages. A deliberate decision was taken not to supply short entries 'covering the entire vocabulary in every field of religious studies', but to provide 'a great network of historical and descriptive articles, synthetical discussions, and interpretive essays'. The extensive bibliographies following the articles are more than mere lists: they are usually narrative in form, with evaluative comments. The 1,300 contributors are drawn from all five continents.

Considerable thought was given to the arrangement of entries and it was early decided to use alphabetical order. But the compilers tell us that 'To avoid the dilemma of "alphabetization" versus "systematization", however, we also planned to follow the ... practice of ... using "composite entries" to group two or more articles under one heading, thus permitting systematic discussion of broad topics.' For instance, the entry 'Afterlife' extends to over 20 pages and comprises four articles each by a different contributor: 'An overview', 'Geographies of death', 'Jewish concepts', 'Chinese concepts'.

Cross-references are plentifully supplied to assist the searcher, but detailed access to the 3,000 articles is best obtained by means of the very thorough 50,000-entry analytical index in volume 16.

These two titles are obviously something more than quick-reference works: some have seen in such comprehensive compilations an extension of the usual role of the encyclopaedia beyond 'first and essential facts' only. They may still be alphabetically arranged, but they appear to have taken on to some extent the role of a treatise, assimilating all of the literature in a particular field and presenting an authoritative synthesis. Indeed, one of the signs that a discipline has come of age is the appearance of a scholarly, multi-volume subject encyclopaedia.

Barnouw, E. (ed.), INTERNATIONAL ENCYCLOPEDIA OF COM-MUNICATIONS. 4 vols. Oxford: Oxford University Press, 1989.

Describing itself as 'a first effort to define the field in a comprehensive way', signalling 'a new stage in the development of the field of communications as an area of knowledge, study, practice, technique and research, and as an academic discipline', and six years in preparation, this handsome new work comprises 569 signed scholarly articles by some 500 contributors from 29 countries.

It defines its field as 'all ways in which information, ideas and attitudes pass among individuals, groups, nations and generations'. This includes some exceedingly diverse topics, e.g. 'Calendar', 'Cuneiform', 'Diaspora', 'Exploration', 'Gandhi', 'Gender', 'Slips of the tongue', 'Spy fiction'.

In a commendable attempt to avoid early obsolescence, the focus is on the long-range perspective, with less attention to specific detail than some users might expect.

The work is patently 'academic' in tone: its editor-in-chief is Professor Emeritus of Drama at Columbia University and it is published jointly with the Annenberg School of Communications of the University of Pennsylvania. The intended audience is 'college students, scholars, professionals and educated laypersons'. There are over 1,100 black-and-white illustrations, mainly photographs. Entries for people are frequent, including the living if born before 1920, but are brief career biographies only. Bibliographies are included with each article: items are mainly in English, but are up-to-date. We are told that 'The Research Bibliographer [on the editorial staff] has verified the accuracy of each entry using standard references.'

After much thought, including consideration by no fewer than three gatherings of communications scholars, alphabetical arrangement was preferred to systematic, with long articles, including some 'composites'. Cross-references between the articles are used to link related subjects, and a 15,000-entry analytical index permits more specific access.

ARRANGEMENT

What above all marks out a reference book from other works is the way it is arranged: it must be deliberately designed for ease of consultation rather than for continuous reading. And it is by its arrangement, as much as by its content, that an encyclopaedia stands to be judged. It is not sufficient that the information provided is comprehensive and fundamental: it must also be easy of access. The usual method is alphabetical by subject; it is instructive to note how the three encyclopaedias just described each arrived at an alphabetical arrangement, though starting from different premises.

Of course, setting out articles in alphabetical order produces an 'arrangement determined by the accident of initial letters', inevitably separating related topics, and some encyclopaedia compilers have therefore come to a different conclusion. Among the multi-volume general encyclopaedias, for instance, *Encyclopédie française* (21 vols.), *Oxford junior encyclopaedia* (13 vols.), and *Joy of knowledge* (10 vols.) are all arranged systematically by subject. Readers are commonly surprised by this; yet historically the systematically arranged encyclopaedia was the first on the scene by many hundreds of years. Among subject encyclopaedias too, one occasionally encounters a systematic rather than an alphabetical arrangement.

Barrett, D. B. (ed.), WORLD CHRISTIAN ENCYCLOPEDIA: A COMPARATIVE STUDY OF CHURCHES AND RELIGIONS IN THE MODERN WORLD, AD 1900 – 2000. Oxford: Oxford University Press, 1982.

Describing itself as 'a comprehensive survey of all branches of global Christianity' and 12 years in the making, this massive volume draws on 500 contributors from 190 countries. We read that 'In order not to fragment the subject unnecessarily by forcing the material into the artificial mould of a simple A – Z alphabetical sequence throughout, this volume divides its treatment of the subject into fourteen major topics.' These include a chronology,

40 pages of statistical tables, a 36-page dictionary of terms, a world bibliography of Christianity, a who's who, a directory of organizations, and, by far the largest, a survey of 232 countries, one by one, arranged A to Z.

INDEXING

Many compilers of subject encyclopaedias seem to assume that if their works are alphabetically organized they are thereby self-indexing. This is by no means the case, as the editors of the great general encyclopaedias have realized for years. The better subject encyclopaedias, particularly the multi-volume works, make great efforts to provide full analytical indexes as well as setting out the individual articles in alphabetical order.

McGRAW-HILL ENCYCLOPEDIA OF SCIENCE AND TECHNOLOGY. 6th ed. 20 vols. New York: McGraw-Hill, 1987.

First published in 1960 and the only major English-language encyclopaedia covering the whole of science and technology at this level, this widely used work shows signs of extensive revision for its latest edition, with an expansion from 15 to 20 volumes, a major overhaul of 28 of the 77 broad subject areas with 450 new and 1,600 totally rewritten articles, and a pleasing improvement of page layout with the use of background colour for tables and diagrams and bold type in the text for differentiation.

The 3,500 expert contributors include 20 Nobel Prize winners, and the editors claim that 'all articles are written for the nonspecialist'. Individual users can obviously form their own opinion. Quite outstanding are the illustrations: with 15,000 (1,900 new, 2,000 revised) for the 13,047 pages, it is plain that few pages lack some graphic adornment. The bibliographies at the end of many of the articles are scholarly and up-to-date, referring the reader to periodical articles as well as books.

To supplement the 50,000 cross-references in the text, the 'Analytical index' making up the last volume contains, we are told, each important term , concept and person mentioned in the 19 text volumes. The publisher's advertising claims that this index is used as a model of the 'perfect index' by several library schools.

As 150,000 entries are required to index the 7,700 articles, users are up to 19 times more likely to find the topic they want if they consult the index first, rather than the main alphabetical sequence.

The existence of the text in machine-readable form also 'makes the information available for electronic distribution', as the preface tells us. On the market since 1987 has been the *McGraw-Hill CD-ROM science and technical reference set*. This comprises on a single disc the *McGraw-Hill concise encyclopedia of science and technology* (New York: McGraw-Hill, 1984) and the *McGraw-Hill dictionary of scientific and technical terms*, 3rd ed. (New York: McGraw-Hill, [1984]). New editions of the printed volumes have since appeared, in 1989 and 1988 respectively; these will doubtless appear in CD-ROM format in due course. The full text (but excluding graphics) of the 20-volume parent set is available online from the West Publishing Company, St Paul, Minnesota, according to the July 1989 issue of the *Directory of online databases* (New York: Cuadra/Elsevier), which also reports that a CD-ROM version is available.

An analytical index of the kind just described is even more necessary with works such as the *Encyclopedia of world art* (see above), which has deliberately adopted a monographic approach, with several of the articles in the main alphabetical sequence extending to 50 pages or more; as its preface concedes, 'At the same time, the advantages for reference of the dictionary-index form are appreciable, and in recognition of this fact, the fifteenth volume of this encylopedia is devoted to a full and thorough index of analytic character.'

Though only in one volume, a work such as A. and J. Kuper (eds.), *The social science encyclopedia* (London: Routledge, 1985) suffers by comparison from the absence of an index, since it too has chosen the long-article approach for many topics. The user seeking information on public opinion polls will find neither an entry nor a cross-reference under 'Public opinion' or under 'Polls'. Yet there is a 500-word article beginning 'Opinion polls ascertain public opinion via direct enumeration ...' under the heading 'Opinion polls'.

Some works also provide an alternative approach in the form

of a systematically arranged index, e.g. the 28-page 'Topical index' grouping the 7,700 article titles of the *McGraw-Hill encyclopedia of science and technology* (see above) under 78 broad subject headings.

In the absence of indexes, an extensive and carefully worked out system of cross-references may provide a partial substitute, but completely adequate examples are rare. Usually the searchers themselves are left to provide the link between related subjects, or to guess the heading under which minor subdivisions of the topic have been subsumed.

Scholes, P. A., THE OXFORD COMPANION TO MUSIC. 10th ed. Oxford: Oxford University Press, 1970.

For over 50 years this has been one of the most popular of the Oxford Companions, and justly so. Much of its appeal derives from the rich anecdotal style of its original compiler, which, since his death in 1958, has been worthily maintained by his successor, John Owen Ward.

Its first tentative title was 'Everyone's musical encyclopaedia', and it is aimed not only at the 'experienced and well-instructed professional musician' (who has always made full use of the work), but also at 'the younger musician, the concert goer, the gramophonist, or the radio-listener'. The compilers tell us 'It is believed that in no article of the book can a technical term be met with of which an explanation is not speedily available by turning to that term in its own alphabetical position.' The unique style and the absence of bibliographies have both attracted criticism, but the extensive and in some instances unusual illustrations are perhaps a surprising feature.

Earlier editions used to describe themselves on their title-pages as 'self-indexed'. There is no index as such, but the method of referencing used as a substitute is worthy of study: 'the larger articles are divided into numbered sections and their separate facts are scrupulously indexed, by means of article and section number, in their alphabetical positions throughout the volume'. Furthermore, 'Abundant cross-references are given in the body of almost every considerable article and also of many a smaller one, and frequently at the end of an article will be found a list of further allusions, elsewhere in the book, to the subject of that article.'

In 1983 appeared D. Arnold (ed.), *The new Oxford companion to music* (Oxford: Oxford University Press), described as a 'drastic updating' of Scholes, drawing on 90 expert contributors and expanded to two volumes. Unusually, the editor, Professor of Music at Oxford, was quite critical of his predecessor, who was largely self-taught, and whose idiosyncratic approach was certainly not to everyone's taste. Curiously, however, Scholes' work (though dropped by Walford and Sheehy in favour of Arnold's) was still available for purchase seven years later, the publishers having reprinted it each year since 1983, an unspoken tribute to a book which our greatest encyclopaedia in the field, S. Sadie (ed.), *The New Grove dictionary of music and musicians* (London: Macmillan, 1980), in 20 volumes, has characterized as 'the most extraordinary range of musical knowledge, ingeniously "self-indexed", ever written and assembled between two covers by one man'.

TREATMENT

A distinction that students will be familiar with from their examination of general encyclopaedias (and perhaps from what has gone before in this chapter) is that between the short-article and long-article approaches. As the preface to the *Encylopedia of world art* (see above) explains: 'A sharp and clear distinction is drawn between the aims of a monographic encyclopaedia and an analytical dictionary index.'

J. Eatwell and others (eds.), THE NEW PALGRAVE: A DICTIONARY OF ECONOMICS. 4 vols. London: Macmillan, 1987.

A subject encyclopaedia despite its title and a milestone in the literature of its subject, this major work does not hesitate to claim comprehensiveness: it 'attempts to define the state of the discipline by presenting a comprehensive and critical account of economic thought'. It is the successor to the great classic, R. H. I. Palgrave (ed.), *Dictionary of political economy* (1894 – 9), and its second edition, H. Higgs (ed.), *Palgrave's dictionary of political economy* (1923 – 6).

So important still a century later is the first Palgrave that a reprint was issued by the publishers simultaneously with this new work, 50 of the original articles are here reprinted unaltered, and all the entries in the first and second editions are listed in an appendix. We are told nevertheless that 'There is so little remaining of the original Dictionary that it would be disingenuous to call this its third edition.'

It is a thoroughly scholarly work for the specialist, with 2,000 entries, signed by over 900 contributors (including 11 Nobel prize winners) from 30 countries. Over 700 of the articles are biographical, and living economists are included if born before 1916. Most are lengthy, with a 'rough and ready correlation between size of entry and importance which the editors attach to the person or subject concerned'. Virtually every article is followed by a meticulous bibliography, often extensive. These lists are intended to serve a dual purpose: 'first, they give details for works referred to in the text of an article; and secondly, they provide additional information on studies on which the authors have drawn as well as recommended reading'.

Among the appendices are a list of entries alphabetically by author, and an analysis of subject entries under 53 heads and of biographies under country. The 37-page index is designed to cover 'significant discussions of key subjects'.

Most single-volume encyclopaedias, on the other hand, are the short-entry type, designed for quick reference.

Banham, M. (ed.), THE CAMBRIDGE GUIDE TO WORLD THEATRE. Cambridge: Cambridge University Press, 1989.

Edited by the Professor of Drama and Theatre Studies at the University of Leeds, this illustrated volume of over 1,100 pages is 'designed to offer . . . a comprehensive view of the history and present practice of theatre in all parts of the world'. Particular attention is paid to comparatively neglected figures or activities, and to popular theatre and entertainment.

Despite its title, it is in fact a subject encyclopaedia, with over 3,000 articles arranged alphabetically. Contributed by over 100 specialists, they are all signed, and are mainly the short-entry type, mostly devoted to theatrical practitioners. There are some longer and more general articles (e.g. 'Shadow puppets', 'Copyright') and a number of national articles (e.g. 'Costa Rica'). Most of these have bibliographies (e.g. 'Stage lighting': 13 books with dates from 1958 to 1985). It will quickly furnish the enquirer with answers to queries such as 'Have you anything on Pepper's Ghost?' (a stage illusion), 'Who was William Gillette?' (American stage actor who played Sherlock Holmes over 1,300 times), 'When was the first Drury Lane theatre opened?' (1663).

Characteristic of many subject encyclopaedias is the inclusion of substantial information outside the basic alphabetical sequence of the text, commonly displayed in tabular or chronological form. *The Oxford companion to classical literature* (see below), for instance, devotes 30 pages to a date chart of classical literature; a table of Greek and Roman weights and measures; plans and illustrations of Greek and Roman houses, theatres, and temples; and ten pages of maps. If the subject matter is appropriate, illustrations and maps may indeed make up a substantial portion of the work.

Buttrick, G. A. (ed.), THE INTERPRETER'S DICTIONARY OF THE BIBLE. 4 vols. New York: Abingdon, 1962. SUPPLEMENT, 1977.

Despite its title 'dictionary' the editor claims that 'these volumes travel far in the direction of a Bible encyclopedia'. It is clearly intended as a comprehensive reference book on the Bible, the Apocrypha and other non-canonical books, including the Dead Sea Scrolls. Its target is the preacher, the scholar, the student, the school-teacher and the general reader: particular care has been taken to avoid technical language, and erudite references and exhaustive footnotes have been excluded. Nevertheless, the 7,500 articles maintain a high standard of scholarship, with distinguished contributors coming mainly from the United States, but with a fair representation also of European and Israeli scholars. Each important article has a select bibliography. They will furnish an instant response to questions such as 'What exactly was the widow's mite?', 'Can you find me something on the Holy Sepulchre?', 'Is it true that John the Baptist was not the inventor of baptism?'

In justification of its subtitle, 'an illustrated encyclopedia', a tenth of the space is devoted to more than 1,000 black-and-white illustrations, 163 maps, many charts, especially chronological, 24 pages of full-colour maps, and many colour illustrations.

USE

As with the general encyclopaedias, the primary use of subject encyclopaedias is by the enquirer (or librarian) in search of specific facts. As user surveys have shown, these fact-finding queries make up the bulk of requests received by libraries of all kinds, and many of them are satisfied from the appropriate subject encyclopaedia. This has been called the 'everyday' approach to information, because the need usually arises in the course of day-to-day activity, and may occur regularly and frequently.

Encyclopaedias are also of value for the 'something on ...' type of enquiry, another common category. These have been described as material-finding queries, as opposed to fact-finding queries, and they also frequently arise on an 'everyday' basis. The editor of *Van Nostrand's scientific encyclopedia* (see above) has explained that 'many users of the book not only seek detailed data on numerous subjects, but also expect well-organized overviews so that any subsequent researching of periodicals and specialized shelf literature can be pursued in the most workmanlike and time-saving manner'. Where enquirers are seeking an introductory outline, or merely concise account to enable them to come to grips with a subject that is new or unfamiliar, they may need to go no further than a good subject encyclopaedia. But even for the more demanding enquirer hoping to make a detailed study of a topic, it can often provide a convenient starting-point.

The compilers of some of the larger subject encyclopaedias see a further reason for consulting their volumes. In the case of the four-volume R. J. Corsini (ed.), *Encyclopedia of psychology* (New York: Wiley, 1984), not only can the work provide 'basic spot information' and 'summary information' but it also 'can serve as a basic textbook for those who want to understand all of psychology in depth'. The compilers of the eight-volume P. Edwards (ed.), *Encyclopedia of philosophy* (London: Collier-

Macmillan, 1967) tell us that 'Some of the longer articles ...
are in effect small books, and even the shorter articles are usually
long enough to allow a reasonably comprehensive treatment of
the subject under discussion.' This has permitted departures from
normal encyclopaedia practice insofar as the editors have
encouraged the expression of individual and even controversial
views from contributors, whilst a number of articles embody
original research.

The librarian in particular can also usefully turn first to a subject
encyclopaedia as a stepping-stone to a more extended search. Not
only should it help to get the topic clearly in focus at the outset,
but it will often suggest further paths to explore. Indeed, for the
beginner, it is a good rule of thumb to open a search with the
encyclopaedia, unless a more obvious starting-point suggests itself.
This role as 'launch pad' for a more extended search is an often
underrated use of the encyclopaedia, both general and special.

Bibliographies

The thrust for such further exploration of the topic under scrutiny
is sometimes provided by the short bibliographies found at the
end of the articles. These are only rarely complete bibliographies,
of course – merely guides to further reading – and they are
perhaps the exception rather than the rule in single-volume works.
The major multi-volume specialist encyclopaedias, on the other
hand, include bibliographies as a matter of course.

Kernfeld, B. (ed.), THE NEW GROVE DICTIONARY OF JAZZ. 2 vols.
London: Macmillan, 1988.

Despite its title, the preface describes it as 'an encyclopedic
work' and it sets out to provide 'comprehensive treatment' not
only of individuals, groups and styles of jazz, but also of
terminology, theory, musical instruments, record companies and
labels, festivals, venues, films, institutions, and individuals who
are not performers. With 250 contributors (mainly academics)
from 25 countries it is an epoch-making work 'in which the
breadth and rigorous methodology that characterize the Grove
projects could be applied for the first time to jazz'. Originally

it was intended to rely largely on material from *The new Grove dictionary of music and musicians* (see above) and its companion set, the four-volume H. W. Hitchcock and S. Sadie (eds.), *New Grove dictionary of American music* (London: Macmillan, 1986), but in the event, 90% of the material is new, and – unusually for an encyclopaedia – incorporates much original research. The result is the 'largest dictionary of the music ever published'.

Jazz is defined more narrowly than some would wish, excluding, for instance, ragtime, gospel music and rock and roll, but this is deliberate, and almost certainly necessary. As the preface confidently proclaims, 'the work as a whole constitutes a definition of jazz'. Of the 4,500 articles, all signed, 3,000 are on individuals, mostly performers, though the personal biographical information is sparse. There are many black-and-white illustrations. Unfortunately there is no index, although an extensive network of cross-references provides a partial substitute.

On the other hand, the bibliographies are quite outstanding. Most articles conclude with a thorough, scholarly bibliography, comprising not only books and articles in journals, but also, for some of the obscurer figures, newspaper items, album liner notes, etc. In addition, Appendix 1 consists of a 2,500-item bibliography of books and periodical titles based on the citations at the ends of the individual articles, supplemented by further titles supplied by the editors 'to make a comprehensive (though not exhaustive) listing'. Some 2,000 of the articles are also furnished with discographies, here more accurately described as 'Selected recordings', chosen to be representative, and cited in very precise detail. And in the case of certain individuals, as appropriate, an indication is also given of 'Oral history material' available 'in one or more major collections'.

Biographies

The appropriate subject encyclopaedia is often a good source to try for narrow or specialized topics that have not yet grown to warrant a whole book of their own. The many biographical entries, for example, in the work just described remind us that enquirers often seek information about people. Like the general encyclopaedias, many (though not all) subject encyclopaedias are valuable sources of biographical information, particularly for minor figures, about whom they may be the only convenient source. The editor of the *Encyclopedia of philosophy* (see above) claims, for instance: 'We have also made it a special point to rescue for obscurity unjustly neglected figures, and in such cases, where the reader would find it almost impossible to obtain reliable information in standard histories or in general encyclopedias, we have been particularly generous in our space allotments.'

Students should note, however, that some encyclopaedias exclude biography as a matter of policy: the ten-volume A. S. Knowles (ed.), *International encyclopedia of higher education* (San Francisco: Jossey Bass, 1977), for example, 'decided that no biographical information would be included because it would be impossible to determine, on an international basis, the names of those who ought to be recognized'. A different excuse is given by D. Greenwald (ed.), *Encyclopedia of economics* (New York: McGraw-Hill, 1982): 'Largely because biographical source material is hard to find, there are no biographical entries.' This contrasts interestingly with *The new Palgrave: a dictionary of economics* (see above), where over a third of the articles are biographies. Biography is omitted from the *McGraw-Hill encyclopedia of science and technology* (see above) because it is 'a work *of*, not *about* science'.

LEVEL

An important distinction between subject and general encyclopaedias is that the former are much more obviously aimed at readers of differing levels of attainment. While it is probably the case that most subject encyclopaedias are written for the only moderately well informed, there are many important titles written for the specialist.

Hammond, N. G. L. and Scullard, H. H. (eds.), THE OXFORD CLASSICAL DICTIONARY. 2nd ed. Oxford: Clarendon Press, 1970.

Still the best one-volume encyclopaedia in its field, it makes plain its comprehensive embrace: 'all fields of ancient Greek and Roman civilization'. Describing itself as 'a compendium of modern scholarship', it is basically a work for the specialist, with extensive bibliographies, including original sources and papers in learned journals. The preface draws attention to P. Harvey, *The Oxford companion to classical literature* (Oxford: Clarendon Press, 1937), as a work more suited to 'the ordinary reader'. In its second edition by M. C. Howatson (Oxford: Oxford University Press, 1989), this Companion has been made even more accessible to the non-specialist. 'Readers of today', the preface tells us, 'are in some respects even more ignorant than those of fifty years ago.' The work now 'requires no knowledge of Greek or Latin' and 'All Greek is transliterated and all Latin and Greek is translated.'

KIRK-OTHMER ENCYCLOPEDIA OF CHEMICAL TECHNOLOGY. 3rd ed. 26 vols., incl. supplement and index. New York: Wiley, 1978 – 84.

With its 9 million words, clearly a major work, and since its first appearance in 1947 now thoroughly tested in use, this is a working tool for professional chemists and chemical engineers. Obviously a long-article encyclopaedia (only 1,332 articles in the 25 text volumes), it draws on the expertise of some 1,400 specialist contributors. Each article is furnished with a bibliography that not only offers general references on the topic but also supplies full documentation, with 536 items cited for the article 'Alkaloids', for example. The massive index comprises 1,270 double-column pages.

This is one of the comparatively few subject encyclopaedias also available online. Vendors include DIALOG, BRS and Data-Star, and the whole of the text is searchable, including the tables. A CD-ROM version is also obtainable from the publishers.

Subject encyclopaedias are frequent targets for criticism on one level; in particular they have been castigated as of little use to specialists. The articles do not go into sufficient depth for their purposes, and the form in which the information is published inevitably prevents it being thoroughly up-to-date. Some of this is unfair, and the critics expect too much. The plain facts of economics frequently dictate that a particular discipline can support no more than one encyclopaedia; compilers must then choose either to direct their efforts at satisfying the limited number of experts in the field, at the expense of the probably more numerous non-specialist users, or, as is usually the case, they may pitch their level at that of the intelligent citizen, to the annoyance of the specialist. Those who try for the cake and the halfpenny run the risk of losing both.

Perhaps the ideal of an encyclopaedia as a tool of equal value to the ordinary user and the expert is as much a dream as the encyclopaedia encompassing the whole of knowledge. This is worth bearing in mind before accepting criticism; it is important for the student to examine each work with care and to measure its achievement against the demands made on it and the uses to which it is put. It is a well-known fact that many of those who come to libraries with 'everyday' queries are seeking information in a subject area peripheral to their primary interest: they are in effect non-specialists in those fields. Many subject encyclopaedias have been carefully designed for precisely such needs; P. Gray (ed.), *The encyclopedia of the biological sciences*, 2nd ed. (London: Van Nostrand Reinhold, 1970), for example, aims 'to provide succinct and accurate information for biologists in those fields in which they are not themselves experts'.

Neither must it be forgotten that an important role of the encyclopaedia, in all disciplines, is to explain its subject to the average intelligent reader, because it is often to an encyclopaedia of the subject that the ordinary curious enquirer turns first. This is where the encyclopaedia editor has the chance to play the role, in the words of Lowell A. Martin, an American librarian and a professor at Columbia University, of 'a mediator, between the world of scholars on the one side and the individual seeking information on the other, between those who know something and those who seek to know'. In science, technology and medicine, in particular, this role as mediator is vital, so dependent is our society on achievements made in those fields.

Havard, C. W. H. (ed.), BLACK'S MEDICAL DICTIONARY. 35th ed. London: Black, 1987.

A widely used and highly respected example of a quick-reference tool, it has been regularly revised since its first appearance in 1906. In this latest edition, the new editor, only the fourth in over 80 years and a consulting physician at two London hospitals, has taken the opportunity to carry out a thorough revision.

It is, as one librarian reviewer felt obliged to point out, 'more an encyclopaedia than a dictionary, with entries ranging from a single line to the seven-page illustrated section on muscles'. There are 4,500 entries in 750 pages of text, and cross-references are extensively used, but there is no index. Some of the terminology is inevitably 'medical', but specialist words are almost always explained under their own headings elsewhere in the volume. It would not of course be the first port-of-call for medically qualified searchers, but the editor believes it will be 'valuable for all those working in fields drawing on medical practice, and to anyone interested in how their body works, and in what is happening in medicine today'.

CURRENCY AND ACCURACY

The common charge that encyclopaedias are rarely up-to-date needs examining with care. As compilations of accepted and digested information, they cannot be at the frontiers of knowledge in every respect, but it is reasonable to look critically at their general performance. The better single-volume encyclopaedias appear in regularly updated editions, and some of the multi-volume works arrange for supplementary volumes, often on an annual basis, e.g. the *McGraw-Hill yearbook of science and technology* serves among other things to update selected subjects in the *Encyclopedia.*

Accuracy in matters of fact, on the other hand, is an area where it is fitting to expect only the highest standards. Amid the thousands of subject encyclopaedias in our libraries, there are some that are worthless and a larger number that are unreliable in some degree. Some years ago a very experienced librarian advised: 'Do not rely on encyclopaedic works; suspect every statement and do your best to verify it.' It is indeed a sound practice to double-check where possible, not only in areas where there may be room for opinion, but also in matters of fact. Sheehy warns that 'as the immediate profits from cheap work are often large and as many buyers do not discriminate between good and poor encyclopaedias, unscrupulous publishers will sometimes utilize hack writers or reprint, with only slight changes, out-of-date material'.

EXPLOITATION

One of the librarian's most important tasks is to maximize the resources at his or her disposal. Mention was made at the beginning of this chapter of the enquirer's uncertainty at the start of a subject search. The way libraries are obliged to display reference books might well contribute to this lack of awareness. A regular library user could scarcely avoid noticing the great general encyclopaedias, grouped together as they usually are on clearly indicated shelves. Subject encyclopaedias, on the other hand, are placed by most library classification schemes according to the subject, and are thus not only dispersed throughout the library but even within their own subject area have to compete for recognition with all the other books on the topic. Some libraries, of course, arrange for an *ad hoc* sequence of purely reference books, or even more specifically of quick-reference books. Yet even here the subject encyclopaedia has to sit cheek-by-jowl with guides to the literature, dictionaries, handbooks, directories, yearbooks, and all the other categories of reference tools.

Confused terminology provides a more fundamental explanation for a user's uncertainty; the plain fact of the matter is that many important subject encyclopaedias are called something else, as has already been noted several times. G. S. Brady and H. R. Clauser, *Materials handbook*, 12th ed. (New York: McGraw-Hill, 1986) and *The Merck index*, 11th ed. (Rahway, New Jersey: Merck, 1989) are not only long-established reference classics, they are also subject encyclopaedias. Indeed, the enquirer who takes the trouble to open them will find on their title-pages that they are subtitled as such: 'an encyclopedia for managers . . .', and 'an encyclopedia of chemicals . . .', respectively.

This concern about terminology is no mere pedant's quibble. Searchers who pass over J. R. Strayer (ed.), *Dictionary of the middle ages* (New York: Scribner, 12 vols. and index vol. 1982 – 9) or the three massive volumes of P. Macquoid and R. Edwards, *Dictionary of English furniture*. 2nd ed. (London: Country Life,

1954), because their titles suggest they may be restricted to the defining of words, would be going sadly astray, as they would in each case be denying themselves the standard encyclopaedia in the subject.

'Dictionary', in fact, is the most frequently misapplied title. In theory, of course, the distinction is crystal clear; it is neatly demonstrated in the two companion volumes by Peter Gray. In the *Encyclopedia of the biological sciences* (see above) he explains: 'This is an encyclopedia, not a dictionary. That is, it does not merely define the numerous subjects covered but describes and explains them.' In his twin work the *Dictionary of the biological sciences* (London: Reinhold, 1966), he explains: 'It was the infeasibility of indexing the Encyclopedia of the biological sciences in a manner that would permit enough individual words to be found that led me to the conviction that a separate dictionary was a necessity.'

In practice, the distinction is often blurred, with much overlapping and even merging. Indeed in certain subjects for most practical purposes the differentiation no longer has any significance. The terms are often used interchangeably, sometimes within the same work: the Royal Horticultural Society, *Dictionary of gardening*, 2nd ed. (Oxford: Clarendon Press, 1956), in four volumes and *Supplement* (1969), is subtitled 'a practical and scientific encyclopaedia of horticulture'. There are works which seek to be both: *The interpreter's dictionary of the Bible: an illustrated encyclopedia* (see above) defines terms (giving pronunciation, etymology, variant spellings) as well as describing and explaining them. There are words that strive to be neither: A. Bullock and O. Stallybrass (eds.), *The Fontana dictionary of modern thought*, 2nd ed. (London: Fontana, 1988) claims that it 'steers a middle course between an ordinary dictionary and an encyclopaedia'.

What does remain distracting, however, are those works calling themselves encyclopaedias, but which are nothing of the kind. A. S. Placzek (ed.), *Macmillan encyclopedia of architects* (New York: Free Press, [1982]) is a four-volume biographical dictionary of 2,500 architects, listed by surname. P. Wasserman, *Encyclopedia of health information sources* (Detroit: Gale, 1986) is a bibliography. The *Encyclopedia of associations*, 24th ed. (Detroit: Gale, 1989) is a directory. *The international geographic encyclopedia and atlas* (London:

Macmillan, 1979) is what most librarians would call a gazetteer, the overwhelming bulk of its 25,000 entries consisting of place-names. Perhaps most inappropriate of all, G. Brown and H. M. Geduld (eds.), *The New York Times encyclopedia of film, 1896 – 1979* (New York: Times Books, 1984), simply reproduces in facsimile in 13 volumes the text of the articles about film (other than reviews and obituaries) that had appeared in the newspaper during the period.

SUGGESTIONS FOR FURTHER READING

Ten of the 16 subject encyclopaedias featured in this chapter have a full bibliographical citation and a descriptive annotation in both Walford and Sheehy; one further title is in Sheehy alone. In choosing what to write about each, therefore, I have assumed that the student will also read carefully what those two commentators have to say. The 11 works also appear in the *ARBA guide to subject encyclopedias and dictionaries* (see above), each with a brief evaluative review, and with citations to reviews elsewhere in the library literature. (The missing works are all too recent for these bibliographies, but will doubtless appear there in due course.)

But there is no substitute for personal acquaintance with individual subject encyclopaedias, either those featured or discussed or briefly mentioned here, or the many similar titles available in our libraries. Yet however similar, each work – even successive editions of the same work – will be found to have a unique identity, and students are advised to focus on the way one differs from the other in the means it employs to achieve its task.

As a reference book, none of the titles here is without faults. The *ARBA guide* (see above) takes particular pains to point these out. What can be said about them all, however, is that they are broadly satisfactory for the purpose for which they were designed, some of them eminently so. Their faults, of course, users should be aware of, but more important are their virtues, and it is on these that I have tried to concentrate in my comments.

5

Biographical Reference Works

Barrie MacDonald

The *Concise Oxford dictionary* definition of 'biography' is 'the written life of a person'. It can be described more fully as the recreation of a person's life, drawing upon memory and written and oral evidence. Above all, biography should be accurate, balanced and objective. However, the ideal biography should not be merely a narrative of the events of a life, but also should give the flavour of personality, as well as the person's achievements, in relation to the period in which they lived and the events in which they participated. 'The aim of biography' according to Sir Sidney Lee, the editor of the *Dictionary of national biography*, 'is the truthful transmission of personality'. 'By telling us the true facts', wrote Virginia Woolf, 'by sifting the little from the big, and shaping the whole so that we perceive the outline, the biographer does more to stimulate the imagination than any poet or novelist.'[1]

Broadly speaking, biography can be divided into two categories: individual biography, at its best the highly creative and interpretive literary form described by Virginia Woolf; and collected biography, now usually intended for reference purposes and the subject of this chapter.

BIOGRAPHICAL REFERENCE PROCESS

Requests for biographical information are amongst the most frequent enquiries a librarian will receive. Many will be straightforward enough to be answered from such standard works as *Chambers biographical dictionary* or *Who's who*; others will require a sound knowledge of biographical reference works, print or electronic, as well as the biographical resources of general reference works and various bibliographical guides to biography, and will result in lengthy searches.

Most important in the reference process is the initial interview, during which the librarian will clarify the enquiry by asking sufficient questions to establish an understanding and common objective with the enquirer.

The first step is to find out any supplementary details the enquirer has about the subject to enable an assessment as to the most suitable sources of the required information. Is the person living or dead? What nationality is the subject? For what achievements is he or she best known? What is his or her profession or occupation? Enquirers often know more than they initially volunteer. The less that is known about a person the more steps in the search, and the more sources the librarian will need to consult. This initial process of assessing which reference sources are likely to contain an entry for a particular person requires experience and a knowledge of appropriate reference material.

The next and essential step before undertaking the enquiry, is to ascertain the amount, level and type of information required. These will also enable the librarian to decide which sources are most appropriate. It would, for example, be as inappropriate to supply *Chambers biographical dictionary*, rather than the *Dictionary of national biography*, to an academic requiring a scholarly article with full bibliography on Queen Elizabeth I, as to offer *DNB*, rather than *Chambers* or *Who did what*, to a 12-year-old schoolgirl wanting to find out about 'Good Queen Bess'.

Not all enquiries will be for complete biographies; some will be for selected, often obscure facts or physical characteristics. Did George III speak with a German accent? In which leg was Byron lame? Which museums have works by Leonardo da Vinci? What do Jane Austen's handwriting and autograph look like? How tall is the Prince of Wales? Thorough knowledge of biographical sources will enable quick decisions as to which of the many entries for these persons is likely to contain the particular item of information. For example, of all the entries for Prince Charles in *Burke's peerage*, *Debrett's peerage and baronetage*, *International who's who* and *Current biography*, only the latter would give his height. Denis Grogan gives many useful examples of biographical reference enquiries.[2]

The reliability and accuracy of even the most authoritative reference works can occasionally be in doubt; therefore potentially suspect details, such as birthdate or education, should be double-checked in as many sources as possible. Enquirers and trainee librarians should be warned of inaccurate works, perhaps with a note on the book. A problem with current biographical works is the currency of the information, such works as *Who's who* being already out of date on publication day due to the delay between compilation and publication; they should therefore be kept up-to-date by regular amendment from newspaper coverage of appointments, honours and obituaries. Thorough preparation for enquiry work, by considered stock selection, up-dating and correction of reference books and compilation of indexes and information files, is as essential to enquiry work as research skills. Herbert Woodbine, editor of the *Library Association record* from 1936 to 1944, wrote 'there are no geniuses in reference work, but that experience does, time after time, show the way to the solution of a problem'.[3]

ASSESSMENT OF BIOGRAPHICAL REFERENCE WORKS

The following points are some of the criteria for assessing biographical reference works:

1 **Purpose**. The title or preface will normally indicate the purpose of the work; whether it is intended to be general, international, national or specialized in scope; and within those categories retrospective or current.

2 **Authority**. An important point in assessing the value of biographical dictionaries is their authority, as indicated by the sponsoring body (often a university or learned society), the author or contributors. Reputable publishers, particularly well-established biography specialists such as A & C Black (*Who's who*), Debrett, Marquis (*Who's who in America*) and Who's Who Verlag of Germany, also guarantee authority.

3 **Coverage**. Is the work comprehensive within its chosen area (as *Crockford's clerical directory* is for the Church of England clergy), or highly selective as with many subject 'Who's whos'?

4 **Selection policy**. The criteria used for selection are particularly important with current works; whether it is solely by merit, as decided by the publisher or editor (as with *Who's who*), or by application, or even for payment in the case of the 'vanity' publications.

5 **Sources of information and method of compilation**. Many 'Who's whos' use the questionnaire method of compiling the entries, whereby each biographee writes and later corrects their own entry, resulting in generally more accurate and comprehensive information, though occasionally subject to omission or falsifying of birthdate, education, divorces or other sensitive details. In other cases the publisher researches the material; both methods have advantages and disadvantages.

6 **Frequency of publication**. An important consideration for current works is their frequency of issue (annual, biennial or irregular), and therefore how up-to-date is the information. If the work is irregular and claims to be a new or revised edition, it is advisable to check it against the previous one. If the work is retrospective does it have regular supplements to update the main set?

7 **Accuracy and reliability**. These are mostly established through experience, though routine examination of the work and reviews in the professional press may help.

8 **Arrangement**. Most biographical dictionaries are arranged alphabetically, some with professions or geographic indexes; though chronological or subject order can provide an alternative approach to biography.

9 **Format and style**. The entries should be clearly presented in an easy-to-use format. The style of entry can vary from the

quick-reference sketch of current 'Who's whos' or the outline biographies of *Chambers biographical dictionary* to the lengthy, scholarly essays of the national biographical dictionaries.

10 **Indexes and cross-references**. Alphabetically arranged works are self-indexing, though classified indexes in such works as the *Dictionary of American biography* can be useful. Classified or chronologically arranged works must have alphabetical indexes. Adequate cross-references are important, especially for foreign or variant forms of names.

11 **Special features**. Bibliographies, portraits, autographs and lists can greatly enhance the value of a biographical work.

12 **Comparison with similar works**. After examining a new work by these criteria, comparison can be made with similar works for duplication, authority, and ease of use in order to assess its value relative to comparable works.

Biographical dictionaries

Louis Shores defines a biographical dictionary as 'essentially a directory of notable persons, usually arranged alphabetically by surname, with biographical identification that ranges from brief outline to extended narrative'.[4] There are three broad categories of biographical dictionaries: **general or universal**, containing persons from all countries; **national, area or local**, for persons from a specified continent, country, region or locality; and **specialized**, for persons from specific social classes, occupations, professions or subject areas. Most works within these categories will be either retrospective or current.

UNIVERSAL BIOGRAPHICAL DICTIONARIES

General

Chalmers, A., THE GENERAL BIOGRAPHICAL DICTIONARY. New ed. 32 vols. London: Nichols, 1812 – 17; Liechtenstein: Kraus, reprint 1976.

Michaud, J. F., BIOGRAPHIE UNIVERSELLE ANCIENNE ET MODERNE. 2nd ed. 45 vols. Paris: Desplaces, 1843 – 65; Graz: Druck- und Verlagsanstalt, reprint 1964.

Hoefer, J. C., NOUVELLE BIOGRAPHIE GENERALE. 46 vols. Paris: Didot, 1852 – 66; Copenhagen: Rosenkilde & Bagger, reprint 1963 – 9.

These three works are important in the history of biographical literature, and are available in facsimile reprints. *The general biographical dictionary*, edited and revised by Alexander Chalmers for publication from 1812 to 1817, after several earlier editions, contains more than 8,000, often lengthy and discursive articles on 'persons of all nations, eminent for genius, learning, public spirit and virtue', with footnote references to other sources. The earlier and more authoritative of the two French works, the *Biographie universelle ancienne et moderne*, was originally published by Jean Francois and Louis Gabriel Michaud of the Royalist printing house in Paris. Alphabetically arranged, its signed articles are scholarly, often very long and with some sources for further reading. The Roman Catholic and Royalist bias of its first edition, reputedly later corrected, is still occasionally apparent in a lack of objectivity; Henry VIII, for example, is described as 'ce tyran voluptueux'. Certainly a French bias is evident in the length of articles, and those on English persons are generally less satisfactory. The 'rival' *Nouvelle biographie generale*, started in 1852 under Johann Hoefer's direction, was intended as a complement to the publisher's *Encyclopedie moderne*; many of its articles are taken from that and other Didot publications, as well as pirated from Michaud, for which the publisher was promptly sued.[5] The articles, though shorter and less scholarly than Michaud, are better presented with more bibliographical references. It is overall a more comprehensive work.

For the majority of libraries, the most accessible and comprehensive general biographical sources, apart from the general encyclopaedias, will be the single-volume dictionaries:

CHAMBERS BIOGRAPHICAL DICTIONARY. Rev. ed. Edinburgh: Chambers, 1984.

WEBSTER'S NEW BIOGRAPHICAL DICTIONARY. Latest ed. Springfield, Massachusetts: Merriam, 1988.

The entries in these two single-volume works are necessarily short, but their comprehensive coverage often provides quick and convenient verification of a person's dates, achievements or occupation, nationality and outline of his or her life, and therefore a useful starting-point for a biographical enquiry. *Chambers biographical dictionary*, first published in 1897, now contains over 15,000 sketches, providing pronunciation guidance for unusual names, dates, brief outline of the person's life and works, with occasional bibliographical references. Subject indexes to the biographical sketches include 'Art and architecture', 'Cinema', 'Exploration and geography', 'Nicknames', 'Science and industry', and other useful groupings. *Webster's new biographical dictionary* is very comprehensive, with over 40,000 brief biographies; it too contains pronunciation guidance, and useful lists of world leaders and monarchs.

Rather better than either for more important contemporaries is the *Macmillan dictionary of biography*, by B. Jones and M. V. Dixon (2nd ed. London: Macmillan, 1985), which has 7,500 short, well-written biographies with bibliographies, and cross-referencing to other entries. From the same publisher, the *Macmillan dictionary of women's biography*, compiled by J. Uglow (2nd ed. London: Macmillan, 1989), is an invaluable source of information on over 1,700 women past and present, and an excellent bibliography of biographical sources.

Some general biographical dictionaries are intended primarily for study purposes or younger readers:

THE McGRAW-HILL ENCYCLOPAEDIA OF WORLD BIOGRAPHY. 12 vols. New York and London: McGraw-Hill, 1975.

'Designed to meet a growing need in school and college libraries', this work contains 5,000 clearly arranged, signed, short illustrated biographies. Broad in coverage, with the Third World and contemporary, as well as historical personages, well represented. It has a 'study guide' volume of biographees listed within a structured, curricula-related, subject and historical outline, with indexes of biographees and subjects. Similar single-volume works are: *Purnell's encyclopaedia of famous people* (Maidenhead: Purnell, 1980), which has over 1,000 illustrated, outline biographies; and *Who did what: the Mitchell Beazley illustrated biographical dictionary* (3rd ed. London: Mitchell Beazley, 1985), whose 5,000 entries briefly list 'the essential achievements of the people who shaped our world'.

Current

Most libraries will have at least one of the following current international biographical dictionaries, which offer quick-reference sketches for important contemporaries. They are useful because, if the nationality of the person is not known or obvious, they save searching through numerous national 'Who's whos', even if a full selection were available. Also not all countries have a 'Who's who', and not all national 'Who's whos' are annual, and therefore as up-to-date.

THE INTERNATIONAL WHO'S WHO. 1935 – . 54th ed. 1990 – 91. London: Europa, 1989. Annual.

THE INTERNATIONAL YEAR BOOK AND STATESMEN'S WHO'S WHO. 1953 – . 37th ed. East Grinstead: Reed Information Services Ltd, 1989. Annual.

WHO'S WHO IN THE WORLD. 1st ed. 1971 – 2; 9th ed. 1989 – 90. Chicago: Marquis, 1988. Irregular.

The international who's who contains over 20,000 entries, representing worldwide coverage of heads of state, government and military officials, diplomats, and prominent persons from the law, business, arts, sciences and the professions. The entries, arranged alphabetically, give name, title, nationality, date of birth, parentage, marriage, children, education, profession, career, present position, honours, publications and address. Lists of world reigning royal families, and the year's obituaries precede the biographical section. A reliable work that is a first source for internationally renowned contemporaries. *The international year book and statesmen's who's who* is a general reference work on international and national organizations, and countries of the world; its third part is a biographical section of about 6,500 entries. Biased towards government officials, diplomats, politicians and military officers, with only a small overlap with the previous work. *Who's who in the world*, published by Marquis, the American biography specialists, is very comprehensive with entries for over 29,000 persons selected for their occupational stature or achievements. Most entries are compiled from biographees' own data, though sketches compiled by Marquis staff through failure of important persons to supply information are denoted by an asterisk.

Two American periodical publishers provide popular biographical articles on people in the news:

CURRENT BIOGRAPHY. 1940 – . New York: H. W. Wilson. Monthly; annual cumulation.

'THE NEW YORK TIMES' BIOGRAPHICAL SERVICE. 1970 – . Ann Arbor: University Microfilms International. Monthly.

Current biography contains lively articles on about 350 international celebrities annually; mostly statesmen, politicians, writers, performers and sports personalities. The entry, checked by the biographee before publication, contains brief data of full names, birthdate and address, a recent photograph, followed by a chatty article quoting liberally from the biographee and others, including personal information unlikely to be found elsewhere (e.g. height and colour of eyes), and concludes with bibliographical references, mostly to periodical and newspaper articles. Each monthly issue has a cumulative index for the current year; the annual volume, which reprints the year's articles in one alphabetical sequence, contains a cumulative index to all preceding volumes of the decade, a professions' index and obituaries of the year. A *Current biography cumulated index, 1940 – 85* (New York: H. W. Wilson, 1986) has appeared. *'The New York Times' biographical service* offers between 100 and 150 photo-reproduced biographical articles, interviews and obituaries from the newspaper each month. Published in loose-leaf format with a monthly, six-monthly and annual index. Particularly useful on people currently in the news, and can rectify omissions in reference books. Now available online through NEXIS.

NATIONAL OR AREA BIOGRAPHICAL DICTIONARIES

Today the standard pattern of biographical dictionaries for most countries is a retrospective dictionary of deceased notables, and one or more quick-reference 'Who's whos' for important contemporaries.

Retrospective

Most important within this category are the 'official' national biographical dictionaries, usually multi-volume works of unimpeachable authority, containing lengthy, scholarly articles, researched from original sources and including substantial bibliographies. Such works, the most authoritative source of biography of a nation's eminent predecessors, are seen as symbols of national prestige.

DICTIONARY OF NATIONAL BIOGRAPHY. 63 vols. London: Smith, Elder, 1885 – 1901; reissue: 22 vols. 1908 – 9; 2ND – 10TH SUPPLEMENTS, 1901 – 85. Oxford: Oxford University Press, 1912 – 90.

This fine achievement of Victorian ambition, perseverance and attention to detail is the most important reference work of English biography, and a pioneer of national biographical dictionaries. The historian G. M. Trevelyan described it as 'the best record of a nation's past that any civilisation has produced'. It was initiated by the original publisher, George Smith, whose heirs presented it in 1917 to the Oxford University Press, which has published it and the various later supplements ever since.[6] Sir Leslie Stephen was appointed the first editor in 1882, to be succeeded by Sir Sidney Lee in 1891. The original work contains over 28,000 notable persons from Great Britain, Ireland, and the Colonies (including America during the Colonial period), from early Britons to the present century. The lengthy, signed articles, researched where possible from original sources and private papers, have extensive bibliographies, often with portraits and memorials indicated. Such distinguished writers as Wilkie Collins and James Ramsey MacDonald were among the 600 specialist contributors. The original work is revised by *Corrections and additions* to the *Dictionary of national biography, cumulated from the Bulletin of the Institute of Historical Research, University of London, covering the years 1923 – 63* (Boston: G. K. Hall, 1966) and has been updated with 10-year and latterly 5-year supplements, each containing a cumulative alphabetical index to all editions since 1901. A micrographic edition of the basic set, plus the supplements up to 1960, is now available as *The compact edition of the Dictionary of national biography* (Oxford: Oxford University Press, 1975. 2 vols., with reading glass). *The concise dictionary of national biography (Oxford: Oxford University Press, 1953 and 1982. 2 vols.), originally the Index and epitome*, contains brief versions of all entries in the full set up to 1970, and is, therefore, both an index to the work and abstract of its articles, as well as a stand-alone biographical dictionary. *The contributors' index to the Dictionary of national biography, 1885 – 1901*, by Gillian Fenwick (Winchester: St Paul's Bibliographies, 1989) contains statistical analysis of contributors and lists of the biographical sketches.

The national biographical dictionaries for Germany, France, Italy and the United States are similar in scope to *DNB*, offering long, well-researched, signed articles with bibliographies. Germany has two overlapping sets: the *Allgemeine deutsche Biographie* (Leipzig: Duncker und Humblot, 1875 – 1912. 56 vols.) containing 23,000 biographies for persons who died before 1899; and the *Neue deutsche Biographie* (Berlin: Duncker und Humblot, 1953 –), which is currently updating the earlier work with more recent articles, and persons who have died since 1899. The French and Italian national biographies are still in progress: the *Dictionnaire de biographie française* (Paris: Letouzey, 1933 –); and the *Dizionario biografico degli italiani* (Rome: Istituto della Enciclopedia Italiana, 1960 –). The *Dictionary of American biography* (New York: Scribner, 1928 – 37. 21 vols.); *Supplements 1 – 8*, 1935 – 70 (New York: Scribner, 1944 – 88) was initiated by the American Council of Learned Societies. The term 'American', widely interpreted, includes persons born in the United States or the older colonies, naturalized Americans and those identified with America through association or contribution. The dictionary and its supplements contain approximately 17,000 signed biographies by such notable contributors as Carl Sandburg. An index volume consists of six indexes: to biographees; contributors; contributors' articles; birth-places of biographees; occupations; and 'distinctive topics' covered. The *Concise dictionary of American biography* (3rd ed. New York: Scribner, 1980) abridges the biographies of the original set, and is a useful quick-reference biographical dictionary.

Not all national biographical dictionaries adopt alphabetical arrangement; some more recent projects have opted for a chron-ological approach. The *Australian dictionary of biography* (Melbourne: The University Press, 1966 – ; *Vols. 1 – 2: 1788 – 1850*. 1966 – 7; *Vols. 3 – 6: 1851 – 90*. 1969 – 76; *Vols. 7 – 12: 1891 – 1939*. 1979 – 90) is a truly national project, supported by the Australian National University. The selection, from convict settlers to pol-iticians and administrators, is very egalitarian. A person is placed in the period when he did his most important work; if that overlaps two periods then the earlier is chosen. A general index volume to the 7,200 biographies in the 12-volume set covering 1788 – 1939 will appear. A similar chronological arrangement is adopted by the *Dictionary of Canadian biography* (Toronto: The University Press, 1966 –) in which each volume covers a specified period from AD 1000 to the present, with the biographee placed according to the period in which they died. Selection, as with the Australian work, is very wide, from pioneers and fur-traders to Governors-General. Each volume contains excellent historical introductions to the period covered, putting the biographies in context, with cumulative name, occupation and geographical indexes to follow. The advantage of a chronological approach is historical per-spective; the works become historical, as well as biographical, reflecting Thomas Carlyle's view that 'History is but the essence of innumerable biographies.'

There are extensive works for many countries that are not the 'official' national biographies, but because of their scope and comprehensiveness are as highly valued:

Boase, F., MODERN ENGLISH BIOGRAPHY. 6 vols. Truro: Netherton, 1892 – 1921. London: Frank Cass; reprint 1965.

It contains over 30,000 short biographies – a greater coverage of national and local celebrities for 1850 – 1900 than *DNB*.

Portraits in books, periodicals and newspapers are listed.

The United States has two similar works, both comprehensive with lengthy articles, portraits and autograph facsimiles: *Appletons' cyclopaedia of American biography* (New York: Appleton, 1888 – 1900. 7 vols.; Detroit: Gale, reprint 1968), now largely superseded by *DAB*; and the *National cyclopaedia of American biography* (Permanent series, 1892 – ; Current series, 1930 – , New York: White), which includes full illustrated biographies for over 66,000 Americans, living and dead, with a cumulated index volume.

Another type of retrospective national coverage dictionary is the 'Who was who', consisting of entries removed from the 'Who's who' on the biographee's death:

WHO WAS WHO, 1897 – 1980. 7 vols. London: Black, 1920 – 81; WHO WAS WHO: A CUMULATED INDEX 1897 – 1980. 1981.

WHO WAS WHO IN AMERICA, 1897 – 1989. 9 vols. Chicago: Marquis, 1942 – 89; HISTORICAL VOLUME, 1607 – 1896. 1963; INDEX 1607 – 1989. 1989.
   These works bridge the gap between the current 'Who's whos' and the older retrospective national biographical dictionaries, and often contain people not included in *DNB* or *DAB*. *Who was who* contains biographical sketches, basically unchanged since their last inclusion in *Who's who*, with date of death added and occasional editing and updating. *Who was who in America* has added a historical volume covering the period 1607 to 1896 to pre-date the main set of removed entries from *Who's who in America*. Later volumes, which also include entries from the Marquis 'regional' 'Who's whos', add details of date of death, place and name of the cemetary where the person was buried.

Obituaries from newspapers, periodicals and yearbooks are invaluable biographical material. Many quality newspapers and journals, for example *The Times*, *Guardian*, *New York Times* and *Illustrated London News*, publish their own indexes for research purposes:

OBITUARIES FROM 'THE TIMES', 1951 – 75. 3 vols. Reading: Newspaper Archive Developments, 1975 – 9.

THE NEW YORK TIMES OBITUARIES INDEX, 1858 – 68. New York: The Times, 1970; NEW YORK TIMES OBITUARIES INDEX, 1969 – 1979. Glen Rock, New Jersey: Microfilming Corporation, 1980.

Obituaries from 'The Times' is both an index to all the newspaper's obituary notices, and a collected biography of selected full obituaries for national and international figures, reprinted without rewriting, and therefore representing the contemporary view of the subject before later reassessment. The *New York Times obituaries index* is a straightforward index to over 350,000 obituary notices from 1858 to 1979, later obituaries being included in the *New York Times biographical service* (see above).

Specially written obituaries appear in *The annual obituary* (1980 – . Chicago and London: St James Press, 1981 –), which covers internationally prominent persons who have died during the year; the evaluative obituaries, containing a descriptive essay followed by a 'Who's who' style sketch and bibliography, are arranged chronologically according to date of death, with alphabetical indexes of professions and obituary writers. Many general yearbooks also contain obituaries, for example *The annual register* (London: Longman, 1758 –).

A recent development in this area of collected biography is the archive of photo-reproduced original biographical articles from historically important (but often long out-of-print) biographical dictionaries:

BRITISH BIOGRAPHICAL ARCHIVE. Munich: K. G. Saur, 1984. 1,236 microfiche (24 ×); negative/diazo/silver film editions.

This microfiche archive contains photo-reproductions of articles for over 200,000 separate individuals from 324 important English-language biographical reference works published between 1601 and 1929, including John Aubrey's *Brief lives, The general biographical dictionary* (q.v.), and *Bryan's dictionary of painters* (see below). A sequence of reproductions of title-pages and prefaces from all source works included, is followed by the main set of original biographies in alphabetical order, each with brief identifying bibliographical citation. Its value is in providing biographies on persons who appear only in these important but elusive collected works, and not in *DNB*, or *Who was who*. The *British biographical index* (Munich: K. G. Saur, 1990. 4 vols.) is a guide to the *British biographical archive* as well as a stand-alone reference work. K. G. Saur have published similar American, Italian, French, German, Scandinavian and Spanish/Portuguese biographical archives.

Finally a category of works which offer different, often highly specialized, approaches to retrospective biography. Interesting examples answer specific questions: 'What did they really look like?', 'What was their handwriting like?', 'What did their contemporaries think of them?', 'Who was it who gave their name to that word?'. *They looked like this* by G. Uden (Oxford: Blackwell, 1965), and its companion volume, *They looked like this (Europe)* (Oxford: Blackwell, 1966) aim to 'give eyewitness accounts of the physical appearances of the great figures of history' by selecting extracts from contemporary diaries, letters and journals. The finding of reproductions of the signatures of historical personages, often a slow process, has been made easier by *Four hundred years of British autographs* by R. Rawlins (London: Dent, 1970), which gathers 1,000 facsimile autographs of monarchs, statesmen and the famous, with brief biographies, descriptions of the autograph, its date and source. The *Penguin dictionary of biographical quotation*, edited by J. Wintle and R. Kenin (Harmondsworth: Penguin Books, 1981), contains 10,000 contemporary or later quotations about 1,300 notable deceased Britons and Americans. Those who gave their names to the language as commonly used words or product names (e.g. Biro, Bowler, Dow-Jones and Sandwich) can be found in *A dictionary of eponyms* by C. L. Beeching (3rd ed. London: Library Association, 1989).

Current

The standard current biographical dictionary in most countries is the 'Who's who', a regularly published collection of biographical sketches of important contemporaries from all walks of life.

WHO'S WHO. 1849 – . 142nd ed. 1990. London: Black, 1990. Annual.

This notable 'first', the model for all later 'Who's whos', began in 1849 as a slim handbook of the titled and official classes, containing only lists of names; it changed to its present format of an alphabetical sequence of biographical sketches in 1897. Currently it contains more than 28,000 biographies, mostly of United Kingdom and Commonwealth citizens, though some internationally prominent figures from other countries are included. It represents a broad spectrum of achievement in politics, central and local government, the armed forces, commerce, industry, the professions, sports, entertainment and the arts, as well as some with hereditary titles. Selection is by the publisher solely according to merit, and once included, the entry normally continues until the biographee's death, so inclusion is of considerable prestige recognizing the person's distinction and influence. The entries are compiled from information supplied by the biographee, both for the first-time entry and then subsequently by their checking and revising the annual proofs. This method usually results in accurate, up-to-date entries, but is occasionally subject to the idiosyncracies of the biographee – birth dates, education, divorces and early career being the usual casualties. The standard format entry usually contains full names, title, honours with dates received, current position, birthplace and date, parents' names, marital state, name of spouse and children, education, career, publications, recreations, address and club.

Modelled on *Who's who*, the following works have the same arrangement and type of entry, with slight variations in scope, frequency of publication, and method of compilation. The very term – 'Who's who' – has become completely international: for example *Who's who in France* (1953 – . 20th ed. 1988 – 9. Paris: Lafitte, 1988. Biennial), despite its English title is in French. West Germany has two works: *Who's who in Germany* (1955 – . 1988 ed. Essen: Who's Who Verlag, 1988. 2 vols.) in English, 'now considered the world's lingua franca'; and *Wer is wer?* (1905 – . 27th ed. 1988 – 9. Frankfurt: Schmidt-Romhild, 1988) containing over 40,000 biographies in German.

Who's who in America (1899 – . 44th ed. 1987 – 8. 2 vols. Biennial) includes 75,000 notables from the United States, Canada and Mexico, with lists of those deleted in the latest edition due to retirement or death, and of those in the Marquis companion regional volumes. A new feature is an italicized statement from first-time entrants of their principles and aims. Accompanying this biennial work are: a supplement of 20,000 new or revised entries for the intervening year; and a geographical and professions index volume. Marquis 'Who's who' data is now online from DIALOG.

Special features, such as lists and illustrations, can be useful additions to the traditional 'Who's who'. *Who's who in Australia* (1906 – . 26th ed. Melbourne: Herald and Weekly Times, 1988. Triennial) contains, in addition to its 10,000 biographies, lists of Australian Government officials, diplomats, Nobel prize-winners and recipients of honours. *Who's who in Canada* (1907 – . 80th ed. Toronto: Global Press, 1989. Annual), has photographs for two-thirds of its biographees, unlike its more comprehensive and authoritative rival, the *Canadian who's who* (1910 – . Vol. 24. Toronto: University of Toronto, 1989).

Another type of geographic area 'Who's who' covers a continent, or group of countries associated through race, culture or geography:

WHO'S WHO IN EUROPE. 6th ed. 1985. Waterloo, Belgium: Editions Servi-Tech, 1985. Irregular.

WHO'S WHO IN THE ARAB WORLD. 1966 – . 9th ed. 1988 – 9. Beirut: Publitec, 1988. Irregular.

For all 28 countries of the continent of Europe, except Turkey, *Who's who in Europe* contains over 40,000 biographies; French is used, except for titles of biographees' publications. Now available online through EURONET. Another work for a continent, the *Africa who's who* (1st ed. London: Africa Journals Ltd, 1981) covers 7,000 Africans in all the Organization of African Unity states, and South Africa and Zimbabwe.

Spanning two continents, *Who's who in the Arab world* is a general reference work, containing an outline of the Arab world, surveys of 20 Arab League countries from Algeria to the Yemen, and a biographical section of 6,000 prominent living Arab personalities. Two similar works covering associated groups of nations also use English as the 'lingua franca': *Who's who in Scandinavia* (1st ed. Essen: Who's Who Verlag, 1981); and *Who's who in the Commonwealth* (Cambridge: International Biographical Centre, 1984).

A final category of area coverage work is the local 'Who's who' for a region, administrative area or town.

WHO'S WHO IN SCOTLAND. 2nd ed. Ayr: Carrick, 1988.

Prominent living Scots from all walks of life either living within Scotland or playing a significant or active role in the country's life are included in *Who's who in Scotland*.

In Victorian Britain, local and civic pride found expression in the illustrated county biographical works, such as *Norfolk notabilities* (1893) and *Suffolk celebrities* (1893). Later, series of town and county 'Who's whos' appeared, *Who's who in Cheltenham* (1910) and *Who's who in Berkshire* (1936) for example, now almost non-existent in Britain apart from occasional occurrences such as *The Birmingham Post & Mail year book and who's who* (41st ed. 1989 – 90. Birmingham: The Post, 1989). Regional or local 'Who's whos' still appear in the United States, such as *Who's who in New York* (1960) and *Who's who in California* (1976), and the Marquis series of regional companion volumes to *Who's who in America* (see above).

SPECIALIZED BIOGRAPHICAL DICTIONARIES

Specialized biographical dictionaries are probably the largest and most diverse group discussed in this chapter, covering almost every subject, occupation and profession, of which only a few can be indicated.

Retrospective

Collected biographies of special groups of persons have a long and interesting history dating back to Greek literature, with early examples, Plutarch's *Parallel lives* (of statesmen and generals) and

Lives of eminent philosophers by Diogenes Laertius, establishing the genre of 'short lives'. By the eighteenth and nineteenth centuries collections of biographies, such as Samuel Johnson's *Lives of the poets* (1779 – 81), were an established literary form, and many appearing then, including Alban Butler's *Lives of the saints* (1756 – 9) and *Lives of the engineers* by Samuel Smiles (1862), are still standard works. From these developed the scholarly biographical dictionaries for various subject areas we have today.

Thieme, U. and Becker, F., ALLGEMEINES LEXIKON DER BILDENDEN KUNSTLER VON DER ANTIKE BIS ZUR GEGENWART. 1st ed. Leipzig: Seeman, 1907 – 50.

Bénézit, E., DICTIONNAIRE CRITIQUE ET DOCUMENTAIRE DES PEINTRES, SCULPTEURS, DESSINATEURS ET GRAVEURS ... 1st ed. 1911 – 23; 3rd ed. 10 vols. Paris: Grund, 1976.

DICTIONARY OF SCIENTIFIC BIOGRAPHY. 16 vols. New York: Scribner, 1970 – 80.

These German and French works are the most comprehensive biographical dictionaries for the graphic arts. Thieme/Becker, with its complementary work, *Allgemeines Lexikon der bildenden Kunstler des XX. Jahrhunderts* by Hans Vollmer (Leipzig: Seeman, 1953 – 62. 6 vols.), is the more comprehensive of the two, containing approximately 50,000 entries. The articles, the longer of which are signed by the contributor, give brief personal details, a narrative of the artist's life and works, with an exhaustive bibliography. The entries in Bénézit contain brief personal details, an outline of the artist's life, a list of museums with works represented, sale prices fetched at auctions and art galleries, and occasional sketchy bibliographies. Despite a European bias, Oriental artists are included. Both works are largely retrospective. There is no comparable English-language work, *Bryan's dictionary of painters and engravers* (4th ed. London: Bell, 1903 – 4. 5 vols.; Washington: Kennikat Press, reprint 1964) despite 20,000 entries, is not as comprehensive and now out of date. A comparable work for scientists is the *Dictionary of scientific biography*, an authoritative work sponsored by the American Council of Learned Societies.

It contains essays for over 5,000 scientists from more than 60 countries and all areas of the sciences, which contain brief personal details, followed by signed articles with quotations, diagrams and formulae illustrating the subject's work, and a bibliography of original and secondary sources.

Subject dictionaries can be useful sources of biographical information.

THE NEW GROVE DICTIONARY OF MUSIC AND MUSICIANS. Edited by Stanley Sadie. 20 vols. London: Macmillan, 1980.

First planned and edited by Sir George Grove, and published from 1878 to 1889 this dictionary, now in its sixth edition and almost completely rewritten, is universal in scope and encyclopaedic in coverage with detailed entries for composers, performers, music scholars and writers, librettists, music patrons and others in the music business. The smaller single-volume subject dictionaries and companions can also be useful, examples being *Baker's biographical dictionary of musicians* (7th ed. New York: Schirmer, 1984), and the *Oxford companion to the theatre*, edited by Phyllis Hartnoll (4th ed. London: Oxford University Press, 1983), described by Walford as 'the standard one-volume encyclopaedia for the theatre'.

Current

Many specialized 'Who's whos' are not regular, and are often short-lived, due to the often limited market of the chosen occupation or area of activity. Only longer-established, regular works will be covered here.

Firstly, current biographical dictionaries for those working within broad categories of occupation – the 'arts' or 'sciences'.

WHO'S WHO IN ART. 1927 – . 23rd ed. Havant: Art Trade Press, 1988. Biennial (latterly).

AMERICAN MEN AND WOMEN OF SCIENCE. 1906 – . 16th ed. 8 vols. New York: Bowker, 1986. Triennial.

Who's who in art aims to produce a comprehensive list of living artists in Britain, but is actually limited to those who wish their names to appear. For artists working in all forms of painting, drawing, graphic art and sculpture, the entries include art qualifications, type of work, art college attended, exhibitions, work in permanent collections, publications, signature and address. Broader in scope is *Who's who in American art* (1935 – . 18th ed. 1989 – 90. New York: Bowker, 1988. Biennial), profiling over 11,000 American, Canadian and Mexican artists, art historians, critics, teachers, dealers and musuem personnel. Similar 'Who's whos' for 'the arts' cover musicians, the theatre and writers. For scientists working in American and Canadian universities, industry, foundations and Government projects, *American men and women of science* in its latest edition contains over 127,000 biographies from the biological and physical sciences. The criteria for selection are: achievement in the particular science; important published research; or organizational position. Entries contain birthdate, specialization, education, career, details of research, publications and address. Online through DIALOG, BRS and TECH DATA. *Who's who in science in Europe* (1967 – . 4th ed. London: Longman, 1984. 4 vols.) contains shorter entries for scientists from Eastern and Western Europe, excluding the USSR, working in universities, research establishments and industry.

Current biographical dictionaries for the professions – traditionally the Church, the Law and Medicine, but now most occupations for which qualifying examinations are necessary including architecture, engineering and even librarianship – are of a standard type, giving general information about the profession, as well as brief biographies of its members.

CROCKFORD'S CLERICAL DICTIONARY. 1858 – . 90th ed. 1987/88. London: Church House, 1987. Irregular.

THE SOLICITOR'S AND BARRISTER'S DIRECTORY. 1984 – . 1989 ed. London: Waterlow Directories, 1989. Annual.

THE MEDICAL DIRECTORY. 1845 – . 145th issue. London: Churchill, 1989. Annual.

Professional directories, as in these for the professions of the

United Kingdom, rarely give personal details in the biographical entries, only information relevant to the profession. *Crockford's*, the standard reference work of the Anglican clergy, has information on how to address the clergy, a biographical section, and indexes of the churches, benefices and Cathedrals of the Church of England. The biographies of the clergy, both active and retired, give name, birthdate, education, degree, dates of ordination and career outline of parochial and other appointments. In *The solicitor's and barrister's directory*, which succeeds *The law list* (1841 – 1976) and *The bar list* (1977 – 83), the entries for barristers are even briefer, giving only name, degree, Inn of Court and date called to the Bar, address and circuit. *The medical directory* lists Health Authorities, medical schools, hospitals in Britain and Ireland, and a biographical section of qualified members of the medical profession, giving details of degrees, medical school attended, current post, previous posts and professional publications.

Collected biographies of writers often contain essay-style entries, with critiques and bibliographies:

CONTEMPORARY AUTHORS. 1962 – . Vol. 127. Detroit: Gale, 1989; NEW REVISION SERIES. 1980 – . Vol. 28, 1989; PERMANENT SERIES. 1975 – . Vol. 2, 1978.

CONTEMPORARY NOVELISTS. 4th ed. London: St James Press, 1986.
  As writers now 'move more rapidly from one area of communication to another, the medium is less significant than the communicator', so the American *Contemporary authors* aims to be a current source on over 82,000 non-technical writers from all media, including the press, broadcasting and films. Entries include personal details, career, awards, checklist of writings, work in progress, comments from the author and further sources of biography and criticism. For over 500 notable living fiction-writers, mostly British and American, *Contemporary novelists* gives a brief biographical sketch, a full bibliography, critical studies of their work, comments from the author and a signed critical essay by an authoritative contributor. Companion volumes

include: *Contemporary dramatists* (4th ed. 1988) and *Contemporary poets* (4th ed. 1985). Increasingly there are 'Who's whos' for writers in particular literary genres: *Twentieth-century crime and mystery writers*, edited by John M. Reilly (2nd ed. London: St James Press, 1986) and *Twentieth-century science-fiction writers*, edited by Curtis C. Smith (2nd ed. Chicago: St James Press, 1986).

'Who's whos' for British politicians illustrate differing, but equally valid, approaches to the same material.

DOD'S PARLIAMENTARY COMPANION. 1832 - . 170th ed. 1989. London: Dod's, 1989. Annual.

'THE TIMES' GUIDE TO THE HOUSE OF COMMONS. 1880 - . June 1987 ed. London: Times Books, 1987.

VACHER'S BIOGRAPHICAL GUIDE. 1987 - . 3rd ed. London: A. S. Kerswill, 1989. Annual.

PARLIAMENTARY PROFILES. Edited by Andrew Roth. 1984 - . 2nd ed. 4 vols. London: Parliamentary Profiles, 1988 - 90.

    Dod's parliamentary companion contains illustrated biographical sketches for members of both Houses of Parliament, concentrating on their parliamentary careers. *'The Times' guide to the House of Commons*, issued after each General Election, contains for each constituency a biography and photograph for the MP, and shorter sketches for the unsuccessful candidates from the main political parties. *Vacher's biographical guide*, stablemate to the long-established *Vacher's parliamentary companion* (1832 -), contains sketches of MPs, Peers and UK Members of the European Parliament, together with cross-reference lists of personal and political interests. More informative, and more irreverent, is Andrew Roth's *Parliamentary profiles*, and its companion *The MPs chart* (1974 -), which aim to provide insight into the position and character of MPs through standard biographical information, but also political outlook, contributions to parliamentary debates and 'traits' (including such quotable comments as 'Iron Maiden in blue chiffon' for Margaret Thatcher).

Biography and lineage of royalty and artistocracy are covered by some long-established genealogical works:

BURKE'S GENEALOGICAL AND HERALDIC HISTORY OF THE PEERAGE, BARONETAGE AND KNIGHTAGE. 1826 – . 105th ed. London: Burke's Peerage, 1970; 4th imp. 1980. Irregular.

DEBRETT'S PEERAGE AND BARONETAGE. 1769 – . 1985 ed. London: Debrett's Peerage/Macmillan, 1985. Irregular.

Burke's peerage has full heraldic details of each member of the Royal Family, royal lineage, biographies and lineage of peers, baronets and knights. *Debrett's peerage* gives details of the life, arms and families of peers and baronets, and though not as detailed as *Burke's peerage*, it has useful sections on orders of knighthood, chiefs and clans of Scotland, and advice on forms of address for titled persons.

Biography and lineage of world royalty and artistocracy are contained in *Annuaire de la noblesse de France et de l'Europe* (1843 – . 92nd vol. London: Annuaire de France, 1982) and its English edition *Royalty, peerage and nobility of the world* (91st vol. London: Annuaire de France, 1976); *Burke's royal families of the world*: Vol. 1, *Europe and Latin America*; Vol. 2, *Africa and the Middle East* (London: Burke's Peerage, 1977, 1980); *Almanach de Gotha* (1763 – 1944. Gotha: Perthes); and *Genealogisches handbuch des Adels* (1951 – . Limburg, C. A. Starke).

Lists of members of societies, exhibitors in art exhibitions, and university and public school alumni, can be useful biographical sources. *The biographical memoirs of the Fellows of the Royal Society* (1955 – . Annual), continuing *Obituary notices of Fellows of the Royal Society* (1932 – 54), contains lengthy essays, with portraits and complete bibliographies. An example of a list of exhibitors is: A. Graves, *The Royal Academy of Arts: a complete dictionary of contributors and their work from its foundation in 1769 to 1904* (London: Henry Graves, 1905; reprint, Weston-Super-Mare: Kingsmead Press, 1989. 4 vols.), and its supplement *Royal Academy exhibitors 1905 – 1970* (Calne, Wiltshire: Hilmarton Manor Press, 1986. 4 vols.). Notable historical lists of students of universities are:

Alumni oxonienses: The members of the University of Oxford, 1500 – 1714/1715 – 1886 by J. Foster (Oxford: Parker, 1891 – 2. 4 vols. Liechtenstein: Kraus Reprint, 1968); and *Alumni cantabrigienses: a biographical list of all known students, graduates and holders of office at the University of Cambridge from the earliest times to 1900* (Cambridge: University Press, 1922 – 54. 10 vols.; Liechtenstein: Kraus Reprint, 1974). British public school pupils also are listed: *Rugby School register 1675 – 1921* (Rugby: The School, 1901 – 29. 5 vols.).

Finally, not all biographical enquiries will be for 'real' people, but for characters from folklore, mythology or fiction. Written by a foremost authority on British and Irish folklore, Katherine Briggs, the *Dictionary of fairies, hobgoblins, brownies, bogies and other supernatural creatures* (London: Allen Lane, 1976; new ed. Penguin Books, 1977) gives 'biographies', with quotations and bibliographies. Characters from Greek and Roman legends can be found in *Who's who in classical mythology*, by M. Grant and J. Hazel (London: Hodder, 1979). For tracing fictional characters, and in which book they appear, *Dictionary of fictional characters*, by W. Freeman (3rd ed. London: Dent, 1973) is a valuable source from which one can then progress in many cases to a reader's guide or companion to a particular author's works, offering fuller biographies of the characters, such as *Who's who in Thomas Hardy*, by G. Leeming (London: Elm Tree Books, 1975).

BIBLIOGRAPHICAL GUIDES AND INDEXES TO BIOGRAPHY

Collected biographies

This section surveys guides and indexes to the contents of general, national and specialized biographical dictionaries, which are invaluable as short cuts to lengthy searches. These guides may refer to rather elusive works not immediately available. However, they can prove useful to identify the subject of a search, and as a direction to further sources.

BIOGRAPHY ALMANAC. Edited by Susan L. Stetler. 2nd ed. Detroit: Gale, 1983.

Hyamson, A. M., A DICTIONARY OF UNIVERSAL BIOGRAPHY OF ALL AGES AND ALL PEOPLES. 2nd ed. London: Routledge, 1951; Detroit: Gale, reprint 1976.

Riches, P. M., AN ANALYTICAL BIBLIOGRAPHY OF UNIVERSAL COLLECTED BIOGRAPHY. London: Library Association, 1934; Detroit: Gale, reprint 1980.

Three works which list the names of biographees, with dates and brief identifying description, with citations for the biographical dictionaries in which they appear. The *Biography almanac* is a guide to over 20,000 'newsmakers from Biblical times to the present' who appear in 325 biographical dictionaries, from the *DAB* to the *International motion picture almanac*. Hyamson contains references to approximately 100,000 biographies appearing in 24 major biographical dictionaries and general reference books, including *The annual register, DNB*, and *Allgemeine deutsche Biographie*. Phyllis Riches contains 56,000 biographies contained in over 3,000 English-language collected biographies, with a full bibliography of works analysed, and chronological and subject indexes.

Similar indexes to the sources of biography are currently in progress:

BIOGRAPHY AND GENEALOGY MASTER INDEX. 2nd ed. 8 vols. Detroit: Gale, 1981. Annual supplements. 1981 – ; Five-year cumulations. 1985 – ; also in microform.

ESSAY AND GENERAL LITERATURE INDEX. 1900 – . New York: H. W. Wilson, 1934 – . Six-monthly, annual, and five-year cumulations.

Lobies, J.-P., INDEX BIO-BIBLIOGRAPHICUS NOTORUM HOMINUM. Osnabruck: Biblio Verlag, 1972 – .

The *Biography and genealogy master index*, originally the *Biographical dictionaries master index* (1975), locates biographical entries in American, Canadian and British current and retrospective biographical dictionaries, subject encyclopaedias, indexes and volumes of literary criticism. A microfiche edition, *Bio-base 1984 master cumulation*, developed from databases used in compiling the hardcopy editions, contains 5,350,000 brief citations in editions of over 500 source works, updated with annual cumulations, the latest (*Bio-base 1985 – 88*) adding a further 1,235,000 citations. DIALOG provides online access to the 6 million references in its *Biography master index* file, the equivalent to the main work and annual supplements to date. The *Essay and general literature index* cites over 4,000 essays and articles annually, many of them biographical, analysed from collected essays and miscellaneous works, published mainly in Britain and the USA, arranged in one alphabetical sequence of authors, titles and subjects, followed by a list of books indexed. *Index bio-bibliographicus*, a massive work gradually appearing in fascicules is both a bibliography of some 2,000 collected biographies from all countries and languages, and an analytical index of their contents.

Individual biographies

Bibliographical details of individual biographies or autobiographies can, of course, be traced in the national bibliographies and 'books-in-print' services; however, some useful specialized bibliographies exist:

Subject bibliographies computer generated from publishers or national library databases now appear:

BIOGRAPHICAL BOOKS 1876 – 1949 and 1950 – 80. New York: Bowker, 1983, 1980.

BIBLIOGRAPHY OF BIOGRAPHY 1970 – 84. London: British Library Bibliographic Services Division, 1985. 44 microfiche.

INTERNATIONAL BIBLIOGRAPHY OF BIOGRAPHY 1970 – 87. 12 vols. London: K. G. Saur, 1988.

Computer-produced from all Bowker databases, *Biographical books* lists individual biographies, autobiographies, letters and diaries published or distributed in the USA, with vocation, author and title indexes. The *Bibliography of biography 1970 – 84* on microfiche is compiled from the British Library/Library of Congress MARC catalogue records for biographical works published in all languages throughout the world, arranged in two sequences of biographees and author/titles. An annual hardcopy *Bibliography of biography 1988* has appeared. Also compiled from MARC records the *International bibliography of biography 1970 – 87* overlaps the previous work, and has over 100,000 entries in two sequences of subject/biographee (giving full bibliographical details, Dewey and Library of Congress class numbers) and author/title.

Catalogues to general or specialized libraries can also be useful guides to individual biography:

National Maritime Museum, CATALOGUE OF THE LIBRARY. Vol. 2: BIOGRAPHY. 2 vols. London: HMSO, 1969.

Royal Commonwealth Society, BIOGRAPHY CATALOGUE OF THE LIBRARY by Donald H. Simpson. London: The Society, 1961.

These handsomely produced catalogues are valuable sources of biography for their subject area. The National Maritime Museum catalogue covers naval and maritime biography, and contains lists of collected biographies, navy lists, individual biographies, autobiographies and journals, with a reference index to 15,000 names appearing in 21 collected works, including *DNB*, Boase, and James Ralfe's *Naval biography of Britain*. The Royal Commonwealth Society Library catalogue has an alphabetical sequence of 6,500 persons born in, or actively associated with, the countries of the Commonwealth, giving brief identifying details and references to books and periodicals in the collection, followed by country and author indexes.

The *British Library general catalogue of printed books* with its *Supplements* is primarily an author catalogue; however it does list books both by and about an author. The *British Museum subject index of the modern works added to the Library, 1881 – 1960*, extended as *British Library general subject catalogue* to 1985, does list individual biographies under specific names; however, collected biographies would be indicated under general subject headings for Biography,

Autobiography, Portraits and such subheadings as Music: Composers.

Guides to specific types of biographical works are important:

Matthews, W., BRITISH DIARIES: AN ANNOTATED BIBLIOGRAPHY OF BRITISH DIARIES WRITTEN BETWEEN 1442 AND 1942. Berkley: University of California Press, 1950.

This excellent source for biography researchers is a chronological listing of published and unpublished diaries, with annotated entries and author index. William Matthews, a diary and autobiography enthusiast, also wrote *American diaries* (1945), *Canadian diaries and autobiographies* (1950) and *British autobiographies* (1955), now updated by *And so to bed: a bibliography of diaries published in English* by Patricia P. Havlice (Metuchen, New Jersey: Scarecrow Press, 1987).

Portraits

Searching for portraits can be a difficult part of biographical research, and although many encyclopaedias and biographical dictionaries contain references to portraits, and even reproduce them occasionally, other specialist guides to portraits will be necessary:

ALA PORTRAIT INDEX. 3 vols. Washington: Library of Congress, 1906; New York: Burt Franklin, reprint 1964.

This index contains references to reproductions of approximately 120,000 portraits of over 40,000 people in books and periodicals. The entry includes a brief identifying description, followed by works containing a portrait of the person.

Catalogues of portraits in art galleries, museums and academic or professional bodies are also useful. Two examples are: *National Portrait Gallery: concise catalogue, 1856 – 1969; 1970 – 1976* (London: The Gallery, 1970, 1977), which contains 3,000 entries with details of sitter, portrait and artist; and *The Royal College of Physicians of London: portraits* (London: J. & A. Churchill, 1964), and *Portraits: catalogue II* (Amsterdam: Elsevier/Excerpta Medica, 1977), with photographs and documentation of over 300 portraits.

Periodicals

BIOGRAPHY INDEX. 1946 – . New York: H. W. Wilson. Quarterly, annual, and three/two-year cumulations.

International in scope, though with an American bias, this currently analyses periodicals, newspapers, collected and individual biographies, diaries and letters. Entries contain brief identification of the biographee, followed by citations, with portraits and illustrations indicated, and an index of professions. Now available online back to 1984 through WILSONLINE, and on CD-ROM. The general periodical indexes, *British humanities index*, and *Readers' guide to periodical literature*, also have biographical references, as do the specialized indexes – *Art index* and *Music index*.

Primary sources

It will often be necessary to direct an enquirer to primary, as well as secondary sources. Much valuable biographical material, such as correspondence, diaries and private papers, is still only in the original manuscript, stored in archives and record repositories. Locations can be found in the 'Index of persons' in the *Guide to the Royal Commission on Historical Manuscripts 1870 – 1911 and 1911 – 1957* (London: HMSO, 1914, 1966), and for newly acquired papers in *Accessions to repositories and reports added to the National Register of Archives* (London: HMSO, 1957 – . Annual).

Subject bibliographies

Slocum, R. B., BIOGRAPHICAL DICTIONARIES AND RELATED WORKS. 2nd ed. 2 vols. Detroit: Gale, 1986.

This definitive subject bibliography of collected biography, contains details of 16,000 biographical dictionaries, bio-bibliographies, biographical indexes, historical and subject dictionaries, and portrait catalogues. International in scope, it is arranged into three sections – universal biography, national or area biography, and biography by vocation – with author, title and subject indexes. A useful subject arranged bibliography, *Biographical sources: a guide to dictionaries and reference works*, by Diane J. Cimbala, Jennifer Cargill and Brian Alley (Phoenix, Arizona: Onyx Press, 1986) provides annotated entries on a wide range of biographical dictionaries.

REFERENCES AND CITATIONS

1 Woolf, V., 'The art of biography', in *The death of a moth and other essays*. London: Hogarth Press, 1942, 126.
2 Grogan, D., *Grogan's case studies in reference work*. Vol. 6: *Biographical sources*. London: Bingley, 1987.
3 Woodbine, H., 'Reference libraries', *Library Association record*, **39** (3), March 1937, 119 – 20.
4 Shores, L., *Basic reference sources*. Chicago: American Library Association, 1954, 99.
5 Christie, R. C., 'Biographical dictionaries', *Quarterly review*, 157, January 1884, 187 – 230.
6 George Smith and the DNB, *Times literary supplement*, 24 December 1971, 1593 – 5.

SUGGESTIONS FOR FURTHER READING

Edel, L., 'Biography: a manifesto', *Biography*, **1** (1), Winter 1978, 1 – 3.
Ellman, R., *Golden codgers: biographical speculations*. London: Oxford University Press, 1973.
Garraty, J. A., *The nature of biography*. London: Cape, 1958.
Gittings, R., *The nature of biography*. London: Heinemann, 1978.
Katz, W. A., 'Biographical sources', in *Introduction to reference work*. Vol. 1: *Basic information sources*. 5th ed. New York: McGraw-Hill, 1987.
Maurois, A., *Aspects of biography*. Cambridge: Cambridge University Press, 1929.
Shelston, A., *Biography*. London: Methuen, 1977.

6

Business and Company Information

Susan Fleetwood

The demand for business and company information has grown at a considerable rate over the last few years. Businessmen are more aware that if they wish to succeed they must acquire as much information as possible on their markets and competitors. Since the recession a steady increase in aggressive marketing has been seen. As well as the business community, other users of business information include candidates for interviews, the general public checking on companies and setting up businesses, and the growing numbers of business students. Increasing demands are being placed on business-information services offered by various types of library. The approach of the Single Market in 1992 is understandably producing a growing need for European information.

At present there is a considerable amount of published information available. Unfortunately this business material is often expensive and libraries on limited budgets are having to struggle to provide an adequate service. It is therefore essential to select material with great care bearing in mind that most publications and information services will need a regular purchasing commitment to guarantee currency. There are few areas of business these days which do not have a directory covering them. Directories may be already out-of-date when first purchased due to the fact that the amount of time needed to collect information and then publish it can be quite lengthy. The introduction of online databases, floppy discs and CD-ROMs has had an enormous impact on business information. The information can be more up-to-date and, most important, it can be manipulated, thus saving hours of laborious searching through publications.

It is essential to remember that this chapter can contain only a small number of major items of business information. Some of these will be too expensive for a number of libraries to purchase, but at least they will act as an indication of what information may be available in the large commercial libraries. Most directories are published annually and where this is so, date and periodicity are not included in the following entries. Many directories will cease or change their name and new publications appear, so it is important to note that bibliographical details given here can be correct only at the time of writing.

TOPOGRAPHICAL AND LOCAL DIRECTORIES

For many years Kelly's directories covered counties and towns throughout Britain. They were an invaluable source of information providing listings of private residents, alphabetical and classified businesses, streets and their occupants in order of house number. Over the years for economic reasons these gradually ceased to be published and from 1976 onwards only the London directory continued. Their demise is a great loss as many enquiries received today could be easily answered if these directories were still published.

KELLY'S POST OFFICE LONDON DIRECTORY. 2 vols. East Grinstead: Kelly's Directories.

First established in 1799 it now includes over 80,000 companies in the London/M25 area and is published in association with the London Chamber of Commerce. Over 200 pages of full-colour maps with a complete index of 65,000 streets are included. Garry Humphreys, Librarian of the City Business Library, criticized the 1988 edition[1] stating that although there is an impression of improvement and expansion many valuable features have been lost. 'There is now no indication of who is on each side of the road, no indications of intersections of other streets, topographical features, blocks of flats, and no alphabetical index of named buildings either.' It is a good idea to retain the 1987 edition which contains these features.

Among other street directories *Thom's Dublin and county street directory* (Dublin: Thom's Directories) is now in its 133rd year and lists every street in alphabetical order with each resident or business.

Throughout the country many chambers of commerce produce alphabetical lists of their members usually with a classified trade index. A number of local councils now produce directories of businesses within their area. In Birmingham the city's Economic Development Unit publishes an annual *Directory of industry and commerce* which covers over 12,000 companies and includes a classified index. The *Birmingham Post and Mail* also produces an excellent yearbook listing local societies, charities, associations, etc.

Thomson local directories (Farnborough: Thomson Directories) are distributed free within the area concerned. They are similar to *Yellow pages*, but not so comprehensive and cover smaller geographic areas. The 144 areas and towns covered include community pages with AA maps and a postcode directory.

TELEPHONE DIRECTORIES

Telephone directories are one of the most valuable sources of business information although they can sometimes be overlooked. The telephone directory for London can often reveal headquarters addresses of major companies, charities and associations as well as including foreign embassies and central government departments. There are currently 103 *British Telecom phone books* plus an index, which are available in hardback, paperback or microfiche. The *Dialling code decoder* provides details of the location of telephone code numbers. *Yellow pages* published annually are available for every area and can often provide information not found in trade directories, such as lists of local retailers and wholesalers. Good cross-references and maps of town centres are included. *Business pages* are also available for a number of areas of the country.

The Library Association has now negotiated with British Telecom that public libraries may claim free copies including microfiche of *Phone books* and *Yellow pages*, dependent on the size of the library and the amount of use made of it. The latest BT developments are *Phonebase*, an online access to alphabetical phone books with over 20 million entries, and *Phonedisc*, the provision of directories on CD-ROM.

Unfortunately foreign telephone directories are not always easy to obtain and it is often difficult to ascertain their frequency and the date of the current edition. BT acts as an agent for a number of countries. *Phonefiche* (Ann Arbor, MI: University Microfilms International) produces telephone directories on microfiche covering the US and Canada and results in a considerable saving of shelf space. It should be borne in mind that there are some places in North America not included in this service.

The layout of telephone directories can vary even in the UK from region to region. A considerable amount of care should be taken when using telephone directories. Many foreign directories do not have printed indexes and need an atlas or gazetteer to trace the correct volume. Some foreign languages have a slightly different alphabetical order from English. Abbreviations used in addresses can also pose problems.

Although due to sheer size it would not be possible to publish international listings of telephone subscribers, the following is a useful directory of European companies:

EUROPAGES – THE EUROPEAN BUSINESS DIRECTORY. Neuilly-sur-Seine: Euredit.

This is available in six languages and includes 140,000 exporting firms in eight countries. Telex numbers are also included. The directory is arranged by product classification and alphabetically by name of company. Over 300,000 copies are distributed free of charge to companies and organizations within the European Community.

The appearance of *US yellow pages* online means that the information can be manipulated. Thus it is easy to trace large jewellery retailers in specified states or towns. *D & B Duns electronic yellow pages* database on DIALOG is updated quarterly. At present it appears to be the largest online database of US businesses, listing nearly 8.5 million and also including SIC (Standard Industrial Classification) code, city population and employee size in addition to the telephone directory information.

It is often necessary to complete the address given in a telephone directory with a postcode. The UK has over 100 separate postcode directories whereas the US has one volume providing Zip codes for the whole country.

TELEGRAPHIC ADDRESS, TELEX AND FAX DIRECTORIES

The demand for information on telegraphic addresses has declined considerably during the last decade. In many cases telex has superseded telegrams and there has been a dramatic rise throughout the world in the use of fax transmission. There is no need to type the message into the equipment and diagrams can also be transmitted. The following directory which has been established for many years caters for the various forms of electronic communication.

MARCONI'S INTERNATIONAL REGISTER. Larchmont, NJ: Telegraphic Cable and Radio Registry.

Includes fax, mail, telephone and cable subscribers. Prominent companies throughout the world are listed alphabetically and are followed by an international trade classification, plus index of cable addresses. A special section includes attorneys under 42 classifications.

JAEGER + WALDMANN INTERNATIONAL TELEX AND TELETEX DIRECTORY. 9 vols. Darmstadt: Telex-Verlag Jaeger + Waldmann.

The major worldwide telex directory. Subscribers are arranged alphabetically within each country. Answerback codes and a classified trades section are included. A companion three volume *International facsimile directory* is also published. Both these directories are now updated twice a year on CD-ROM.

For most countries the providers of the telex and fax services publish their own directories. British Telecom publish directories for the United Kingdom and a number of networks such as ITT and Western Union cover the United States.

Although the directories mentioned here are of the highest reputation there are a number of fraudulent companies, who have been operating for some years from various parts of the world. They solicit payment for entries in directories which often do not exist. It is therefore very important to check carefully any proforma invoice received from telex or any other directory publisher.

GENERAL BUSINESS DIRECTORIES

Due to the vast numbers of companies operating throughout the world any worldwide business directories will be highly selective. The majority of the companies listed will of necessity be a reasonable size.

PRINCIPAL INTERNATIONAL BUSINESSES. Parsippany, NJ: Dun's Marketing Services.

This one volume work contains international information on 55,000 companies in 140 countries. Businesses are listed alphabetically under country and also by product classification. Annual sales volume, number of employees and details of chief executives are also included. An alphabetical listing of businesses throughout the world is particularly useful if the enquirer is uncertain of the country where the company operates.

D & B international Dun's market identifiers is online on DIALOG (Palo Alto, Ca.; Oxford: DIALOG Information Services). Does not include USA, China or Soviet-bloc countries, but contains 530,000 public, private and government controlled companies in 133 countries. Updated quarterly.

THE TIMES 1000. London: Times Books.

An annual review of leading world industrial and financial companies. Tables include the 1000 largest industrial companies in descending order of turnover and Europe's top 20 industrial groupings.

A long-established and indispensable one volume directory for checking company addresses and tracing manufacturers of products in the United Kingdom is the following in its 103rd edition.

KELLY'S BUSINESS DIRECTORY. East Grinstead: Kelly's Directories.

An alphabetical listing of over 84,000 British companies and a classified section of 15,000 concise subject headings. A trade-names index is also included. This directory does not contain any detailed company information. *Kelly's business link* is available free on controlled circulation and includes over 12,000 businesses who promote their services in *Kelly's business directory*.

Often more detailed information is required and the following major British directories will be able to provide it:

KEY BRITISH ENTERPRISES. 3 vols. London: Dun & Bradstreet.

Identifies the top 25,000 companies. Two updates are published each year. The information on each company comprises an alphabetical listing with ownership, trade names, export markets, directors and SIC code. There is also a listing of companies by SIC and a geographical listing by country in SIC order.

KBE is available online (London: PFDS) and the information can be manipulated easily by the use of various criteria.

KOMPASS REGISTER. 3 vols. East Grinstead: Kompass Publishers.

The registers are available for 22 foreign countries. The UK edition contains comprehensive information on over 40,000 companies and more than 41,000 different products and services. The classification used for products is the same for the whole series of registers. Detailed financial data on the status of the leading 30,000 companies include assets and professional ratios.

Kompass online (East Grinstead: Reed Information Services) is also available on DIALOG and other gateways. The UK company file also includes other directories such as *Dial industry*, *British exporters* and *Directory of directors*.

A series of *Kompass regional sales guides* is published in seven volumes in association with the Institute of Marketing. Salestargeting information is provided on 50,000 UK-based companies. These guides differ from the register in that they identify departmental heads in addition to directors. More than 250,000 named contacts are included. It is possible to purchase individual regional guides.

INTERNATIONAL STOCK EXCHANGE YEARBOOK. London: Macmillan Publishers; Stock Exchange Press.

The authoritative source of over 3,000 companies quoted on London's International Stock Exchange, this is published under the sanction of the Council of Europe. Company information details acquisitions, mergers and takeovers in addition to major shareholdings. Profitability, performance and dividends are also included.

ICC REGIONAL COMPANY SURVEYS. Hampton: ICC Business Publications.

Over 50 regions of the country are covered by this series of county and regional profiles of company performance. Three years of financial statistics are included. A postcode index allows companies to be pinpointed and a SIC index enables local companies trading in the same industry to be monitored. All this information is available on disc. Detailed factsheets on around 100,000 companies are also produced.

ICC is online on a number of host systems including DIALOG, Data-Star and PFDS. Their own system can also be accessed on Viewdata. There are plans to expand the number of companies covered and Danish company data have just been added to the Viewdata service.

MACMILLAN'S UNQUOTED COMPANIES. 2 vols. London: Macmillan Publishers.

Financial profiles of Britain's top 20,000 unquoted companies with individual turnovers in excess of £3 million per annum. Three-year trading periods plus industrial-sector performance tables. Comparisons can be made between individual companies and the average for their industrial sector.

Jordan & Sons have been established since 1863 and act as company registration agents and providers of company information. A *New company information service* is issued weekly to subscribers. Companies can be selected either by geographical location or type of business. Financial surveys include *Britain's top 4000 privately owned companies*, which present information in tabulated form similar to ICC publications. Various industry surveys are also produced. Jordans is online on a number of host systems with current company information (including dissolved companies) since 1964, updated weekly. Full financial information is available on companies with a turnover of £1 million + or pre-tax profits over £50,000 or shareholder funds of £1 million + . The *Jordans shareholder service* has details of shareholders owning more than 0.15% of issued shares in nearly 2,000 companies.

Very often it is necessary to investigate a company's relationship with other companies. It may be a parent company or exist as a subsidiary or associate. There may also be connections with companies abroad.

WHO OWNS WHOM UK & REPUBLIC OF IRELAND. 2 vols. London: Dun & Bradstreet.

Includes subsidiaries and associates of parent companies registered in UK and Republic of Ireland, foreign parent companies with subsidiaries in UK and Republic of Ireland, and an alphabetical index to subsidiaries and parent companies. Other publications in this series cover Australasia and the Far East, Continental Europe and North America.

The international database is available on PFDS. It is continuously updated and allows the searcher to build up a file of historical information on the parentage of subsidiaries.

It is often necessary to find biographical details of various directors and personalities eminent in the field of business.

DIRECTORY OF DIRECTORS. East Grinstead: Thomas Skinner.

This invaluable directory now in its 110th edition contains details of 59,000 directors, who control Britain's major companies.

Over 16,000 companies with board members including status are included. Financial highlights of the major companies are also provided.

Who's who in the City (London: London & International Publishers) details individuals working in the financial community and extends to a large number of people based in regional financial centres. There is a companion volume *Who's who in industry*.

As 1992 approaches it is essential to be able to provide as much European business information as is possible within the financial resources of the library.

DUNS EUROPA. 3 vols. London: Dun & Bradstreet.

English language profiles of the leading 35,000 manufacturing, wholesale and retail, financial and business services companies in the EEC plus Austria and Switzerland. The top 10,000 companies are ranked by sales turnover and also in each major industrial category. Also included are statistical profiles by country, SIC and European Currency Unit.

Duns also produce a series of directories concentrating on the largest companies in various countries of Western Europe.

EUROPE'S 15,000 LARGEST COMPANIES. London: ELC International.

Companies are ranked by turnover and then listed alphabetically. ELC directories also cover Scandinavia, Asia, and the UK and are available on disc and online on PFDS.

MAJOR COMPANIES OF EUROPE. 3 vols. London: Graham & Trotman.

Key information on over 8,000 companies. The publishers also produce similar works for the Arab world, Far East and US.

Kompass register for the UK has been described earlier in this section. Registers are available for a total of 23 countries. The *European companies file* online contains details of over a quarter of a million companies taken from the directories. *European Kompass* will shortly be available on CD-ROM with 300,000 companies covering 11,000 products, which will be updated twice a year. *ABC Europ production* is available on Data-Star and includes

140,000 European companies which make it a major competitor to Kompass.

The United States is well served by directories and company-information services and space permits only a few major publications to be listed here.

THOMAS REGISTER OF AMERICAN MANUFACTURERS. 23 vols. New York: Thomas Publishing.

Volumes 1 – 14 include more than 50,000 separate product and service headings. Volumes 15 – 16 contain over 145,000 US company profiles with asset ratings, company executives and locations of sales offices. A number of companies provide a complete profile of their subsidiaries and divisions and entire product lines. A brand name index is also included. Volumes 17 – 23 catalogue data from more than 1,400 companies. The *Register* is online on DIALOG and updated twice a year. CD-ROM version will be available shortly.

MACRAE'S CORPORATE INDEX. 3 vols. New York: Macrae's Blue Book.

A much smaller directory than *Thomas* including company addresses with capital ratings. Trade-names index has both registered and non-registered names. There is also a two volume product classification.

D & B MILLION DOLLAR DIRECTORY. 6 vols. Parsippany, NJ: Dun's Marketing Services.

Current financial and marketing information on 160,000 companies. There is also a *Billion dollar directory*. Online on DIALOG and CD-ROM. *D & B – Dun's market identifiers* is an extensive database on DIALOG covering more than two million US companies.

The remaining areas of the world are covered by directories such as *Trado Asian African directory* (New Delhi: Trado Publications) and *Asia/Pacific directory* (Auckland: Universal Business Directories).

INDIVIDUAL TRADES DIRECTORIES
AND BUYERS' GUIDES

The range of individual trades directories available is now quite
considerable and most libraries will not be in a position to maintain
large collections. Libraries can no longer limit their collections
to local demand as industries and business services have become
so diverse within many areas. International directories will cover
many countries but in the space allowed information cannot be
very specific. European directories on specific industries are
becoming increasingly popular. Difficult decisions will have to
be made regarding the range of coverage to be made and whether
it is possible to purchase European or international editions as
well as those for the UK.

A number of established publishers produce series of directories.
Financial Times international year books (Harlow: Longman) includes
world insurance, oil, gas, and industrial companies. *Benn's
directories* (Tonbridge: Benn Business Information Services) range
over hardware, the timber trade, leather, gas industry, the paper
trade and many more.

An example of a directory which has adapted to the European
marketplace is the following:

EUROPEAN FOOD TRADES DIRECTORY. London: Newman Books.
  Although mainly European and UK it does extend coverage
to overseas producers, outlets and services. Over 2,000 companies
operating in 27 countries are included. There is an excellent very
specific product listing and trade name index.

In the last few years a series of specialist European marketing
directories have been published by Euromonitor Publications,
London covering a wide range of industries. These include
consumer goods, the retail industry, electrical appliances and the
drinks industry. Each directory which covers every Western
European country contains a list of companies within the particular
industry, a summary of statistics and a directory of information
sources. It is particularly useful to have so much information on

an industry within the one volume. The only problem for the librarian is where to locate it on the shelf – with the directories or in the statistical sequence.

Some journals produce buyers' guides either as a separate regular publication or as an integral part of the journal. *Toy directory* (Watford: *Toy Trader*) is published as a separate publication from the journal. A franchise sales directory is included each month within *Franchise world*. *Trade directory information in journals* (4th ed. London: British Library Business Information Service, 1984) provides a very useful listing comprising an alphabetical list of journals plus index of industries, trade and products.

Trade associations can be a rich source of lists of companies operating within certain industries. Professional organizations can also provide information on their individual members. Most of these are available to the public, but occasionally the publications may be on controlled circulation.

With the increase in aggressive marketing techniques there is a growing demand for mailing lists. It is possible to tailor these to a businessman's specific requirements through manipulating the information in many online databases. Some of these have already been described. *Industrial market locations* on PFDS provides information not usually found in printed directories. It is updated six times a year and covers some 145,000 manufacturing and warehousing establishments. Details include whether the company has fork-lift trucks, staff canteens and packaging departments. *BRAD direct marketing – lists, rates and data* (Barnet: McLean Hunter) is published twice a year. The lists contained can range from bowls enthusiasts to petrol filling stations. *Benns direct marketing services* (Tonbridge: Benn Business Information Services) is a similar publication.

DIRECTORY OF BRITISH ASSOCIATIONS AND ASSOCIATIONS IN IRELAND. 10th ed. Beckenham· CBD Research, 1990.

This is the major British work with over 6,300 full entries covering national associations, societies and institutions in all fields of activity. Membership data, objects, activities and publications are included plus an excellent subject index and list of abbreviations of associations. This new edition includes all the new telephone codes for London. Also in the series *Directory of European industrial trade associations, Pan-European associations*, and *Centres and bureaux*.

TRADE NAMES SOURCES

Many products on the market do not carry details of the manufacturer's address, but rely solely on a trade name or mark. These can often be difficult to trace especially if they are not registered or appear on imported goods. In the UK as in some other countries it is not necessary to register a trade name. Manufacturers must lose sales as a result of only a trade name appearing on their products.

In 1958 the Trades Mark Registry of the Patent Office supplied certain libraries with new trade name information on paper slips. This service lasted about 20 years and it is very unfortunate that it has never been resumed. Their weekly *Trade marks journal* provides the latest information on trade mark registrations and applications in the UK. This information is also given on the *British trade marks* database on PFDS. Marks which have lapsed since January 1976 are also included. Online has made it much easier to trace this information. Some general business directories contain a trade name section and individual trades directories often include listings. Trade names can also be traced by scanning trade journals especially the advertisements and by using trade fair catalogues.

UK TRADE NAMES. 10th ed. East Grinstead: Kompass Publishers, 1988.

An important feature of this indispensable directory, which contains over 75,000 UK trade names, is the inclusion of companies who act as agencies for overseas firms. It is important to note that entries for industries engaged in the preparation of food, drink, tobacco and pharmaceuticals are not included. However there are a number of directories covering these industries which do have trade name listings.

For the United States there is information included in *Thomas register of American manufacturers* and *Macrae's corporate index*. The *Trademark register of the United States* lists current trademarks registered and received since 1881. *Tradescan* has Federal and State registrations databases on DIALOG. These are updated weekly and amount to nearly one million marks. Gale Research produce the two volume *Trade names dictionary* which is a guide to over 250,000 consumer oriented, trade, brand and product names. Worldwide coverage is provided by the weekly *Les marques internationales*, which is a record of registrations with the World Intellectual Property Organisation. A very recent trade mark database is IMSMARQ (London: IMSMARQ), which includes trade mark files for all classes of goods and services from Denmark, Finland, Germany, Italy, Sweden, UK and shortly USA. There is also a common law file of all pharmaceuticals worldwide.

COMPANY INFORMATION

Most information on companies can be gleaned from the documents which they are required to lodge with the company registration authority in each country. Companies House based at Cardiff with a London search facility handles companies registered in England and Wales. Scotland and Northern Ireland have their own registrars. It is possible to obtain microfiche and photocopies of annual accounts and returns by personal visit to the offices or by post and fax. Satellite offices offering these facilities have also been established throughout the country.

Companies House produces some very important directories and indexes, which are available on microfiche or roll film. The *Main directory* is revised every three months and contains information on approximately one million companies incorporated in Great Britain. Information about foreign companies registered in Great Britain is also included. Company name, number, registered office address, date of incorporation, accounting reference date and made-up date of the latest set of accounts and annual return are provided. Weekly cumulative supplements provide amendments and additions. (It is important for the most up-to-date information to check these before the *Main directory*.) An *Alphabetical index of companies* including industrial and provident societies is published monthly. A quarterly *Numeric index of companies* allows searching through their registered numbers. The *Index of dissolved/change of name companies*, which covers the past 20 years, is invaluable.

Companies House intends to create a computerized register of company directors and secretaries, which will eventually amount to around four million names. The practice of company registration varies throughout the world. In the United States registration is by state and many European countries use chambers of commerce.

Company annual reports

Librarians can usually obtain annual reports from companies they are interested in. These reports often contain information on products and the organization of the company as well as financial statements. A considerable amount of staff time and shelf space is necessary to maintain a large collection. Decisions will need to be made on which companies to select and the length of time to keep back issues. MIRAC Service (Warminster: McCarthy Information) provides microfiche copies of reports and accounts of around 3,500 publicly quoted companies on the International (London) Stock Exchange. USM and OTC companies are also included. The *Financial Times* acts as an agent for *Disclosure* reports on 12,000 US Securities Exchange Commission Companies. *ICC full text accounts* on PFDS provide a database of British publicly quoted companies. European companies are to be included in the future.

Card services

Before the advent of information technology, card services were the means of keeping business information up-to-date and they still provide a very valuable service. The drawbacks for libraries are that they tend to be expensive and require time for filing. However libraries who do provide these services find them very well used. One of the best known and established services is Extel, whose cards cover over 7,500 British and foreign companies. Since commencing publishing cards in 1919 they have long been market leaders as a source of company accounts.

EXTEL UK LISTED COMPANIES. London: Extel Financial. Loose-leaf.

Details of over 3,000 companies listed on the UK and Irish Stock Exchanges. An annual card includes balance sheet, activities, chairman's statement and dividend record. News cards update when necessary. The *Analysts' service* for 1,300 companies provides a ten-year record of analysed and adjusted financial statements. Around 2,000 of the larger unquoted companies are covered by a separate service. Other services include *The third market*, *The unlisted securities market*, *Over-the-counter* and major foreign companies.

Extel information is now available in various formats. *Exstat* updates weekly on various online host systems and includes companies in the UK, Europe, Australia and Japan. An important feature is that up to 13 years' data are given for each company. MicroEXSTAT is the easy to use micro-based version. MicroVIEW provides information on a PC, including company news and securities pricing. Extel cards with the full text of both annual and news cards are to go online on Profile.

McCARTHY CARDS. Warminster: McCarthy Information Services. Loose-leaf.

McCarthy Information is now part of the *Financial Times* Group. The cumulative cards provide a comprehensive press comment service. Items on companies and industries are extracted from a wide range of over 60 British and foreign newspapers and journals. Company fact sheets are now published for the top 1,000 quoted companies. As well as press comment on quoted and unquoted companies there is also coverage of major companies in Australia, Europe and North America. The information is available on microfiche and online through Profile. The database is updated daily and contains full text of around 160,000 articles. It is less extensive than *Textline* (London: Reuters).

STANDARD & POOR'S CORPORATION RECORDS. 6 vols. New York: Standard & Poor's. Loose-leaf.

Over 45,000 leading public and private US (and some non-US) companies, usually with sales in excess of one million dollars. The information is published periodically in loose-leaf format. Company descriptions and supplementary news items plus an index are included. Also available online on DIALOG as *Standard & Poor's corporate descriptions*.

Credit ratings

It is becoming increasingly necessary to check the credit worthiness of companies. Various services now provide this information.

INFOCHECK. London: Infocheck. Microfiche.

The register on fiche contains filed information on limited companies with up to 75 useful ratios and a review of up to four years' accounts. A credit limit recommendation is also included. The information is constantly being increased to cover other companies. At the time of writing around 240,000 fully analysed reports were available. The service is online on a number of host systems including PFDS.

DUNSPRINT. London: Dun & Bradstreet.

This enormous database on its own host system provides very detailed financial and credit information on over 16 million companies throughout the world's key trading areas. Dun & Bradstreet also produce directories providing credit ratings covering various countries.

Two extensive and well-used credit information services on Viewdata are *CCN* (Nottingham: Guardian Business Information, CCN) and *Infolink* (Croydon: Infolink). As well as a financial analysis they provide information with continuous updating on county-court judgements, liquidations, winding-up dates and directors. Both systems hold millions of records on individuals as well as companies.

Financial analysis

FAME. London: Jordan & Son. CD-ROM.

Financial analysis made easy is a new development which provides data for five years and is updated bi-monthly. Financial information on 70,000 UK companies and brief descriptive information on a further 55,000. These data can be searched using various criteria and it is possible to do a statistical analysis, which can be graphically displayed on screen or printed. It is extremely easy to use. *Online business information*[2] commented that 'FAME has set the standard for value-added European CD-ROM business databases'.

Analysis (London: Analysis Corporation) database updated each day can be manipulated in a similar way to FAME, but also includes full text of articles from McCarthy press cuttings through a gateway. Subscribers can review share price performance and use graphic analysis.

Market research reports such as those produced by Jordans and Key Notes (ICC) often include major company profiles. Full text of *Key notes* is available on PFDS. *Business ratios* from ICC are a series of over 200 ratio reports which provide financial analysis of individual company performance and an insight into the overall industry structure and developments. Each company can be compared against its competitors by up to 20 performance ratios. ICC also publish *Financial survey company directories* which can include up to 1,500 companies in each survey.

Stockbroker reports

An increasing amount of information on companies and industries can be found in stockbroker reports. Often the information contained in these reports is not easily available elsewhere.

ICC DIRECTORY OF STOCKBROKER REPORTS. London: ICC Information Group. Loose-leaf.

All stockbroker reports published during the year are arranged alphabetically by company name and industry sector and this information is updated monthly. Full text of the reports is available online on a number of host systems.

PRODUCT INFORMATION

Directories with classified sections indicating which companies manufacture certain products have already been described in the preceding pages. However it is often necessary to find further information on the products than just the name and address of the manufacturers or suppliers.

Trade journals can provide news of established or new products in articles or advertisements. *Willing's press guide* (East Grinstead: British Media Publications) and the monthly *BRAD – British rate and data* contain classified ratings of trade journals. In addition various products are exhibited at trade fairs, both in this country and abroad, and obtaining the catalogues is a useful addition to the library's stock of trade literature. Details of trade fairs taking place throughout the world are listed in the monthly *Exhibition bulletin*.

Annual reports of companies in addition to containing financial statements often include details or even photographs of products. In addition companies may publish house journals, catalogues, data sheets, handbooks and price lists. This literature can be extensive and therefore decisions will need to be made regarding a selection policy. The collection could be restricted to local industries. It is very important that if a collection of trade literature is commenced that it is kept up-to-date. Some companies have started to lodge their business archives with public libraries.

A few services exist to provide trade information but without the need for extensive shelf space or staff time.

BARBOUR MICROFILES (Windsor: Barbour Microfiles). Updated quarterly.

The files are available on microfiche with a hard-copy index. The *Product microfile* includes around 5,500 catalogues from almost 1,000 selected manufacturers covering all product types in the UK construction industry. The *Technical microfile* is a companion file with around 6,000 technical publications covering standards and codes, legislation, specifications and government reports.

TECHNICAL INDEXES (Bracknell: Technical Indexes)

The indexes provide product information, standards and specifications, which are regularly updated, for designers and engineers. They are available in a number of formats including microform, CD-ROM, online and other computer-based systems as well as some printed product data books.

DISCOVERING SOURCES OF INFORMATION

In this chapter it has been possible to mention only a very small number of business publications that are on the market. There has been a considerable increase in the availability of business information since the previous edition of this work. Various listings and updating services help us to keep aware of new titles and editions. It is very important to ensure that we have the current edition of a publication on our shelves. A number of directories during the year will change their names to reflect increased or different areas of coverage.

Since 1953 the following publication has been produced at regular intervals and has proved invaluable as an aid to directory selection for libraries.

CURRENT BRITISH DIRECTORIES – a guide to directories published in the British Isles. 11th ed. Beckenham: CBD Research, 1988.

Directories include such items as buyers' guides, membership lists, registers, who's who, etc. Local and specialized directories are included and there is a publishers' index. The subject index is useful not only as an aid to choosing directories within a certain subject area for purchase, but also as an index to the library's own stock. A classification mark can be put against the directories stocked by the library. In the preface C. A. P. Henderson[3] warns against fraudulent directories: 'such "directories" are based entirely on paid entries (i.e. only firms who pay for inclusion are listed); many exist in name only and never appear in print; those that do are generally and justifiably regarded as worthless either as reference books or as advertising media'.

Legislation has been enforced, but the problem is still serious. To protect the public the Association of British Directory Publishers was established in 1970 (their membership handbook lists all member companies with more than 600 different reference works). The Association is affiliated to the European association which was formed in 1966.

THE TOP 3000 DIRECTORIES AND ANNUALS. Reading: Alan Armstrong & Associates.

As well as UK publications this also includes many foreign directories and a selection of reference works and guides. Entries are annotated and there is a good subject index. To illustrate the increase in directory publishing the previous edition covered 1,000 directories. *Croner's trade directories of the world* (New York: Croner Publications) provides a worldwide listing with loose-leaf monthly supplements. Some indication of the information included in the directories is also given. CBD also provides a series of directories of foreign publications. *Current African directories*, 1972, *Current Asian and Australasian directories*, 1978 (in both cases new editions are in preparation) and *Current European directories*, 1981.

For North America *Directory of directories* (Detroit: Gale Research), now in its fourth edition, is an annotated guide to approximately 9,600 business and industrial directories. A subject listing and title index is also included. A companion volume contains information on around 7,000 directory publishers.

Library accession lists such as City Business Library's *Courier* provide useful checklists and the *British national bibliography* and its overseas equivalents should not be forgotten. However unlike the other works mentioned they give little idea about content.

With so many online databases, disc and CD-ROM products emerging on the market it is vitally important to keep aware of these new developments. Fortunately there are an increasing number of publications providing this information. *Online business sourcebook* (Cleveland: Headland Press), this semi-annual publication is an important evaluative guide to electronic databases. British and European services are emphasized, but the rest of the world is also covered. Discs and CD-ROM are also included. Headland Press also publish equally important monthly periodicals *Online business information* and *What's new in business information*.

Brit-line – directory of British databases (Maidenhead: McGraw-Hill), *Directory of online databases* (New York: Cuadra/Elsevier) and *Businessline* (London: Euromonitor) are all excellent sources of information about online. The *CD-ROM directory* (London: TFPL) has increased its titles to over 800 in 1990 – 30% of which originate in Europe. Current information on new online databases and directories can also be found in periodicals such as *New library world* and *Library & information news*.

REFERENCES AND CITATIONS

1 Humphreys, G., 'Misguided directories'. *Refer: journal of the ISG*, **5** (2), Autumn 1988, 6 – 7.
2 *Online business information*. May 1989, 93.
3 Henderson, C. A. P. (ed.), *Current British directories*. 11th ed. Beckenham: CBD Research, 1988, IX.

SUGGESTIONS FOR FURTHER READING

Bakewell, K. G. B., *Business information and the public library*. Aldershot: Gower Publishing, 1987.

Campbell, M. J. (ed.), *Manual of business library practice*. 2nd ed. London: Bingley, 1985.

European company information: EEC countries. 2nd ed. London: London Business School Information Service, 1989.

Legal industrial espionage. 2nd ed. 1988 – 9. Newbury: Eurofi, 1988.

Tudor, J., *Macmillan directory of business information sources*. 2nd ed. London: Macmillan Publishers, 1989.

Wall, R. A. (ed.), *Finding and using product information*. Aldershot: Gower Publishing, 1986.

7

News and Current Events

Frances Tait

News and newspapers are essential as the major sources for current information, for reference and historical research and as a general commentary on life at the time. Major political, economic and other historically significant events usually find their way into more formal printed sources – initially news digests, then annual surveys and yearbooks, chronologies and, years later, they may be covered by learned research publications and other studies of a particular subject or period. However, many aspects of the news such as reports of crimes, gossip, fashion, sport, social issues, science, the arts and passing references to individuals can all be equally important to researchers and may never appear in any other source.

Until recently, newspapers have been an unwieldy source of information to handle with few indexes and almost insurmountable problems of storage, and back files have been difficult to locate if they existed at all. However major developments have been brought about by the extraordinary speed and sophistication of modern communication systems and the increasing power of computers. The business and finance communities need current, up-to-the-minute information and, with satellite transmission, journalists need information instantly to support their reporting of concurrently developing events across the world. The development of online news databases, accessible internationally, and greater acknowledgement by academics of the role of the media in reporting news have also played their part.

Most news never appears anywhere other than in the newspapers of the following day, so, unless it is available online, it is 'lost' for ever except to those few organizations who have the need, the time and the money to maintain large libraries of press cuttings, or who purchase the few printed indexing services. However there are limitations to retrieval accuracy both in print and online. In both cuttings files and indexes, retrieval is possible only through fairly broad subject headings and selected biographical files; almost the opposite occurs in unindexed online full-text databases which are most effective for retrieving fairly specific pieces of information rather than mounting broad subject searches.

If there is no online file or index the only way to find the information needed in a newspaper is first to identify the date of an event in chronologies or year reviews, then to trace titles likely to have reported the event and finally to locate a file of the original in a local library or in the British Library.

This chapter concentrates on news as a source of current information but for tracing historical events chronologies, year reviews, yearbooks, indexes and locations of back files are also discussed. No attempt is made to chart in detail the several name changes of some of the titles referred to; consequently the date given for the first edition indicates that the current publication can be traced back continuously to that date although there may have been name changes over the years. Walford and Sheehy (see references at end of Chapter 1) provide guides to similar and ceased titles.

NEWSPAPER DATABASES

Once newspapers began to be compiled and printed electronically it was a natural and easy step to transfer the electronically encoded information into online databases and these are now the most common method of accessing news in libraries. Many important national newspapers, press agency 'wires', weekly specialized trade journals, newsletters and other periodicals are now available on databases. Unfortunately 'popular', regional and local papers are not yet well covered by the commercial databases.

Care must be taken in checking exactly what the database of a particular newspaper contains. Although the publishers and database hosts will claim that their database is 'full' text, which leads to the assumption that every word printed in the paper is included, close questioning of the publisher or close examination of the user manual may reveal that certain categories of material have been omitted for various reasons, including copyright. Often whole sections of the newspaper, such as the arts or sports pages, are excluded, as well as verbatim press agency reports, syndicated articles, letters to the editor, and freelance and commissioned contributions. The other major omissions are photographs, maps, graphs, diagrams and tables, all of which can make a valuable contribution to the understanding of an article, and for these the only recourse is to the original printed version.

The following are amongst the major full-text database hosts:

PROFILE (formerly *World reporter*). Sunbury-on-Thames: *Financial Times.*

NEXIS. Dayton, Oh.: Mead Data Central.

DIALOG. Palo Alto, Ca.

Of these probably the most important for British national newspapers is PROFILE dating from the *Guardian* 1984 – , and, for American sources, NEXIS with the *Washington Post* from 1977. Other databases with particularly good US regional and local newspaper coverage include DIALOG, DATATIMES and VU/ TEXT.

Two specialized UK databases aimed at the business community should also be mentioned, even though they are not files of complete newspapers:

TEXTLINE. London: Reuters.

McCARTHY INFORMATION on PROFILE.

In both databases articles of interest to business are selected from a wide range of national and international newspapers and periodicals and provided either in full-text or abstract form. The advantage of these databases is that articles and companies are indexed, so retrieval can be more accurate than in unindexed full-text files. TEXTLINE's coverage of the UK regional press is particularly to be noted.

In Europe, amongst others, Data-Star (with *La Suisse*) is in the full-text field as well as L'EUROPÉENNE DE DONNES (with *Le monde* and, in English, Agence France Presse), and GENIOS (with *Handelsblatt*).

'Newsletters' have recently become a major growth area in publishing and these can be important for news purposes. Because businesses and governments need to know the political and economic climate of a country or industry with which they are dealing, daily and weekly newsletters provide particularly good coverage in these areas, but there are also specialized newsletters for many other subjects including religion and Hollywood. Newsletters convey the very latest developments by reporting news items – both original and from the press – press releases, extracts from annual reports and authoritative comment by journalists and specialist contributors. Although they are usually expensive and often too specific to be found in general libraries, newsletters are fairly widely available online and can be searched as individual titles or as a group. Examples of the latter are:

PTS NEWSLETTER DATABASE. Cleveland, Oh.: Predicasts, on DIALOG and Data-Star.

NEWSNET. Bryn Mawr, Pa. on NEWSNET.

FT BUSINESS REPORTS on PROFILE.

PTS and Newsnet cover 250 – 300 newsletters each. The newsletters on NEXIS can also be searched as a specialized group and both NEXIS and DIALOG host a considerable number of other full-text business newspapers and journals.

Database hosts are ever expanding and more files are constantly becoming available. With internationally available access a particular host will not necessarily have exclusive rights to a newspaper and the dates of the files also vary. To find out which newspapers and news agencies are currently available, and where they are to be found, there are general database directories which are listed in Chapter 19 and, from 1989, a specialized directory, *Full-text sources online*, has been published twice yearly by BiblioData, Needham Heights, Ma.

NEWS BROADCASTS

None of the broadcast news transmitted in Britain on radio or television by the British Broadcasting Corporation or independent companies is published. The American *ABC news transcripts* (microfiche) and *Index*, have been published since 1970 by Research Publications, Reading.

News broadcasts from countries of the world for which alternative sources of information are not readily available are well covered in print. For the purposes of monitoring broadcast news throughout the world the British and American governments have divided the world between them, exchanging all information received. The countries the BBC listens to, funded by the British government, include the USSR, Eastern Europe, the Middle East and North Africa. All major radio news broadcasts are monitored as they are transmitted, the information is supplemented with further reports from television broadcasts, news agency output and press material, and then translated into English and published as:

SUMMARY OF WORLD BROADCASTS, Reading, BBC. 1939 – . Four parts: USSR; Eastern Europe; Far East; Middle East, Africa and Latin America.

The *SWB* is published six days a week and excerpts of the full text of important speeches, communiqués, commentaries and official rebel propaganda on a wide variety of subjects are included but there is no editorial interpretation, analysis or comment. The *Weekly economic reports* for each area provide summaries of items of interest to business and the *Monitoring report* outlines the major reports in all the four main parts. The *SWB weekly world broadcast information* gives comprehensive news about developments in radio, television, satellite communications and news agencies worldwide, and includes broadcasting schedules with details of frequencies and current affairs programmes and news of political clandestine broadcasters.

All the *SWB* publications are available on subscription but, unfortunately, in original printed form their use is more-or-less limited to current awareness as there is no index to the 100,000 words published each day. However the full text is available on NEXIS (1979 –), PROFILE and TEXTLINE which at least provides for keyword subject searching. The *SWB* can also be a unique source for references to proper names although if a foreign name is not retrieved using the usual British spelling it is probably because American transliteration systems are used.

The equivalent American service is disseminated as the eight regional Foreign Broadcast Information Service *Daily reports*, available from NTIS and, over a month later, on microfiche and on CD-ROM from NewsBank, New Canaan, Ct. NewsBank also publishes *Indexes* to the *FBIS daily reports* arranged under country, international organization and personal name, but these are difficult to use for a subject search as information is indexed primarily under country and relational country subheadings. However, this is a valuable source for information about relations between two specific countries including diplomatic, economic, legal, military, terrorism and human rights relationships. The *Index* is to be issued on CD-ROM which may aid the subject approach.

NEWS DIGESTS

For a general picture of current affairs the news digest services provide factual summaries usually abstracted from the press, broadcasting, official and other sources. Two digests of international news typify this group:

KEESING'S RECORD OF WORLD EVENTS. Harlow: Longman, 1931
(July) – .

FACTS ON FILE WORLD NEWS DIGEST. New York: Facts on File, 1940
(30 October) – .

Keesing's (known as *Keesing's contemporary archives* until 1987) is
published monthly. Each issue begins with a comprehensive digest
of the previous month's world news. Major items are given
extended coverage and there are also concise factual articles,
arranged by continent. The reference section contains background
briefings on every country, principal international organizations
and political themes: these are all updated at least once a year
and useful maps, background chronologies to events, new cabinets
and ruling councils are also included. The index cumulates
throughout the year but in most cases items are indexed only under
country. *Keesing's* is online on PROFILE 1983 – and on
microfiche. Although it seems to be less widely known at home
than it should be, special reference should be made to the Foreign
and Commonwealth Office's *Monthly survey of current affairs*, 1967 –
which is international in scope with a firmly British approach.

Facts on file is similar to *Keesing's* although it is published weekly
and therefore usually more up-to-date. Naturally stronger on
American news, *Facts on file* offers a similarly wide coverage but
also has items on economics and business and a more lightweight
miscellaneous section on sport and the arts. It is online on
DIALOG 1982 – and NEXIS 1975 – .

Of many regional digests, one of the most important to world
watchers is the *Current digest of the Soviet press*, 1949 – weekly,
Columbus, Oh. which is online NEXIS 1983 – , DIALOG
1982 – . *Keesing's UK record*, a bi-monthly, began publication in
1988. Other regions of the world are covered by a scattering of
regular news and factual summaries such as *Asian recorder*, New
Delhi, 1955 – , weekly, and *Africa research bulletin*, Crediton, Devon,
1964 – , monthly, two series – political and economic.

INDEXES AND ABSTRACTS

Indexes and abstracts are essential for a comprehensive subject approach to news. However, for daily journalism they are not up-to-date enough as publication is usually a couple of months after the appearance of the original newspaper; and also, what may have been considered unimportant and omitted by an abstractor might be the most crucial sentence to a journalist – for what it does not say as much as for what it does. So, particularly when dealing with news, it should always be remembered that abstracts and indexes are secondary sources.

Two conventions of newspaper indexing briefly referred to earlier, which may not be familiar to the general user, are common practice in news indexes and news libraries: subject headings relate only to the country of publication of the index and the topic in general or internationally, items about the subject relating to any other specific country will be found only under the name of that country, and relations between two countries – on any subject – will be under the country which is first in alphabetical order.

A particular weakness of newspaper indexes is edition changes. Because newspapers vary their content and page layout between editions, the index may fail to locate items in the copy to hand: for instance if it is not the same edition as that indexed, items may not appear at all or may be on different pages from those listed. However, published indexes usually match the microfilmed edition of the paper.

Unfortunately there are still only three comprehensive published indexes to individual British newspapers:

THE TIMES INDEX. Reading: Research Publications, 1785 – .

MONTHLY INDEX TO THE FINANCIAL TIMES. Reading: Research Publications, 1981 – (also 1913 – 1920).

THE GUARDIAN INDEX. Ann Arbor, UMI. 1986 – .

Of these *The Times index* is the most generally available in reference libraries together with the microfilm of the newspaper, and it can be used to research dates which can then be checked out in other newspapers of the time for alternative accounts of an event. From 1790 – 1941 *Palmer's index to The Times newspaper* was published and this has now been extended back to 1785 under

The Times index title although it actually covers *The Times'* predecessor *The Daily Universal Register* from 1785 – 7. *The official index* to *The Times* was in competition with *Palmer's* from 1906 to 1941. From 1973 onwards *The Times index* also includes *The Sunday Times, The Times literary supplement, The Times educational supplement* and *The Times higher educational supplement*. It is compiled and published monthly with annual cumulations. Over the years the indexing has improved greatly; it used to have a reputation for being idiosyncratic with only a modest number of cross-references and assumed great intelligence, and diligence, on the part of the user in divining the most likely heading to have been selected by the indexer for the information required. Now items are indexed from several aspects in a single sequence under personal name, subject, country or locality.

The monthly index to the Financial Times has, naturally, a fairly substantial overlap with *The Times index* but also complements the coverage. While its strength is worldwide company, financial and industrial news, the *FT* is also much respected for its reviews of the arts. It will also often turn up information about national and foreign businessmen and political figures which is not available elsewhere. In addition to the currently published index an early index to the *Financial Times* appeared briefly from at least 1913 to 1920. *The Guardian index*, monthly, is a welcome recent addition to index sources.

The *Clover newspaper index*, Biggleswade, 1986 – indexes the major national dailies and Sundays. *Research index*, Dorking, 1965 – , is intended for business users and includes national newspapers as well as periodicals; it is fortnightly and online on PERGAMON FINANCIAL DATA SERVICES 1985 – . The major online news abstracting service in Britain since 1980 has been TEXTLINE which selects items of interest to business from the national, regional and international press but it is now increasingly becoming full-text.

Newspaper indexes come and go, the compilers usually defeated by the high-cost, labour-intensive task, and this applies particularly to the local press. The BL Newspaper Library has a record of over 1,000 indexes most of them unpublished and transitory, and often dependent on the resources of the local public library. One of the rare published indexes is the *Glasgow herald index* 1906 – 68 which has recently been updated to 1987 and these later indexes are also to be published.

There are a few indexes to European newspapers. These include *Le monde index* 1944/5 – Research Publications, *Zeitungs – Index* 1974 – Munich, Saur, which indexes 19 newspapers and *El pais indice*, Madrid, Prisa. For Arab news, the Arab Information Bank is on DIALOG in English, and summarizes articles from the Arab press.

There are a number of published indexes to American newspapers, and although called 'indexes' many also contain brief abstracts, for example:

THE NEW YORK TIMES INDEX, 1851 – . UMI.

THE WASHINGTON POST INDEX, 1971 – . UMI.

CHRISTIAN SCIENCE MONITOR INDEX, 1945 – . UMI.

THE LOS ANGELES TIMES INDEX, 1977 – . UMI.

THE WALL STREET JOURNAL INDEX, 1955 – . Dow Jones.

The *New York Times index*, 1851 – , is semi-monthly, most of the others are monthly and all cumulate. *The Wall Street Journal index* includes *Barrons* and, for those who need to know, lists the daily closing Dow Jones averages for the month. Most of the printed American indexes are not found in Britain except at the BL Newspaper Library. Online *Newspaper abstracts* 1984 – on DIALOG represents the comprehensive version of UMI's indexes and abstracts of 20 major regional, national and international newspapers and UMI have announced *Newspaper abstracts ondisc* on CD-ROM. *National newspaper index* 1979 – , Information Access Company, on DIALOG, also indexes items in five of the major US newspapers. For local American newspapers NewsBank, New Canaan, Ct provides copies on microfiche of major articles from over 450 titles, with an index in printed form and on CD-ROM.

For the Canadian press, *Canadian news index* 1977 – covers seven daily newspapers.

Although it is not a specialized index to newspapers, the Public Affairs Information Service, New York, should not go unacknowledged in this section because its two monthly publications *PAIS bulletin* 1914 – and *Foreign language index* 1968 – provide exceptional international coverage of social conditions, government, international relations, business and economics. The Service indexes periodicals, books, government documents and reports issued anywhere in the world in English, French, German, Italian, Portuguese and Spanish. Both publications are indexed and entries annotated, in English, and both are cumulated with author indexes. They are also available online on DIALOG, DATA-STAR and on CD-ROM.

General directories of newspapers and periodicals usually indicate if and where a title is indexed. If more comprehensive information is needed on American indexes Milner's *Newspaper indexes: a location and subject guide for researchers*, 3 volumes, Scarecrow, 1977 – 82, can be consulted.

CHRONOLOGIES

The use of chronologies is one way of tracing dates which can be used to refer back to printed copies of newspapers and periodicals, although sometimes a brief entry in a chronology is sufficient in itself. Annual chronologies are frequently included in yearbooks and almanacs but more comprehensive separately published historical chronologies with good indexes often provide a better, faster answer. Most chronologies include not only major political, economic and social events but also cover developments in the arts and sciences. Within an overall arrangement by date they are usually subdivided into subject sections, but it is to be regretted that chronologies do not always give the specific dates of events, often preferring a general reference to the month. Even the compilers of chronologies admit that sometimes errors creep in because of the amount of information that has to be traced and transcribed, so it is often necessary to check dates in more than one source to be certain of the correct one.

Examples of comprehensive chronologies are:

Trager, J., THE PEOPLE'S CHRONOLOGY: A YEAR-BY-YEAR RECORD OF HUMAN EVENTS FROM PRE-HISTORY TO THE PRESENT. London: Heinemann, 1980. (3 million BC to 1973).

Grun, B., THE TIMETABLES OF HISTORY: A CHRONOLOGY OF WORLD EVENTS. London: Thames and Hudson, 1975. (5000 BC to 1974).

Williams, N., CHRONOLOGY OF THE EXPANDING WORLD 1492 – 1762. London: Barrie and Rockliff, 1969.

Williams, N., CHRONOLOGY OF THE MODERN WORLD 1763 TO THE PRESENT TIME (i.e. 1965). London: Barrie and Rockliff, 1966.

All the publications are arranged chronologically but Grun is particularly interesting for comparative development purposes as its tabular double-page-spread format with separate headings for different subjects makes it easy to see what else was happening at the time of a particular event, e.g. history and politics, literature, religion, visual arts, science and daily life.

Other recent, less comprehensive, contributions to this field are:

CHRONICLE OF THE WORLD, 1989. (3.5 million years BC to 1945); CHRONICLE OF THE 20TH CENTURY, 1988. (1900 – 87); CHRONICLE OF THE YEAR 1988 – . Harlow: Longman.

These three publications are all similar in style, and produced for popular appeal. Each story is written as if it were being told by a modern journalist reporting the event at the time. They are extensively illustrated in colour and black-and-white with pictures, diagrams and maps. *The twentieth century: an almanac* by R. Ferrell, London: Harrap, 1986 also covers this century up to 1984 and has good black-and-white illustrations.

Newspapers should also be remembered as an excellent and inexpensive source of year chronologies well worth retaining. At the end of December or in early January most publish lists of the year's events, often well illustrated, and frequently there are specialized articles reviewing the year in a particular subject area – not just politics and international developments, but also the arts, sport and the sciences.

YEAR REVIEWS

With a longer look and more time at their disposal, annual reviews can present a better perspective, summarizing trends in various fields. Providing the year of search is known, a check through several of the year reviews makes a strong reference source for events, although for contextual purposes reference to preceding and subsequent years is needed and, helpfully, some year reviews provide a cumulative index in each volume. The year on the spine of these publications is frequently the year of publication and the contents actually relate to the previous year.

Four major general reviews can be singled out:

THE ANNUAL REGISTER: A RECORD OF WORLD EVENTS. London: Longman, 1758 – .

THE AMERICANA ANNUAL. Danbury, Ct: Grolier, 1923 – .

BRITANNICA BOOK OF THE YEAR. Chicago: Encyclopaedia Britannica, 1938 – .

UNIVERSALIA. Paris: Encyclopaedia Universalis, 1973 – .
    While all these volumes contain brief chronologies of the year their main function is to provide a general review of events either by country or subject or both.
    The annual register is the doyen of the group, and its feature articles are perhaps better for catching the flavour of a year than for factual reference. The main body of each annual volume consists of surveys by specialist contributors with a major chapter on the United Kingdom and shorter general articles on every other country plus articles on broad issues such as international organizations, defence, the sciences, the arts, sport, economic and social affairs. It also reprints some documents and speeches of

international importance and has a six-year economic and social statistical survey of the UK and the USA with international comparisons, and an obituary section.

Other year reviews are linked with encyclopaedias. Most are well-illustrated, wide-ranging and detailed. *Britannica*, *Universalia* (in French) and *The Americana* are fairly typical, taking the form of a large number of articles on the affairs of the year arranged by subjects, a section of biographies and obituaries, and a detailed ten-year index. Since 1985 about a third of the *Britannica* annual volume has been headed 'Britannica World Data' and provides a country-by-country statistical portrait of the world by major thematic subject enabling easy comparison between countries, and listing the national statistical sources used.

Year reviews are also frequently included in yearbooks and special note should be made of those in the *Europa* regional series. Other annual regional and national surveys include *L'Annee politique, economique et sociale en France* 1876 – . Paris: Editions du Moniteur, and *Africa contemporary record: annual survey and documents*, New York and London: Africana, 1968 – .

YEARBOOKS

General information about foreign countries and specific facts about their government, politics, population, trade and geography are frequently required and these can most quickly and conveniently be produced from an international or national yearbook. However caution should be exercised in certain areas of enquiry, e.g. names of ministers, officials and ruling councils, as a publication a year old cannot be up-to-date. Unlike year reviews the date on the spine of yearbooks is often the year after the actual publication date. The most recent information, if it is published anywhere, is likely to be in a newspaper or news digest but an Embassy is the most authoritative source for current information.

The following titles are amongst the most important:

THE STATESMAN'S YEAR-BOOK. London: Macmillan, 1864 – .

THE EUROPA WORLD YEAR BOOK. London: Europa, 1926 – .

Of these the *Statesman's year-book* is the most compact and *Europa* the most comprehensive, but both provide basic information about all countries of the world including government, politics, defence, geography, population, economy, trade and communications. The *Statesman's year-book*, which concerns itself nowadays less with history than with current facts and statistics, has a short further reading list for each country, and also includes special features relating to the previous or present year.

The *Europa world year book*, for a general reference work, is particularly strong on information about the international scene. A useful international comparisons table shows, for each country, the area, population, life expectancy, and GNP. For all the major international organizations it gives the address, membership, finance, organization and activities, principal historical events, specialized agencies and, for some, the charter is included too. In addition there is an extensive section grouping other international organizations by subject, e.g. agriculture, arts, religion, tourism. The majority of *Europa* is a country-by-country survey and is probably the most comprehensive general source of this type of information in the English language. Each country is divided into three sections – an introductory survey including location, climate, language, religion, recent history and government; an extensive statistical survey of the country including population, industry, agriculture, finance; and a 'Directory' which is an excellent source for information and names and addresses relating to the constitution, government, a wide variety of national organizations, diplomatic representation, the judicial system, religion, broadcasting, etc. The national lists of newspapers and periodicals can be checked for the titles of publications which can be consulted for detailed reports of specific events. Other publications which give information about countries and governments, although not all are annual so their currency needs to be checked, include *Handbook of the nations* 1979 – , Gale, and *International year book and statesmen's who's who* 1953 – , Reed.

Each of the regions of the world is the subject of at least one annual reference work, e.g. the *Europa* series. These titles, which follow the style of the *Europa world year book* and expand some of the data contained in it are:

AFRICA SOUTH OF THE SAHARA 1971 – ; THE MIDDLE EAST AND NORTH AFRICA 1948 – ; THE FAR EAST AND AUSTRALASIA 1969 – ; SOUTH AMERICA, CENTRAL AMERICA AND THE CARIBBEAN 1986 – ; WESTERN EUROPE 1990 – ; USA AND CANADA 1990 – .

These all follow the same format, with part 1 being short review essays on the background of the region, part 2 being regional organizations, and part 3 being country surveys. The latter all conclude with a good bibliography of basic reading.

The *Commonwealth yearbook* 1967 – compiled by the Foreign and Commonwealth Office, published by HMSO, gives a wide range of data on organizations and member countries of the Common-wealth and also has comparative tables which include social, economic, population and educational statistics and immigration into Britain. World of Information in Saffron Walden publish yearbooks concentrating on economic and business information needs, e.g. the *Africa review* and the *Middle East review*.

Space precludes mention of all the national yearbooks which earn their keep among the stock of reference libraries. Not all countries publish them, some are official government publications which are sometimes available gratis from Embassies and others are compiled by commercial publishers. The United Kingdom's official annual is *Britain: an official handbook*, 1946 – , a work of immense detail and catholicity of choice published for the Central Office of Information by HMSO. This attempts to describe, in narrative form, all aspects of current British life, government and other major institutions and also includes some statistics. Amongst the many foreign national yearbooks, all similar to *Britain*, are the *People's Republic of China year-book*; *South Africa: official yearbook of the Republic of South Africa*; *Year-book Australia*; *Israel yearbook*; *Turkey almanac*; *Pakistan official yearbook*; *Korea annual*. Many have excellent colour illustrations and some, e.g. Turkey and China, even include the words and music of their national anthems.

151

Although the international and regional yearbooks give some information about international organizations, for a review of the year's work of the United Nations and European organizations there are two official annuals:

YEARBOOK OF THE UNITED NATIONS. New York: UN 1946 – .

ANNUAIRE EUROPEEN/EUROPEAN YEARBOOK. Dordrecht and London: Nijhoff 1948 – .

The *UN yearbook* comprehensively covers the main activities of the UN and each related UN organization during the year but publication is very delayed, and the 1984 volume was not published until 1988. The *European yearbook*, with a parallel text in French and English, published under the auspices of the Council of Europe, is more up-to-date with the 1987 volume appearing in 1989, and it includes a substantial bibliography for further reading.

ALMANACS

These indispensable and handy annual volumes have a fascinating history going back to Roger Bacon and Rabelais, but the main purpose today of the English-language ones is not so much for calendar and astronomical data, as for the compendia of current facts of all kinds about the minutiae of modern living and officialdom. Two worth special mention, very similar in approach, which should be found side-by-side in any reference collection are:

WHITAKER'S ALMANACK. London: Whitaker's, 1868 – .

THE WORLD ALMANAC AND BOOK OF FACTS. New York: Pharos, 1868 – .

Whitaker's is virtually a mini-encyclopaedia, perhaps the archetypal form, still quaintly describing itself on the title page as 'an almanack for the year of our Lord ...'. The range of information is a remarkable triumph of compression and comprehensiveness and so, if baffled by an enquiry, try *Whitaker's* first. Back issues should be retained for the sake of non-repeated items, and for the chronologies. The index, at the front until the 1989 edition, is good but not without fault and a user has to be prepared to use lateral thinking. The slim *Daily mail year book*, London: Harmondsworth, 1900 – , is by no means to be despised because it is inexpensive, and although it has a limited range, it is sometimes easier to use than *Whitaker's* because it is possible to scan quickly through its well-arranged broad subject sections searching for particular information.

The principal US almanac, *The world almanac*, is equally venerable, and naturally better on American aspects, though its scope is worldwide. It is especially good for US national and local politics and statistics and for chronologies including disasters, storms, volcanic eruptions, kidnappings, oil spills and assassinations. Other miscellaneous items include a noted personalities section, movies, best sellers, heights of tall buildings, and notable bridges in the US.

PRESS GUIDES

Many of the international and national yearbooks referred to earlier list newspapers published in a particular country, and national directories of newspapers and periodicals are published in some countries. The two principal lists published in Britain which can be used for research purposes to identify newspapers being published at the time of a particular event are:

BENN'S MEDIA DIRECTORY. Tonbridge: Benn, 1846 – .

WILLING'S PRESS GUIDE. East Grinstead: British Media Publications, 1871 – .

Both have changed publishers and titles over the years: *Benn's*, known for many years as the *Newspaper press directory*, was started by Charles Mitchell, an advertising agent, and *Willing's* was *May's* until 1890. Well before the turn of the century they covered overseas newspapers, and for many years Mitchell included a newspaper map of the United Kingdom. Nowadays *Benn's* and *Willing's* both have sections on UK newspapers, arranged by location or region, and foreign newspapers appear under the name of the country of publication. An interesting historical survey of these and other newspaper directories of the Victorian era appears in the *Journal of newspaper and periodical history*, 3 (2), 1986, 20 – 8.

Internationally, the *Editor and publisher international year book*, New York, 1924 – is a specialized directory of newspapers published in the United States and throughout the world. The best-known American periodicals directory is Gale's *Directory of publications* 1869 – , formerly *Ayer's*, and in France the *Annuaire de la presse et de la publicité* has been published since 1878. Other directories referred to in Chapter 8 cover newspapers as well as periodicals. National press periodicals directories are noted in Walford and Sheehy.

LOCATING NEWSPAPERS

Locating recent copies of the major 'serious' national newspapers has never been too much of a problem as some will be held in local public reference libraries. Most libraries will have at least a file of *The Times*, probably on microfilm, and *The Times index*. Back files of the 'popular' and local press are, unfortunately, very rare.

The only comprehensive library of newspapers in the UK is the British Library, which has an outstanding collection. Photocopies can be provided if the exact bibliographical details of an article are known, but the Library is not staffed to undertake detailed research so a personal visit to the Reading Room is normally necessary to trace vague references or to make subject searches. Information in newspapers is more-or-less inaccessible unless a date is known and sources referred to earlier in this chapter have to be used to provide the key to the extraordinary and fascinating treasury of information otherwise kept locked in a newspaper. The Newspaper Library has a good collection of the comparatively few indexes that are published and back sets of *Benn's* and *Willing's* press guides which will guide an enquirer to the relevant national, local and foreign titles published at the time of the event.

The main collection of newspapers in the British Library is in the Newspaper Library at Colindale in North London, which houses daily and weekly newspapers and periodicals including London newspapers from 1801 onwards, English provincial, Welsh, Scottish and Irish newspapers from about 1700 onwards and large collections of Commonwealth and foreign newspapers in Western and Slavonic languages from all countries. British national newspapers for the last six months, and other UK papers for the last two to three years, are not usually available as access to them is not permitted until they have been bound or microfilmed. The *Catalogue of the Newspaper Library, Colindale*, London: British Library, 1975, in eight volumes, lists UK papers held up to the end of 1970 and overseas titles to the end of 1971 arranged by place and title. Two collections of press cuttings have been acquired by the Newspaper Library: the Royal Institute of International Affairs' collections from the British and foreign press 1915 – 69 and the *Daily Express* biographical files of people who died between 1900 and 1980.

Pre-1801 London newspapers are housed in the BL in central London together with some other remarkable historical collections. The Burney Collection of 700 volumes of newspapers from 1603 – 1800 is particularly valuable for research as, most unusually, the papers are arranged by date so that different titles of the same date are bound together. The oriental collections, also in central London, hold newspapers published in oriental scripts and take in the countries of the Near East, the Indian sub-continent and the Far East. The BL's India Office Library holds South Asian newspapers in English.

For other locations *The world list of national newspapers*, compiled by Rosemary Webber, London: Butterworths 1976, contains in excess of 1500 national newspapers from 120 countries in British libraries. There are a smattering of union lists for specific types of newspapers in British libraries. For American newspapers the *American newspaper holdings in British and Irish libraries*, British Association for American Studies, 1974, is a good starting-point and Hewitt's *Union list of Commonwealth newspapers in London, Oxford and Cambridge* was published in 1960 by Athlone Press.

It has never been easy to identify and locate UK local newspapers apart from those held at Colindale, but the British Library now has the Newsplan project, a major cooperative programme between local and national libraries which aims to survey, microfilm and preserve local newspapers. Reports on the South West, the East Midlands and the Northern Region have already appeared giving essential details about each local newspaper, such as dates, title changes and publishers, information on hard-copy and microfilm holdings and recommendations about future preservation. There are also a number of regional union lists of British newspapers which are usually compiled and published by the local public library and/or under the auspices of the British Library. A few examples are a *Directory of Scottish newspapers*, 1984, *South Yorkshire newspapers*, 1754 – 1976, *Durham and Northumberland*, 1982, *Nottinghamshire*, 1987, and *Kent*, 1982; the latter three form part of the *Bibliography of British newspapers*. The best starting-point for help in locating a local or regional newspaper is undoubtedly the public library in the area.

Many back files of newspapers are available in microform. The British Library Newspaper Library has an extensive microfilming programme, primarily of historical newspapers, and issues a detailed catalogue of those which can be purchased; some filming is also undertaken on request. Other major suppliers of newspapers on microfilm are Research Publications, Reading, and UMI, Ann Arbor; both of these companies issue catalogues of their publications and comprehensive microform and CD-ROM directories list these and other newspapers.

The offices of newspapers themselves can occasionally supply back copies but probably only the most recent. An enquiry to a newspaper's library may or may not produce a helpful response: it must be remembered that, like all special libraries, newspaper libraries exist first and foremost to serve their own journalists and little time is available to assist an outside enquirer, however important the request. Some commercial information services exist based on press-cuttings libraries. The BBC, *Financial Times*, Press Association and *Daily Telegraph* will all provide information from their cuttings libraries and other sources, for a fee. Press-cuttings agencies which provide a tailor-made service are listed in *Willing's* and *Benn's* press directories but these companies do not usually supply a retrospective service.

NEWSPAPER HISTORY

To follow up any aspect of British newspaper history there is an excellent, comprehensive bibliography:

Linton, D., THE NEWSPAPER PRESS IN BRITAIN: AN ANNOTATED BIBLIOGRAPHY. London: Mansell, 1987.

It contains over 2,900 references on all aspects of the subject from individual local and national newspaper histories, to journalists', cartoonists' and proprietors' biographies and autobiographies, to the politics, sociology, industrial relations and management of newspapers. This exhaustive study of books and periodical articles is arranged by author with an index to subjects, titles and people. One appendix is a chronology of British newspaper history from 1476 – 1986 and the other gives the location of important collections of documents and other archives on the subject. The introduction makes interesting reading in itself and surveys other earlier bibliographic contributions to the subject. There are many histories of individual newspapers, of which the most detailed is the five volumes of *The history of The Times*, London: The Times, 1935 – 66, others are listed in Linton and usually published to coincide with a significant anniversary of a newspaper. For current work in the field of newspaper history the *Journal of newspaper and periodical history*, **1** (1), 1984 – , publishes well-researched articles on the topic, book reviews, abstracts of theses and an annual review of research work.

Of several books on the international history of newspapers a particularly well-illustrated and detailed one is by Anthony Smith, *The newspaper: an international history*, London: Thames and Hudson, 1979, which also includes a reading list. Smith charts the history of newspapers from before the first daily publication in the world, *Einkommende Zeitung* ('Incoming News'), in 1650 to the late 1970s when the old press barons had mostly surrendered their empires, and before the publishing and technological upheavals of the 1980s lead to the demise of 'Fleet Street', for so long a world-renowned name in daily newspapers.

Newspapers and news can be frustrating sources of information because of the difficulty of finding the information needed amongst the vast mass of printed material which is being added to, and changing, every minute. Searching back through newspapers can be an arduous and time-consuming task but at the same time it is also an absorbing area of research as, inevitably, fascinating long-forgotten and irrelevant information is scanned before the required report is eventually, triumphantly located.

SUGGESTIONS FOR FURTHER READING

There are very few books on news librarianship. The key British work is still *The modern news library* by Geoffrey Whatmore, London: Library Association, 1978. Although this is now out-of-date in some respects, it is still essential reading for basic principles. A recent American addition to the literature is L. Nupham's *Newspapers in the library: new approaches to management and reference work*, New York: Haworth, 1988. David Nicholas' two research publications *Online searching: its impact on information users*, London: Mansell, 1987, and *Online information sources for business and current affairs*, London: Mansell, 1989, are informative about how people need and use news information and related online databases.

8

Periodicals

Hazel Woodward

DEFINITIONS

Harrod's librarians' glossary (6th ed. Aldershot: Gower, 1987) defines a periodical as 'A publication with a distinctive title which appears at stated or regular intervals, without prior decision as to when the last issue shall appear. It contains articles, stories or other writings, by several contributors.' In current usage, the terms periodical and journal are synonymous, while the term magazine is reserved (in UK usage) for more popular, mass-circulation titles.

Periodicals are subsumed within the wider category of serials. The British Standard *Specification for the presentation of serial publications, including periodicals* (BS 2509: 1970) defines a serial as 'a publication issued in successive parts, bearing numerical or chronological designations, and intended to be continued indefinitely'. If this definition is strictly interpreted, the term serial encompasses an extremely wide range of publications, including periodicals, newspapers, society transactions, conference proceedings, newsletters, technical and research reports, yearbooks and annuals, and national and international government publications. Such coverage in one chapter would clearly not do justice to this complex area, and this chapter will therefore concentrate upon reference material specifically relating to periodicals and their associated indexes.

REFERENCE USE

Periodicals are an important element of the reference collection, especially in academic, commercial, industrial and research libraries. Current issues of periodicals are of particular importance in those areas of scholarly communication relating to science, technology, business and politics, where the latest up-to-date information is essential for research and development. Furthermore, articles within periodicals frequently discuss highly specialized topics and include information which is not yet (and may never be) available in monograph publications. In those libraries which retain back runs of periodicals, the older volumes may have relevance to historical research and furnish contemporary opinion on a given topic or person.

PROBLEMS OF ACCESS

Many of the problems associated with access to periodical titles stem from the massive, international growth of published literature. The first periodicals appeared in the latter half of the seventeenth century (a well-known example is the *Philosophical transactions of the Royal Society* which began in 1665), and the publication format flourished throughout the eighteenth and nineteenth centuries. Thomas[1] states that 27 periodicals were being published in the USA by 1810. By the twentieth century, the increasing flow of new titles had turned to a flood, creating the so-called 'information explosion', with increasing numbers of periodicals, in ever-more specialized subject areas, being published. This is well illustrated by examining the 1st edition (1932) of *Ulrich's international periodicals directory* (New York: Bowker) which listed 6,000 titles, and comparing it to the 28th edition (1989) which lists 111,950 titles. Such proliferation of information has had a major impact upon current library periodical collections. Even major national libraries can no longer hope to acquire, maintain and retain comprehensive periodical collections.

The other significant factor which has affected the size and scope of collections during the last decade is the escalation of subscription prices. A detailed, statistical survey of periodical prices is published annually by Blackwells in the *Library Association record* (London: Library Association); figures show that, in just ten years, the average price of a periodical has risen from £44.18 in 1979 to £136.99 in 1989. Over this same period, library budgets have at best remained static and at worst decreased in real terms. An initial response to the problem was to buy fewer monographs, but eventually most libraries have been forced into cancelling significant numbers of periodical subscriptions.

It is ironical that, while academics, researchers and librarians have increasing access to published information via online databases, CD-ROM databases and library networks, escalating subscription prices and shrinking library budgets mean that fewer and fewer titles are purchased from the ever-growing range available. This has resulted in increasing reliance being placed upon document delivery from external sources, and in the UK this usually involves obtaining photocopies of articles from the British Library Document Supply Centre (BLDSC). A list of *Current serials received* (Boston Spa: BLDSC, 1989), which comprises just the titles and shelf numbers of all current serials received by the BLDSC and the Science Reference and Information Service (SRIS), is available to libraries. A companion publication, which also includes bibliographical information, is *Serials in the British Library*. This contains data derived from three MARC files – BNBMARC back to 1950 – and the current catalogues of the British Library Humanities and Social Sciences and the British Library Science Reference and Information Service. In addition, the British Library has recently announced the publication of a new CD-ROM *Boston Spa serials*, containing over 366,000 serial records from the collections of the British Library, Cambridge University Library and the Science Museum Library.

TYPES OF PERIODICAL

Periodicals publications exist to satisfy a variety of different needs and interests, ranging from current affairs and hobbies magazines through to learned academic and scientific journals. They can be broadly grouped into the following categories:

Commercially published periodicals

Periodicals published as a commercial venture comprise the largest category. Once subscriptions are established, magazines and journals can provide a lucrative source of revenue for publishing houses. At one end of the spectrum are the low-cost, mass-circulation titles such as *Practical photography* (Peterborough: EMAP National Publications) and *Country life* (London: IPC Magazines). At the other end of the spectrum are the high-cost, low-subscription titles from academic journal publishers. Major international publishers such as Elsevier and Pergamon currently publish several hundred different titles, mainly aimed at the academic library market. Their titles cover very specialized areas of academic interest, for example *Regulatory peptides* (Amsterdam, Netherlands: Elsevier Science) and *Women's studies international forum* (Oxford: Pergamon).

A wide variety of publishers' directories are available to libraries, including *Magazine industry market place: directory of American periodical publishing* (New York: Bowker, 1988) which covers about 5,400 periodicals and their publishers, and the more general *Publishers' international directory* (14th ed. Munich, West Germany: Saur, 1987). It is unfortunate that the publication *Sources of serials* (2nd rev. ed. New York: Bowker, 1981) has not been updated since 1981; this title includes 65,000 publishers and corporate authors arranged under 180 countries and lists some 96,000 current serial titles.

Learned society journals

Journals emanating from academic and professional organizations and institutions constitute an important segment of the journal market, although there has been a trend in recent years for the production and distribution of learned society journals to pass to commercial publishers. For example, the British Ecological

Society's *Journal of ecology* is actually published by Blackwell Scientific. Nevertheless, large numbers are still published by professional organizations and many of these journals are regarded as core titles within their academic discipline, for example the range of *IEE proceedings* published by the Institution of Electrical Engineers, London, and the various *Transactions* of the Royal Society of Chemistry, Cambridge.

Letters journals

Letters journals, such as *Tetrahedron letters* (Oxford: Pergamon), may also fall within the category of journals published as a commercial venture. However, unlike traditional journals, they do not contain full-length articles, only short, preliminary communications on new developments and initiatives in research, frequently in the areas of science and technology. The aim of such titles is to speed up the publication and distribution of scholarly information. Publications with a similar aim frequently include the word 'communications' in their title, for example *Polymer communications* which is published as a supplement to *Polymer: the international journal for the science and technology of polymers* (London: Butterworths).

House journals

A house journal is a publication produced by a company primarily to communicate information to its staff and shareholders. Some house journals are little more than ephemeral newsletters, but others do contain important contributions to knowledge. Bank reviews, for example the *National Westminster Bank quarterly review*, frequently contain useful information and articles on a variety of economic issues, and the publications of major manufacturing companies, for example *Heat engineering* (Clinton, NJ: Foster Wheeler Corporation), can provide useful trade and business information. House journals are often available free of charge, although there is an increasing tendency for companies to levy a subscription charge to libraries. P. M. Dunning and D. M. Sawyer's *House journals held by the Science Reference Library* (2nd ed.

London: British Library Science Reference Library, 1985) is a useful checklist. Further titles may be traced through Adeline M. Smith's *Free magazines for libraries* (3rd rev. ed. McFarland and Co., 1989).

Synoptic journals

Journals containing synopses of articles, where the full text is supplied on demand as an offprint or in microform, are an unusual but noteworthy type of periodical. Few new titles are published in this category, but the Royal Society of Chemistry, Cambridge, has succeeded in establishing *Journal of chemical research: synopses* as a successful publishing venture since 1977. The synopses are published in printed format and the full text is available on microfiche or in miniprint.

Newsletters

The printed newsletter is a brief publication conveying up-to-date news and information, usually relating to a specific society or business organization. Such newsletters are normally free or low-cost, low-circulation publications. A more recent trend is for commercial publishers to produce newsletters for specific interest groups, for example *Advanced information reports: an international newsletter for publishers and information users* (Amsterdam, Netherlands: Elsevier), and such titles may carry a higher subscription price. Newsletters are frequently omitted from the standard periodical directories; however they can be traced through *Newsletters in print* (4th ed. Detroit: Gale, 1988), which provides detailed entries for over 10,000 sources of information on a wide range of topics. Entries are arranged in seven broad categories comprising 31 specific subjects. The *Oxbridge directory of newsletters* (6th ed. New York: Oxbridge, 1988) is a similar publication which covers over 15,000 US and Canadian newsletters.

Translation journals

International scholarly and research literature is published in many different languages and translation journals are a major source of information on foreign-language journal articles. A translation journal may be either a cover to cover translation of a periodical title into another language (usually English), or a journal which offers selected articles in translation. A useful guide is *Journals in translation* (4th ed. Boston Spa: BLDSC and the International Translation Centre, 1988) which includes a titles listing and a keyword index; titles available from the BLDSC are indicated, as are other sources from which copies may be ordered.

Progress in . . .

This category of periodical appears in a variety of guises and includes titles beginning *Progress in . . .*, *Developments in . . .*, *Advances in . . .* and *Year's work in . . . .* The majority of these titles began publication as annual or irregular reviews of the literature in a particular subject area, for example *Year's work in English studies* (London: John Murray). Some titles in this category, however, now appear on a more frequent basis; for example *Progress in surface science: an international review journal* (Oxford: Pergamon) which is published 12 times a year.

PERIODICAL FORMATS

While the printed periodical still dominates the publishing scene, there are an increasing number of alternative formats available to libraries.

Microforms

Journals on microfilm and microfiche have an important role to play in library collections. Microforms are normally acquired either as a space-saving device or because older and rarer periodical titles are no longer available in printed format. A small number of publishers (for example Pergamon) produce hard-copy and microfiche versions of their titles simultaneously. It is more usual, however, for libraries to acquire back runs of periodicals on microform. University Microfilms Inc. (UMI) are one of the largest microform publishers, and their annual catalogue *Serials in microform* gives details of a wide range of publications; the 1989 volume includes over 16,000 serials titles and 7,000 newspapers. *Guide to microforms in print* (Westport, Conn.: Meckler, 1989) is also an annual listing of microform titles, comprising books, journals, newspapers and other serial publications. Published in two volumes, volume one is an author/title listing and volume two is a subject guide based upon Library of Congress classification.

Online full-text databases

An increasing number of full-text journals are available via a variety of online systems, including BRS, STN International DIALOG, and Mead Data. As far back as 1983, the American Chemical Society mounted 18 journals, initially on BRS, as a full-text file. Many examples are now accessible from a variety of host systems; a typical example is the *Comprehensive core medical library* which is part of an online service that provides physicians and medical researchers with the complete text of important references and journals. Lists of online full-text journals are incorporated in the documentation of individual host systems; alternatively, for a more comprehensive list, consult *Full-text sources online* (Oxford: Learned Information) which claims to be the definitive reference source on the subject. It is published twice a year and is available on a subscription basis.

Full-text journals on CD-ROM

CD-ROMs are the major growth area in journal publishing. In 1987 the *CD-ROM directory* (2nd ed. London: TFPL, 1987) listed only a handful of full-text journals, including predictably such titles as *CD-ROM librarian* (Westport, Conn.: Meckler) and *The electronic library* (Oxford: Learned Information). By 1989 a far greater range of titles was available, particularly in the areas of business and finance. UMI's *Business periodicals ondisc* contains the full text of 300 business and management journals: coverage is from 1987 onwards and discs are updated every two months. Due to the upsurge in popularity of this format, new titles are constantly being published, making directories out-of-date even before publication. Nevertheless, the annual *CD-ROMs in print* (Westport, Conn.: Meckler, 1989) is a useful source of information, which consists of an optical product directory arranged in alphabetical order by disc title, with eight supporting indexes. The subject index classifies each CD-ROM by one or more of 37 subjects.

PERIODICAL BIBLIOGRAPHIES

For reference purposes, libraries require a range of guides and bibliographies in order to make the best use of, and provide access to, periodicals and periodical literature. In addition to the library's own list of periodical holdings, the following types of reference tool should be available:

(a) Bibliographies of periodicals which provide information on their correct titles, frequencies, title changes, publisher, history, editors, prices, etc.
(b) Union lists of periodicals which supply information about the location of titles. Union lists will normally be either of a geographical nature (e.g. local and regional lists) or of a subject nature. Catalogues of the holdings of major libraries and specialized collections will also be found useful.

Current general bibliographies

Due to the vast and diffuse worldwide periodical publishing output, no single directory can claim to be comprehensive. Thus, each library will need to stock a range of bibliographies most suited to its user needs. An extremely large number of periodical bibliographies are published.

General national and international listings of titles should be available in most libraries. Although press guides are covered in more detail in another chapter, passing reference must be made to *Willing's press guide* (115th ed. East Grinstead: British Media Publications, 1989) and its US equivalent the *Standard periodicals directory* (12th ed. New York: Oxbridge Communications, 1989).

Other useful information is contained within media guides such as *Benn's media directory* (Tonbridge: Benn Business Information Services, 1987) published in two volumes covering UK media and international media, and the monthly publication *BRAD: British rate and data* (Barnet, Herts: MacLean Hunter).

Two major listings vie for supremacy of coverage in this general category. The first (because it has been established longer) is *Ulrich's international periodicals directory* (28th ed. New York: Bowker, 1989). Published annually in three volumes with quarterly supplements, *Ulrich's* currently lists over 111,950 titles. Up until 1987 *Irregular serials and annuals* was published as a sister volume, but all data are now included in one sequence. The main sequence is a classified list of titles, accessed by a title index and an ISSN index. Other listings include an index to publications of international organizations, cessations and serials available online. Detailed information about individual titles includes year first published, ISSN, publisher and address, price, language, editor, title changes, format and circulation. A particularly useful feature is the inclusion of which indexing and abstracting services cover the title. Ulrich is available both online and on CD-ROM.

The serials directory (4th ed. Birmingham, Al.: Ebsco Publishing, 1990) claims 'to provide easy access to more information on more serials titles than any other printed source available'. It is based upon Ebsco's (subscription agents) internal database and the Library of Congress CONSER file. Like Ulrich, it is arranged by subject category with a title and ISSN index, and it provides a similar range of detail about each title – including indexing and abstracting information. Publication of *The serials directory* (which is also available on CD-ROM) coincides with a growing awareness in the serials industry that subscription agents' databases contain a wealth of bibliographical data which can be an extremely useful information source to both librarians and publishers. Many of the major international agents produce extensive printed catalogues of serial titles, which are available to customers free of charge (e.g. Blackwells, Swets, Dawsons, Faxon), and increasingly agents are also providing online access to their databases (for example DataSwets).

Two other publications of a slightly more specific nature should be highlighted in this section. David Woodworth's *Current British journals* (5th ed. Boston Spa: UK Serials Group and BLDSC, 1989) is a classified listing of British journals with both a title index and a subject index. All relevant bibliographical information is provided for each title, and each entry has a short paragraph describing the subject coverage of the title. *Magazines for libraries* (6th ed. New York: Bowker, 1989) is aimed at school, college and public libraries. Arranged under broad subject headings, this publication provides helpful and sometimes critical descriptions of a wide range of international journals.

General serial bibliographies can be a useful tool for librarians in terms of selection of new titles and overall collection-development decisions. However, apart from the rather general *Magazines for libraries*, bibliographies do not normally attempt to evaluate the relative merits of individual titles within their subject areas. Some guidance may be obtained from directories which list the abstracting and indexing services which cover individual titles, as important core journals will be included in the coverage of the major abstracting services relating to that subject area. For evaluation purposes, many librarians utilize the ranked lists of journal titles, arranged in broad subject groups, published annually in *Journal citation reports* (Philadelphia: Institute for Scientific Information).

Current subject bibliographies

A vast number of bibliographies of periodicals covering specific subject areas is available. Librarians working in special or departmental libraries might identify bibliographies relating to their subject of interest by checking general bibliographical tools such as the *British national bibliography* (London: British Library National Bibliographic Service) which has a separate section in its classified sequence for serial bibliographies. *Journal citation reports* (ISI) can also be used to identify core lists of titles in specific subject areas. It is worth noting that several publishers specialize in current bibliographical material: Bowker, for example, publish a range of titles such as *Law books and serials in print*; *Scientific and technical books in print* and *Medical and health care books and serials in print*.

These publications are compiled from Bowker's *Books in print* database and the Bowker International Serials Database (from which is produced *Ulrich's international periodicals directory*). Another prolific publisher in the field of serials bibliography is Greenwood Press in London. Their current catalogue lists numerous titles such as *Marine science journals and serials: an analytical guide*; *History journals and serials* and *Jewish serials of the world: a research bibliography of secondary sources*.

Retrospective bibliographies

Various attempts have been made over the years to produce historical bibliographies of periodicals. Bibliographies covering the very early years of journal publishing include W. S. Ward's *Index and finding list of serials published in the British Isles: 1789 – 1832* (Lexington: University of Kentucky Press, 1953) which lists over 5,000 items, and H. C. Bolton's *Catalogue of scientific and technical periodicals, 1665 – 1895* (2nd ed. Washington: Smithsonian Institution, 1897). Two other publications which now act as important general bibliographies, but which started life as union lists, are R. S. Crane and F. B. Kaye's *Census of British newspapers and periodicals, 1620 – 1800* (Reprinted. London: Holland, 1966) and *British union catalogue of periodicals* (London: Butterworths, 1955 – 80) frequently referred to as BUCOP. This latter title is an extremely important source for historical bibliography and is normally available in most medium-sized to large libraries. BUCOP claimed to be 'a record of the periodicals of the world, from the seventeenth century to the present day, in British libraries'; it ceased publication in 1980 and is succeeded by *Serials in the British Library* which was discussed above.

Other important sources include the *New Cambridge bibliography of English literature* (5 vols. Cambridge: University Press, 1969 – 77) and *Tercentenary handlist of English and Welsh newspapers, magazines and reviews* (London: *The Times*, 1920. Reprinted. London: Dawsons, 1966). A detailed analysis of the history and development of scientific and technical periodicals from 1665 – 1790 is provided by Kronick.[2] Major directories covering more recent periods of history are Michael Wolff's *The Waterloo directory of*

Victorian periodicals, 1824 – 1900 (Oxford: Pergamon, 1980) and *World list of scientific periodicals published in the years 1900 – 1960* (4th ed. London: Butterworths, 1963 – 5). Containing more than 60,000 titles in the natural sciences the *World list* ceased publication after the fourth edition 1963 – 5, and was incorporated in BUCOP.

Retrospective bibliographies dealing with specific types or subject groups of periodicals can also be very important to historical research. Examples include *Women's magazines, 1693 – 1968* (London: Michael Joseph, 1970); *The little magazine: a history and a bibliography* (New Jersey: Princeton University Press, 1946); and *Serial publications in the British parliamentary papers, 1900 – 1968: a bibliography* (Chicago: American Library Association, 1971).

Union lists

Because of the existence of the BLDSC, and the resulting centralization of the UK interlibrary loan network, current union lists of periodical titles are not such a major and prolific feature of serials librarianship as in North America, where the interlibrary loan system is organized on a regional basis. This is further discussed in an article by Woodward.[3] The main aim of union lists of periodicals is to provide locational information about the holdings of a group of libraries. In a large library system spread out over a wide geographical area, a union list is essential if college and departmental libraries are to be informed of periodical holdings in other parts of the system. The *University of London union list of serials* (London: The University Library) for example, has been in operation since 1979 and is updated twice yearly on microfiche. Other extensive library systems, such as Essex County Library and Cambridge University, have also produced similar union listings.

Union lists are extremely expensive – in terms of staff time – to set up and maintain, and they are difficult to compile if participating libraries operate a range of differing manual systems or incompatible automated systems. These factors, combined with the reluctance of library users to travel to other libraries, and the findings of recent research by MacDougall[4] which demonstrate that it is cheaper to obtain a photocopied article from the BLDSC than from other local libraries, probably explain the scarcity of current, general, regional union lists.

However, in specialized subject areas compilation of union lists has thrived. This may be due to the fact that provision within BLDSC of highly specialized journal literature is incomplete, particularly in relation to foreign titles and obscure back runs. It is therefore useful to have additional bibliographical and locational information in the form of union lists. Examples include C. Travis and M. Alman's *Periodicals from Africa: a bibliography and union list of periodicals published in Africa* (Boston: G. K. Hall, 1977. Supplement, 1985); U. S. Williams's *Union catalogue of Persian serials and newspapers in British libraries* (New York: Ithaca Press, 1985); and Catherine Deering's *Union list of American studies periodicals in UK libraries* (Boston Spa: BLDSC and Standing Conference of National and University Libraries, 1983).

Library catalogues

Published library catalogues range from the extensive holdings of major national libraries to the rather more specialized holdings of smaller libraries such as government departments and research institutes. Some, such as the Oxford University's *Catalogue of English newspapers and periodicals in the Bodleian Library, 1622 – 1800* (Oxford: Bibliographical Society, 1936) are useful for historical bibliography; others such as the *List of serial publications in the British Museum (Natural History) library* (London: Trustees of the British Museum, 1980 –) aim to be a current listing. Lists emanating from smaller libraries perform a similar function to subject union lists; many examples are available, including *Serials in the College of Librarianship Wales Library* (Aberystwyth, Wales: College of Librarianship, 1988); and *Commonwealth Agricultural Bureaux serials checklist* (Wallingford, Oxon: CAB International, 1988).

GUIDES TO THE CONTENTS OF PERIODICALS

With the increasing number of periodical titles being published and the inability of libraries to keep abreast of this publishing output, two major problems face scholars and researchers. The first is keeping up-to-date with the periodical literature published in a particular subject discipline. The second is conducting a comprehensive, retrospective search of the literature over a given period of time. In order to assist the researcher in these tasks, an enormous range of secondary services or abstracting and indexes services has proliferated. Examples of some of the major services will now be examined.

Current awareness services

A popular, but basic method of current awareness which is practised by many library users is browsing through the current issues of journals on the library shelves: however it must be recognized that such browsing activities are not a particularly efficient or effective method of keeping up-to-date with the bulk of the literature. In addition to internal current-awareness initiatives operating within individual libraries and current-awareness services offered by online hosts, an extremely useful group of publications entitled *Current contents* (Philadelphia: Institute for Scientific Information) are published in the following subject areas: *Agriculture, biology and environmental sciences*; *Arts and humanities*; *Life sciences*; *Physical, chemical and earth sciences*; *Clinical medicine*; and *Engineering, technology and applied science*. *Current contents* are published on a weekly basis and simply comprise copies of contents pages of journals. Their importance lies in the fact that they do not undergo sophisticated editing procedures and therefore the information they contain is up-to-date. ISI have recently launched each of the *Current contents* on disc, and these will also be updated on a weekly basis.

Similar types of publications, also based on the speedy reproduction and dissemination of contents pages, exist across a variety of subject areas. These include the weekly *Contents of recent economic journals* (London: Department of Trade and Industry Library Services) which covers English-language journals in the field of economics, and the fortnightly *Contents pages in management* (Manchester: Manchester Business School Library and Information Service).

Indexing and abstracting services

Most periodicals of any reference value produce indexes of their own, usually at annual intervals. Occasionally cumulative indexes will be compiled covering five or ten years; remarkably *The engineer* (London: Morgan-Grampian) produced a 100-year index in 1956. However, when breadth of coverage is essential, indexes to individual journals are not particularly useful and researchers should consult one, or several, of the printed indexing and abstracting services.

Indexes and abstracts are continuing bibliographic publications which aim to provide coverage of the literature in a given field of knowledge. They may be discipline-oriented, i.e. covering a particular subject discipline such as psychology, biology or chemistry, or they may be mission-oriented, i.e. covering an inter-disciplinary area of interest such as the oil industry. The basic difference between an abstracting service and an indexing service is that abstracting journals provide an abstract (or résumé) of the cited article, whereas indexing journals provide only a citation. There are even examples of hybrid publications, such as the recent Butterworth publication *ASSIA – Applied social sciences index and abstracts.*

In order to guide the user to the most appropriate index or abstract, a number of directories are available, such as *The index and abstract directory* (Premier ed. Birmingham, Al.: Ebsco Publishing, 1989). Section one of this publication lists some 30,000 serial titles which are covered by one or more indexing or abstracting services, by subject. Section two is arranged alphabetically by the name of the indexing or abstracting service, and lists all serial titles covered by that service. Of more specific coverage are Dolores Owen's *Abstracts and indexes in science and technology: a descriptive guide* (2nd ed. Metuchen, NJ: Scarecrow Press, 1985) and L. A. Harzfeld's *Periodical indexes in the social sciences and humanities: a subject guide* (Metuchen, NJ: Scarecrow Press, 1978).

Indexing services

Probably the best known of early periodical indexes is W. F. Poole's *An index to periodical literature 1801 – 1881* (4th ed. Boston, Mass: Houghton, 1891). The original two-volume work was extended by the publication of five supplements up to 1907. The index included 479 US and British periodicals with entries mainly by subject. A more recent attempt to provide a key to the nineteenth-century journal literature is Walter E. Houghton's impressive work, *Wellesley index to Victorian periodicals 1824 – 1900* (5 vols. London: Routledge and Kegan Paul, 1966 – 89). Each of the first four volumes takes a selection of important titles, gives a brief introduction to that title and then provides the contents list of each individual issue. The recently published index in volume 5 consists mainly of a bibliography of contributors, plus an index of initials and pseudonyms.

Another early attempt to harness the growing literature was the *Readers' guide to periodical literature* (New York: H. W. Wilson, 1900 –). The cumulated volumes (vol. 1 covering 1900 – 4) are still available from H. W. Wilson, and the early volumes make fascinating study, covering such diverse titles as *Century magazine*, *Engineering magazine*, *Music*, *Harper's bazaar* and *Popular science monthly*. From this humble beginning, the H. W. Wilson Company has gone on to become one of the leading publishers of periodical indexes, and their catalogue now lists over 20 important indexing services, including *Applied science and technology index*, *Business periodicals index*, *Education index*, *Index to legal periodicals*, *Social sciences index*, and the still-extant *Readers' guide to periodical literature*! Wilson indexes normally appear either monthly or quarterly, with annual cumulations; only English-language material is covered and there is a definite bias towards North American coverage. All Wilson indexes are available online and many are now being issued on CD-ROM.

The UK has no comparable publisher, but there exists a multitude of periodical indexes from a wide variety of publishers. *British humanities index* (London: Butterworth) is a useful quarterly publication, with annual cumulations, covering articles appearing in newspapers and journals published in Britain. 'Humanities' is interpreted broadly to include the arts, economics, history, philosophy, politics and society. The index grew out of *Subject index to periodicals* (London: Library Association, 1915 – 61) which split into three parts, all of which are still published. The other resulting titles from the split are the bi-monthly *Current technology index* (London: Butterworth) – formerly *British technology index* – and the quarterly *British education index* (Leeds: Leeds University Press). All three indexes are simple to use; they contain specific headings with sub-headings and 'see' references. An author index is also provided.

Other major indexing services include *Index medicus* (Washington D.C.: US National Library of Medicine), which is the principal medical indexing service covering some 2,888 biomedical journals. Monthly author and subject indexes are issued, with multi-volume cumulations. Supplements include *Medical subjects headings* (MeSH) and *List of journals indexed in index medicus*. For smaller libraries *Abridged index medicus* is available covering approximately 100 journal titles. The database is widely available online and a number of different publishers have produced a CD-ROM version.

Current index to journals in education is a monthly guide to the current periodical literature in education, covering articles published in approximately 740 major educational and education-related journals. It is part of the ERIC database, sponsored by the Educational Resources Information Center (ERIC), US Department of Education. A sister publication *Resources in education*, also forms part of the ERIC database and covers current research findings, projects and technical reports, speeches, unpublished manuscripts and books. The ERIC database can also be accessed both online and on CD-ROM.

Mention should be made in this section of citation indexes. Citation indexes are published by the Institute for Scientific Information, Philadelphia, and comprise the following three titles: *Science citation index (SCI)*; *Social science citation index (SSCI)* and *Arts and humanities citation index (AHCI)*. Whereas most periodical indexes use some form of subject approach to tracing information, in a citation index the subject of a search is a reference, rather than a word or subject heading. The search begins with the author of a reference identified through a book, bibliography, footnote, encyclopaedia, etc. and this is then checked in the *Citation index* section. When the author's name and appropriate reference is located, the entry will then list all the current citations to that work. Having noted this list of citations, the searcher then turns to the *Source index* section to obtain the complete bibliographical data for the citations. An additional search strategy is offered by the *Permuterm subject index* which, as the name suggests, is a permuted title-word index to the article titles. Every significant word is paired with every other significant word in the same title, thus producing a 'natural language' indexing system. Thus, if a relevant starting title is not already known, one can be found through the keyword index.

There have been a number of attempts to catch up retrospectively with journal material which is inadequately covered in existing services. Such publications require an enormous amount of research and consequently cover very specific subject areas. Titles include Barry Bloomfield's *An author index to British 'little magazines' 1930–1939* (London: Mansell, 1976); K. I. MacDonald's *The Essex reference index: British journals on politics and sociology* (London: Macmillan, 1975); and L. Batty's *Retrospective index to film periodicals* (New York: Bowker, 1975).

Abstracting services

The advantage that abstracting services have over indexing services is that they can save the researcher considerable time locating and scanning unsuitable references. Borko states that 'at best, abstracts can save about nine-tenths of the time needed to read the original documents'.[5]

One of the earliest abstracting services was *Science abstracts* (London: Institution of Electrical Engineers) which began publication in 1898. It was not long (1903), however, before the growth of published information demanded that the title split into two series: Series A – *Physics abstracts*, and Series B – *Electrical and electronics abstracts*. In 1966 Series C was added – *Control abstracts*. For 90 years *Science abstracts* has been recognized as the English-language information service in the fields of physics, electrotechnology and, more recently, computing. In 1967 INSPEC (Information Service for the Physics and Engineering Communities) was formed as the Information Division of the Institution of Electrical Engineers. To maintain its position and to deal with the ever-increasing growth in published information, INSPEC developed a computer-based information-retrieval system for its abstracting services. Currently four INSPEC titles are published: *Physics abstracts*; *Electrical and electronics abstracts*; *Computer and control abstracts*; and *IT focus – information technology update for managers*. These titles currently record, respectively, some 120,000, 60,000, 45,000 and 3,000 recently published scientific and technical papers, and the database is growing at the rate of 200,000 records per year. Journal articles comprise about 80% of the total items.

Chemical abstracts (Columbus, Oh.: American Chemical Society) is another major abstracting service which has its origins at the beginning of the twentieth century, starting in 1907. The official statement of *Chemical abstracts* is as follows: 'It is the careful endeavour of Chemical Abstracts to publish adequate and accurate abstracts of all scientific and technical papers containing new information of chemical and chemical engineering interest and to report new chemical information revealed in the patent literature.' The abstracts are selected from more than 12,000 scientific journals from more than 150 countries and about 75% of references are to journal articles. *Chemical abstracts*, which is available both in printed form and online, contains informative abstracts of the original documents, i.e. the intention is to provide the user with enough information on the contents to establish whether the original is worth consultation.

Despite its title, *Engineering index* (New York: Engineering Information Inc.) is actually an abstracting journal. Claiming to be 'the index to the world's engineering developments' this service is published monthly with annual cumulations; three-year cumulations are also available. Citations and abstracts are arranged under main subject headings selected from the SHE (Subject Headings for Engineering) authority list. Users can search for information by subject heading in the abstracts section, by subject in the accompanying subject index, or by author in the author index. *Engineering index* is available online, and work is in progress to produce the CD-ROM version.

In the biological and life sciences *Biological abstracts* (Philadelphia: BIOSIS) is the major abstracting service. Published fortnightly, the printed work contains an abstract section which can be browsed by concept headings (listed at the front of each issue), an author index and a subject index. The subject index appears quite daunting, due to the fact that the typeface is extremely small and the layout is in narrow columns. Keywords are printed in bold face in the centre of the column and subject context words are located to the right and left of each keyword. Other indexes to this work include the *Biosystemic index*, used to find entries by taxonomic category, and the *Generic index*, used to find entries according to genus or genus-species name.

The social sciences, management and economics are all served by a variety of abstracting services, although few can claim to be as comprehensive as their counterparts in the sciences and technology. The Anbar abstracting service (Bradford: MCB University Press) commenced in 1961 to cover the field of management. It is split into eight separate parts: *Accounting and data processing abstracts*; *Marketing services and production abstracts*; *Marketing and distribution abstracts*; *Personnel and training abstracts*; *Top management abstracts*; *Service industries management*; *Mergers and acquisitions*; and *Information management and technology*. Each title appears 12 times a year and there is an annual index for each title. The *Cumulative joint index* covers all eight abstracting journals and appears four times a year. An annual index covering all the titles forms part of the yearbook *The compleat Anbar*, which contains reprints of all abstracts, along with an author index. The classification scheme is somewhat unusual and can be unwieldy; however, the abstracts themselves often contain lively critical comment. *Psychological abstracts* (Arlington, Va: American Psychological Society) began publication in 1927 and is now an established core abstracting title, providing access to the world's literature in psychology and related behavioural and social sciences. Published monthly, the abstracts are listed under 16 major classification categories with an author and brief subject index. An expanded cumulation is published at the end of each volume. *Economic titles/abstracts* (Dordrecht, Netherlands: Martinus Nijhoff) is a semi-monthly review (with an annual index) providing information of interest to business, trade, economic libraries and research institutes. It is the printed version of the online database *Foreign trade and economics abstracts.*

Although a large proportion of abstracting services cover the sciences, social sciences and technology, the arts and humanities are not entirely neglected. A major service covering historical literature is *Historical abstracts: a bibliography of the world's historical literature* (Santa Barbara, Ca: ABC-Clio). The abstracts are published quarterly in two parts: Part A – modern-history abstracts, and Part B – twentieth-century abstracts. 2,100 major history journals of the world are scanned, and geographical coverage is worldwide, with the exception of the US and Canada which are covered by *America: history and life* (Santa Barbara, Ca: ABC-Clio).

CONCLUSION

Periodicals present a range of problems to the library manager. New titles are constantly being published, current titles change or split into several parts, unannounced supplements appear and prices spiral at an alarming rate. Such constant momentum and change also means that they are very difficult to control bibliographically, posing problems for librarians and end-users alike. Concern about the low use of many journal titles within library collections has also prompted many librarians to question the cost-effectiveness of current provision.

A potential solution to the problem which has been discussed extensively in the professional literature is electronic article delivery. Theoretically, instead of being printed and published in the traditional way, full-text periodical articles could be stored in some vast database, which could be accessed remotely by individual libraries. Articles would be retrieved on demand and libaries would pay only for articles required by their users. The British Library is currently conducting research in this area (the ADONIS project) with a sample of 219 biomedical journals stored on CD-ROM. Findings from the research project are reported by Braid.[6] A further detailed study of journal versus article delivery was conducted at Loughborough University. This research involved detailed use studies and costing exercises on a variety of models of journal provision. It concluded, however, that 'a complete switch to electronic journals article transmission in the present state of technological development and financial provision would leave the librarian and reader at a severe disadvantage'.[7] It therefore appears unlikely that the printed periodical and its associated bibliographical guides and indexes will disappear from the library shelves in the near future.

REFERENCES AND CITATIONS

1   Thomas, I., *History of printing in America*. New York: The author, 1874, Vol. 2, 292.
2   Kronick, D. A., *A history of scientific and technical periodicals: the origin and development of the scientific and technical press, 1665 – 1790*. 2nd ed. New Jersey: Scarecrow Press, 1976.
3   Woodward, H. M., 'Union lists: the UK perspective', *Serials review*, 1 – 2, 1988.
4   MacDougall, A. F., Wheelhouse, H. and Wilson, J., *A study of various aspects of cooperation between East Midlands university and polytechnic libraries*. BLRDD Report 5989. British Library, 1989.
5   Borko, H. and Bernier, C. L., *Abstracting concepts and methods*. London: Academic Press, 1975.
6   Braid, J. A., 'The Adonis experience', *Serials*, **2** (3), November 1989, 49 – 54.
7   MacDougall, A., Woodward, H. M. and Wilson, J., *Modelling of journal versus article acquisition by libraries*. Report to the British Library Research and Development Department, BNBF Report 23, Loughborough: Loughborough University Pilkington Library, 1986.

SUGGESTIONS FOR FURTHER READING

Bourne, R. (ed.), *Serials librarianship*. London: Library Association, 1981.
Chatterton, L. and Clack, M. E. (eds.), *The serials information chain: discussion, debate and dialogue: proceedings of the North American Serials Interest Group*. New York: Haworth Press, 1988.
Desmaris, N., *The librarian's CD-ROM handbook*. Westport, Ct: Meckler, 1989.
Gellatly, P. (ed.), *Serials librarianship in transition: issues and developments*. New York: Haworth Press, 1986.

Graham, M. and Buettel, F. (eds.), *Serials management: a practical handbook*. London: Aslib and the UK Serials Group. Announced (Summer 1990).

Osborn, A. D., *Serial publications: their place and treatment in libraries*. 3rd ed. Chicago: American Library Association, 1980.

Page, G., *Journal publishing: principles and practice*. London: Butterworths, 1987.

Taylor, D., *Managing the serials explosion: the issues for publishers and librarians*. New York: Knowledge Industry Publications, 1982.

Tuttle, M. and Cook, J. (eds.), *Advances in serials management*. Vol. 1. Greenwich, Ct: Jai Press, 1986.

Tuttle, M., *Introduction to serials management*. Greenwich, Ct: Jai Press, 1983.

9

Reports and Theses, Conferences and Symposia, Standards and Patents

C. Peter Auger

Reference material relating to reports, conferences and symposia, theses, standards and patents places an extra degree of responsibility on the librarian. The reason is that when readers with queries about these materials have been correctly introduced to the appropriate sources, they are nevertheless frequently unable or unwilling to pursue their enquiries with quite the same facility that they show when directed to more conventional and certainly more familiar works such as dictionaries, directories or encyclopaedias. Difficulties for readers arise partly because publications in these areas are genuinely not easy to use, and partly because they are unfamiliar. In addition, the reference material embodies to a greater or lesser degree information and documents which may be subject to various obstacles, restrictions and constraints not encountered elsewhere, such as the frequent issue of amendments and updates (standards specifications), the requirement to demonstrate a 'need to know' (research reports), the non-availability of listed publications (conference papers withdrawn before presentation), authors' rights to be consulted (theses), and publications in the form of a legal document (patents). Yet such sources, especially in the fields of science and technology, often provide information not obtainable elsewhere, sometimes because it is too new to have reached conventional channels of publication, and sometimes because it is too detailed or specialized to warrant the expense and delay of formal editing and assessment. Thus the librarian is more likely to be asked for extra guidance, and in consequence needs to have a good understanding of the material in question.

Many libraries, even when they have definite acquisition policies towards such materials, have tended to shy away from the task of cataloguing, indexing and arranging the publications involved, and have instead established special collections arranged on some broad fundamental characteristic, with a heavy reliance on externally produced indexes and guides. In some areas bibliographic control is indifferent or inconsistent; documents may as a result appear under more than one identity. Added to this are the problems of considerable variety in physical format, which prevent collections from being shelved alongside other printed material, because for example they are issued as preprints (conference papers), microfiche (reports), typescripts (theses), or as flimsies with a limited life (draft standards).

Despite this heterogeneity, however, the publications under consideration justify their juxtaposition in the present chapter by virtue of one important common feature; they are all amenable to treatment as series of publications, wherein each individual item has its own unique identifier, most often in the form of an alphanumeric code (British Standard 9000; SAE Paper 880574; NASA Report SP-470; European Patent EP 0328080; and so on).

In recent years attempts have been made to describe much of this material as 'grey literature', that is to say materal which is difficult to acquire and not normally available through the book trade. In an attempt to ameliorate the situation, a European database called SIGLE (System for Information on Grey Literature in Europe) was set up following the York Conference in 1978 and became operational in 1981. It is now regularly supplied with brief bibliographical entries of appropriate items contributed by various national centres in Europe. In the United Kingdom this responsibility falls to the British Library Document Supply Centre, which has an announcement journal devoted solely to grey literature (see below).

The concept of grey literature is a useful one which is generally gaining acceptance, but most authorities, in drawing up a

definition, would exclude standards and patents, which nevertheless feature in this chapter. On the other hand there is an
increasing tendency to count as part of the grey literature certain
categories of central and local government publications, which
are discussed elsewhere in this book.

REPORTS

The term 'report' in its everyday sense is well understood as
indicating an account given, or an opinion formally expressed,
after an investigation or an appraisal. When, however, reports
are looked at collectively as a form of literature, then a question
of definition becomes a little more difficult. In the context of
reference material, reports may be regarded as accounts from
government establishments, scientific institutions and industrial
laboratories, about work performed and results achieved, rendered
to their clients and sponsors. This is certainly the case with reports
in the fields of science and technology, where they are frequently
known as research and development (R & D) reports; and in
recent years the format has spread increasingly to other areas,
especially education and economics.

Reports often contain extensive descriptions of experiments,
investigations, studies and evaluations, fully supported by figures,
graphs and tables, and more recently, computer-derived print-
out. Normally reports do not remain silent about unsuccessful
projects, and since they are written during, or immediately after
the activities they describe, they contain results and data on the
very latest stages of research in a particular area. They are
therefore of great importance as a communication medium in
those regions of science and technology where changes are being
made at a very rapid rate, as for example electronics and
aerospace. It is no coincidence that such fast-moving subject areas
are also of great importance to governments for reasons of defence
and military strength. Consequently many reports start life as
documents issued by the agencies of the armed services, or by
government departments. Indeed the origins of many series of
reports, still being issued today, can be traced back to the massive
research programmes conducted during World War II.

Much of the world's report literature originates in the United States, and due to the fact that the greater part of this literature is issued on the authority of various government establishments and agencies, that is to say with the support of public funds, as many as possible of the resulting reports are sooner or later made available to the public. Availability is always subject to the overriding factor of national security. When a report is considered unsuitable for public release because of security considerations, it is customarily described as being 'classified', and as a consequence not available to readers who are unable to demonstrate a 'need to know'.

Reports, even when entirely free from security and distribution restrictions, are still regarded by journal editors and commercial publishers alike as unpublished documents, which have not been subjected to the rigours of refereeing or editorial control. Consequently they have tended to be ignored in the majority of conventional abstracting services and national bibliographies. Instead it has been the custom for a great many years to publish details of newly issued reports in specialized announcement journals, the presentation and content of which are quite different from those of other current awareness sources.

Reports constitute the largest category of documents within grey literature, and a major announcement medium covering a very wide range of disciplines, and embracing foreign as well as United States documents, is:

GOVERNMENT REPORTS ANNOUNCEMENTS AND INDEX (GRA&I). Springfield, Va: US Department of Commerce, National Technical Information Service (NTIS). 26 issues per annum.

GRA&I is a highly structured abstracting publication, the format of which has been designed for librarians and technical information specialists. NTIS is the central source for the public sale of US Government-sponsored research, development and engineering reports, and for sales of foreign technical reports and other analyses prepared by national and local government agencies and their contractors or grantees.

Each entry in *GRA&I* usually records a document's accession number, corporate author, title, personal author, date, pagination, contract number, report number and availability. Also included is an abstract, supplemented by a note of the indexing terms used. Indexes to *GRA&I* are issued annually as a set comprising several volumes. Abstracts are arranged by the NTIS subject classif- ication, a scheme which uses 38 broad subject categories which are further separated into over 350 subcategories.

In addition to the twice-monthly issues of *GRA&I*, other means are used by NTIS to announce the availability of new publications, notably a series of weekly newsletters:

ABSTRACT NEWSLETTERS. Springfield, Va: US Department of Commerce, NTIS.
Abstract newsletters announce in 26 subject categories summaries of most unclassified federally funded research as it is completed and made available to the public. Abstracts of reports appear in as many categories as appropriate and do so within a few weeks of their receipt from the originating agencies. Titles of *Abstract newsletters* vary from *Administration and management* to *Urban and regional technology and development*.

Whereas *GRA&I* and its associated services are extremely wide in their subject coverage, there are several announcement journals which concentrate on a narrower, albeit still broad area of activity. Inevitably there is a fair degree of overlap between *GRA&I* and the more specialized journals. Firstly there is:

SCIENTIFIC AND TECHNICAL AEROSPACE REPORTS (STAR). Washington: US Government Printing Office. Issued on the 8th and 23rd of each month.
Publications abstracted in *STAR*, which is prepared by the NASA Scientific and Technical Information Facility operated for the National Aeronautics and Space Administration by RMS Associates, include scientific and technical reports issued by NASA and its contractors; other US Government agencies; corporations; universities; and research organizations throughout the world. The value of *STAR* lies in its thoroughness of coverage and its subject scope, which includes all aspects of aeronautics and space

research, supporting basic and applied research, and applications. Aerospace aspects of earth resources, energy development, conservation, oceanography, environmental protection, urban transportation and other topics of high national priority are also included.

NASA points out that *STAR* should be used in conjunction with its sister publication, which covers the conventionally published literature in the same fields. Its title is:

INTERNATIONAL AEROSPACE ABSTRACTS (IAA). New York: American Institute of Aeronautics and Astronautics. 24 issues per annum.

Secondly, the increasingly important energy field is covered by:

ENERGY RESEARCH ABSTRACTS (ERA). Washington: US Government Printing Office. 24 issues per annum.

ERA began publication in 1977 and is compiled by the Office of Scientific and Technical Information of the US Department of Energy (DOE). It may be regarded as the successor to *Nuclear science abstracts (NSA)*, an announcement service published between 1948 and 1976 and still today regarded as a reference work of the highest value. *ERA* continues to devote a large amount of its coverage to nuclear energy, but its contents reflect DOE's broader charter for energy systems, conservation, safety, environmental protection, physics research, biology and medicine.

For reports in the field of nuclear energy proper, there is still:

INIS ATOMINDEX. Vienna: International Atomic Energy Agency. 26 issues per annum.

INIS atomindex is prepared as part of the Agency's International Nuclear Information System (INIS) and its purpose is to construct a database identifying publications relating to nuclear science and its peaceful applications. INIS defines 'non-conventional literature' as 'all literature other than journal articles or commercially produced books'.

Away from the realms of science and technology, a notable reports announcement service is:

RESOURCES IN EDUCATION (RIE). Washington: US Government Printing Office. 12 issues per annum.

RIE, formerly known as *Research in education*, is sponsored by the Educational Resources Information Centre (ERIC), part of the US Department of Education. ERIC is a nationwide information network for acquiring, selecting, abstracting, indexing, storing, retrieving and disseminating reports relating to education. It consists of a coordinating staff in Washington, and 16 clearing-houses at universities or professional organizations across the country. ERIC acts as both a document-provision agency and a bibliographic service, with a heavy emphasis on reports and projects. *RIE* calls its abstracts résumés and highlights those publications announced that have been selected as having special significance for educators. All résumés are numbered sequentially by an accession number beginning with the prefix ED, for *E*RIC *D*ocument.

Research workers in Britain tend to rely heavily on the American announcement journals, but can, when the occasion demands, turn to publications devoted in the main to United Kingdom material. The first of these used to be:

R&D ABSTRACTS. Orpington, Kent: Department of Industry. 26 issues per annum.

R&D abstracts was compiled and issued by the Technology Reports Centre (TRC) until the termination of its reports-handling activities in 1981. *R&D abstracts* was directed at industry in general, but a service still available to Ministry of Defence contractors engaged in research and development work is:

DEFENCE RESEARCH ABSTRACTS. Glasgow: Defence Research Information Centre. Details on application to DRIC.

The key source of information about British reports which are available without restriction to all readers is:

BRITISH REPORTS TRANSLATIONS AND THESES (BRTT). Boston Spa: British Library Document Supply Centre (BLDSC). 12 issues per annum.

BRTT has developed from its predecessor *BLL announcement bulletin*, to become a bibliography of material falling within the category of grey literature, which is defined as semi-published documents such as reports, theses and translations – items in fact which can be difficult to identify and locate. *BRTT*'s aim is to help increase the awareness of such material and so promote its wider use, and it does this by listing British reports literature and translations produced by British Government organizations, local government, universities and learned institutions. *BRTT* also lists most doctoral theses accepted at British universities and selected British official publications of a report nature not published by Her Majesty's Stationery Office.

The BLDSC is a major contributor to SIGLE (System for Information on Grey Literature in Europe) and all the material listed in *BRTT*, except translations, appears in the SIGLE database, accessible through BLAISE.

Although reports can be catalogued in the same way as published literature, using personal and corporate authors for the main entries, they are normally identified and filed by report numbers of one sort or another. Considerable efforts have been devoted to imparting some measure of bibliographical control on the reports literature, and in certain areas well-known report-number series present few difficulties to users, as for example the AD reports issued by the US Department of Defense. AD stems from ASTIA Document, and ASTIA itself stands for the Armed Services Technical Information Agency.

There are several reference guides to such report-numbering schemes, notably:

Aronson, E. J., REPORT SERIES CODES DICTIONARY. 3rd ed. Detroit: Gale Research Company, 1986.

The *Dictionary*, which updates the compilation originally produced by the Special Libraries Association in New York, provides details of over 20,000 report-series codes used by nearly 10,000 corporate authors.

DICTIONARY OF ENGINEERING DOCUMENT SOURCES. Santa Ana, Ca: Global Engineering Documents, 1985.

This dictionary cross-indexes reports codes assigned to technical documents by both government and industry sources.

THESES

A thesis may be regarded as a statement of investigation or research, presenting the author's findings and any conclusions reached, and submitted by the author in support of his or her candidature for a higher degree, professional qualification or other award. On the basis of this definition it becomes apparent that a thesis has several features in common with a report: both present details of investigations and research, both offer findings and conclusions, both are submitted to an overseeing body (the university or college in the case of a thesis, the sponsoring agency in the case of a report), and both are unpublished documents.

The thesis often describes investigations of an advanced nature, reflecting the writer's attempt to extend and explore the limits of knowledge in his chosen subject. As such, a thesis can be an important document for other research workers, since it will contain results not available elsewhere, even though such results must be regarded as primarily intended to show a candidate's grasp of a given subject and the research methodology involved. Many theses eventually appear, in an amended form, as journal articles or monographs and are frequently cited as individual items in the literature.

Since 1950 the standard reference work on information about current British theses has been:

INDEX TO THESES WITH ABSTRACTS ACCEPTED FOR HIGHER DEGREES BY THE UNIVERSITIES OF GREAT BRITAIN AND IRELAND AND THE COUNCIL FOR NATIONAL ACADEMIC AWARDS. London: Aslib. 4 issues per annum.

The *Index* covers around 9,000 theses each year, and since 1950 has been produced by Aslib with the active collaboration of the universities concerned. From volume 35 onwards, Aslib entered into an agreement with Expert Information Limited to launch an expanded and improved version of the *Index* to include the full text of abstracts and a greatly enhanced subject index.

In its new format, the *Index* is being published in four parts per volume; volume 35 was completed in August 1987 and published in 1988. A CD-ROM version was announced in 1989, to incorporate details going back to 1716.

This date is significant, because at present if the reader wishes to find out about British theses before the start of the *Index*, it is necessary to consult:

Bilboul, R., RETROSPECTIVE INDEX TO THESES OF GREAT BRITAIN AND IRELAND 1716 – 1950. Santa Barbara, Ca: Clio Press, 1976.

In the United States, where the preferred term is dissertation, the principal source of reference is:

DISSERTATION ABSTRACTS INTERNATIONAL (DAI). Ann Arbor, Michigan: University Microfilms International. Monthly or quarterly.

DAI began publication in 1938 as *Microfilm abstracts*, became *Dissertation abstracts* in 1952, and changed again in 1969 to its present title. In 1966 the publication was split into two sections, Section A (The Humanities and Social Sciences, monthly) and Section B (The Sciences and Engineering, monthly). In 1976 a third section, Section C (Europe, quarterly) was started and initially it represented European institutions only, but in 1989 the title was changed to Section C (Worldwide) to cover institutions in all parts of the globe.

Each entry in *DAI* comprises the following information: title of the dissertation, author's name, year, awarding institution and the order number allocated by the publishers. This number acts as a unique identifier in the manner similar to that of a report number. A feature of *DAI* is comprehensiveness of the abstracts, each of which is usually about half a page in length.

An aid to retrospective searching of dissertation material is to be found in:

COMPREHENSIVE DISSERTATION INDEX (CDI). Ann Arbor, Mi.: University Microfilms International.

What the publishers call the 'landmark' collection consists of 37 volumes covering the years 1861 – 1972, and lists more than 417,000 dissertations under keyword headings and within a separate author index. Two further cumulations have been published, one covering the years 1973 – 82 and citing nearly 351,000 dissertations in 38 volumes, and one covering the years 1983 – 7, with over 162,000 citations in 22 volumes. Supplements are issued annually.

In the United Kingdom it is the usual practice for candidates to present their theses in typescript form, with only a handful of bound copies being produced. On the Continent however it has long been the custom to have theses printed, sometimes with as many as 200 copies of a title. This procedure greatly simplifies the establishment of collections by exchange.

Each European country keeps its own records of theses, as for example the cumulation:

GESAMTVERZEICHNIS DEUTSCHSPRACHIGER HOCHSCHUL-SCHRIFTEN (GVH), 1966 – 80. Munich: K. G. Saur.

GVH appeared in 24 volumes between 1982 and 1987, and is to be supplemented by an index of a further 16 volumes. The main section covers dissertations, post-doctoral theses and university publications from the Federal Republic of Germany, East Germany, Switzerland and Austria.

CONFERENCES AND SYMPOSIA

Papers in a preliminary form made available prior to or at meetings and conferences, where they are presented by their authors in person, are usually termed preprints or meetings papers. The practice is especially common in the United States, and many large American technical societies issue preprints in advance of their meetings, where each paper is identified by a serial code, not unlike a report number. After the meeting or conference has taken place, the papers are reviewed, and all or a certain proportion selected for inclusion in a society's permanent records, or in the conference organizer's official transactions. Those not selected for such treatment are simply listed, sometimes abstracted by announcement services, quite often cited in bibliographies and of course requested by readers. A peculiar feature of meetings papers is that not all the items promised to a conference organizer (and so assigned preprint numbers) are actually submitted in written form; some may be presented orally, some indeed may never be presented at all. Nevertheless, because they have been allocated preprint numbers, they are quoted in lists and bibliographies as though they were available.

The physical forms which conference literature can take include the preprint noted above: the bound conference volume, available either during or shortly after the event; a conference record as part of or a supplement to an established journal; conference records issued as part of the reports literature; and conference records in which extended abstracts only are provided, a practice adopted for example in the United States by the Electrochemical Society.

Generally the library will want to have access to two main types of information about conferences and meetings: firstly, what events are due to take place, and secondly, what form will the official record take?

On the first count it is possible to consult various published lists such as:

FORTHCOMING INTERNATIONAL SCIENTIFIC AND TECHNICAL CONFERENCES. London: Aslib. 4 issues per annum.

However, given the transitory nature of the information involved, it is probably more effective to ignore the printed sources, at least when conducting a comprehensive search, and rely instead on online databases. Two useful services are:

MEETING AGENDA, compiled by CEN-SACLAY, Service de Documentation, Commissariat a l'Energie Atomique, Gif-sur-Yvette, France, and accessible through the host Questel, which contains announcements of congresses, conferences, meetings, workshops, exhibitions and fairs due to take place around the world.

FAIRBASE, produced by Fairbase Database Limited, Hanover, Germany, and accessible through various hosts, which provides details of fairs, exhibitions and meetings due to take place in over 100 countries.

Once conferences and meetings have taken place, the problem then becomes one of identifying the permanent form in which the proceedings are eventually published. In the United Kingdom, the National Lending Library (as it then was) began in 1965 to publish the *Index of conference proceedings received by the NLL*. Today the British Library Document Supply Centre compiles:

INDEX OF CONFERENCE PROCEEDINGS. Boston Spa: BLDSC. 12 issues per annum.

The *Index* has annual, 5-year, 10-year and 18-year cumulations, and 16,000 conferences covering all subjects are added annually, contributing to a record which is approaching a quarter of a million items. All types of conference proceedings are noted, including those that appear in journal form, those reporting individual conferences and published as books, and those published as part of normal serials. The indexes are arranged alphabetically by subject key terms taken from the title and organizing or sponsoring body of the conference.

In the United States a number of publications offer information on conferences and meetings, including:

CONFERENCE PAPERS INDEX. Bethesda, Maryland: Cambridge Scientific Abstracts. 7 issues per annum.

The *Index* covers the life sciences, the physical sciences and engineering on a worldwide basis, and cites approximately 48,000 conference papers annually.

INDEX TO SCIENTIFIC AND TECHNICAL PROCEEDINGS (ISTP). Philadelphia, Pa: Institute for Scientific Information (ISI). 12 issues per annum.

The compilers of this index estimate that about 10,000 scientific meetings take place each year, and that three quarters of them (conferences, seminars, symposia, colloquia, conventions and workshops), result in a published record. ISTP indexes publish proceedings from around the world and from a range of scientific disciplines.

Finally, it is possible to consult:

DIRECTORY OF PUBLISHED PROCEEDINGS. Harrison, NY: Interdok Corporation.

Often referred to simply as *Interdok*, the *Directory* is issued in three series, namely: *Series PCE* – *Pollution control and ecology*; *Series SEMT* – *Science, engineering, medicine and technology*; and *Series SSH* – *Social sciences and humanities*.

STANDARDS

Standards are officially approved specifications applicable in various sectors of trade and industry and they cover such topics as methods of testing, terminology, performance and construction requirements and codes of practice. Usually they are prepared by agreement among the interested parties concerned and are subsequently used to simplify and rationalize production and distribution, to ensure uniformity, reliability and safety and to eliminate wasteful variety. Standards can also be considered as constraints which hinder the development of new and improved ideas and so act as a brake on scientific and technical progress.

On balance however standards must be regarded as vital to the success of any advanced industrial society and the various collections available at national and international levels are ample evidence of the vital contribution they make to the manufacturing and commercial aspects of everyday life.

The average standard specification is not a lengthy document – usually a pamphlet of a few pages, typically with details of methods, measurements, definitions, properties and processes. It invariably has an identifying alphanumeric code which in many cases can acquire an international significance. Many different bodies – national standards organizations, trade associations and government departments – issue standards.

In the **United Kingdom** the official organization with the responsibility of preparing and publishing standards and encouraging their use is the British Standards Institution (BSI). The key to BSI activities lies in:

BRITISH STANDARDS CATALOGUE (previously known as the *British Standards yearbook*). London: BSI. Annually.

The *Catalogue* lists current BSI publications and gives a brief description of each. Publications are arranged in numerical order within each series, and the series can be identified from the alphabetical characters which precede the number of the standard. BS, the general series, contains the most standards and information about it occupies the bulk of the work.

Current publications are identified by the use of bold type whilst publications withdrawn can be recognized by the use of light type. The policy of BSI is for every standard to be reviewed by the technical committee responsible not more than five years after publication. The *Catalogue* lists over 10,000 BSI publications and each year some 700 new or revised standards are issued. In order to keep subscribers up to date, BSI issues:

BSI STANDARDS CATALOGUE SUPPLEMENT. London: BSI. Monthly.

The *Supplement* contains details of new and revised specifications, amendments, publications withdrawn and European standards. The wider aspects of standardization are described in:

BSI NEWS. London: BSI. Monthly.

In addition to general features on topics such as quality and health and safety, the periodical lists new and revised publications and has a special section on new work started.

Although there are a number of other bodies in Britain which prepare their own standards, most work through BSI. An example of these exceptions is:

IEE WIRING REGULATIONS. London: Institution of Electrical Engineers, 1981, with 1987 amendments.

Most other industrialized countries have their own national standards organizations and their publications are widely quoted in the literature. In **Germany** the Deutsches Institut für Normung (DIN) issues:

DIN KATALOG FÜR TECHNISCHE REGELN. Berlin: Beuth Verlag. Annually.

The *Katalog* consists of two volumes prepared by the Deutsche Informationszentrum für technische Regeln (DITR), and provides details of standards in both German and English. Over 4,000 DIN standards have been translated in full into English, and are indicated in the *Katalog* by the letter code En. New standards and information on drafts and revisions are covered in:

DIN MITTEILUNGEN ELECTRONORM. Berlin: Beuth Verlag. 12 issues per annum.

France too is active in standardization, and the official body responsible for issuing standards is the Association Française de Normalisation (AFNOR), which produces:

AFNOR CATALOGUE. Paris: AFNOR. Annually.

The compilation contains details of 13,500 French standards and is similar in format to the BSI *Catalogue*.

In the **United States** there are very many bodies which are active in the preparation of standards, and although there is a central organization, the American National Standards Institute (ANSI), its main function is to coordinate and approve the publication of standards developed by qualified technical and professional societies, trade associations and other groups, which voluntarily submit them to ANSI for approval. Lists of ANSI standards are available from the Institute's headquarters, and news of current activities is to be found in:

ANSI REPORTER. New York: ANSI. 26 issues per annum.

The United States Department of Commerce, through the National Bureau of Standards, has issued a directory which identifies over 750 bodies which develop, publish and revise standards in the public and private sectors:

STANDARDS ACTIVITIES OF ORGANISATIONS IN THE UNITED STATES. (*Special publication 681*, edited by R. B. Toth). Washington: US Government Printing Office, 1984.

Although the advantages of national standardization programmes are considerable, the ultimate benefits are derived when standards receive **international** recognition. The Organisation Internationale de Normalisation (ISO) has its headquarters in Switzerland, and publishes:

ISO CATALOGUE. Geneva: ISO. Annually.

The current *Catalogue* lists 7107 published international standards, and the sales agents are ISO member bodies in countries around the world – in the case of the United Kingdom, the member body is the BSI. ISO also issues:

KEY-WORD-IN-CONTEXT KWIC INDEX OF INTERNATIONAL STANDARDS. Geneva: ISO. 3rd ed. 1987.

In certain areas of standardization, notably metals and alloys, considerable attempts have been made to cross-reference national standards by means of compilations which compare specifications according to various criteria such as composition and physical properties, enabling a user to select a national standard which is an equivalent or near-equivalent of a standard issued by another body. A recent example is:

Unterweiser, P. M. and Cobb, H. M., WORLDWIDE GUIDE TO EQUIV-ALENT IRONS AND STEELS. 2nd ed. Metals Park, Oh.: ASM International, 1987; and WORLDWIDE GUIDE TO EQUIVALENT NON-FERROUS METALS AND ALLOYS. 2nd ed. 1987.

Both collections of data include details from 28 standards and standards-issuing organizations, and the layout is based on the UNS (Unified Numbering System) scheme for metals and alloys.

PATENTS

A patent is an official document setting out in great detail an inventor's solution to a particular problem, and granting that inventor the sole right for a specified period of years to make, use or sell the invention disclosed. All such inventions must meet certain criteria of novelty, and must be capable of industrial application. Normally the librarian is not concerned with the drafting, filing, exploitation and contesting of patents, since these tasks are the province of the inventor himself, the patent agent and the patent examiner.

Because however patent specifications often reveal technical information at a much earlier date than other literature, because they often review and examine the prior art which led up to the invention, and because taken collectively they can be indicative of trends in a given subject field, no literature search on an industrial topic can be considered complete unless British and foreign patents have been taken into account.

All major industrialized countries have a national patents system, because it has long been recognized that the protection obtained in return for disclosure acts as a stimulus to the inventive spirit, and so benefits technical progress in a most positive manner. In the United Kingdom details of all applications filed, specifications published and patents sealed are announced in:

OFFICIAL JOURNAL (PATENTS). London: Patent Office. 52 issues per annum.

In addition it is possible to consult:

ILLUSTRATED ABRIDGMENTS OF PATENT SPECIFICATIONS (Patents Act 1949) and ILLUSTRATED ABSTRACTS OF PATENT APPLICATIONS (Patents Act 1977). London: Patent Office.

The *Abridgments* and *Abstracts* are published in pamphlet form in 25 parts corresponding to the divisions of the United Kingdom classification key, and constitute a record of developments in all branches of invention, useful to research students and specialists alike. The Patent Office also issues a range of other publications, and in the context of this chapter, one book in particular is of great usefulness, namely:

PATENTS: A SOURCE OF TECHNICAL INFORMATION. London: Patent Office, 1986.

This concise work is written for industry, research and development units, universities, polytechnics, inventors, engineers and scientists. It is frequently updated.

A great deal of information on patents can be obtained from specialist patents abstracting and indexing organizations, as for example:

WORLD PATENTS ABSTRACTS. London: Derwent Publications Ltd. 52 issues per annum.

World patents abstracts is one of a series of printed patent services available from Derwent, and each week some 13,000 patent specifications from 29 patent issuing authorities are received and processed. The result is a database providing details of over 7 million patent numbers, corresponding to 3 million separate inventions.

It is customary for companies and organizations which employ inventors to file patent applications in leading industrial countries throughout the world, each of which has its own patent system. In the course of time British applications can result in granted patents in say the United States, Europe and Japan, thus providing global protection for an invention. Conversely many overseas countries file applications with the British Patent Office, and increasingly with the European Patent Office in Munich. Thus there is a strong international aspect to patents, one manifestation of which is the system of International Classification Marks, the principles of which are contained in:

INTERNATIONAL PATENT CLASSIFICATION, and the companion volume OFFICIAL CATCHWORD INDEX. 4th ed. Geneva: World Intellectual Property Organisation (WIPO). 1984.

The *International classification*, which is published on behalf of WIPO by Carl Heymanns Verlag, Munich, came into force in 1985. It consists of nine volumes, the last of which is a guide, survey of classes and summary of the main groups. The *Catchword index* is intended to indicate the part or parts of the *Classification* in which matter relating to any given subject is likely to be found, as for example LIGHTERS (barges) or LIGHTERS (devices for igniting).

The Patents Act of 1977 was designed firstly to improve the United Kingdom domestic law and secondly to enable the British and European patent laws to co-exist, for the London Patent Office operates simultaneously with the European Patent Office. Details of the latter's activities are to be found in:

OFFICIAL JOURNAL OF THE EUROPEAN PATENT OFFICE. Munich: EPO. Monthly.

The first issue of the *Journal* appeared in December 1977, and it is mainly devoted to the announcement of decisions of the Board of Appeal of the EPO. Details of published applications, arranged according to the *International classification*, are contained in:

EUROPEAN PATENT BULLETIN. Munich: EPO. 52 issues per annum.

CONCLUSION

All the categories of reference material described above demand a considerable amount of study and application if the user is to be able to make full and effective use of the resources which individually and collectively they have to offer. Reports call for an understanding of the world of research and development establishments; these require an insight into the methods of awarding higher degrees; conference papers necessitate an appreciation of the eagerness of scientists and engineers to enhance their public reputation; standards depend on a grasp of the diversity of standards bodies; and for patents some knowledge of the concepts of intellectual property is essential.

The observations made and the examples quoted are but an indication of the scope and nature of what is in part grey literature, and in part well-established highly specialized forms of reference material. Fuller accounts of many of the aspects touched upon can be found in the titles given in the following list.

SUGGESTIONS FOR FURTHER READING

Auger, C. P., *Information sources in grey literature*. London: Bowker Saur, 1989.

International Federation of Library Associations and Institutions, *Guide to the availability of theses*. ('Guides to the sources of the history of nations', vol. 29). Munich: K. G. Saur, 1985.

McClure, C. R. *et al.*, *Linking the US National Technical Information Service with academic and public libraries*. Norwood, NJ: Ablex Publishing Corporation, 1986.

Morehead, J., *Introduction to United States public documents*. 3rd ed. Littleton, Col.: Libraries Unlimited Inc., 1983.

Sullivan, C. D., *Standards and standardization: basic principles and applications*. New York: Marcel Dekker Inc., 1983.

Williams, J. E., *A manager's guide to patents, trade marks and copyright*. London: Kogan Page, 1986.

10

Maps, Atlases and Gazetteers

Susan V. Howard

Mapmaking has a long history, dating back to the pre-historic era, when materials such as rocks, wood and clay tablets were used to create depictions of the known environment; Bagrow dates the earliest extant Babylonian map at *c.* 3800 B.C. and maps were also produced in ancient China, Egypt, Greece and Rome.[1] Progress in cartography was sporadic until the great advances which were made in Europe during the Renaissance. Geographical discoveries and technological innovations enabled more accurate maps to be drawn, and the development of printing led to their dissemination to a wider audience. Until the eighteenth century mapmaking was principally a private concern, but a need for accurate, up-to-date maps of large areas stimulated the establishment of national surveys. Early maps were usually topographic and were commissioned for a variety of practical purposes, including land-ownership claims, trade routes, military campaigns and colonial expansion; thematic mapping did not develop on a large scale until the nineteenth century.

Today cartography is firmly established on a scientific basis and maps are produced both by national survey organizations and by commercial publishers using derived data. Specialist institutes and private companies also produce maps. The traditional map was a two-dimensional representation of all or part of the earth's surface or substrata on a sheet of paper; maps are now available in other media, such as on microform or magnetic tape, although the vast majority of map production is still on hard copy.

Maps do, of course, play an important role in the study of geography, but they are also an essential tool in everyday life and as such have a place in the collections of all types of library, where they will be used to answer a wide range of enquiries, from complex academic and planning problems to the simple request for the best route from A to B.

Selection will depend upon the perceived and expressed needs of the users of a particular library. This chapter seeks to illustrate the various types of map available in both sheet and atlas form; also included is a consideration of gazetteers, which are often used in conjunction with maps. Representative examples only can be given: for fuller listings, specialist bibliographies and standard works such as Walford's *Guide to reference material* should be consulted. The librarian will also need to make use of other works for guidance on the storage, acquisition, cataloguing and classification of maps; Nichols has written one such guide.[2]

SELECTION

Present-day production of maps and atlases is enormous, thus presenting the librarian with a major problem in the selection of current material. No single guide can be claimed to be entirely satisfactory and a number of sources will need to be consulted.

GEOKATALOG. Stuttgart: Geocenter Internationales Landkartenhaus. Vol. 1 1972 – ; Vol. 2 1976 – .

This is the sales catalogue of Europe's largest map supplier and is the most comprehensive source available for international mapping. The first volume is an annual publication, listing maps, atlases and guidebooks which are mainly of use for recreational and tourist purposes. The loose-leaf second volume is a continuous publication and includes official cartographic publications, arranged by countries. Index sheets for map series are included. The entries are in German, but English translations of the abbreviations used are given and there are notes for use in English. Volume 2 is regularly updated by *Geokartenbrief*.

A less comprehensive, but more accessible work is:

Parry, R. B. and Perkins, C. R. (eds.), WORLD MAPPING TODAY. London: Butterworths, 1987.

It is to be hoped that revised editions of this extremely useful book will be published on a regular basis. Arranged alphabetically by country within continents, it lists the principal maps, atlases and gazetteers which were available at the time of publication. Introductory essays give an overview of mapping in each country and it includes key maps for map series and addresses of the main national and commercial map producers.

Catalogues and accessions lists of major map collections are another useful source of information, both for current and retrospective acquisition.

British Library. CATALOGUE OF PRINTED MAPS, CHARTS AND PLANS. 15 vols. London: British Museum, 1967. TEN-YEAR SUPPLE-MENT, 1965 – 74. 1978.

This catalogue contains entries for the maps, atlases, globes and related materials held in one of the world's largest cartographic collections. Items are listed under the names of specific places, areas and geographical features. For more current acquisitions, consult:

BRITISH LIBRARY CARTOGRAPHIC MATERIALS FILE: CURRENT ACCESSIONS 1975 – . London: British Library, 1975 – .

This microfiche catalogue, which is updated monthly, is divided into three sequences: geographical names; names/titles; subjects. As well as listing current map accessions, it also includes entries for 160 remote-sensing and digital databases located throughout the United Kingdom.

It is perhaps worth mentioning here that in 1989 the British Library began the compilation of a machine-readable catalogue of its entire atlas collection.

American Geographical Society, INDEX TO MAPS IN BOOKS AND PERIODICALS. 10 vols. Boston, Mass.: G. K. Hall, 1967. FIRST SUPPLEMENT, 1971; SECOND SUPPLEMENT, 1976; THIRD SUPPLEMENT, 1987.

These volumes are arranged alphabetically by geographical area and subject and give full bibliographic details of the source of the maps. G. K. Hall have also published the *Research catalogue of the American Geographical Society* (Boston, Mass., 1962; *Supplements* 1972, 1974 and 1978), which in part acts as a cumulation of:

American Geographical Society, CURRENT GEOGRAPHICAL PUBLICATIONS. Boston, Mass.: AGS, 1938 – .

Issued ten times a year, this periodical covers all accessions to the library and is divided into four sections: Topical; Regional; Maps; Selected books. The maps section is arranged regionally, according to the AGS map classification scheme.

Bodleian Library, Map Section, SELECTED MAP AND BOOK ACCESSIONS. Oxford: Bodleian Library, 1958 – .

This monthly listing from a legal-deposit library arranges entries by countries within continents.

The review sections of cartographic and geographical journals provide critical descriptions of new material. Examples include the *Cartographic journal* (Cambridge: British Cartographic Society, 1964 –); *SUC bulletin* (Reading: Society of University Cartographers, 1965 –); *Geographical journal* (London: Royal Geographical Society, 1893 –) which includes a *Cartographic survey* in its review section.

A number of national bibliographies include sheet maps, as well as atlases and gazetteers, and the catalogues of both official and commercial map publishers should be scanned.

GENERAL MAPS

Maps can be divided into two major groups: thematic maps, which will be discussed later in this chapter, and general topographic maps. Topographic maps are representations of the land surface, including both natural and man-made features. They are produced at a variety of scales but are not usually smaller than 1:100,000. These maps are used for a number of recreational, educational and business purposes, and as such will form the basis of any map collection.

In many countries, these general topographic maps are produced from original data by national survey organizations. In Western Europe, a number of these had their origins in the late eighteenth century, when there was a need for accurate mapping for military purposes. In Britain, the Ordnance Survey was first established in 1791 as the Trigonometrical Survey, and produced its first one-inch map in 1801. After various editions and revisions, the Ordnance Survey moved over to metric maps in 1974. A detailed history has been compiled by Seymour.[3]

The maps published by the Ordnance Survey are listed in its annual *Map catalogue*; this is updated monthly by the *Publication report*. Indexes are available for all series and should be made accessible to library users for identification of the required sheets. The map series produced are listed below:

Pathfinder Scale 1:25,000. These maps, which include public rights of way for England and Wales and delineate field boundaries, are suitable for walking, planning and educational purposes.

Outdoor leisure Scale 1:25,000. These maps are based on the *Pathfinder* series and cover 31 popular recreation areas, such as the Lake District and the New Forest. In addition to the topographic detail of the *Pathfinder* series, they also include tourist information, such as camp sites and picnic areas.

Landranger Scale 1:50,000. These 204 sheets, which replaced the one-inch series, are the Ordnance Survey's best-known publication. They include tourist information and contours at 10m intervals and are suitable for both walking and motoring.

Tourist Scale 1:63,360. This series consists of 11 sheets covering tourist areas, including several National Parks. Hill-shading is used.

Routemaster Scale 1:250,000. Nine sheets cover the country. Tourist information and road distances are included. They are

suitable for touring and business and are regularly updated.
Routeplanner   Scale 1:625,000. This covers Great Britain on one
sheet, printed on both sides, with inset maps of scenic areas,
motorway junctions and major urban areas. It is updated
annually, and has been available as a digital map since 1986.

The *Pathfinder*, *Landranger*, *Routemaster* and *Routeplanner* series are
all published in outline or colour editions and are available as
folded maps or flat sheets suitable for wall mounting.

The Ordnance Survey also publishes larger-scale maps which
are of use to planners and others requiring greater detail. These
are:

Nationwide large-scale maps   Scale 1:10,000. These are the largest-
scale maps to cover the whole country. Contours are given at 10m
intervals in mountainous areas, and 5m intervals elsewhere.
Urban-area large-scale maps   Scale 1:1,250. There are over 50,000
maps at this scale, which is the largest scale published by the
Ordnance Survey. This series covers all the major urban areas
of Great Britain in considerable detail.
Rural-area large-scale maps   Scale 1:2,500. These maps cover all
of Britain, apart from urban, mountainous and moorland areas.

The 1:1,250 and 1:2,500 maps are available on hard copy, on
magnetic tape and on microfilm. Updating services are available.
Survey information on and from microfilm (SIM) provides copies of
published maps; more up-to-date information is available from
the *Supply of updated but unpublished survey information* (SUSI) service.
Both services are available from Ordnance Survey agents; a list
of these agents can be obtained from the Ordnance Survey. The
digital database is still being created and it is hoped that the whole
of the United Kingdom will be covered by 2015.

The map series produced by the Ordnance Survey have been
described in some detail, since they will be of greatest use in most
British libraries. However, most national survey organizations
in Europe publish map series at scales of 1:25,000, 1:50,000 and
1:100,000, as well as larger-scale maps for more specialist use.
Cartobibliographies listed at the beginning of this chapter include

addresses for these organizations, from which current catalogues can be obtained. Examples of other European national survey organizations include:

France: *Institut Geographique National.*
Italy: *Instituto Geografico Militare.*
Switzerland: *Eidgenössische Landestopographie.*

In the Federal Republic of **Germany**, the situation is different: maps are produced within each Länd by the individual land-survey administrations.

In the **United States**, the principal mapping agency is the United States Geological Survey, which produces geological and resource maps as well as being responsible for topographic mapping. Most of the United States has now been covered by a 1:24,000 series, which will eventually include 53,838 sheets. Details of the maps produced can be found in *New publications of the US Geological Survey*, a monthly publication with annual cumulations. A comprehensive work detailing the mapping of America is M. M. Thompson's *Maps for America* (Washington: US Geological Survey, 1981).

Guides to the use of maps include a series of map-reading books produced by the Ordnance Survey and also J. B. Harley's *Ordnance Survey maps: a descriptive manual* (Southampton: Ordnance Survey, 1975).

THEMATIC MAPS

Thematic maps are representations of a particular feature or spatial distribution. Data can be derived from physical surveys, as in the case of geological and land-use maps, or from statistical data, used in the production of socio-economic maps.

Geological

Most of Europe had been covered by detailed geological maps by the late nineteenth century.[4] As is the case with topographic maps, most geological series are produced by national survey organizations.

In Great Britain, the body now responsible for geological mapping is the British Geological Survey; most maps are published by the Ordnance Survey, and are obtainable from either organizations. The basic map series is:

GEOLOGICAL SURVEY OF GREAT BRITAIN. Scale: 1:50,000.

This series is replacing the old one-inch series, some of which is still available. The maps are published in three editions: drift, solid and combined. The maps have accompanying monographs known as the *1:50,000 sheet memoirs*, which in most cases are entitled *Geology of the country around (place-name)*. Other series also exist, including maps of the United Kingdom and its continental shelf at a scale of 1:250,000 in three editions: solid geology, seabed sediments and quaternary. Details of the maps available are listed in the British Geological Survey's *Geological report*; the memoirs and other publications can be located in *HMSO sectional list 45*.

Other geological survey organizations include:

France: Bureau de Recherches Géologiques et Minières. *Cartes géologiques de la France*. Basic series: 1:50,000.
Italy: Servizio Geologico d'Italia. *Carta geologica d'Italia*. Basic series: 1:50,000.
United States: United States Geological Survey. *Geologic quadrangle maps*. Scale 1:24,000.
In the Federal Republic of **Germany**, large-scale maps are produced by the Länder at scales of 1:25,000, 1:50,000 and 1:100,000.

Land-use maps

Land-use maps employ a number of categories to represent the use of the earth's surface at a given time. Land-use surveys have been carried out, or are in the process of being carried out, in much of the world, following the establishment of the World Land-Use Survey Commission by the International Geographical Union in 1949.

In Great Britain, the first land-utilization survey was organized by Sir L. Dudley Stamp in the 1930s; the *Second land utilisation survey* (London: Second Land Utilisation Survey, 1961 –) was carried out under the direction of Dr A. Coleman.[5] The maps identify 70 categories of land use and are available at a scale of 1:25,000, the categories being overprinted in colour on the Ordnance Survey 1:25,000 series. Intended to show that the introduction of planning machinery had rectified the misuse of land identified in the first survey, these maps have instead proved that this aim has not been achieved.

In recent times, remote sensing has been an important tool in land-use surveys, one example of its use being the United States Geological Survey's land-use and classification maps, at a scale of 1:250,000.

Closely related to land-use surveys are soil surveys. The resultant maps classify soil types and also give some indication of their agricultural potential. In Great Britain, two organizations are responsible for soil surveys; examples of their work being:

SOIL MAP OF ENGLAND AND WALES. Harpenden: Soil Survey of England and Wales, 1983.
  This consists of six loose-leaf sheets at a scale of 1:250,000. *Regional bulletins* have been published to accompany each map sheet.

SOIL AND LAND CAPABILITY MAP OF SCOTLAND. Aberdeen: Macaulay Institute for Soil Research, 1982.
  There are seven sheets at a scale of 1:250,000, each with an accompanying text.

Other soil-map publishers include:

Italy: Touring Club Italiano.
France: Service d'Études des Sols et de la Carte Pedalogique de France.
United States: Soil Conservation Service.
The Länder are responsible for soil mapping in the Federal Republic of Germany.

Charts

Traditionally, the term 'chart' has been used to describe maps used by navigators: the earliest extant chart dates from *c*. 1300. Marine charts show coastlines, water depths, rocks, channels and other features of importance to sea traffic. They are compiled by a number of national hydrographic survey organizations and oceanographic research establishments. The Admiralty Hydrographic Department has produced charts covering the whole world, at a wide variety of scales. These fall into three categories: small-scale charts of large areas, such as the Atlantic Ocean; larger-scale charts of coastal areas; detailed charts of harbours and estuaries. Details can be found in the annual *Catalogue of Admiralty charts*.

More recently, aeronautical charts have been produced, which show surface-relief features as a guide to navigation. World aeronautical charts are published by the United States Defense Mapping Agency at scales ranging from the *Tactical pilotage chart* series at 1:500,000 to the *Jet navigation chart* series at 1:2M.

Road maps

Road maps are intended for the purposes of recreational and business motoring. Whilst people tend to buy such maps rather than consult them in libraries, they may have a place in a library collection for the purpose of study, or as a guide to availability for library users. It is important that the collection be kept up-to-date, in view of the number of bypasses and motorway extensions that are continually under construction.

In many countries, the principal publishers of road maps are commercial organizations and it is advisable to buy maps produced by the country itself, for they are likely to be more accurate and up-to-date. Some examples are:

Italy: *Grande carta stradale d'Italia* series published by the Touring Club Italiano. Scale: 1:200,000; Italy in covered in 15 sheets. Federal Republic of **Germany: Die general Karte** series published by Mair. Scale: 1:200,000; 26 sheets.

France: *Cartes IGN* published by the Institut Geographique National. Scale: 1:100,000; 72 sheets.
Great Britain: *National and leisure map* series published by Bartholomew. Scale: 1:100,000; coverage of tourist areas only.

Other publishers for Europe include the Automobile Association, RAC Publications and Michelin. The Ordnance Survey publishes road maps of Britain, including motorway maps for the M25 and London, and for Manchester, Sheffield, Leeds and York at a scale of 1:126,720.

ATLASES

Traditionally, atlases could be defined as collections of maps of uniform dimensions bound together in a single volume or volumes. Today, many are published serially in a loose-leaf format and electronic atlases are a recent innovation.

Whilst more specialized atlases will be required for the study of geography and history, any public library will need a selection of world atlases for general reference use.

The basic contents of an atlas are of course the maps and an index for the location of places, but other features will also be found. The amount of accompanying text will vary from a brief introduction to lengthy essays; in some cases, the text:map ratio is such that it is doubtful that the work should be called an atlas at all. On the whole, the essays on topics such as earth sciences and the statistical data found in many general atlases will be little used; for these readers will refer instead to standard reference works. In the case of historical atlases, substantial amounts of text may be necessary to explain properly what is depicted in the maps.

In the selection of atlases, several points need to be borne in mind; Sheehy has given a useful list.[6] It is important that the information presented is up-to-date: an atlas containing Rutland or Rhodesia may have some historical interest, but will not be suitable for answering quick-reference enquiries. Clarity of colour and typography, and comparability of scale are also important.

General reference atlases

The general reference atlas, containing topographic coverage of the whole world and often also containing a thematic section, is the most familiar form of atlas.

TIMES ATLAS OF THE WORLD: Comprehensive ed. 7th ed. London: Times Books, 1985. Reprinted with revisions 1988.

This is undoubtedly the major general-reference atlas and has gone through a number of revisions since it was first published in 1967. This edition contains 123 plates of maps at a variety of scales. Continental scales range from 1:12.9M for Europe to 1:15M for the USSR and Australasia. Larger scales are used for individual countries and regions: the London area is mapped at 1:100,000, China at 1:5M. A variety of projections are used and the mapping has good clarity. The index contains 210,000 names, spelt according to the principles of the British Permanent Committee on Geographical Names. In many cases, English conventional names have been added. This edition includes a large number of name changes.

NEW INTERNATIONAL ATLAS. Rev. ed. Chicago: Rand McNally, 1986.

This is another good general atlas, published as a cooperative venture, with text in English, French, German and Portuguese to underline its international approach. Scales tend to be smaller than in the *Times atlas*, but they do allow for comparative study: continents are at 1:24M, major regions at 1:12M, smaller areas at 1:6M and 1:3M, key areas 1:1M, and urban areas, mainly European and North American at 1:300,000. The mapping is clear, and there is a thematic section. The index lists over 160,000 place-names.

There are a number of second-tier atlases which are useful for quick-reference enquiries. The *Times atlas* is available in a concise edition and *The Penguin atlas of the world* (Rev. ed. London: Viking, 1987) uses the mapping from the Rand McNally atlas listed above. John Bartholomew and George Philip publish a range of atlases for use at a variety of levels. One good example is:

PHILIPS GREAT WORLD ATLAS. London: George Philip, 1987.

This contains clear, up-to-date information, using scales ranging from 1:80M for world maps to 1:1M for the Netherlands, Luxembourg and Belgium. Scales used vary between continents, but are comparable within continents. The index has over 56,000 entries and there is a thematic section.

Mention should also be made of the various thematic atlases which are available. Some are global in scale, whilst others deal with a particular topic in a country or region. For example:

TIMES ATLAS AND ENCYCLOPAEDIA OF THE SEA. 2nd ed. London: Times Books, 1989.

A revised edition of the 1983 *Atlas of the oceans*, this covers all aspects of the ocean environment, from physical and biological information to merchant shipping and naval warfare. There are over 600 maps and the text is illustrated with numerous diagrams.

At a more detailed and local scale is the *Atlas of the seas around the British Isles* (Lowestoft: Ministry of Agriculture, Fisheries and Food, 1981), a ring-bound volume with 73 charts.

WORLD ATLAS OF AGRICULTURE. Novara: Istituto Geografico de Agostini, 1969 – 76.

This loose-leaf atlas which plots land use throughout the world is accompanied by four volumes of text: Europe, USSR, Asia Minor; South and East Asia, Oceania; the Americas; Africa.

National atlases

National atlases are collections of topographic and thematic maps presenting an overview of a particular country, often using data derived from official censuses. The earliest were produced during the late nineteenth century and several European countries had national atlases by the Second World War. Production in the rest of the world was stimulated by the establishment of the Commission on National Atlases by the International Geographical Union in 1964. Several have since gone out-of-print without the intended revisions being made. However, a number of countries have published new and revised national atlases: Stams has listed those published up to 1978,[7] and other carto-bibliographies can be used to find more recent examples. National atlases are generally published with the aid of government sponsorship, necessitated by the level of funding required to accumulate up-to-date, detailed information. In recent years, computer technology has been used in their production, although most are still published in the traditional format.

NATIONAL ATLAS OF CANADA. 5th ed. Ottawa: Energy, Mines Resources Canada, 1985 – .

The first edition of the *National atlas of Canada* was published in 1906; this latest edition is being prepared digitally, with the intention of creating a Digital National Atlas Database giving public access to the research material. It is a serial production of loose-leaf sheets, which will eventually give a comprehensive coverage of 44 subject areas or realms of information, including topography, climatology, ecology, agriculture, tourism and industry. Most of the maps published so far are on a scale of 1:7.5M, with a good use of colour and very clear cartography. New editions and revisions will be published when the necessary data are available; consequently the production of a finite set of maps is not envisaged.

ATLAS DER SCHWEIZ. 2nd ed. Wabern: Bundesamt für Landestopographie, 1981 – .

The trilingual national atlas of Switzerland is a serial loose-leaf publication, with maps at a scale of 1:500,000 and accompanying text.

No comparable national atlas exists for Great Britain. The production of such an atlas has been under discussion for some time; a committee to consider the project was set up in 1938 by the British Association for the Advancement of Science.[8] Plans for a national atlas continued for several years and in 1975 the first sheets of the Department of the Environment's *Atlas of the environment* were published. Based on the 1971 census at a scale of 1:1.7M these sheets could be regarded as the beginning of a national atlas, but the project was abandoned in 1979. A less ambitious publication is:

ORDNANCE SURVEY NATIONAL ATLAS OF GREAT BRITAIN. Southampton and London: Ordnance Survey and Country Life Books, 1986.

The 64 topographic maps are clearly presented at a scale of 1:250,000. The thematic coverage, highlighting 30 topics, is fairly superficial, and is accompanied by a written text. The index contains 33,000 place-names.

Although not a national atlas in the traditional sense, the *Domesday project* can be used to fulfil the functions of one.[9] This collaborative venture, led by the BBC, was launched in 1986 and was designed to reflect the state of Britain at that time. With the use of a microcomputer, the information can be retrieved from an interactive video system consisting of two discs: the National Disk and the Community Disk. These disks contain 30 million words, 54,000 photographs, 21,000 files of spatial data which can be used to create coloured thematic maps, an hour of moving film and 24,000 maps, including complete Ordnance Survey coverage of the United Kingdom at a scale of 1:50,000.

Road atlases

A wide variety of road atlases is published, mainly by commercial organizations. The same general points apply here as were outlined for road maps. Many road atlases are revised annually. MICHELIN ROAD ATLAS OF EUROPE. London: Hamlyn, 1988.

This road atlas covers both Western and Eastern Europe, at scales intended to reflect the density of the road network: Western Europe is mapped at 1:1M, Scandinavia at 1:1.5M and Eastern Europe at 1.3M. All motorways and major roads are included, as well as many minor roads, space permitting. Tourist information and holiday routes are included and there are 70 maps of major towns. A useful section gives information on the driving regulations of the European countries.

ORDNANCE SURVEY MOTORING ATLAS OF GREAT BRITAIN. 7th ed. Southampton and London: Ordnance Survey and Temple Press, 1989.

This annually updated atlas covers Great Britain at a scale of 1:190,080 and includes 45 town plans.

Collins publish a number of road atlases, including the English edition of the Rand McNally atlas of the USA, Canada and Mexico, and road atlases of France and Italy, produced in association with the Institut Geographique National and Istituto Geografico de Agostini respectively.

Street atlases are available for closer detail, including a series covering south-east England published by the Ordnance Survey and G. Philip.

Historical atlases

Historical atlases are contemporary mappings of historical data and as such are dependent on the available research for their accuracy and completeness of coverage. Some are thematic in approach; Times Books, for example, have produced atlases of the Bible and of the Second World War. Others seek to present the historical development of the world, or of a particular country or administrative unit. The most comprehensive example on a global scale is:

Barraclough, G. and Stone, N. (eds.), TIMES ATLAS OF WORLD HISTORY. 3rd ed. London: Times Books, 1989.

This atlas is worldwide in concept and seeks to depict broad movements, such as the spread of religions and European colonial expansion, rather than to compete with national historical atlases. It provides a good overview of world history from the origins of man to the 1980s and, unlike many older world historical atlases, is not strongly Eurocentric in its coverage. The 500 maps use a variety of projections and display the clarity of mapping and good use of colour associated with other Times Books publications. A glossary gives information about particular peoples and events, and there is an extensive index.

Several national historical atlases exist. An outstanding example is:

Harris, R. Cole (ed.), HISTORICAL ATLAS OF CANADA. Vol. 1: FROM THE BEGINNINGS TO 1800. Toronto: University Press, 1987.

Two more volumes, covering the nineteenth and twentieth centuries, are in preparation. This atlas begins with the pre-history of Canada, and then in five further sections considers the impact of European exploration, trade and settlement. In each section, a concise, clearly written introduction is followed by a series of double-page map spreads. This authoritative and attractively presented volume also includes a lengthy bibliography.

HISTORICAL ATLAS OF THE UNITED STATES. Washington: National Geographic Society, 1988.

This is another attractively produced work, published in the Society's centennial year. It is divided into five thematic sections, covering people, boundaries, economy, transportation and settlements, and the subjects are treated historically within each section. There are 380 maps and the text is lavishly illustrated with photographs and reprints of historic maps. A wide range of topics is included, covering the period 1400 to 1988.

For several years, the University of Oklahoma Press has been publishing a fine series of state historical atlases. These are all similar in format, and a recent example is:

Scott, J. W. and De Lorme, R. L., HISTORICAL ATLAS OF WASH-INGTON. Norman: University of Oklahoma Press, 1988.

This atlas traces the history of the state of Washington from prehistoric times to the twentieth century. Each of the 77 maps, mostly drawn at the same scale, is faced by a page of explanatory text. The atlas is divided into 15 thematic sections, covering topics such as Indian history, the fur trade, population growth and economic development. In most cases, the thematic information is superimposed on a relief-shaded map.

In contrast, little attention has been given to the production of historical atlases of English countries. One of the rare examples is:

Dymond, D. and Martin E., AN HISTORICAL ATLAS OF SUFFOLK. Ipswich: Suffolk County Council Planning Department and Suffolk Institute of Archaeology and History, 1988.

This atlas, which presents a wealth of information for the local historian, plots the history of Suffolk since 1550 in 62 distribution maps. The accompanying text expands on such topics as agriculture, industry and urban growth.

Good examples of historical atlases of towns are:

Lobel, M. D. (ed.), HISTORICAL TOWNS. Vol. 1. London and Oxford: Lovell Johns-Cook, Hammond and Kell, 1969; Vol. 2. London: Scholar Press, 1975; LONDON FROM PREHISTORIC TIMES TO c1520. Oxford: Oxford University Press, 1989.

The first two volumes trace the history and development of 12 British towns, including Glasgow, Hereford and Cambridge. For each town, an essay on its development is followed by a series of maps tracing the history from medieval times to *c*.1800. The volume on London covers an earlier period.

These volumes were produced as part of an international series, suggested by the International Commission for the Study of the History of Towns.

EARLY AND LOCAL MAPS

Early and local maps are the subject of considerable interest; they can be regarded as investments, as works of art and as tools for historical research. As representations of the earth's surface, they are inevitably less accurate than contemporary publications, reflecting as they do both the geographical knowledge and cartographic techniques of the time in which they were created; it is also important to bear in mind the purpose for which the maps were made, since there may well exist bias in the information which is portrayed.

Many national and university libraries have built up outstanding collections of early maps and there are several catalogues and bibliographies which can be consulted for details. It should be noted that before the nineteenth century, the majority of printed maps appeared in atlases, rather than as individual sheets.

Shirley, R. W., THE MAPPING OF THE WORLD: EARLY PRINTED WORLD MAPS 1472 – 1700. London: Holland Press, 1983.

During the period 1472 – 1700, approximately 650 maps of the **world** are known to have been printed. This bibliography is arranged chronologically with an index of map-makers. The maps, many of which are illustrated, are described, and locations are given for those held in the British Library, the Library of Congress and the Bibliothèque Nationale; other locations are given for very rare maps only.

Useful general lists include the published catalogue of the Map Library of the British Library, the Library of Congress's *List of geographical atlases* (8 vols. Washington: Library of Congress, 1909 – 74) and the National Maritime Museum's *Catalogue of the Library, Vol. 3: Atlases and cartography* (2 vols. London: HMSO, 1971).

Listings also exist at the national level. The centre of map production from the late sixteenth century was the **Netherlands** and a very fine bibliography exists:

Koeman, I. C., ATLANTES NEERLANDICI. 6 vols. Amsterdam: Theatrum Orbis Terrarum, 1967 – 85.

This is a bibliography of atlases and pilot books published in the Netherlands. The first five volumes cover the period up to 1880, and Volume 6 is a supplement covering the period 1880 – 1940. Well over 1000 atlases are described, listed alphabetically by map-maker and publisher, with indexes by year of publication, author, engravers, and by geographical names.

French maps can be located in:

Pastoreau, M., LES ATLAS FRANCAIS XVI – XVII SIECLES. Paris: Bibliothèque Nationale, 1984.

This contains descriptions and locations of the atlases produced in France from 1500 to 1700, using present-day France as the boundary for inclusion. It is arranged alphabetically by cartographer, providing a brief biography for each. It has a geographical index and list of locations.

English cartography dates from the thirteenth century, with the maps of Matthew Paris. Little development occurred until the mid-sixteenth century, when Christopher Saxton published the first complete set of county maps between 1574 and 1579. Over the next three centuries, other county maps appeared, which can be traced in the following bibliographies:

Skelton, R. A., COUNTY ATLASES OF THE BRITISH ISLES, 1579–1850. Vol. 1. Folkestone: Dawson, 1978 (reprint).

Hodson, D., COUNTY ATLASES OF THE BRITISH ISLES PUBLISHED AFTER 1703. 2 vols. Tewin: Tewin Press, 1984–9.

Chubb, T., THE PRINTED MAPS IN THE ATLASES OF GREAT BRITAIN AND IRELAND 1579–1870. Folkestone: Dawson, 1974 (reprint).

Skelton's work was intended as a multi-volume description of county maps from Saxton to the Ordnance Survey. The first volume covers the period up to 1703; Hudson carried on the work after Skelton's death and his two volumes cover 1704–63. Chubb's work can be used to cover the later period. Skelton's descriptive bibliography follows a strictly chronological approach with cross-referencing to other editions; Hodson, like Chubb, brings all editions of an atlas together within a basically chronological format. These volumes provide an extensive bibliography of British atlases.

A number of **county** cartobibliographies have been produced. One of the most recent is:

Kingsley, D., PRINTED MAPS OF SUSSEX 1575–1900. Lewes: Sussex Record Society, 1982.

This gives descriptive entries for 200 maps in a chronological arrangement. In an appendix, it lists the 18 comprehensive county cartobibliographies which were published between 1901 and 1977.

Early **local** maps were generally made for practical purposes, the most common example being estate maps which date from the sixteenth century. About 30,000 are extant, and they display great differences in scale, detail and accuracy. Other types of local map include enclosure maps, tithe maps and town plans. Repositories of such maps include the British Library, Public Record Office, National Library of Wales and the Scottish Record Office: their catalogues should be consulted. A good general location guide is Watt's *Directory of UK map collections* (2nd ed. London: McCarta, 1985).

Other countries hold local maps in their national libraries, and they will be listed in the appropriate catalogues.

Early Ordnance Survey maps have been reprinted. David and Charles have published individual sheets, and the old series is being published in book form:

Margary, H., THE OLD SERIES ORDNANCE SURVEY MAPS OF ENGLAND AND WALES. 10 vols. Lympne Castle: Harry Margary, 1975 – .

The intention is to produce a complete set of the early versions of the maps in book form; by 1987, five volumes had been published. Each volume contains an essay on the mapping of the particular area, and *c.* 12 original map sheets.

GAZETTEERS

A gazetteer is an alphabetical list of place-names, including both natural and man-made features. The entries in a gazetteer give some reference to the locations of the features and in many cases will also be annotated with additional information. Gazetteers are used for two main purposes: locating places and checking the approved names of places.

Gazetteers are published both by national organizations and by commercial firms. They range in scale from world gazetteers to those of a national or local nature; in general, the smaller the scale, the more extensive the coverage will be. Gazetteers published between 1945 and 1982 will be found in Emil Meynen's *Gazetteers and glossaries of geographical names* (Wiesbaden: Steiner, 1984). This has a section on world and continental gazetteers, and is thereafter arranged nationally. Current geographical bibliographies will provide more recent examples.

The standardization of geographical names has long been a problem. In 1960 the United Nations established a Group of Experts on Geographical Names and in 1967 the UN recommended the creation of standard gazetteers, but so far few countries have produced them. Two other organizations concerned with the standardization of names are the United States Board on Geographical Names and the British Permanent Committee on Geographical Names for Official Use, which have produced a large number of gazetteers for foreign countries.

The indexes to atlases fit the basic definition of a gazetteer and can be used as such. One separately published gazetteer derived from an atlas is:

THE TIMES INDEX-GAZETTEER OF THE WORLD. London: *The Times*, 1965.

No update exists for this gazetteer, which is based on the mid-century edition of the *Times atlas*. It has 345,000 entries, making it the largest of the world gazetteers. It does not include descriptive annotations, but gives locations by means of latitudinal and longitudinal coordinates, with grid references to those places which are also in the atlas. Although many of the place-names for developing countries will be out-of-date, this gazetteer still has a useful function.

Another well-known large-scale gazetteer which has not been updated is L. E. Seltzer (ed.), *Columbia-Lippincott gazetteer of the world* (New York: Columbia University Press, 1962). Again, its use is limited by the lack of current information, but with 130,000 entries it is still of some value. More up-to-date world gazetteers include:

WEBSTER'S NEW GEOGRAPHICAL DICTIONARY. Revised ed. Springfield, Mass.: Merriam, 1986.

Despite its title, this is in fact a gazetteer. It contains about 50,000 entries, with a USA bias; entries include a guide to pronunciation.

Munro, D. (ed.), CHAMBERS WORLD GAZETTEER. 5th ed. Cambridge: Chambers, 1988.

Much smaller than the gazetteers mentioned above, with 20,000 entries, this work does give up-to-date statistical information as well as brief descriptions.

Examples at a national and continental level include:

ORDNANCE SURVEY GAZETTEER OF GREAT BRITAIN. 2nd ed. London: MacMillan, 1989.

As a locational aid, this is outstanding: all of the names shown on the 1:50,000 *Landranger* series are listed. Over 250,000 places are given with their grid references, sheet number and a feature code. This is also available on microfiche.

Mason, O. (comp.), BARTHOLOMEW GAZETTEER OF PLACES IN BRITAIN. 2nd ed. Edinburgh: Bartholomew and Son, 1986.

With its 40,000 entries, this gazetteer cannot compete with the gazetteer mentioned above for extent of coverage, but it does give brief descriptions of the places included, with a locational reference to the 120 pages of maps. For quick-reference enquiries, it is a valuable tool.

In Canada, a series of gazetteers of the provinces and territories have been published in hard copy and on microfiche using the automated database. One example is:

GAZETTEER OF CANADA: BRITISH COLUMBIA. 3rd ed. Ottawa: Energy, Mines and Resources Canada, 1985.

Over 42,000 entries include all the officially registered names of physical features, as well as a wide range of man-made features. References are given to a map section drawn at a scale of 1:50,000.

NATIONAL GAZETTEER OF THE UNITED STATES. Reston, Va: US Geological Survey, 1983 – .

This serial gazetteer, many volumes of which are available on microfiche or computer tape as well as in hard copy, is being published state by state.

MASTER NAMES FILE. Belconnen: NATMAP, 1989.

This is the Australian equivalent of the *Ordnance Survey gazetteer*. It is an annually updated microfiche listing of place-names from the 1:250,000 and 1:100,000 series produced by the Division of National Mapping.

Kirchherr, E. C., PLACE-NAMES OF AFRICA 1935 – 1986. Metuchen, NJ and London: Scarecrow Press, 1987.

This is a useful volume giving all the names by which the principal African states have been known between 1935 and 1986.

Older gazetteers should be selectively retained for information on places which no longer exist, or which have changed their names, since they will be useful for the purposes of historical research. One nineteenth-century work which is still consulted for its use to local historians is S. A. Lewis' *Topographical dictionary of England* (7th ed. 4 vols. London: Lewis, 1848 – 9); this gives fairly detailed descriptions for a large selection of places. Some historical gazetteers have been published, such as:

Darby, H. C. and Versey, C. R., DOMESDAY GAZETTEER. Cambridge: Cambridge University Press, 1975.

This gives Domesday place-names, variant spellings and modern equivalents for over 13,000 places which are mentioned in the Domesday Book, arranged by county.

Ellis, H. J. and Brickley, F. B. (eds.), INDEX TO THE CHARTERS AND ROLLS IN THE DEPARTMENT OF MANUSCRIPTS, BRITISH MUSEUM. 2 vols. London: British Museum, 1900 – 12.

This lists the place-names and religious houses, with their modern equivalents, which occur in manuscripts acquired up to 1900.

The English Place-Name Society was founded in 1923 to survey English place-names and issue annual volumes, county by county; coverage is not yet complete. Names are arranged by civil parishes within hundreds, with an alphabetical index. Street and field names are included as well as settlements, and non-current place-names are also listed. One recent example is:

Cameron, K., THE PLACE NAMES OF LINCOLNSHIRE, PART 1.
Nottingham: English Place-Name Society, 1985.
This volume covers the County of the City of Lincoln.

Maps, atlases and gazetteers are all sources of information which may be used singly, together, or in conjunction with other works, not necessarily of a geographical nature. For this reason, it is not appropriate to house maps separately from other sources of information. The precise contents of any collection must obviously be attuned to local needs, and whilst collections should be constantly updated to provide accurate, current information, older material should not automatically be discarded, because it may be of relevance to historical enquiries.

REFERENCES AND CITATIONS

1 Bagrow, L., *History of cartography*. Revised and enlarged by R. A. Skelton. 2nd ed. Chicago: Precedent Publishing, 1985, 31.
2 Nichols, H., *Map librarianship*. 2nd ed. London: Bingley, 1982.
3 Seymour, W. A. (ed.), *A history of the Ordnance Survey*. Folkestone: Dawson, 1980.
4 Ireland, H. A., 'History of the development of geologic maps', *Bulletin of the Geological Society of America*, **54**, 1943, 1227 – 80.
5 Coleman, A. and Balchin, W. G. V., 'Land-use maps', *Cartographic journal*, **16** (2), 1979, 97 – 103.
6 Sheehy, E. P., *Guide to reference books*. 10th ed. Chicago: American Library Association, 1986, 958.
7 Stams, W., *National and regional atlases*. Enschede: Sneldruk for the International Cartographic Association, 1985.
8 'Reports of research committees: a national atlas', *Advancement of science*, **1** (2), 1940, 361 – 8.
9 Rhind, D., 'The Domesday machine: a nationwide geographical information system', *Geographical journal*, **154** (1), 1988, 56 – 68.

SUGGESTIONS FOR FURTHER READING

Crone, G. R., *Maps and their makers*. 2nd ed. Folkestone: Dawson, 1978.
Harley, J. B. and Woodward, D. (eds.), *The history of cartography: vol. 1*, Chicago and London: University of Chicago Press, 1987.

This is the first volume of a projected six-part work, and covers prehistoric, ancient and medieval Europe and the Mediterranean.

Hindle, B. P., *Maps for local history*. London: Batsford, 1988.

A very readable volume describing the different types of maps and plans which are available.

Hodgkiss, A. G. and Tatham, A. F., *Keyguide to information sources in cartography*. London: Mansell, 1986.

A useful volume, this contains an extensive cartobibliography and the addresses of major map publishers.

Hodgkiss, A. G., *Understanding maps*. Folkestone: Dawson, 1981.

Smith, D., *Antique maps of the British Isles*. London: Batsford, 1982.

This volume contains descriptions of the different types of map available and gives guidance on conventional signs and the map trade.

Thrower, N. J. W., *Maps and man*. Englewood Cliffs, NJ: Prentice-Hall, 1972.

A history of cartography in relation to the development of civilization.

Transactions of the Institute of British Geographers, 11, 1986, 290 – 325.

A series of articles covering various aspects of the Domesday Project.

11

Local History

Chris E. Makepeace

T he growth of interest in local history over the last 30 years has been reflected in the number of local history libraries that have been established, in the use made of local material in libraries and record offices and by the rapid and sustained growth in the publishing of local history books by both local and national publishers. In fact, the name 'local history' is something of a misnomer as it involves the study of all aspects of the community and 'not merely a single class, industry, or section of it'.[1] Hence, the name 'local studies' is sometimes applied to the subject.

LOCAL STUDIES LIBRARIANSHIP

Local studies work can be one of the most complex parts of a library on account of the many different types of material which are used and which require detailed indexing and cataloguing to be fully exploited. There are several publications which examine the problems of local studies librarianship:

Carter, G. A., A. J. HOBBS' LOCAL HISTORY AND THE LIBRARY. 2nd ed. London: Deutsch, 1973.

Dewe, M. A. (ed.), MANUAL OF LOCAL STUDIES LIBRARIANSHIP. Aldershot: Gower, 1987.

Lynes, A., HOW TO ORGANISE A LOCAL COLLECTION. London: Grafton, 1974.

Nichols, H., LOCAL STUDIES LIBRARIANSHIP. London: Bingley, 1979.

Local history and the library, originally published in 1962, was revised in 1973 to take account of the rapid growth of interest in local history. Many of the problems Carter examines, such as the relationship between local studies collections and archives departments and record offices and the wide range of material used in local-history departments, still hold true today. The book includes sections on the use of local research material and photography as well as an example of a local classification scheme and an extensive bibliography.

Similar ground is covered in *The manual of local studies librarianship* but it takes account of developments which have taken place since 1973. Amongst the subjects examined are the acquisition of material, indexing, oral recording and visual materials. A second volume, in preparation, will examine specific types of material such as maps and minor publications, and their use in libraries, and should be an important contribution to local studies librarianship.

Lynes and Nichols also examine the problems of local studies librarianship, but concentrate on those associated with the development and running of such departments. Lynes includes chapters on types of material, their treatment and staffing, whereas Nichols examines these areas as part of more general chapters dealing with some of the different types of work which local studies librarians need to undertake to exploit their stock to the fullest advantage. Both authors have included useful bibliographies.

Comment and discussion on current problems in local studies librarianship as well as short articles on various aspects of the professional approach to the subject are to be found in the *Local studies librarian*[2] and *Locscot*.[3]

In addition to material on the area covered by the library, there

231

will also be a need to have access to books on national history so that research can be put in its correct historical context. An indication of some of these titles can be found in *Sources of local history*,[4] *Local history handlist*[5] and in the opening section of *A companion to local history research*.[6]

Local history for beginners

Those using local material sometimes require assistance when they are starting out on their researches. What tends to be confusing to those becoming involved in local research for the first time is the variety of both book and non-book material, such as maps, broadsheets and illustrations, that can be used as well as the wide range of both local and national sources, some of which will not be available locally. For those starting out on local history research two useful publications are:

Celoria, F., TEACH YOURSELF LOCAL HISTORY. London: English Universities Press, 1958.

Iredale, D., DISCOVERING LOCAL HISTORY. Princes Risborough: Shire Publications, 1977.

Both these books aim to introduce the subject to the interested person. Celoria's book is very wide-ranging and is one which can be used by both the beginner and someone with a little experience. Iredale, on the other hand, states that his book is intended for someone 'wanting to discover, though not necessarily to write, local history' (p. 3). Both authors draw attention to the type of material that can be consulted and make suggestions as to the way research projects can be developed.

The importance of consulting a wide range of both local and national sources was first put forward in:

Hoskins, W. G., LOCAL HISTORY IN ENGLAND. Rev. ed. London: Longman, 1988.

When this book was first published in 1959, it was regarded as an important step forward in the study of local history, as it drew attention to both local and national sources which local historians could use. Although not outlining the origins of the different sources, Hoskins illustrated their use with carefully chosen examples and included an extensive bibliography of general works which local historians might need to consult and, by implication, to which a local-history library should have access. Hoskins developed several of his themes in later publications like *Fieldwork in local history*.[7]

One of Hoskins' arguments was that fieldwork should be used in conjunction with traditional sources. Others who have argued along the same lines include:

Dunning, R., LOCAL HISTORY FOR BEGINNERS. Rev. ed. Chichester: Phillimore, 1980.

Ravensdale, J. R., HISTORY ON YOUR DOORSTEP. London: BBC, 1982.

Riden, P., LOCAL HISTORY: A HANDBOOK FOR BEGINNERS. London: Batsford, 1983.

These three books examine the sources that can be used to investigate a limited number of 'popular' subjects and suggest that as well as undertaking research in the library or record office, there is much to be gathered by going out and looking for evidence on-site. Dunning says he limited the number of sources he mentions, to assist 'the beginner who is looking for material near at hand . . . to give a fair coverage . . . and to demonstrate that an important part of local studies involves working out of doors' (p. xi). Riden, on the other hand, aims to provide 'a simple introduction to the study of local history . . . for part-time amateur enthusiasts with no previous experience of historical research' (p. 9). Ravensdale's book, published to accompany a television series, follows up points made in the programme in more detail, but not at a level to be off-putting for a beginner. All three books contain useful bibliographies of general background works on history and local history.

Sources which local historians might need to consult are examined in:

Campbell-Kease, J., A COMPANION TO LOCAL HISTORY RESEARCH. Sherborne: Alphabooks, 1989.

Rogers, A., APPROACHES TO LOCAL HISTORY. 2nd ed. London: Longman, 1977.

Stephens, W. B., SOURCES FOR ENGLISH LOCAL HISTORY. 2nd ed. Cambridge: Cambridge University Press, 1981.

Sources for English local history is not a general bibliographical guide, but 'an introduction to the detailed study of the general history of a region ... or local area' (p. 1). It includes an examination of national as well as local sources of printed and manuscript information for eight subject areas. However, little attention is paid to the use and importance of non-book material, except maps, which could result in important sources being overlooked.

Approaches to local history is an in-depth examination of the various sources which exist for mid-Victorian England and provides a framework within which research on the period can be undertaken. The sources referred to are not restricted to manuscripts and books, but include many examples of the use of non-book material such as broadsheets and illustrations. Although there is no bibliography, the chapter notes can be used to create a list of additional reading.

Campbell-Kease seeks to 'describe the principal material available for the study of local history, indicate where it may be found, and set it against the broader framework of national and regional events' (p. 11). The various sections examine national sources, as well as those for historic periods, particular subjects and related areas such as palaeography and archaeology. Campbell-Kease also includes a section on the writing of local history. Further advice on this subject is contained in:

Iredale, D., LOCAL HISTORY RESEARCH AND WRITING. Chichester: Phillimore, 1980.

Dymond, D., WRITING LOCAL HISTORY: A PRACTICAL GUIDE. London: Bedford Square Press, 1981.

Iredale and Dymond examine the question of writing a local-history book from different standpoints. Iredale looks at the research techniques and sources which may be used, whereas Dymond concentrates on the techniques of writing of a good book. There is also a useful section in Iredale which gives advice on working in libraries and record offices as well as a bibliography and a list of helpful addresses.

Many local-history books are published by local publishers, organizations or societies. Consequently, it is unusual to find a series covering the whole country relating to a particular subject, like the history of towns, although societies may publish series on their own town as the New Mills Local History Society has done for its area. (One exception is the series *Portrait of . . .*, published by Hale.) It should be noted, however, that in recent years there have been several publishers who have published books of photographs of individual towns where the only difference in the title has been the name of the town. Although not a series as such, if the various titles are taken together, they present a picture of the development of different communities over the last 100 years. Much of the importance and usefulness of this type of book lies in the quality of the photographs and the information content of the accompanying captions, some of which are little more than basic statements whilst others are more substantial and informative.

Publishers whose market is national have tended to concentrate on either county or regional histories or on sources. For example, Batsford's local history series includes titles on maps[8] and photographs,[9] which are areas on which there are no other adequate books published. This series has also recognized that there are differences in the sources used by local historians in Scotland and as a result has included two titles specifically related to Scotland.[10]

Although some national publishers have published histories of towns, the more general policy approach has been to look at counties and publish books on individual counties like Phillimore's *Darwen county history of . . .* . However, such county histories tend to be basic outlines of the county's history rather than a detailed examination of it. The exception to this are the *Victoria county histories.*

The Victoria county history project[11] was started in 1899 with the aim of publishing a definitive history of every county in England. Despite the fact that work started on the series over 90 years ago, there are still counties which have not been completed and others where publication has only just started.

During the time that work has been in progress, there has been a gradual change in emphasis in local history, which has been reflected in the content of the later volumes. For example, there is now less emphasis in the later volumes on the established church and land ownership than in the earlier ones. Despite the changing emphasis, the format for all counties is the same: the first two or three volumes consist of a series of general articles on the history of the county and on specific subjects followed by brief histories of individual communities. Originally, there were no volumes dealing exclusively with a single town or city, but this has changed and now several major towns have their own volume. Unfortunately, with the exception of Essex,[12] no county has a general bibliographical volume.

It is not only histories of counties which have attracted the attention of publishers. Reprints of source material like the Domesday Book, by Phillimore's, or the first edition Ordnance Survey maps, by David and Charles, or the larger-scale Ordnance Survey maps, by Alan Godfrey, have become commonplace in the last 20 years. So also has the publication of books, often on a county basis, on particular topics. For example, Penguin's series *Buildings of England*, which includes much material helpful to local historians and also of general interest. Sometimes it is a mixture of region and county as with David and Charles' *Industrial archaeology of the British Isles*, or it may be purely regional as is the case with the same publishers' series *Canals of the British Isles* and *Regional history of the railways of Great Britain*. All of these series not only make important contributions to the history of the subject, but are also valuable sources of secondary information for local historians.

Those involved in social and urban history at a national level often draw on local communities for examples. The result is that many books on social history often contain local material, or may even be devoted to a particular locality, although the title does not indicate this. For example *Building the industrial city*[13] includes important contributions on Huddersfield, the West Riding of Yorkshire, Liverpool and Scotland, whilst *The poor and the city: the English poor law in its urban context*[14] has sections on Sunderland, Bradford, north-east England and east London. It is important, therefore, to remember that local history information is not only to be found in local books, but can also be found in general historical works.

Record offices and societies

Another area on which local information may be sought concerns addresses and locations of record offices and repositories and details of local societies. Addresses of record offices are relatively easy to trace, but the location within the town is often more difficult. A useful publication which includes address, telephone number and a sketch map showing the location is *Record offices and how to find them.*[15]

It can be more difficult to trace information on societies, especially national ones or ones outside the library's immediate area. A useful guide to local societies is:

Pinhorn, M., HISTORICAL ARCHAEOLOGICAL AND KINDRED SOCIETIES IN THE UNITED KINGDOM: A LIST. Isle of Wight: Pinhorn, 1986.

This pamphlet is divided into three sections. The first is an alphabetical list of societies and the addresses of secretaries. This main section is followed by societies arranged by county and finally a list of societies which cover more than one county. It is not an exhaustive list, but can be helpful when information for a non-local area is requested. It should also be remembered that officials of societies change and that the address given may not be the most recent. Details of changes in address and of new and omitted societies is to be found in each issue of *Local history* (see below).

Periodicals

There are two periodicals which are specifically published for the local historian:

THE LOCAL HISTORIAN.[16] London: British Association for Local History.[17] 1952 - . Quarterly.

LOCAL HISTORY. Nottingham: R & S Howard, 1984 - . 6 times per year.

The *Local historian* was started to assist local historians 'to progress more surely and swiftly and to achieve more reliable results' (**1** (1), p. 1). Although the major part of each issue is devoted to articles on various aspects of local history, there is a substantial bibliographical section containing reviews and listing recently received publications, many of which appear in *BNB* only some considerable time after publication.

Local history was started with the intention of publishing 'both scholarly works and news stories' (**1**, p. 1) on local history. As well as articles of a practical nature, there is news of local history activities and an extensive section, 'Listings', which consists of a large number of short reviews of new local publications, arranged by county and including details of where to obtain them. These periodicals are not competitors but complementary to each other. Both are important publications in the field of local history.

New local publications often take a considerable time to reach *BNB*. It is, therefore, necessary to watch local newspapers and periodicals for reviews. Sometimes reviews appear in yearbooks like *Urban history yearbook*[18] or regional publications such as the *Manchester region history review*.[19] Additionally, both these publications include general articles and an annual bibliography of new publications received.

BIBLIOGRAPHIES

Although bibliographies are an important means of tracing what has been published on a particular subject, published ones are not as important in local history as in other fields because many tend to be produced for the individual library's own use. Those which are published usually cover a region or a county, such as Lancashire,[20] Dorset[21] or Cumberland and Westmorland,[22] or

for a local event which has national significance, such as Peterloo.[23]
There is no national local history bibliography published, as there
was in the nineteenth century when Anderson compiled *The book
of British topography* (2nd imp. Wakefield: 1976), which lists all
local history publications up to 1881. Neither is there a current
bibliography of local history bibliographies like A. L. A. Humphreys' *A handbook to county bibliographies ... relating to the counties
and towns of Great Britain* (2nd imp. London: Dawson, 1974).
Although local history bibliographies tend to be 'place specific',
those which are published and which cover a county or wider area,
require good place and subject indexes. They also need to be
updated as new material is published. It is possible to do this by
means of supplements, like those issued for the *East Anglian
bibliography*,[24] but unless the supplements are incorporated into
a revised edition, or are cumulated regularly, the bibliography
can become unwieldy to use.

The growth in urban history has resulted in an increase in the
amount of bibliographical work on the subject. The earliest
bibliographical work on urban history was:

Gross, C., BIBLIOGRAPHY OF BRITISH MUNICIPAL HISTORY. 2nd
ed. Leicester: Leicester University Press, 1966.

Martin, G. H. and McIntyre, S., A BIBLIOGRAPHY OF BRITISH AND
IRISH MUNICIPAL HISTORY. Leicester: Leicester University Press, 1972.

Although first published in 1900, Gross has become the starting-
point for modern urban bibliographical work, such as that
undertaken by Martin and McIntyre. An important feature of
Gross' work is that he recognized that periodicals included
important articles on urban history and so he included these as
well as books and pamphlets. The bibliography includes sections
on archival material and general works, general works on urban
history and histories of individual towns. The index enables entries
for specific places, which do not appear under its location entry,
to be easily traced.

A bibliography of British and Irish municipal history is the first volume
of a series of bibliographies on urban history and as such is the
introduction, listing general works on urban history. The five

sections include one on bibliographies and another on guides to libraries and record offices. Where necessary, the sections are sub-divided to make the bibliography easier to use. There is also a comprehensive index which enables entries on specific places to be quickly located.

In addition to those bibliographies which relate to particular districts or to urban history, there is a limited amount of local coverage in some general history bibliographies. For example, *Bibliography of historical works issued in the United Kingdom* (5 vols. London: Institute of Historical Research, 1957 –) and *Writings on British history* (25 vols. London: Cape for Institute of Historical Research, 1937 –), have both included sections on local history since they were started. Others, however, like *Oxford bibliography of British history* (6 vols. Oxford: Oxford University Press, 1952 – 77), have introduced such sections after they were started and are having to include them in the earlier volumes when they are revised. Local material can also be found in those biblio-graphies which cover particular periods, like Bonser's biblio-graphies on Roman[25] and Anglo-Saxon[26] Britain. Neither should it be forgotten that specialist subject bibliographies, such as G. Otley's *A bibliography of British railway history* (London: HMSO, 1983; *Supplement*, 1988), may also contain many local references.

Many important contributions to local history are to be found in the publications of societies, but it can be difficult to trace them if the publishing society is not local. Since 1933, analytical entries for many national and specialist periodicals have been included in *Writings on British history* (London: Cape for Institute of Historical Research). For those which were published between 1901 and 1933, there is:

Mullins, E. L. P., A GUIDE TO THE HISTORICAL AND ARCHAEO-LOGICAL PUBLICATIONS OF SOCIETIES OF ENGLAND AND WALES, 1901 – 33. London: Institute of Historical Research, 1966; Athlone Press, 1968.

This publication lists the contents of 6,560 volumes published by societies between 1901 and 1933. Under the name of each society are details of their publications and, where necessary, notes indicating the contents of particular volumes. The comprehensive index allows the user to identify relevant local material without difficulty.

THESES

Another important source of local information is theses submitted for higher degrees, details of which can be found in:

HISTORICAL RESEARCH FOR UNIVERSITY DEGREES IN THE UNITED KINGDOM. London: Institute of Historical Research. 1971 – . Annual (2 vols. per year).

Horn, J. M., HISTORY THESES, 1970 – 1980. London: Institute of Historical Research, 1984.

Jacobs, P. M., HISTORY THESES, 1901 – 1970. London: Institute of Historical Research, 1976.

History theses brings together information on theses submitted between 1901 and 1980 which was previously to be found in several different places. The entries are divided into broad historical periods and then sub-divided into subjects, including local history. Each entry gives the title of the thesis, the author's name, the date of submission and at which university. There is also information on how copies can be obtained. The index enables theses on particular areas or subjects to be easily traced.

Details of theses submitted after 1980 and those which are being written are to be found in the annual, two-volume *Historical research for university degrees*. The first part details those theses which have been completed and submitted and is indexed in a similar manner to *History theses*. The second part lists theses in progress, the name of the author, the title of the thesis and to which university the student is attached. There is no index, making entries on specific places difficult to trace.

RECORDS FOR LOCAL HISTORY

It is important for those involved with local history to be aware of the existence and content of local material which is not held locally but at places like the Public Record Office and the county record office, and to know a little about their interpretation and use. This has assumed more importance with the increased availability of copies of this type of material in microform or as photocopies.

National records

National records, mainly found in the Public Record Office, are often overlooked by local historians. The Public Record Office guide[27] merely lists the various types of record there and the periods covered. There is no information on their origins, use or details of published guides. However this can be found in a series of leaflets which deal with particular subjects and types of record[28] and in *An introduction to the use of public records.*[29]

Not all national records will be relevant for local historians. Details of those which are can be found in:

Morton, A. and Donaldson, G., BRITISH NATIONAL ARCHIVES AND THE LOCAL HISTORIAN: A GUIDE TO OFFICIAL RECORD PUBLICATIONS. London: Historical Association, 1980.

Riden, P., RECORD SOURCES FOR LOCAL HISTORY. London: Batsford, 1987.

Morton and Donaldson's pamphlet concentrates on material in the Public Record Office and the Scottish Record Office where there is a published transcript or calendar. It gives a brief outline of the origins of some of the material referred to and also on the arrangement of the calendar. The appendix contains a list of published calendars of national records.

Riden gives a detailed account of the local information which can be found in national records, laying stress on 'centrally preserved sources' up to 1974. The book includes details of the Public Record Office classification numbers and an indication of the subjects covered by the records. There are many useful footnotes and an extensive bibliography.

Private records

Private records, that is those not in the public domain, can be important sources of local information, but it was not until the establishment of the Royal Commission on Historic Manuscripts in 1869 that the full extent of these collections was known. The Royal Commission's *Guides to the reports*[30] lists collections which have been surveyed, but does not go into detail about the contents, which are detailed in the actual report on the collection. As well as the reports of the Royal Commission, some academic institutions which have archival collections have published guides to their holding. For instance, Warwick University's *Guide to the modern records centre,*[31] shows that there are many records there which relate to different parts of the county and whose whereabouts would not have been known unless the guide had been published.

Assistance in locating records can be obtained from the National Register of Archives. The NRA was established in 1945 to coordinate the production and distribution of archive calendars, to advise individuals and institutions on where they could deposit their archives and to assist researchers in tracing particular archive collections.[32]

Local records

Local records, found in the county record offices or in archives departments within the larger libraries, constitute the archival material which local historians will most frequently encounter. Copies of guides to the local record offices, which list the material there, and copies of annual reports, which often list newly acquired material, should be available in all libraries which deal with local studies enquiries. Useful guides to the type of material which may be found in record offices are:

Emmison, F. G., ARCHIVES AND LOCAL HISTORY. 2nd ed. Chichester: Phillimore, 1978.

Emmison, F. G. and Smith, W. J., MATERIAL FOR THESES IN LOCAL RECORD OFFICES AND LIBRARIES. 2nd ed. London: Historical Association, 1980.

West, J., VILLAGE RECORDS. 2nd ed. Chichester: Phillimore, 1982.

West, J., TOWN RECORDS. Chichester: Phillimore, 1983.

Archives and local history is a general introduction to the various classes of archive found in record offices and how to use a record office. Although many types of material are mentioned, there is little on their origins or use. Neither is there any indication of what each record office holds, but this information can be found in Emmison and Smith's pamphlet.

Village records examines the archive sources which can be used to trace the history of a village. West not only shows the information which can be obtained from different types of record, but also includes copies of original documents together with a transcript, details of peculiarities in the text and handwriting and a list of printed transcripts. The book also includes a glossary of unfamiliar or archaic words as well as an extensive bibliography. *Town records* examines the various sources, such as newspapers, maps and directories, which can be used when working on the history of a town. There is an extensive reading list as well as details of urban records which have been published. West's two books, taken together, refer to most of the local records which the librarian will be asked about or need to know about.

Parochial records

Parochial records are an important source of local information up to the early nineteenth century. Parishes were responsible for such things as highway maintenance and poor law. Details of the various types of record and their use is explained in:

Tate, W. E., THE PARISH CHEST. 3rd ed. Cambridge: Cambridge University Press, 1969 (reprinted 1983).

This important book examines the origins of various types of parochial record concerned with local administration and explains their use for local historians and others. There is a helpful glossary of unfamiliar terms and an extensive bibliography.

There are many other types of archival material which are useful to local historians. Some types of material have been examined in detail in pamphlets which deal exclusively with a particular type. These include title deeds,[33] quarter session records,[34] tithes[35] and local taxation.[36] Other pamphlets which include many references to archival material, illustrate their use in answering particular types of enquiry, such as seeking information on the history of a house.[37]

In the nineteenth century, the transcription and publication of archival material was the only way of making original material more widely available. A list of these transcripts is to be found in:

Mullins, E. L. F., TEXTS AND CALENDARS: AN ANALYTICAL GUIDE TO SERIAL PUBLICATIONS. 2 vols. London: Royal Historical Society, 1958 – 83.

These two volumes list those transcriptions and archive calendars which have been published by national, regional or local societies. The entries are arranged under the society's name and where appropriate, there are details of the contents of individual volumes. The index enables individual places, persons and types of document to be traced irrespective of the publishing society.

USING ARCHIVAL SOURCES

The use of archival sources can create difficulties for those not familiar with such subjects as the dating of documents, Latin words and phrases and even with the handwriting. Some of these difficulties can be overcome by using:

Richardson, J., THE LOCAL HISTORIAN'S ENCYCLOPAEDIA. Rev. ed. New Barnet: Historian Publications, 1986.

The encyclopaedia is divided into sections covering particular topics such as agriculture, architecture, heraldry, and dates of market charters, schools and railways. However, to make full use of this important work, it is necessary to use the index as some entries are to be found in locations where they are not expected. The sections on dating and Latin and archaic words are useful, although not as comprehensive as the specialist works like *Handbook of dates for students*[38] and *Latin for local history.*[39]

Although many libraries may not have a great deal of manuscript or archival material, the increased availability of microfilm and photocopies has made it necessary for local studies departments to be able to provide some assistance with **handwriting**. Simple guides to reading sixteenth- and seventeenth-century handwriting include *How to read local archives, 1550 – 1700*[40] and *Reading Tudor and Stuart handwriting.*[41]

NEWSPAPERS AND PERIODICALS

Newspapers

Newspapers and periodicals are also important sources of local information. Newspapers contain not only news, but also announcements, editorial comment on the news, feature articles and advertisements, all of which are important to local history research. Although libraries will have back files of local newspapers, there will be gaps. Helpful in establishing what gaps exist is:

British Library, CATALOGUE OF THE NEWSPAPER LIBRARY. 8 vols. London: British Library Board, 1975.

This eight-volume catalogue is divided into three sections: London newspapers, newspapers and periodicals published in provincial towns and finally an alphabetical list by title. The volumes covering the provincial towns are arranged in alphabetical order of town and the titles alphabetically under each town's name. It includes many papers which existed only a short time and others which have been preserved only in the British Library. This catalogue is the most comprehensive list of newspapers and periodicals to have been compiled at national level, but gaps do exist here as well.

There are also regional lists of local newspapers which can be helpful in that they also indicate where copies can be seen within the area covered. Such regional lists, like *Newspapers first published before 1900 in Lancashire, Cheshire and the Isle of Man* (London: Library Association Reference, Special and Information Section North West Group, 1964), often include the holdings of local newspaper offices as well, which increases their comprehensiveness.

Indexes are important to exploit the full potential of newspapers. However, most indexes are local in their scope, like *The Leicester newspapers, 1850 – 1874*.[42] The one national index, published by *The Times*[43] includes local references and should not be overlooked as an important reference tool.

Periodicals

Periodicals are also important sources of local information. Although local periodicals are often indexed, national ones tend to be forgotten about, although those like the *Illustrated London news* (London 1842 –) include many local news items. There are also important specialist periodicals, like the *Builder* (1842 – 1956), which contain many local items. Those articles which relate to architectural competitions have been included in *Victorian architectural competitions*.[44] Information on current periodicals is easy to trace, but for ones which no longer exist the British Library's *Catalogue of the newspaper library* is very useful.

PARLIAMENTARY PAPERS

Parliamentary papers, that is public and private Acts of Parliament, reports of Royal Commissions, Sessional Papers and evidence presented to Parliamentary committees, are important sources of local information. Useful introductory guides to the various types of material include:

Bond, M. F., GUIDE TO THE RECORDS OF PARLIAMENT. London: HMSO, 1971.

Bond, M. F., THE RECORDS OF PARLIAMENT: A GUIDE FOR GENEALOGISTS AND LOCAL HISTORIANS. Canterbury: Phillimore, 1964.

Ford, P. and Ford, G., A GUIDE TO PARLIAMENTARY PAPERS. 3rd ed. Shannon: Irish Universities Press, 1972.

Powell, W. R., LOCAL HISTORY FROM BLUE BOOKS. London: Historical Association, 1962.

Bond's *Guide to the records of Parliament* is a comprehensive guide to the manuscript and printed Parliamentary papers in the Palace of Westminster, some of which are found nowhere else. However, it does not include information on their origins or their use by local historians. For this it is necessary to consult one of the other books on the subject, which also include useful descriptions of how Parliamentary material is numbered. The only one which indicates those items of particular use to local historians is *Local history from blue books*, which gives details of libraries with extensive holdings and lists of sessional papers which the local historian might find useful.

DIRECTORIES

Directories are another important source of local information in listing names and addresses of individuals and businesses, giving general information on the town or area and including many advertisements. Late eighteenth- and early nineteenth-century directories tended to be regional in their coverage, but from the mid-nineteenth century, they usually cover a single town or county. Useful guides to directories are:

Norton, J. E., GUIDE TO THE NATIONAL AND PROVINCIAL DIRECTORIES OF ENGLAND AND WALES ... PUBLISHED BEFORE 1856. London: Royal Historical Society, 1950.

Shaw, G. and Tipper, A., BRITISH DIRECTORIES: A BIBLIOGRAPHY AND GUIDE TO DIRECTORIES PUBLISHED IN ENGLAND AND WALES (1850 – 1950) AND SCOTLAND (1773 – 1950). Leicester: Leicester University Press, 1988.

These two publications complement each other. Both include accounts on the compilation of directories. Norton lists 878 provincial directories,[45] based on the holdings of major libraries, which means that important directories held only by small libraries have been omitted. There is a full bibliographical description for each entry, enabling different editions to be identified. The index lists only counties and not individual towns, which can be a disadvantage, although this information can be traced through one of the many regional lists, like that for the West Midlands,[46] which have been compiled.

Shaw and Tipper continue where Norton stopped, except in the case of Scotland, which Norton did not include. Individual towns are listed under their counties so it is possible to trace those directories which relate to a particular town. Coverage is not restricted to the well-known publishers, but includes many local ones as well. Together, these two books form an important guide to this printed source of local information.

GENEALOGICAL RESEARCH

With the increased popularity of family history, those involved in local history work have had to become more aware than ever before of the methodology of undertaking genealogical research and the sources used by family historians. There are many books on the subject, such as *In search of ancestry*,[47] *Genealogy for beginners*,[48] *Tracing your ancestors*,[49] *Genealogical research in England and Wales*[50] and *Discovering your family history*,[51] which seek to explain the various sources that can be used and how to undertake research. In addition to books, there are pamphlets relating to family history research in particular areas, for example York[52] and Knowsley,[53] and on different sources, many of which have been produced by the Family History Society and which are very helpful. For librarians there is:

Harvey, R., GENEALOGY FOR LIBRARIANS. London: Bingley, 1983.
   This book provides guidance for librarians who might be asked to assist amateur genealogists and family historians. It examines the problems librarians face and the sources which family

historians use. Although there is no bibliography, the text gives details of many important sources which can assist the librarian and the family historian.

Rogers, C. D., THE FAMILY TREE DETECTIVE. 2nd ed. Manchester: Manchester University Press, 1985.

There are many problems which family historians encounter in the course of their research. Sometimes the staff of the local studies library are called upon to resolve these problems and explain the reason why the information content of the same type of record varies. This book sets out to look at some of these problems and to explain them. There is a useful bibliography which includes publications dealing with some of the less well-known sources.

In recent years, parish registers have become more widely available on microfilm. A useful guide to what is available is:

THE NATIONAL INDEX OF PARISH REGISTERS. London: Phillimore, 1968.

This series aims to list all the parish registers which are available to be consulted. The first three volumes form an introduction to the various types of register and ancillary sources such as monumental inscriptions and wills. The remaining volumes cover the country on a regional basis. Within each region, parishes are listed under their respective counties. There are no details of where the registers can be consulted. However, this information is recorded in *Parish register copies* (2 vols. London: Phillimore, 1971) which lists registers in the Society of Genealogists' library as well as in libraries and record offices.

Printed sources which might be helpful to genealogists are listed in:

Humphrey-Smith, C. R. A GENEALOGIST'S BIBLIOGRAPHY. Rev. ed. Chichester: Phillimore, 1985.

This bibliography is arranged by county, and gives details of the local record repositories before listing published transcripts on subjects such as feet of fines and marriage licences. It is a useful guide to sources which might be overlooked and also includes a useful glossary of terms and an extensive bibliography.

For more general genealogical information, *The genealogist's encyclopedia*[54] provides a general background to the subject, dealing with such subjects as heraldry, the clan system and sources of information, both in England and abroad, for those engaged in genealogical research.

CENSUS REPORTS

Census enumerators' returns and census reports are also important sources of local information. The census reports are purely a statistical account of the population of an area whilst the enumerators' returns give personal information which is not released for 100 years after the census. Many libraries have acquired microfilm copies of the enumerators' returns for the years 1841 to 1881. A list of these libraries is published in:

Gibson, J. S. W., CENSUS RETURNS 1841 – 1881 ON MICROFILM: A DIRECTORY OF LOCAL HOLDINGS. 4th ed. Plymouth: Federation of Family History Societies, 1982.

This list of libraries and record offices with copies of the census enumerators' returns is arranged by county and lists those places with microfilm copies and which censuses are held and whether there are any indexes.

The accuracy of the information in the census depends on the way in which it was carried out. Accounts of this are included in *Guide to census reports: Great Britain 1801 – 1966,*[55] which includes examples of the forms used for each census, and *Making sense of the census: the manuscript returns for England and Wales, 1801 – 1901,*[56] which includes a section on the make-up of a nominal page and a glossary of terms. This is especially valuable as there is often doubt about what is meant by some of the terms used. A more general account of the importance of nineteenth-century censuses is in *The census and social structure.*[57]

It can be difficult to obtain accurate information on population before 1801, but some of the sources which can be used are outlined in *Sources for the history of population and their uses*,[58] which also includes an explanation of their problems. The results of work using pre-1801 sources, as well as details of analysis of census returns, can be found in *Local population studies* (1947 –. Twice yearly).

PLACE-NAMES

There is also a need to know where to find information on place-names. Much of the research that has been undertaken is by the English Place-Name Society, and is found in their series on place-names of England, which is published on a county basis. Each county's series begins with a general introduction and then examines the place- and field-names found there. Where a less detailed account is required, there is:

Ekwall, E., CONCISE OXFORD DICTIONARY OF ENGLISH PLACE-NAMES. 4th ed. Oxford: Oxford University Press, 1974.

This dictionary gives both the derivation of individual place-names and the meaning of some of the more common place-name elements such as '-ton' and '-ley'. Each entry has a list of various spellings, the date of the first recorded use and the language from which the word is derived. It does not include field- or street-names.

Those who wish to put places into their historical context have to consult M. Gelling's *Signposts to the past: place names and the history of England* (London: Dent, 1978), which provides a useful background to the subject.

BIOGRAPHICAL INFORMATION

Biographical information is also important in local studies work. General works like the *Dictionary of national biography*[59] include relatively few people of local significance, although there are more local people included in *Modern English biography*.[60] A valuable source for local biographies is the various county biographical dictionaries published around the beginning of the twentieth century. A useful introduction to this source, and others, is '*Some neglected sources of biographical information*'.[61]

NON-BOOK MATERIALS

In addition to printed material, local-studies libraries also have extensive collections of non-book materials such as maps, illustrations and ephemera. The problem with this material is that much of it tends to relate to a particular locality and is listed only locally.

Maps

The one exception to this is maps which form an important and well-use part of the stock. The best-known maps are those published by the Ordnance Survey, but these are only the most recent type to be published. County maps have been issued since the sixteenth century.

Publications on maps tend to treat non-Ordnance Survey maps separately from Ordnance Survey maps, but two recent publications have broken with this and look at all types of maps:

Hindle, P., MAPS FOR LOCAL HISTORY. London: Batsford, 1988.

Smith, D., MAPS AND PLANS FOR THE LOCAL HISTORIAN AND COLLECTOR. London: Batsford, 1988.

Although the titles might give the impression that the contents of these two books are similar, this is not the case. *Maps for local history*, although covering the various types of maps that have been published, concentrates on county, estate, enclosure and tithe maps, town plans, transport maps and Ordnance Survey maps. *Maps and plans for the local historian and collector*, on the other hand, covers a wider range of maps, including military maps, marine charts and settlement plans. Both authors examine the origins of the various types of map and include bibliographies. Hindle also provides some information on special collections of maps and a list of reprinted county maps.

Until the publication of these two books, the basic introduction to non-Ordnance Survey maps was:

Harley, J. B., MAPS FOR THE LOCAL HISTORIAN: A GUIDE TO BRITISH SOURCES. London: Standing Conference for Local History, 1972.

This book had its origins in a series of articles published in the *Amateur historian*[62] which was intended to be an introduction to non-Ordnance Survey maps. The articles examined six different types of map and drew attention to problems that are encountered when using them. There is an extensive bibliography not only of cartographical works, but also of publications which list maps for a particular area.

The most widespread of the non-Ordnance Survey maps are those for individual counties, often produced for atlases. However, they were frequently re-issued without any change being made except to the imprint. There are several bibliographies of county atlases:

Chubb, T., PRINTED MAPS IN THE ATLASES OF GREAT BRITAIN AND IRELAND ... 1579 – 1870. London: Dawsons, 1927. Reprinted 1974.

Rogers, E. M., LARGE SCALE COUNTY MAPS OF THE BRITISH ISLES, 1596 – 1850: A UNION LIST. 2nd ed. Oxford: Bodleian Library, 1971.

Skelton, R. A., COUNTY ATLASES OF THE BRITISH ISLES, 1579 – 1850. London: Carta Press, 1970.

Chubb and Skelton follow a chronological approach in their bibliographies. Whereas Chubb lists subsequent editions under the original edition, Skelton lists them under the date when they were published. Neither bibliography is easy to use if details of maps for a specific county are required, but Skelton's work does make it possible to identify different editions.

Rogers adopts a different approach in that the maps are listed by county with each entry giving the date of publication, scale, surveyor and the libraries which hold copies, which is more satisfactory when a topographical approach is required.

In addition to general lists of county maps, there are important publications listing maps relating to specific counties. For example, in 1912 the Bristol and Gloucester Archaeological Society published one such map bibliography on the printed maps of Gloucester.[63]

For Ordnance Survey maps an invaluable guide is:

Harley, J. B., THE HISTORIAN'S GUIDE TO ORDNANCE SURVEY MAPS. London: Standing Conference for Local History, 1964.
    Harley outlines the history of the Ordnance Survey after which he comments on the various editions of the small-scale Ordnance Survey maps. There is also a section on the large-scale town plans which are especially useful to urban historians but instead of being listed, those areas with such maps are shown on a sketch-map together with the date of publication.

Photographs

Maps constitute only a small proportion of the non-book materials in a local studies collection. Many collections also include substantial holdings of illustrative material, especially photographs.
    Photographs are important as they show changes in the locality which have taken place over a period of time as well as providing information on costume, architectural detail of specific buildings, street furniture, transport, events and advertisements. Often the same photograph can provide several different pieces of information. Even modern photographs can be of value as things change very rapidly when redevelopment occurs. The best way to discover the usefulness of illustrations is to spend a short time studying individual ones looking for information, which can often result in a reasonably accurate date being ascribed to an undated illustration.[64] An account of a modern photographic-record survey and an assessment of it after 21 years is to be found in the *Manchester review*.[65] For those who want to undertake a photographic-record survey of their area or make copies of material that has been lent to the library and where there are no in-house photographic facilities, a useful book is:

Houlder, E., RECORDING THE PAST: A PHOTOGRAPHER'S HAND-BOOK. Studley: *Local history* in association with K. A. F. Brewin Books, 1988.

This book is 'a practical, no-nonsense guide' (cover blurb) intended to help local historians and, by implication, local-studies librarians take better photographs. It includes a section on equipment, but more useful to librarians are those tips which are given on matters such as taking photographs of inscriptions and copying other photographs.

On a more general level, dealing with the content of photographs, is:

Oliver, G., USING OLD PHOTOGRAPHS: A GUIDE FOR THE LOCAL HISTORIAN. London: Batsford, 1989.
This publication looks at the various types of photograph which exist and the use local historians make of them. Attention is drawn to the amount of information which can be gleaned by studying a photograph and this is reinforced by the use of specific examples.
As many collections of illustrations are related to a particular locality and not by famous photographers, little attention has been paid to recording details of the scope of photographic collections in local studies departments. Two publications which do provide some guidance on this are:

Barley, M. W., A GUIDE TO BRITISH TOPOGRAPHICAL COLLEC-TIONS. London: Council for British Archaeology, 1974.

Wall, J., DIRECTORY OF BRITISH PHOTOGRAPHIC COLLEC-TIONS. London: Royal Photographic Society, 1977.
These books look at different aspects of illustration collections. Barley concentrates on prints and makes only a brief reference to photographic collections, whereas Wall deals specifically with photographs. Barley is arranged by county with individual towns listed under the county and he includes material in both libraries and art galleries. Wall follows a subject arrangement and does not include very much information on the full extent in individual collections.

Ephemera

Within any local collection there is a large body of material which is difficult to categorize as it consists chiefly of single sheets of paper. It is referred to variously as 'miscellaneous material' or, more recently, as 'ephemera'. It is difficult to produce a full list of such material, but one is to be found in:

Makepeace, C. E., EPHEMERA: A BOOK ON ITS COLLECTION, CONSERVATION AND STORAGE. Aldershot: Gower, 1985.

This book defines ephemera before making a detailed examination of the various types and how it can be collected and treated within the library. The appendix includes a lengthy list of various types of ephemera whilst the bibliography includes both general works and books on specific types of ephemera. Other books on the subject include:

Clinton, A., PRINTED EPHEMERA: COLLECTION, ORGANIZATION, ACCESS. London: Bingley, 1981.

Rickards, M., THIS IS EPHEMERA: COLLECTING PRINTED THROWAWAYS. Newton Abbot: David and Charles, 1977.

After a general introduction on ephemera and its problems, Clinton looks at the ephemera produced in three distinct areas. He deals with collecting policies as well as the uses to which the material can be put. Rickards' book, on the other hand, is intended for the private collector, but he does provide a useful indication of where ephemera can be found and the wide range of material which interests the private collector.

In addition to those books which deal with ephemera generally, there are a number which deal with specific types. Amongst these are *Printed ephemera*,[66] *Collecting printed ephemera*[67] and *Ephemera of travel and transport.*[68]

Tape-recordings

Tape-recordings are a significant source of oral information that has gained in importance with the advent of the cassette recorder. Libraries have been able to build up collections of reminiscences, sounds and eye-witness accounts for preservation. The case for oral history is put in P. Thompson's *The voice of the people: oral history* (Oxford: Oxford University Press, 1972) whilst the journal of the Oral History Society *Oral history*[69] gives an indication of the work that is currently being undertaken.

Often the amateur can be put off making recordings by the use of technical jargon, but much of the mystique has been stripped away in:

Howarth, K., AN INTRODUCTION TO SOUND RECORDING FOR THE ORAL HISTORIAN AND SOUND ARCHIVIST. Radcliffe: The author, 1977.

This booklet introduces oral history and explains, in simple terms, some of the technical details of the work, including how to make sound recordings that are satisfactory.

A local history library is a microcosm of the main library. Its subject field impinges on almost every department of the library and hence its staff have to be familiar with a wide range of material and sources. It is not only local material with which they must be familiar, but also general material. Although a library may deal in detail only with their own area, staff will need to be familiar with where to find general information on other areas and where to direct enquiries for further information. The expansion of interest in local history has resulted in an explosion of new publishing as well as a growth in requests for information on related subjects such as listed buildings and archaeology.[70] Many of the items referred to in this chapter can be used both by the specialist seeking to ensure that the collection is as comprehensive as possible and by the reference-library staff seeking an answer or to provide a guide to an area on which they are not familiar.

REFERENCES AND CITATIONS

1   Everitt, A., *New avenues for English local history.* Leicester: Leicester University Press, 1970, 5.

Local history

2 *Local studies librarian*. Library Association Local Studies Group. 1982 – . Twice yearly.

3 *Locscot*. Library Association Local Studies Group Scottish Branch. 1984 – . Twice yearly.

4 Library Association County Libraries Group, *Sources of local history*. 4th ed. London: Library Association, 1971.

5 Hale, A. T., *Local history handlist*. 5th ed. London: Historical Association, 1982.

6 Campbell-Kease, J., *A companion to local history research*. Sherborne: Alphabooks, 1989.

7 Hoskins, W. G., *Fieldwork in local history*. London: Faber and Faber, 1982.

8 Hindle, P., *Maps for local history*. London: Batsford, 1988.

9 Oliver, G., *Using old photographs: a guide for the local historian*. London: Batsford.

10 Moody, D., *Scottish local history: an introductory guide*. London: Batsford, 1988.
Moody, D., *Scottish family history*. London: Batsford, 1989.

11 A full account of the series is to be found in Pugh, R. B., *The Victorian county history of the counties of England*. London: Institute of Historical Research, 1970. See also Pugh, R. B., The *Victoria county histories. Local historian*, **13** (1), 15 – 22.

12 *Victoria county history of Essex: bibliography*. London: Institute of Historical Research, 1959.

13 Doughty, M. (ed.), *Building the industrial city*. Leicester: Leicester University Press, 1986.

14 Rose, M. E., *The poor and the city: the English poor law in its urban context, 1834 – 1914*. Leicester: Leicester University Press, 1985.

15 Gibson, J. and Peskett, P., *Record offices and how to find them*. 2nd ed. Plymouth: Federation of Family History Societies, 1982.

16 Formerly *Amateur historian*.

17 The British Association for Local History is the successor to the Standing Conference for Local History.

18 *Urban history yearbook*. Leicester: Leicester University Press, 1974 – . Annual.

19 *Manchester region history review*. 1986 – . Manchester: Manchester Polytechnic. The bibliography is contained in the Spring issue each year. It is published twice a year.

20 *Lancashire bibliography*. 11 vols. Manchester: Joint Committee for the Lancashire Bibliography, 1961 – .

21 Douch, R., *Handbook of local history: Dorset with supplement and corrections*. Bristol: Bristol University Extra Mural Department, 1961.

22 Hodgson, H. W. A., *A bibliography of the history and topography of Cumberland and Westmorland*. Carlisle: Carlisle and Westmorland Archives Committee, 1968.

23   Leighton, M. (comp.), *Peterloo Monday 16th August 1819: a bibliography*. Manchester: Manchester Libraries Committee, 1969.

24   Library Association Eastern Branch, *East Anglian bibliography*. 1960 – . Quarterly.

25   Bonser, W. A., *Romano-British bibliography*. 2 vols. Oxford: Blackwell, 1964.

26   Bonser, W. A., *An Anglo-Saxon and Celtic bibliography*. 2 vols. Oxford: Blackwell, 1957.

27   *Guide to the contents of the Public Record Office*. Rev. ed. 3 vols. London: HMSO, 1963 – 8.

28   Public Record Office, *Leaflets*. 2 vols. Compiled from individual leaflets.

29   Galbraith, V. H., *An introduction to the use of public records*. Oxford: Oxford University Press, 1963.

30   Royal Commission on Historical Manuscripts, *Guide to the reports and collections of manuscripts*. 3 vols. London: HMSO, 1914, and *Guide to the reports of the Royal Commission 1911 – 1957*. 4 vols. London: HMSO, 1966.

31   Storey, R. and Druker, J., *Guide to the modern records centre*. University of Warwick Occasional Papers No. 2. Coventry: Warwick University, 1977.

32   Ranger, F., 'The National Register of Archives', *Journal of the Society of Archivists*, **3**, 452 – 62.

33   Dibben, A., *Title deeds*. London: Historical Association, new ed., 1990. Cornwall, J., *How to read old title deeds*. Shalfleet Manor: Pinhorn, 1964.

34   Emmison, F. G. and Gray, I., *County records*. London: Historical Association, 1974.

35   Evans, E. J., *Tithes and the Tithe Commutation Act 1836*. London: Standing Conference for Local History, 1978.

36   Beckett, J. V., *Local taxation and the problems of enforcement*. London: Standing Conference for Local History, 1980.

37   Harvey, J. H., *Sources for the history of houses*. London: British Records Association, 1974.

38   Cheney, C. R., *Handbook of dates for students of local history*. London: Royal Historical Society, 1970.

39   Gooder, E. A., *Latin for local history*. London: Longman , 1975.

40   Emmison, F. G., *How to read local archives, 1550 – 1700*. London: Historical Association, 1973.

41   Mumby, L., *Reading Tudor and Stuart handwriting*. Chichester: British Association for Local History, 1988.

42   Greenall, R. L., *The Leicester newspapers, 1850 – 1874: a guide for historians*. Leicester: Department of Adult Education, University of Leicester, 1980.

43   *Times index*. 1785 – . London: *The Times*.

44   Harper, R. H., *Victorian architectural competitions: an index to British and Irish architectural competitions in the Builder, 1843 – 1900*. London: Mansell, 1983.

45   For London directories there is Goss, C. W. F., *The London directories, 1677 – 1855*. London: Archer, 1932.

46   Radmore, D. F. and Radmore, S., *Guide to the directories of the West Midlands*

to 1850. London: Library Association Reference, Special and Information
Section, West Midlands Section, 1971.

47 Hamilton-Edwards, G., *In search of ancestry*. Rev. ed. London: Phillimore,
1974.

48 Willes, A. J., *Genealogy for beginners*. 2nd ed. London: Phillimore, 1970.

49 Camp, A. J., *Tracing your ancestors*. Rev. ed. London: Gifford, 1970.

50 Smith, F. and Gardner, D. E., *Genealogical research in England and Wales*.
3 vols. Salt Lake City: Bookcraft, 1956 – 66.

51 Iredale, D. and Barrett, J., *Discovering your family tree*. 4th ed. Princes
Risborough: Shire Publications, 1985.

52 Bowling, R. G., *Researching family history in York Reference Library*. York:
North Yorkshire County Library, 1989.

53 Burgess, B. M. (comp.), *Tracing your family history in the Knowsley area at
Huyton Library*. Huyton: Department of Leisure Services, Knowsley, 1989.

54 Pine, L. G., *The genealogist's encyclopedia*. Newton Abbot: David and
Charles, 1969.

55 Office of Population, Censuses and Surveys, *Guide to census reports: Great
Britain, 1801 – 1966*. London: HMSO, 1977.

56 Higgs, E., *Making sense of the census: the manuscript returns for England and
Wales, 1801 – 1901*. London: HMSO, 1989.

57 Lawton, R. (ed.), *The census and social structure*. London: Cass, 1978.

58 Stephens, W. B., *Sources for the history of population and their uses*. Leeds:
Leeds University Institute of Education, 1971.

59 For full details see Chapter 5.

60 Boase, F., *Modern English biography*. 2nd imp. 6 vols. London: Cass; reprint
1965.

61 *Bulletin of the Institute of Historical Research*, **34**, 1961, 55 – 66.

62 *Amateur historian*, **7**, 6 – 8; and **8**, 2, 3, 5.

63 Chubb, T., *A descriptive catalogue of the printed maps of Gloucester, 1577 – 1911*.
Gloucester: Bristol and Gloucester Archaeological Society, 1912.

64 Makepeace, C. E., 'Dating and locating unidentified photographs', in
*Proceedings and papers of 1981 symoposium of the European Society for the History
of Photography*. Bath.

65 Milligan, H., 'The Manchester photographic survey', *Manchester review*,
8, 1958, 193 – 204.
Makepeace, C. E., 'Twenty-one years of continuous record survey',
Manchester review, **12**, 1972, 43 – 8.

66 Lewis, J., *Printed ephemera*. London: Faber, 1969.

67 Lewis, J., *Collecting printed ephemera*. London: Studio Vista, 1976.

68 Anderson, J. and Swinglehurst, E., *Ephemera of travel and transport*. London:
New Cavendish Books, 1981.

69 *Oral history*. Colchester: Oral History Society. 1972 – .

70 Aston, M. and Rowley, T., *Landscape archaeology*. Newton Abbot: David
and Charles, 1974.

Brown, A., *Fieldwork for archaeologists and local historians*. London: Batsford, 1987;

Pearce, D., *Historic buildings and planning policies*. London: Council for British Archaeology, 1979.

SUGGESTIONS FOR FURTHER READING

Bagley, J. J., *Historical interpretations*. 2 vols. Newton Abbot: David and Charles, 1972.

Bettey, J. H., *Church and parish: a guide for local historians*. London: Batsford, 1987.

Bettey, J. H., *The English parish church and the local community*. London: Historical Association, 1985.

Bradley, L., *A glossary for local population studies*. Matlock: Local Population Studies, 1978.

Brunskill, R. W., *Illustrated handbook of vernacular architecture*. London: Faber, 1971.

Brunskill, R. W., *A systematic procedure for recording vernacular architecture*. Vernacular Architecture Group, 1975. Also published in *Transactions of the Ancient Monuments Society*, **13**, 1965 – 6.

Brunskill, R. W., *Traditional buildings of England*. London: Gollancz, 1981.

Buckley, K. A., *British ancestry tracing*. Sutton Coldfield: The author, 1978.

Burkett, J. and Morgan, T. S., *Special materials in libraries*. London: Library Association, 1963.

Chapters 7 and 8 deal with local history and maps.

Burton, A. and May, J., *Landscape detective*. London: Allen and Unwin, 1986.

Camp, A. J., *Wills and their whereabouts*. Canterbury: Phillimore, 1963.

Carter, G. A., 'Libraries and local history', *The librarian and book world*, **45** (7 – 8), Aug/Sept 1956.

Child, M., *English church architecture: a visual guide*. London: Batsford, 1981.

Cole, J. A. and Armstrong, M., *Tracing your family tree*. London: Guild Publishing, 1988.

Cook, T. G., *Local studies and the history of education*. London: Methuen, 1972.

Cowell, S., *The family history book*. 2nd ed. Oxford: Phaidon, 1989.

Crafts Advisory Council, *Conservation source book*. London: Crafts Advisory Council, 1979.

This contains the names and addresses of organizations involved in many aspects of conservation. It includes a section on archives and books. A handy reference tool.

Currier-Briggs, N. and Gambier, R., *Debrett's family historian: a guide to tracing your ancestry*. London: Debrett and Webb and Bower, 1981.

Dawson, G. E. and Kennedy-Skipton, L., *Elizabethan handwriting, 1500 – 1659*. Chichester: Phillimore, 1981.

Drake, M. (ed.), *Population studies from parish registers: a selection of reading from Local Population Studies*. Matlock: Local Population Studies, 1982.

Dymond, D., *Archaeology for the local historian*. London: Historical Association, 1967.

Field, J., *Discovering place-names*. Princes Risborough: Shire Publications, 1980.

Field, J., *English field names: a dictionary*. Newton Abbot: David and Charles, 1972.

Finberg, H. P. R., *The local historian and his theme*. Leicester: Leicester University Press, 1952.

Finberg, H. P. R. and Skipp, V. H. T., *Local history: objective and pursuit*. Newton Abbot: David and Charles, 1967.

Fisher, J. L., *A mediaeval farming glossary*. London: Standing Conference for Local History, 1968.

Galbraith, V. H., *An introduction to the study of history*. Newton Abbot: David and Charles, 1967.

Garden, G., *A sense of the past*. London: Ward Lock, 1985.

Garratt, M. (ed.), *Sure coffers: some sources for the history of religion in the North West*. Knowsley: Library Association Local Studies Group North West Branch, 1987.

Hall, R. de Z., *A bibliography on vernacular architecture*. Newton Abbot: David and Charles, 1972.
    Useful entries, but no place index. It is necessary to check regional entries as well as the general entries.

Hobbs, J. L., *Libraries and the material of local history*. London: Grafton, 1949.

Hoskins, W. G., *English landscapes*. London: BBC, 1973.

Hoskins, W. G., *One man's England*. London: BBC, 1978.

Hoskins, W. G., *The making of the English landscape*. London: Hodder and Stoughton, 1955.

Houlder, E., 'Computing for the local historian: an introduction', *Local history*, 22, July 1989.

Industrial archaeology. Newton Abbot and Tavistock: David and Charles and Graphmitre, 1964 – 83.
    Contains many local items not recorded elsewhere.

Industrial archaeology review. Oxford and Ironbridge: Oxford University Press for Association of Industrial Archaeology, 1977 – .
    Contains many local items not recorded elsewhere.

Iredale, D., *Discovering your old house*. Princes Risborough: Shire Publications, 1977.

Iredale, D., *Enjoying archives*. Newton Abbot: David and Charles, 1973.

Kirby, A., *A guide to historical periodicals in England and Wales*. London: Historical Association, 1970.

Mackay, J., *Collecting local history*. London: Longman, 1984.

Matthews, A., *The chief elements used in English place-names*. English Place-Name Society, Vol. 1, part 2. Cambridge: Cambridge University Press, 1971.

Mawer, A. and Stenton, F. M., *An introduction to the survey of English place-names*. English Place-Name Society, Vol. 1, part 1. Cambridge: Cambridge University Press, 1926.

Muir, R. and Muir, N., *Fields*. London: Macmillan, 1989.

Mumby, L. M., *Short guides to records*. London: Historical Association, 1972.

Neuberg, V. E., *The past we see today*. Oxford: Oxford University Press, 1972.

Newton, K. C., *Mediaeval local records*. London: Historical Association, 1971.

Nichols, H., 'Maps and plans for local history: 1 Introduction', *Local history*, **25**, March 1990.
Other parts to be in subsequent issues of *Local history*.

Owen, D. M., *The records of the established Church of England*, British Records Association, 1970.

Pannell, J. P. M., *Techniques of industrial archaeology*. Newton Abbot: David and Charles, 1966.
Contains a useful introduction to the subject and includes a chapter on sources. This is the first volume of a series which covers the industrial archaeology of the country on a county-by-county basis.

Peace, C. G. and Mills, D. R., *Census enumerators' books: an annotated bibliography based substantially on the 19th-century census enumerators' books*. Milton Keynes: Open University, 1982.

Perry, G. A., Jones, E. and Hammersley, A., *A handbook of environmental studies*. London: Blandford, 1971.

Platt, C., *Mediaeval archaeology in England*. Shalfleet Manor: Pinhorn, 1969.
The title hides the fact that this is a useful bibliographical work which draws attention to some of the sources which mediaeval archaeologists use.

Reaney, P. H., *Origins of English place names*. London: Routledge, 1960.

Rogers, A., *Group projects in local history*. London: Dawson, 1977.
A useful publication which is well illustrated and has sections by individual specialists. There is a very useful bibliography and many references to publications in the footnotes which accompany each chapter.

Sippings, G., 'Formulating an acquisitions policy', *Local history*, **15**.

Smith, A. H., *The place-name elements*. 2 vols. London: English Place-Name Society, 25 and 26.

Smith, J. F., *A critical bibliography of building history*. London: Mansell, 1978.
Very useful as it contains many entries for local places which might not be recorded elsewhere. There is also a place index.

Smith, J. T. and Yates, E. M., 'On dating of English houses from external evidence', *Field studies*, **2** (5), 1968.

Smith, L., *Investigating old buildings*. London: Batsford, 1985.

Standing Conference for Local History. *Hedges and local history*. London: SCLH, 1971.

Steel, D. and Taylor, L., *Family history in focus*. Guildford: Guild Press, 1984.

Thirsk, J., *Sources of information on population, 1500 – 1769: unexplored in local records*. Canterbury: Phillimore, 1965.

Local history

Thompson, K., 'Palaeography made easy', *Local history*, **11**, April/May 1986.
Waites, B., 'Children in local history', *Local history*, , March 1985.

12

Current and Retrospective Bibliographies

David Lee

Most of the chapters in this book include some bibliographies relevant to their theme. It is the aim of this and the next chapter to concentrate on the nature and function of bibliographies.[1] Bibliographies – that is, lists of books – are central to the life of the librarian and the information-handler. That they are not so apparently central to most readers gives the librarian a function and a duty, to know bibliographies at first hand, by use, and then to communicate their value to potential users. In addition, bibliographical work can be a very large part of some librarians' working lives, sometimes as part of a cooperative bibliography scheme, either subject- or area-based. In studying bibliographies, it is useful to test them against books you know or subjects in which you are interested. Comparison of the treatment of a book or class of material can be instructive.

The term 'bibliography' is one which has been used in many ways, a favourite football knocked about, often quite cleverly, by the pedant.[2] Here we mean simply a list of books, but as the newest essay writer learns to add a 'bibliography' to his or her work, we should say that to be called a bibliography the list of books and other materials should be fairly ambitious.

Serious bibliographical listing has gone on for centuries; it is natural that the growth of printing brought about a need for scholars to know what was being published (current bibliography) and what had been done (retrospective). In the present chapter we shall look in turn at both these aspects, and in the following chapter examine the development of subject bibliography, which can also be either current or retrospective.

By a 'current bibliography' we mean one which comes out on a periodical basis and which is likely to be continued, particularly at a national level. Whilst all bibliography is to a large extent retrospective, we use that term here to mean those which address themselves to the books of the past.

CURRENT NATIONAL BIBLIOGRAPHIES

A natural basis on which to list materials is by country, given that there is often a dominant language (though we should not forget that the days of Latin scholarship gave rise to some interesting universal bibliographies). Most countries by the twentieth century have created a national bibliography, current or retrospective or both. A fuller list than we shall give here may be found in the second edition of this book,[3] in Walford's *Guide*,[4] and in that invaluable Unesco publication *Bibliographical services throughout the world.*[5] Also to be consulted are:

Gorman, G. E. and Mills, J. J., GUIDE TO CURRENT NATIONAL BIBLIOGRAPHIES IN THE THIRD WORLD. 2nd ed., revised. London: Hans Zell, 1987.

Includes a section on regional bibliographies, i.e. those of a rather larger area than one country, such as the *CARICOM bibliography* (Georgetown, Guyana: Caribbean Community Secretariat, 1977 – , two per year), which is in classified order.

Bell, Barbara L., AN ANNOTATED GUIDE TO CURRENT NATIONAL BIBLIOGRAPHIES. Alexandria, Va: Chadwyck-Healey Inc., 1986.

Covers a selection only of current national bibliographies, linking with Universal Bibliographical Control (UBC), see page 288.

National bibliographies sometimes arose through the natural publicity activities of the publishers/booksellers, and sometimes they were instituted by librarians and other cultural administrators. Quite often parallel current bibliographies exist for a country. Amongst these is Britain, which has not only an official national bibliography, the *British national bibliography* (see below), but also a first-class trade bibliography in:

WHITAKER'S BOOK LIST, the title since 1987 of the former *Cumulative book list*. London: J. Whitaker & Sons, annual.

This describes itself as 'the complete list of all the books published in the UK during the period'. Cumulates from *Books of the month*, and is a handy annual quick-reference volume for library purposes. It includes some 60,000 titles a year, including reprints, and is available in various formats.

On the world front, however, it is the legal-deposit framework which is more likely to provide the home for a national bibliography than the publishing industry itself. Often the national bibliography of a country is associated with its national library as the natural centre for the legal deposit of materials. Completeness, in broad terms at least, is the aim of both such a library and a bibliographical network.

Some natural development occurs: a current bibliography, if accurately compiled and drawing widely upon materials (books, pamphlets, periodical titles, government publications, 'grey literature') will become, if cumulated carefully and totally indexed, a retrospective bibliography. A good example of the process may be seen in:

BRITISH NATIONAL BIBLIOGRAPHY. London: British Library, 1950 – . CD-ROM version on three discs 1950 – 76, 1977 – 85 and 1986 – , re-issued quarterly by Chadwyck-Healey.

A weekly classified list, with author/title and subject indexes which cumulate monthly. The classified list and the indexes are further cumulated annually and at one time there were further, very large printed cumulations. Since the advent of online and CD-ROM formats, the printed cumulations may not be forthcoming; they had become rather cumbersome and the CD-ROM versions are geared to a variety of search languages.

The institution of *BNB* was a revolution in the library world, in that it provided a classified list which could be scanned for book-selection purposes, and the detailed indexes meant that the other purpose of the current bibliography, tracing and checking details, could be done with ease. The differences from Whitaker's *Bookseller* and *Cumulative book list* were sufficient to allow a place for both, these as a trade bibliography uncluttered by unnecessary detail, and *BNB* as a more official librarianly tool. There have always been exclusions from *BNB*: 'The objects of the *BNB* are to list new works published in the British Isles, to describe each work in detail and to give the subject matter of each work as precisely as possible', but periodicals other than the first issue, maps, music and most government publications are excluded.

From the start, *BNB* used Dewey DC as a classification, albeit modified, and adhered to a cataloguing code; there was always this relationship with cataloguing as well as bibliographical work. In the earliest days, *BNB* was even printed one-sided to allow the mounting of entries – and *BNB* cards followed. In later years we have seen the development of the MARC format for the same ultimate purpose of aiding library cataloguing.

This thorough progress, however, logical though it may seem, is not the only possibility. The trade bibliography may well not wish to become more ambitious in a scholarly way or may feel that the process is being done elsewhere.

CUMULATIVE BOOK INDEX: a world list of books in the English language. New York: H. W. Wilson, monthly except August.

This has been published since 1928, supplementing the *United States book catalog* 4th edition, and is a most useful trade bibliography including much of what one is searching for. It has a longer list of exclusions however than *BNB*. It is charged for, incidentally on a service basis, like other Wilson publications, i.e. largely based on libraries' book funds and the use they are likely to be able to make of the service. It is quite frankly a checking tool, and does not give even LC cataloguing information, unlike:

AMERICAN BOOK PUBLISHING RECORD: an American national bibliography. Bowker, 1960 – .

Caters for libraries by being in Dewey DC order. It has now gone retrospective to 1876, and normally cumulates into five-year volumes, from a monthly publication. Entries are in DC groups, and there are LC subject headings. There are author and title indexes.

On the other hand, a national library collecting more widely, and yet producing a national bibliography, may really prefer a listing which is not limited by nation. Quite a number of books are puzzling in provenance, in terms of their originating bodies. Books often name a number of countries on their title pages and more than one publisher, or, reversing the process, two otherwise identical books may boldly declare their (quite different) countries and publishers on their title pages, because of trade agreements negotiated at Frankfurt Book Fair and elsewhere. A library catalogue or current listing is not therefore necessarily a national bibliography though it may emanate from the country's national library.

NATIONAL UNION CATALOG. US BOOKS. Microfiche, 1983 – .

Is, however, in effect the national bibliography of the United States.

It is worth summarizing what are the uses of a current bibliography.[6] They may be summarized as:

1   **a finding tool** for a specific item, by author, title, subject, series, and perhaps other possibilities such as publisher. Limited bits of the total information about a book may be remembered by the reader. Form of an item also may be important – see the chapters on periodicals, audiovisual, etc. This type of use will be made often by librarian, bookseller and reader. Incidentally the value of the ISBN is worth noting, as a shorthand notation of the book's publisher and individuality. The Standard Book Numbering system began only in 1968 and is run in the UK by the bibliographical publisher J. Whitaker.

2 **a book-selection tool**. A major value of the current bibliography, whether trade- or library-originated, is to provide the librarian with a publication which he/she can go through, as a first-line tool or as a last check on output from a country or group or language. In times of financial stringency this aspect may be of less importance to the average librarian, but the increase in the size of library authorities in Britain in the 1970s should mean that the process is still needed. Parts at least of such publications may be checked by the academic and special librarian. It is one of the essential tools of a genuine book-selection policy, the landing on one's desk of the weekly (or whenever) current bibliography. Whitaker's altered the format of their weekly list to make it more attractive to run through with an eye to selection. A further service is now provided by Whitaker's *Book preview*, 'the most comprehensive source of pre-publication judgements of key British books'. A longstanding work of similar type and wider scope is *British book news*, a monthly from the British Council, whose bibliographical surveys on particular topics are of great value.

3 **a cataloguing tool**. Thanks to the MARC set-up in its various forms, the current bibliography (and some retrospective) can be invaluable in computerized cataloguing systems.[7] There has been movement in recent years in various countries to tie in the current national bibliography with a 'cataloguing in publication' (CIP) programme, whereby details of a forthcoming book may be made known through the current bibliographies, and cataloguing records prepared.

BOOKS IN ENGLISH. London: British Library, 2-monthly, with annual and longer cumulations, covering 1971 – 80 on 600 microfiche, and 1981 – 5.

These are in author/title order, but give full subject information according to Library of Congress and *BNB* practice. Following Anglo-American Cataloguing Rules (AACR2), this bibliography is intended for library cataloguing, particularly where automated.

The first function makes us demand accuracy and sharpness; the second gives the publisher a duty to make the bibliography easy to use in its typography and arrangement; the third again requires accuracy and speed of appearance.

To carry out these functions, two things are required:

(a) **frequency of publication**. The ideal size depends on the amount of material which is likely to be recorded, but in a country of prolific publication, such as the UK (66,619 titles published in 1989), weekly publication is ideal so that one issue contains a manageable amount of material. Many national bibliographies throughout the world are published at much longer intervals, not necessarily even annually. A problem undoubtedly arises in such instances that the books listed therein are no longer available.

There may, of course, be a variety of forms in which the national bibliography is produced: printed journal, card, online, etc. It may be that no single form will emerge as 'victor', as each has its advantages.

(b) **cumulation** of at least the index as soon as possible, so that tracing material is not delayed. This is where computerized work scores over the traditionally printed version in that labour-intensive work can be avoided at the printers without fresh errors being incorporated.

Judgement of current bibliographies is not easy to make, except by use, and it does sometimes become apparent that a particular bibliography has been a failure, or a failure for part of its life. One feature of trade bibliographies is that they often are a necessity for the trade, and perhaps less subject to financial policy on the part of national cultural organizations. Continuity, however, can never be assumed to have taken place, or to be secure for the future.

The preparation of a current bibliography is no easy task. In the case of a commercially produced listing, the cooperation of publishers is required to send in their material, or at least details of it. Hence it is more common to find current national bibliographies linked with the national library, which will have legal deposit; i.e. all books (perhaps within certain categories) must be deposited with them, for copyright reasons. As may be imagined, the two aspects, processing new material for a current bibliography on the one hand and treating the work as an item of library stock, intended for library use, on the other, are not entirely easy to reconcile. It is always to be hoped that the current listing will also be able to be used for the deposit library's own cataloguing system.

'IN PRINT' VOLUMES

One particular aspect of current/restrospective bibliography is the preparation of 'in print' lists, that is, of material which is still available at the time of compilation. Close cooperation with publishers is required for these, which are produced commercially rather than by national libraries. It is in the trade's interest to have these right for day-to-day use. It must be remembered that an item can go 'out of print' before it is even listed, so a list of 'in print materials' must never be treated as if it were an all-inclusive retrospective bibliography. Not all books, even if they sell well, are reprinted.

'In print' bibliographies are extremely useful from a practical point of view, often being the quickest way to a desired item. They are manageable, though much larger now than they used to be, and something readers can be encouraged to use. There are more types of 'in print' bibliography now than there used to be, some even being produced on a subject basis, such as *International legal books in print, 1990 – 1991* (Sevenoaks, Kent: Bowker-Saur, 1990), and *Religious books in print* (London: Whitakers).

WHITAKER'S BOOKS IN PRINT. 4 vols. in its current edition. London: Whitaker.

Retitled in 1978, from *British books in print*, this now lists about half a million titles. A further microfiche shows *Books 1976 – 1990 now out of print*. The CD-ROM versions of these two are titled *BOOKBANK* and *BOOKBANK OP*.

BOOKS IN PRINT. 7 vols. Sevenoaks, Kent: Bowker-Saur, 1988 – 9. Supplemented in 2 vols., 1989 – 90. Also available in CD-ROM and microfiche forms.

The American equivalent of the British *Whitaker's books in print*, this contains author, title, subject and publisher sequences.

INTERNATIONAL BOOKS IN PRINT. English-language titles published outside the United States and the United Kingdom. 9th ed. Sevenoaks, Kent: Bowker-Saur, 1990. 4 vols. covering authors/titles in two volumes and subjects in two volumes, this includes works from 100 countries, not the US and UK.

VERZEICHNIS LIEFERBARER BÜCHER (VLB). 19th ed. Sevenoaks, Kent: Bowker-Saur, 1989 – 90.

'The only comprehensive guide to German-language publishing', this lists German books in print.

LES LIVRES DISPONIBLES. Paris: Éditions du Cercle de la Librairie.

The French equivalent, with author, title and subject (DC) sequences. 'Librairie' in the publisher statement means bookshop and not library. This is now available on CD-ROM and through the ubiquitous French online system Minitel.

CATALOGO DEI LIBRI IN COMMERCIO. Milan: Editrice Bibliografica.

The Italian equivalent with author, title and subject sequences. All these series, English, French, Italian, German and others are most impressive and invaluable in dealing with overseas material. They are just examples of a type existing for many countries throughout the world. Their organization and production is remarkable, though when the type size gets as small as that in *Libros Espanoles en ventos* you begin to see why non-printed formats may become more acceptable in future.

A very large network of people and systems is involved today in current national bibliography, and it has reached considerable complexity to which automation is a strong answer. Online and CD-ROM have come into their own in the more developed services – *BNB*, *Deutsche Bibliographie* and *Bibliographie Nationale Française* are some recent examples. It should not be forgotten, however, that some national bibliographies are still small hand-knitted affairs, if of great value to their users.[8] At this point we will turn to the development of bibliographies dealing with publications of the more distant past.

RETROSPECTIVE BIBLIOGRAPHIES

A retrospective bibliography[9] is in a sense created by the cumulation of a current bibliography, as with *BNB* from 1950 or *CBI* from 1928, but this is not the only way. As there may be old bibliographies of books like these, so there are deliberately compiled bibliographies of old books.[10] This can be seen by a contrast between two items, both dealing with nineteenth-century output:

THE ENGLISH CATALOGUE OF BOOKS. London: Sampson Low, 1864 – 1901; *Publishers' circular*, 1906 – . Reprint. New York: Kraus, 1963.

This listing of books is very much a trade publication, with considerable variation in fullness and in arrangements in the various volumes. Although the *Publishers' circular* and its cumulations continued well into the twentieth century, it is as a prime source for nineteenth-century printed books that it is most useful. A retrospective volume covering 1801 – 36 was published in 1914 (reprinted New York: Kraus, 1963), edited by R. A. Peddie and Q. Waddington, based on current trade bibliographies of the nineteenth century, and there were index volumes which concentrated on the titles and subjects. The not infrequent errors and complexities make the *English catalogue* akin to a rather interesting nightmare.

NINETEENTH-CENTURY SHORT-TITLE CATALOGUE (NSTC). Newcastle-upon-Tyne: Avero, through Chadwyck-Healey, 1984 – . Series I (6 vols.) and series II (to be in 50 volumes).

Inspired by the *Eighteenth-century STC* (see below), *NSTC* began in 1983, based on six major British libraries, and far removed from a trade bibliography in type. This is in solid printed form and aims to include all materials from 1801 to 1918, a period of massive expansion in publishing. Series I covers 1801 – 15 and series II 1816 – 70. The volumes, like most short-title catalogues, are in alphabetical order of author, but *NSTC* unusually has an elaborate DC-based subject index, which is rather daunting. The Chadwyck-Healey *Nineteenth-century project* reprints, in microfiche form, many books from that period, and is an important link between listing and availability.

Thorough current bibliographies were quite late on the scene[11] and a lot of output, in book materials alone, remained to be recorded. Bibliographers, usually in libraries with great resources, have moved to fill the gaps.[12] It is interesting that in Britain bibliographers have moved on century by century, from the fifteenth to the nineteenth, sometimes hand-in-hand with book collectors. In view of the effort which goes into current output recording, a retrospective bibliography of the twentieth century may seem unthinkable, but when it does come it will be different from the cumulated current bibliographies.

Some of the old classic retrospective bibliographies still worth knowing include:

Lowndes, William Thomas,THE BIBLIOGRAPHER'S MANUAL OF ENGLISH LITERATURE. Various editions from 1837 onwards. 6 vols. London: H. G. Bohn, 1885. Reprint, London: Pordes, 1968.

An alphabetical list of authors and their books, with locations in some cases, essentially aimed at collectors and their suppliers. Lowndes also planned *The British librarian*, but little of this appeared (1828 – 39). It was strong on annotation, always helpful to collectors. Lowndes' influence was strong in encouraging publishing societies.

Watt, Robert, BIBLIOTHECA BRITANNICA; OR, A GENERAL INDEX TO BRITISH AND FOREIGN LITERATURE. 4 vols. London: Constable, etc., 1824. Reprint New York: Burt Franklin, 1965.

Two volumes concern authors, in alphabetical order with their books chronologically; the other two are alphabetical by subject, a rare occurrence of this format. Four quarto volumes which it is easy to imagine on the shelves of the scholarly nineteenth-century collector, giving him his authors and subjects at a glance.

Brunet, Jacques Charles, MANUAL DU LIBRAIRE ET DE L'AMATEUR DES LIVRES. 5th ed. 6 vols., plus 2 vols. Paris: Firmin Didot, 1860 – 5, 1878 – 80.

There are classified lists in this work, akin to Lowndes. This annotated work goes back to the headiest days of book collecting, which may be said to have begun in the later eighteenth century.

THE NEW CAMBRIDGE BIBLIOGRAPHY OF ENGLISH LITERATURE. 5 vols. Cambridge: Cambridge University Press, 1969 – 77.

This is the bibliography of literature in a 'literary' rather than in a wider sense, and is arranged in broad periods. Rather than concentrating in each period upon authors, genre is emphasized. Critical works are included upon each author, and the whole is a most useful bibliography of a sphere librarians may still be expected by the public to know about. The final volume is an index, the 1940 edition was fuller on 'non-literary literature', and there is a cut-down version *The shorter new Cambridge bibliography of English literature* (1981).

Having noted some standard bibliographies, we may now turn briefly to the development of bibliographical listing beyond the needs of 'mere collectors'. In establishing the method of describing books, as opposed to the trade listing of them, the major work was done with early printed books, and particularly with incunabula, that is, books of the fifteenth century. Among important bibliographies are:

Hain, L. F. T., REPERTORIUM BIBLIOGRAPHICUM, in quo libri omnes ab arte typographica inventa usque ad annum MD . . . 2 vols. Stuttgart: Cotta, 1826 – 38.

A most influential bibliography, based on German collections and still quoted in other catalogues and lists, its value was in the standardization of items included. It also provided a springboard for the work of others such as W. A. Copinger in Britain and D. Reichling in Germany. Hain's work was in author order, without any introduction, but the following work offered a different approach.

Proctor, Robert, AN INDEX TO THE EARLY PRINTED BOOKS IN THE BRITISH MUSEUM FROM THE INVENTION OF PRINTING TO THE YEAR MD. 2 parts, with later supplements. London: Kegan Paul, 1898 – 1903.

Very heavy work in the British (Museum) Library enabled Proctor to place books in a different order, of greater value to the student of printing and bibliography. This 'Proctor order' consists of country, town and printer, and is akin to schools of painting. Proctor did relate to Hain and much of the anonymous printing of early days shown there was now able to be allocated on typographical evidence. The entries themselves are quite short.

Two further works are worth knowing in this sphere, which is one still very heavily worked on by scholars.

GESAMTKATALOG DER WIEGENDRUCKE, herausgegeben von der Deutschen Staatsbibliothek zu Berlin. 2nd ed. Stuttgart: Hiersemann; New York: Kraus, 1968 – .

GW or *GKW*, as it is colloquially known, is a by-word for detailed accuracy in description, on which an English explanation can be found in volume 8 of this edition. The entries are full and arranged by author. This forms something of a contrast to the short-title catalogues, noted below, which are the first things one turns to with older books.

British Museum, CATALOGUE OF BOOKS PRINTED IN THE XVTH CENTURY NOW IN THE BRITISH MUSEUM. London, 1908 – . Reprint 1963 includes handwritten amendments.

This is also full in its descriptions, but, not surprisingly, follows Proctor's order. Work on it continues, part 12, an Italian supplement appearing in 1985. Thanks to the work of book collectors in earlier centuries, the British Library is very rich in incunabula from all European countries, and in preparing this catalogue concentration has been on those centres rather than Britain itself. The value of the 'standardization' aspect of works such as *GW* and *BMC* cannot be over-emphasized, and the task of many librarians dealing with early works largely consists of comparison with them.[13]

For practical verification purposes, the great descriptive catalogues are not the first port of call, and to help us there is a whole category of lists known as **short-title catalogues**. It must not be forgotten, however, that the fullest descriptions will be needed for definite identification in the end. Amongst the short-title catalogues are:

Pollard, A. W. and Redgrave, G. R., A SHORT-TITLE CATALOGUE OF BOOKS PRINTED IN ENGLAND, SCOTLAND AND IRELAND, AND OF ENGLISH BOOKS PRINTED AROUND 1475 – 1640. 2nd ed. 2 vols. London: Bibliographical Society, 1976 – 86.

The original edition (1926) contained 26,000 books, but the revision should add another 10,000 books when completed. It is the standard work to check for English books of an early date, and is frequently cited, as 'STC', by booksellers' catalogues and other bibliographies. The old STC numbers were fortunately retained in the new edition, as it had provided a basis for a number of finding lists, of which Ramage, D., *A finding-list of English books to 1640 in libraries in the British Isles* ... (Durham: Council of the Durham Colleges, 1958) is particularly useful for the UK, and *A checklist of American copies of 'Short-title catalogue' books*, by W. W. Bishop (Ann Arbor: University of Michigan Press, 1950) for the United States.

An *Index of printers, publishers and booksellers* ..., by P. G. Morrison was produced by the Bibliographical Society of Virginia in 1961, and a draft *Chronological index* by Philip Rider (1989) is circulating. The long introduction to the original STC is most interesting on the recording of early books.

STC was followed chronologically in period by:

Wing, Donald G., SHORT-TITLE CATALOGUE OF BOOKS PRINTED IN ENGLAND, SCOTLAND, IRELAND, WALES AND BRITISH AMERICA AND OF ENGLISH BOOKS PRINTED IN OTHER COUNTRIES, 1641 – 1700. 2nd ed. 3 vols. New York: Modern Languages Association, 1972 – 88.

This also in its earlier edition gained an index, by Paul Morrison (1955), though these long lists of book-trade personnel are very daunting at first sight. 'Wing' may be consulted online, through BLAISE.[14] Like STC numbers, 'Wing numbers' are often quoted, the work covering a period of great publishing activity, though in fact the original numbers were not entirely sacrosanct in the second edition and the old edition (3 vols., 1945 – 51) needs to be kept on the shelf.

EIGHTEENTH-CENTURY SHORT-TITLE CATALOGUE (ESTC): THE BRITISH LIBRARY COLLECTIONS. 113 microfiche, 1984, also available on BLAISE. To be published on CD-ROM in 1990.

Moving on from early printed books to the period when publishing really expanded was a milestone, and the whole basis of rare-book cataloguing was revolutionized by use of the computer and new rules[15] devised to conduct the work. The British Library has published *The ESTC: the British Library collections* (1983), several useful guides and a newsletter.[16] Research Publications has, since 1982, been publishing a microfilm collection of these eighteenth-century books, not as full as *ESTC*, and based on a few major libraries. It publishes a guide in several volumes, continuing, which contains three sequences, main entries, titles and subjects. Whereas author, date, place and certain types of publication can be consulted on microfiche, in the online version, title, imprint, locations and language can also be accessed.[17]

INCUNABULA SHORT-TITLE CATALOGUE. BLAISE-line.

Although earlier in period covered, this began quite late, in 1981.[18] This was preceded by and based on the following work, and its supplement:

Goff, F. R., INCUNABULA IN AMERICAN LIBRARIES: A THIRD CENSUS. New York: Kraus for Bibliographical Society of America 1964, reprinted 1973.

The reprint is heavily annotated in the hand of the compiler.

Ideally it should be possible to trace all older materials in a country by whatever aspects the user desires – author and other personnel concerned with editing, title, alternative title, subject, form, format, publisher, printer, place of publication. A description of content and physical make-up is required, but not perhaps a critical annotation, which is rather the sphere of the subject bibliographer. Bibliographical description now ideally includes at least a facsimile title page, the pseudo-facsimile being rather less than satisfactory.[19]

Whilst it is not hard to imagine the possibility of this ideal world, it is much less easy to bring a programme to a satisfactory conclusion. Amongst the difficulties are the uniqueness of individual copies in early days and lack of certainty about an edition. Even in modern times the word 'edition' has been badly abused by some publishers. The scholars' refinement of bibliographical description has continued and literary critics/historians have needed to have information about a book which no bibliographer has found it necessary (or easy?) to record. A bibliography which shows the ultimate relationship between analytical (critical) bibliography and intelligent listing is:

Greg, W. W., A BIBLIOGRAPHY OF THE ENGLISH PRINTED DRAMA TO THE RESTORATION. 4 vols. London: Oxford University Press for the Bibliographical Society, 1939 – 59.

The more concentrated in period a bibliography is, the more detailed the descriptions are likely to be and librarians should see just what can be listed about a book. Unique copies of printed books do exist, and even in the nineteenth century, where standardization might be expected, variants are legion, as reading numbers of *Studies in bibliography* and similar journals will soon show.[20]

Retrospective bibliographies may be available for countries, for the output of a particular period, of materials in a particular form, on a particular subject, and for classes of material. Subject bibliographies are dealt with in the next chapter. Amongst other standard bibliographies which are well worth knowing are:

Halkett, S. and Laing, J., DICTIONARY OF ANONYMOUS AND PSEUDONYMOUS ENGLISH LITERATURE. Enlarged ed. 9 vols. Edinburgh: Oliver and Boyd, 1926 – 62.

A much-used bibliography in order of the first word of title (excluding articles), giving details of the putative author. Such works are not just of earlier years, volume 8 actually covering 1900 – 50. A third edition of the work is being produced, which takes the works in chronological periods linked to *STC* and similar authorities. The work is being edited under a slightly different title, by John Horden and the first part was published by Longman in 1981.

PRIVATE PRESS BOOKS, 1959 – . Pinner, Middlx: Private Libraries Association, 1960 – . Occasional.

Not large in any year, this lists what may be ephemeral productions, but may be quite substantial works, under the presses which produce them.

The contents of individual libraries continue to receive attention from retrospective bibliographers and studies of these are a useful contribution to cultural history. They are listed in the various volumes of Denis F. Keeling's bibliographies (see page 318). One example from many is:

Harrison, John and Laslett, Peter, THE LIBRARY OF JOHN LOCKE. Oxford Bibliographical Society, monograph 13. Oxford: Oxford University Press, 1965.

With a major thinking figure like John Locke, knowledge of the contents of his library is essential in understanding the development of the man's mind, and this is the main value of this kind of work. In this case, there is an essay on the author's book-acquisition habits and also some discussion of what individual works meant to the philosopher himself.

British Museum, CATALOGUE OF THE PAMPHLETS, BOOKS, NEWS-PAPERS AND MANUSCRIPTS RELATING TO THE CIVIL WAR, THE COMMONWEALTH AND RESTORATION, COLLECTED BY GEORGE THOMASON, 1640 – 1661. 2 vols. London: British Museum, 1908.

This is one of the great bibliographies if you need English Civil War material, for the collector was a bookseller who picked up what he could during this troubled period. It is arranged chronologically but authors and titles can be traced. University Microfilms has made the actual materials available, as with the contents of a number of other bibliographies included here. Its printed index was done in 1981.

The provenance of books (i.e. their former ownership) is of great interest to the bibliographer, whether the books were in private or collective care. There are several books devoted to the study of library catalogues.[21] The doyen of provenance studies was Neil R. Ker:

Ker, Neil R., MEDIEVAL LIBRARIES OF GREAT BRITAIN: A LIST OF SURVIVING BOOKS. 2nd ed. London: Royal Historical Society, 1964. Supplement by Andrew G. Watson. 1987.

This is a work of great scholarship, in which the still existing volumes from monastic libraries were sought in current collections and listed. It gave rise to much further study. Pearson, David, *Provenance indexes for early printed books and manuscripts: a guide to present resources* (Huntingdon: The author, corrected reprint 1988) is a useful help for finding whether scholarly libraries have indexes of the provenance of the books they hold. In the same sphere, subscription lists of older books are helpful, and *A check-list of eighteenth-century books containing lists of subscribers*, by R. C. Alston and others has been produced by Avero (1983). Work on this aspect of the book trade has been built up at Newcastle-upon-Tyne University since 1972.[22] The whole sphere of manuscript bibliography has also developed fast in recent years, for earlier manuscripts,[23] documentary sources and modern literary manuscripts.

To return to printed books, it is worth noting that other parts of the UK have produced bibliographies of books printed in their countries. There are also many studies of the output of individual presses, and of printing in individual towns or counties, just as many libraries, particularly academic, have printed lists of their older books, whatever their origin.

Rees, Eiluned, LIBRI WALLIAE: A CATALOGUE OF WELSH BOOKS AND BOOKS PRINTED IN WALES, 1548 – 1820. 2 vols. Aberystwyth: National Library of Wales, 1987.

An author catalogue, with the great problem of differentiation between many authors of the same name, which has caused the editor to interfile titles alphabetically under names which are of the same appearance. This bibliography has excellent indexes, including book-trade personnel, on which the book contains essays, and a chronological index. There is, incidentally, an annual bibliography of interest in the Celtic field:

BIBLIOTHECA CELTICA: A REGISTER OF PUBLICATIONS RELATING TO WALES AND THE CELTIC PEOPLE AND LANGUAGES. Aberystwyth: National Library of Wales, 1910 – . Annual.

With coverage from 1909, this has been published in various series, and we are now in the third. It is a classified list, with author index, and acts as a current and retrospective bibliography. The *Irish publishing record, 1967* – (Dublin: University College of Dublin, 1968 – . Annual) is similarly classified, by DC.

Aldis, H. G., A LIST OF BOOKS PRINTED IN SCOTLAND BEFORE 1700 ... Edinburgh: Edinburgh Bibliographical Society, 1904. Reprint, National Library of Scotland, 1970.

Although there is an author index, this is chronologically arranged, perhaps fitting for an author who had such a strong interest in the book trade. Good use has been made in the reprint of modern technology, which has enabled corrections to be made, together with additions. As with Welsh publications, there is a further, more current bibliography:

BIBLIOGRAPHY OF SCOTLAND, 1976/77 – . Edinburgh: National Library of Scotland, 1978 – .

This has a topographical section, a subject section and a name index. Rather unusually it includes periodical articles, making it an important subject bibliography. On the Gaelic side we have:

Ferguson, M. and Matheson, A., SCOTTISH GAELIC UNION CATALOGUE: A LIST OF BOOKS PRINTED IN SCOTTISH GAELIC FROM 1567 – 1973. Edinburgh: National Library of Scotland, 1984.

The United States is naturally quite well covered by retrospective bibliographies, as well as by current bibliographies which have cumulated, such as the *American catalog of books, 1876 – 1910*, and the *Cumulative book index*, from 1898.

Evans, Charles, AMERICAN BIBLIOGRAPHY ... 1639 – 1800. 12 vols., plus 2 vols. (1955 – 9). Chicago: The author, 1903 – 34.

This complex work is a chronological list (like Aldis for Scotland), and a supplementary volume (no. 14) was needed to give authors and titles. There are in fact further index and supplementary volumes, and the vast detail of the information given makes it an essential work unlikely to be superseded. Just as the great catalogues of incunabula required short-title catalogues, so did Evans, and the 'Short-title Evans', in author order, is:

NATIONAL INDEX OF AMERICAN IMPRINTS THROUGH 1800. 2 vols. Worcester, Mass.: American Antiquarian Society and Barre Publishers, 1969.

As with the *Eighteenth-century short-title catalogue* in the UK, there has been a publishing programme in microform, to provide availability of rare materials, and references are given to this.

Sabin, Joseph, and others, A DICTIONARY OF BOOKS RELATING TO AMERICA FROM ITS DISCOVERY TO THE PRESENT TIME. 29 vols. New York: Sabin, 1868 – 92; Bibliographical Society of America, 1928 – 36.

This Bibliotheca Americana is a most interesting work on American literary output, not limited to the United States, but it is not easy to use because of its variety of arrangements and unevenness of compilation. An *Author-title index* was prepared by J. E. Molnar in 1974 (3 vols. Metuchen, NJ: Scarecrow Press) though its use of the Sabin numbers makes one wish those numbers were listed on the spines of the original work. *The new Sabin* has been published by Whitston Publishing Co. of Troy, NY, since 1974, and involves fresh examination of all the original material.

Lack of space does not allow for description of the major bibliographical works of other countries,[24] but the bibliographical habit is well established in all European countries, and they are well worth studying. Worth mention, in terms of lists likely to be found in major British libraries, are the British Library short-title catalogues of foreign-language books. These, which also exist for France, Germany and the Netherlands/Belgium, are valuable for verification, and include:

SHORT-TITLE CATALOGUE OF BOOKS PRINTED IN ITALY AND OF ITALIAN BOOKS PRINTED IN OTHER COUNTRIES FROM 1465 – 1600 NOW IN THE BRITISH MUSEUM. London: British Museum, 1958. Reprinted 1986, with supplement 1986 and addenda 1990.

Rhodes, Dennis, CATALOGUE OF BOOKS PRINTED IN SPAIN AND OF SPANISH BOOKS PRINTED ELSEWHERE IN EUROPE BEFORE 1601 NOW IN THE BRITISH LIBRARY. 2nd ed. London: British Library, 1989.

UNIVERSAL BIBLIOGRAPHIES

If national bibliography grew with the 'rise' of nations, as countries made an effort to control their cultural heritage, so too an international dimension came into bibliography with the growth of conscious internationalism in the late nineteenth century. But one should mention that some of the early bibliographies (Hain, for instance, see page 277) had been more than national, as scholars throughout Europe communicated, particularly through the Latin language.

Brunet, J. C., MANUEL DU LIBRAIRE ET DE L'AMATEUR DES LIVRES. 5th ed. 6 vols. Paris: Firmin-Didot, 1860 – 5.

Graesse, J. G. T., TRÉSOR DES LIVRES RARES ET PRÉCIEUX. 7 vols. (including supplement). Dresden: Kuntze, 1859 – 69.
   Brunet's work in a sense may be seen as a universal bibliography, in that it is not really bounded by country (though in reality it does work in a Eurocentric framework), and Graesse's is a similar work, annotated for collectors.

There is a sense in which the catalogues of large libraries may be seen as universal bibliographies, achieving their generality without losing the specificity of individual library copies. The stocks of the British Library in London, and the Bibliothèque Nationale in Paris both include so many works of at least European culture that they must be regarded as such.

BRITISH LIBRARY CATALOGUE to 1975. 360 vols., and supplement of 6 vols. Munich: Saur. Also to be available on three CD-ROM discs.

This incorporated the old *General catalogue of printed books (GK3)* and its supplements and is sometimes known as *GK4.*[25]

BRITISH LIBRARY GENERAL CATALOGUE OF PRINTED BOOKS 1976 – 82. 50 vols. London: British Library, 1983. 1982 – 5. 26 vols. 1986.

LIBRARY OF CONGRESS. MAIN CATALOG 1898 – 1980

An enormous catalogue, occupying over 10,000 microfiche, and perhaps the closest to a universal bibliography in the world. Complemented by the SHELFLIST (1979), on 3215 fiche, including well over 6 million cards, with LC numbers.

NATIONAL UNION CATALOG, PRE-1956 IMPRINTS. 754 vols. 1968 – 81.

Based on the Library of Congress Catalog, this covers some 20 million books and many metres of shelf space. Since its publication, further volumes covering the period from 1956 have appeared, covering 1956 – 67, 1968 – 72, 1973 – 7, and 1978 onwards. Although printed volumes are available, microfiche give a substantial saving in space.

New York Public Library, DICTIONARY CATALOG OF THE RESEARCH LIBRARIES 1911 – 1971. 800 vols. New York: The Library, 1979 – 83.
This monster work is dealt with on page 297.

Bibliothèque Nationale, CATALOGUE GÉNÉRAL DES LIVRES IMPRIMÉS: AUTEURS. 231 vols. Paris: Imprimerie Nationale, 1897 – 1981.

This is another major catalogue which is available in microfiche form.

The range of large library catalogues available is very wide and keeps extending, though their price makes them likely to be bought only by other major libraries. A recent example is:

Bavarian State Library, ALPHABETICAL CATALOGUE 1501 – 1840 (BSB-AK). 60 vols. Munich: Saur, 1987 – 90.

It is interesting also to consider what attempts have been made beyond the efforts of these huge libraries to create a true international bibliography. We are led soon to the name of Paul Otlet in this connection. He believed that the world would progress along a more united front if each country knew each other's state better, and that some 'control' over knowledge of literary output could be kept. All should cooperate and an organization was created, the International Institute of Bibliography, to facilitate this. It is curious to think that these ideas were current before all sorts of practical improvements in librarianship were seen. Paul Otlet was a fanatic, very fertile in ideas.[26]

The Institute was founded in 1895, well before World War I, and did quite a large amount of work, but the conditions of the twentieth century have hardly been good for such cooperation. Nevertheless the ideals have not been totally ignored. The International Federation of Library Associations (IFLA) has encouraged UBC (Universal Bibliographical Control) since it was discussed at a symposium in 1958.[27] UBC is concerned with both current and retrospective bibliography, and seeks to encourage standardization, as for instance in the ISBD (International Standard Book Description).[28]

USE OF RETROSPECTIVE BIBLIOGRAPHIES

If current bibliographies have a role in both the verification of titles and in book selection, retrospective bibliographies concentrate on the former and add a dimension of historical research. It is likely that the user will be trying to trace the existence of an item or perhaps of a corpus of work. One aspect that has grown has been interest in book-trade history and the book in society.[29] Whereas verification can often be satisfied by a simple author/title/publisher/date line, deeper work demands fuller description.

Location of an item is a valuable feature of some retrospective bibliographies and indeed quite a few are in effect union catalogues of a number of libraries with good holdings in a field. In the rare-book field, Moelwyn I. Williams' *A directory of rare-book and special collections in the UK and the Republic of Ireland* (London: Library Association, 1985) is of great value in tracing their existence. A new edition is in active preparation. Union catalogues of such libraries can then be built upon to form even wider retrospective bibliographies. An interesting example is:

McLeod, Margaret S. G., THE CATHEDRAL LIBRARIES CATA-LOGUE: BOOKS PRINTED BEFORE 1701 IN THE LIBRARIES OF THE ANGLICAN CATHEDRALS OF ENGLAND AND WALES. Vol. 1. London: British Library, 1985.

A publication done in association with the Bibliographical Society, this is a personal *tour de force*, based on heavy work at the cathedral libraries, and on the *STC* and Wing. Naturally there are books in the cathedral libraries not in *STC* or Wing – and so the work goes on.

An aspect of books of the past is that of their value to collectors and dealers. There are several well-known sequences of records of values and indeed books have been better covered in this respect until recent years than most categories of other antiques.

BOOK AUCTION RECORDS, 1902 – . At present published Folkestone, Kent: Dawson.

BOOK PRICES CURRENT, 1887 – . London: Serjeants Press.

AMERICAN BOOK PRICES CURRENT, 1916 – . At present published Washington: Bancroft-Parkman.

Each of these series has cumulated indexes from time to time, and aims to show author/title, price, sale, etc. Although there is a strong element of 'sale price = value' attached to these works, they also have a use as bibliographies of older, rarer material. This type of search calls for computerization, and *Bookquest*, an online service, has been offered by Faxon Company, from 1990. It was formerly named *ABACIS* (Antiquarian Book and Collectibles Information Systems).

LIBRARY PROBLEMS WITH BIBLIOGRAPHIES

Bibliographies as a class of material present a few problems to the librarian, which are not shared by other printed reference material. These problems are found in two areas: access and training.

As bibliographies tend to be a librarian's tool, there is a temptation to shelve them away from the reader's eye, behind desks, in other rooms and so on. This tendency should be resisted. Many readers are aware of some major items such as the British Library catalogues and *Whitaker's books in print*, and should be encouraged to use even more. The growth of presentation in new media such as CD-ROM,[30] microfiche and online should not make access harder (in making this comment I am ignoring financial considerations). Many readers see the use of fiche in other spheres, even quite small bookshops now often sporting *Books in print* on fiche. As for the computer and CD-player, they are more and more a part of everyday life.

Quite where on the shelves bibliographies should be is another problem. The major works obviously need a large library to house them in printed book form and a separate bibliographic area is useful for these general works. Subject bibliographies, dealt with in the next chapter, may also be placed with bibliographies in such circumstances, but there is otherwise a good case for them to appear near their relevant subjects (using the .016 suffix in DC-based libraries). The most specialized bibliographies are likely to be housed in HQ's bibliographic section in an extended system, such as a county library, but this is unfortunate, in my view, for the readers.

We are at present undergoing a productive period in bibliography compilation and production, and publishers deserve all the encouragement they can get, whatever the physical format of their work. The readers should be allowed to see them.

As for training, this is necessary, for little bibliographical training is likely to have been given to most readers.[31] Librarians themselves need to be given opportunity to learn and understand bibliographies – verification work at point-of-contact needs following up by heavy work with the untraced requests, specific and subject. But in the hardly generous staffing atmosphere we work in, readers themselves in all kinds of library need some staff encouragement to browse amongst the bibliographies and do as much work for themselves as possible.

When the material has been traced, then it may need to be obtained, but that is beyond the scope of this chapter, into practical librarianship.

REFERENCES AND CITATIONS

1 Krummel, D. W., *Bibliographies, their aims and methods*. London: Mansell, 1984;
   Robinson, A. M. Lewin, *Systematic bibliography: a practical guide to the work of compilation*. 4th ed. London: Bingley, 1979;
   Stokes, Roy, *The function of bibliography*. 2nd ed. Aldershot: Gower, 1982.
   The British Library annual research lectures, 1982 –. British Library, 1983 –. Free.
   These offer an interesting conspectus of views on the growth of information and its handling. An essential background to bibliographical understanding.
   McKenzie, D. F., *Bibliography and the sociology of texts*. Panizzi lectures, 1985. British Library, 1986.
2 Cowley, J. D., *Bibliographical description and cataloguing*. London: Grafton, 1939;
   Esdaile, A., *A student's manual of bibliography*. 5th ed. by Roy Stokes. Metuchen, NJ: Scarecrow Press, 1981;
   Greg, W. W., 'Bibliography: an apologia', *The library*, 4th series, **13**, 1932 – 3, 113 – 43;
   Greg, W. W., 'Bibliography: a retrospect', in *Bibliographical Society, 1892 – 1942: studies in retrospect*. 1945, 22 – 31;
   Gaskell, P., *A new introduction to bibliography*. Oxford: Clarendon Press, 1972;
   Blum, Rudolf, *Bibliographia: an inquiry into its definition and designations*. Chicago: American Library Association; Folkestone, Kent: Dawson, 1980.
3 Higgens, G. L. (ed.), *Printed reference material*. 2nd ed. London: Library Association, 1984.
4 Walford, A. J., *Guide to reference material*. 4th ed. Vol. 3. London: Library Association, 1987.
5 Unesco, *Bibliographical services throughout the world*. Based on replies to questionnaires, these volumes cover up to five years each, after the 1950 – 59 edition. The latest covers 1983 – 84, published 1987.
6 *Bibliographic records in the book world: needs and capabilities, proceedings of a seminar . . . 1987*. BNB Research Fund report no. 33.
7 MARC Users Group, *Databases for books: their uses for selling, acquiring and cataloguing*. London: Library Association, 1983.

8 Bell, B., 'Progress, problems and prospects in current national bibliographies: implementations of the ICNB recommendations', *Journal of library and information science* (Delhi, India), **12** (2), December 1987, 104 – 27; Carpenter, Michael (ed.), *National and international bibliographic databases: trends and prospects.* Binghamton, NY: Haworth Press, 1988.

9 Beaudiquez, M., *Retrospective national bibliographies: an international directory.* (IFLA publication no. 35). Munich: Saur, 1986.
   Lists the main works, as part of UBC.

10 Maxted, I., 'Historical and non-current bibliography', in *British librarianship and information work, 1981 – 1985*, ed. by D. W. Bromley and A. Allott. London: Library Association, 1988. Vol. 1, 303 – 25.
   Gives a good account of the relationship between historical bibliography and the listing of books.

11 Schneider, G., *Theory and history of bibliography.* 1934.
   The standard, heavy historical work.

12 Myers, R. and Harris, M., *Pioneers in bibliography.* St Paul's Bibliographies, 1988.
   The great bibliographers (series), from Scarecrow Press of Metuchen, NJ, includes Henry Bradshaw, A. W. Pollard, T. F. Dibdin, D. C. McMurtrie, R. B. McKerrow and M. Sadleir, all major figures, not all discussed in this essay.

13 Tanselle, G. T., 'Descriptive bibliography and library cataloguing', *Studies in bibliography*, **30**, 1977, 1 – 56.

14 See *BLAISE manual* for details of coverage. Leaflets also available from British Library.

15 *The eighteenth-century S.T.C.; the cataloguing rules*, compiled by J. Zeeman. 2nd ed. London: British Library, 1986.

16 *Factotum: ESTC newsletter.* 3 per year, free from ESTC Office, British Library;
   Crump, M. and Harris, M., *Searching the eighteenth-century* . . . . London: British Library, 1983;
   Alston, R. C., *Searching ESTC online: a brief guide.* London: British Library, 1982;
   Alston, R. C. and Jannetta, M. J., *Bibliography, machine-readable cataloguing and the ESTC.* London: British Library, 1978.

17 Alston, R. C., 'The grammar of research: some implications of machine-readable bibliography', *British Library journal*, **11** (2), 1985, 113 – 22.

18 Hellinga, L. and Goldfinch, J. (eds.), *Bibliography and the study of 15th-century civilisation* . . . London: British Library, 1987.
   A collection of papers on ISTC and its importance.

19 The main works on bibliographical description are Bowers, F., *Principles of bibliographical description.* Princeton, NJ: Princeton University Press, 1949, reprinted Winchester: St. Paul's Bibliographies, 1986;
   McKerrow, R. B., *An introduction to bibliography.* Oxford: Clarendon Press, 1927.

20 *Studies in bibliography*. Charlottesville: Bibliographical Society of the University of Virginia. Annual.
Bibliographical Society of America. *Papers*.
In Britain, in addition to the Bibliographical Society, which publishes *The library*, there are bibliographical societies in other parts of the country: Edinburgh, Cambridge, Oxford, etc.

21 Taylor, Archer, *Book catalogues: their varieties and uses*. 2nd ed. Winchester: St. Paul's Bibliographies, 1986;
Jayne, Sears, *Library catalogues of the English renaissance*. Godalming, Surrey: St Paul's Bibliographies, 1983;
Nelson, Bonnie R., *Guide to published library catalogs*. Metuchen, NJ: Scarecrow Press, 1982.

22 Robinson, F. J. G. and Wallis, P. J., *Book subscription lists: a revised guide*. Newcastle-upon-Tyne: PHIBB, 1975, with supplements.

23 Ker, N. R., *Medieval manuscripts in British libraries*. 3 vols. Oxford: Oxford University Press, 1969 – 83.

24 See note 9 above.

25 Chaplin, A. H., *GK: 150 years of the 'General catalogue of printed books in the British Museum'*. Aldershot: Scolar Press, 1987;
McCrimmon, B., *Power, politics and print: the publication of the BM Catalogue 1881 – 1900*. Hamden, Ct: Linnet Books; London: Bingley, 1981.

26 Rayward, W. Boyd, *The universe of information: the work of Paul Otlet for documentation and international organisation*. Moscow: International Federation for Documentation (FID), 1975.

27 Anderson, Dorothy, *Universal bibliographical control*. Verlag Dokumentation for IFLA, 1974. International Office for UBC, *Encyclopedia of library and information science*. Vol. 37, supp. 2, 1984, 366 – 401.

28 *IFLA guidelines for the application of the ISBDs to the description of component parts*. IFLA, 1988.

29 *Annual bibliography of the history of the printed book and libraries (ABHB)*, 1 – , 1970 – . Various publishers, now Dordrecht: Kluwer.

30 Helal, A. H. and Weiss, J. W. (eds.), 'The impact of CD-ROM on library operations and universal availability of information', in *11th International Essen Symposium . . . 1988: Festschrift in honour of Dr Maurice B. Line*. Essen University Library, 1989.

31 Mann, Thomas, *A guide to library research methods*. New York, London: Oxford University Press, 1987.
Particularly good on bibliographies;
Kirkham, Sandi, *How to find information in the humanities*. London: Bingley, 1989.
Integrates the paper and electronic sources;
Gash, Sarah, *Effective literature searching for students*. Aldershot: Gower, 1990.
Martyn, John, *Literature searching attitudes of research scientists*, British Library research paper no. 14, 1987.
A study of one aspect of the use of literature.

13

Subject Bibliographies

David Lee

E
ven if the general bibliographies for a country do allow for a subject approach, there is still room for subject bibliographies as such. In national current bibliographies subjects are catered for almost accidentally by the allocation of a subject heading or a class number to the general bibliographical entry, and although in retrospective bibliographies the subject side is likely to be more self-consciously applied, it is only in true subject bibliography that the needs of the user can really be addressed.

Below, some general bibliographies with a subject approach are noted. A fault of the general, however, is that material relevant to the subject user may be diffused by a classification rather than gathered by it, or the grouping may be too unspecific. There is also normally a lack of critical annotation in the general bibliography. The subject bibliography tends to be created by a person or organization which feels the need to review critically the literature of the field: broad, as in the case of the *MLA international bibliography of books and articles on the modern languages and literatures*, one of the world's great current bibliographies; or narrow, as in *Green belt, green fields and the urban fringe: the pressure on land in the 1980s*, a work by Lesley Grayson for the British Library's Science Reference and Information Service (1990). It is the aim of this chapter to give some idea of the variety of the subject bibliographies which have been created, noting some famous landmarks and illustrating, by other examples, their types and trends.[1]

Subject bibliographies are legion. The *British national bibliography* includes well over 10,000 between 1950 and 1990, so no librarian is likely to know them all. He or she must, however, know the main general sources, have a firm idea of the types which are likely to exist in a subject and be able to trace them. Some subject bibliographical structures the librarian will learn during his or her training; others will need developing during his career. Techniques in the machine retrieval of bibliographical material will also need to be developed, for they have changed rapidly in the last few years. Bibliographical work has its fascination and those who wish to engage in it are likely to find opportunity, either in individual libraries (where posts of bibliographer are sometimes advertised) or as a member of a cooperating group.

When you examine the variety of bibliographies, you can see why there are so many and why compilers are drawn to this branch of literary and critical endeavour. The categories which will be dealt with in this chapter are:

(a) general bibliographies with a subject approach, including library catalogues and guides to reference books;
(b) selective bibliographies, including series and handbooks to the literature;
(c) comprehensive subject bibliographies;
(d) special library catalogues, knowledge of which may depend on knowledge of the libraries themselves;
(e) current bibliographies;
(f) analytical indexes, which are akin to subject bibliographies;
(g) bibliographies of bibliographies.

GENERAL BIBLIOGRAPHIES WITH A SUBJECT APPROACH

In seeking material where the author is not known, general bibliographies may be the first base. *British national bibliography* has, from 1950, given a subject approach to British publications on a classified (DC) basis. The American *Cumulative book index*, from 1928, has had a wider world coverage under alphabetical subject headings. To have the two approaches is useful; they represent a common difference between practice in the two continents.

The weekly and monthly trade and reviewing journals have a different function from the bibliographies, in that they are aids to selection by librarians and booksellers and usually lack a detailed and consistent subject approach. They rely much on keywords in titles, an approach which may often work but is not rigorous enough for the serious search. The *Subject guide to books in print*, published annually by Bowker (1988 – 9, 4 vols.), uses LC headings for tracing material and is supplemented by the *Books in print supplement*. The service is also available online or as microfiche. Another work from Bowker, *Subject guide to international books in print*, extends the scope. In Britain the Whitaker's range is of great value but the subject aspect is limited, thanks to a reliance on the keyword.

For works published before 1928, one has mainly to turn to library catalogues (see below), as earlier bibliographies are of little value from the subject angle – the *English catalogue of books* for instance. The attempts of Watt, Brunet and Lowndes are historically interesting but not of genuine value to the subject searcher. These and other older bibliographies are included in the previous chapter. Those two important bibliographies of older material, the *ESTC* and *NSTC* have rather different approaches to subjects. The latter has an adaptation of the Decimal classification. Though this may look daunting, with long strings of item numbers, at least there is a subject approach, useful for those concerned with subject bibliography. *ESTC* in its fullest version will offer rather more subject approaches (see page 280).

General library catalogues

The large repositories of books are collections of material on all subjects, and their catalogues are akin to bibliographies for their national literatures. The British Library (founded 1753) began with author lists only, but later came to subjects in both formats, classified 1824 – 34 and alphabetical from 1874.

The BRITISH LIBRARY SUBJECT INDEX OF MODERN BOOKS ACQUIRED, 1971 – 1975. 14 vols. plus supplements. London: British Library, 1986.

In printed form, edited for many years by F. J. Hill,[2] this is the last volume of the *BL subject index* in its old guise.

SUBJECT CATALOGUE 1975 – 85. 75 vols. Munich: K. G. Saur, 1986. Also available as 450 microfiches in a binder.

This is the successor series, in large handsome volumes based on the main guide-book catalogue of the Round Reading Room.

Peddie, R. A., SUBJECT INDEX OF BOOKS PUBLISHED BEFORE 1880. 4 vols. London: Grafton, 1933 – 48.

The bibliography to consult for earlier works, it is not limited in content to the British Library. The supplements in some volumes should not be missed.

British Library. GENERAL CATALOGUE OF PRINTED BOOKS TO 1975. 360 vols., or three CD-ROM discs. SAZTEC/Chadwyck-Healey, 1989 – 91.

With well over 5 million records, this will be a prime source, allowing searches not only by author and title, but also by keyword and by subject, amongst other possibilities. At the time of publication, the discs cost £9,000, but the printed version roughly twice as much. Either is a major investment for cost-conscious libraries.

LIBRARY OF CONGRESS SUBJECT CATALOGUE. Published quarterly since 1950. Title in earlier days was *Library of Congress catalog: books: subjects.*

This is of some size, 1970 – 4 for instance taking up 100 large volumes. Now available on microfiche. It is a current subject bibliography, using Library of Congress alphabetical subject headings. Cooperative cataloguing allows the inclusion of other libraries' materials, a most useful feature.

NEW YORK PUBLIC LIBRARY. Dictionary catalog of the research libraries. 800 vols. Boston: G. K. Hall, 1979.

An astonishingly useful general catalogue of the world's literary output.

The LONDON LIBRARY SUBJECT INDEX

Listing its books under subject headings (the library is alphabetico-classed in its shelf arrangement), this is an important and convenient British source. In recent years the handsome printed volumes have been supplemented on microfiche, based on computerization of the library's accessions.

At one time subject catalogues or class lists were quite often printed but now they are uncommon. It is a rare library which can claim that its catalogue is a comprehensive subject bibliography, and even rarer that such should be available for purchase. The Institute of Chartered Accountants added material it did not possess to make its catalogue *Historical accounting literature* (1975) into a bibliography. Other special library catalogues are dealt with more fully below.

General guides to reference books

One of the most useful categories of bibliography is the general guide, which helps the librarian when the library stock appears to be deficient and he/she does not know the subject literature. There are two guides which try to keep up-to-date as handbooks:

Sheehy, E. P., GUIDE TO REFERENCE BOOKS. 10th ed. 3 vols., with occasional supplements. Chicago: American Library Association, 1986.

Walford, A. J., GUIDE TO REFERENCE MATERIAL. 5th ed. 3 vols. London: Library Association, 1989 – .

Sheehy's work is the 10th edition of a classic which goes back to 1902 as Kroeger, Mudge or Winchell; Walford's is in its fifth edition, 1989 – . Volume 1 covering science and technology has so far appeared. Both lists are classified and annotated. Walford is 'intended for librarians, in the building up and revision of reference library stock; for use in general and special library enquiry work; as an aid to students taking examinations in librarianship, and for research workers, in the initial stages of research' (Introduction). Sheehy's aims are almost identical.

The two books are invaluable aids to what exists and may be

in a system rather than the individual library. The *American reference books annual (ARBA)* (Englewood, Col.: Libraries Unlimited, 1970 –), which has several cumulative indexes, is a useful update on new bibliographies in all fields.

General guides to reading are not usually of great help to librarians, but the following should be known:

Sonnenschein, W. S., THE BEST BOOKS. 3rd ed. 6 vols. London: Routledge, 1910 – 35.
  Containing 150,000 entries and indexed in volume 6, this is a striking achievement, not superseded in its type. The American *Reader's adviser: a layman's guide to literature* (13th ed. 6 vols. New York: Bowker, 1986 – 8) has its devotees. There is a complete index in the last volume.

SUBJECT BIBLIOGRAPHIES – SELECTIVE

Most bibliographies are selective, for the obvious reasons that the work must appear manageable to the reader and must be able to be finished by the compiler. There are very many selective bibliographies at the ends of books and articles and many others, some quite large, which are whole books. A glance at *Whitaker's books in print* will show under the term 'bibliography' the range of subjects covered and I will not attempt here to classify them. Their origins are legion – for instance experts in a field may like to set down their bibliographical knowledge and reduce the size of their other books. An author who has compiled some detailed book has necessarily acquired a good knowledge of the literature and may produce a second, bibliographical, book. A good example here is Amar Kaur Jasbir Singh, *A guide to source materials in the India Office Library and records for the history of Tibet, Sikkim and Bhutan 1765 – 1950* (London: British Library, 1988) for the author had already written a history, *Himalayan triangle*, on the subject. Harold B. Carter in his *Sir Joseph Banks (1743 – 1820): a guide to biographical and bibliographical sources* (1987) 'presents the main body of material on which [he has] drawn in the writing of the biography of Sir Joseph Banks for which it is a form of extended bibliography'.

Some writers are simply absorbed by the literature. The food and wine writer André L. Simon, for instance, produced a number of elegant bibliographies, of which *Bibliotheca vinaria* (London: Holland Press, 1979), first published in 1913 as the Wine Club's library catalogue, has the author's manuscript amendments in the new edition.

An interesting type of selective bibliography is exemplified by:

INTERNATIONAL REVIEW OF PERIODICAL LITERATURE: BRITISH HISTORY. Chadwyck-Healey, 1988 – .

One of a new series of annual reviews of literature, in which an expert panel will review the literature, from journals only. In the literature-conscious humanities one can imagine that this kind of venture could become more common.

A library with a strong subject collection may feel it a duty to publish a bibliography of its speciality. The Westminster City Libraries have published Catherine Cooke, *The contents of a lumber room: a catalogue of the Sherlock Holmes collection* (1986), though the lack of an index and too little annotation do rather spoil the ship. The University of Texas has a unique collection of literature on early photography:

Gernsheim, Helmut, INCUNABULA OF BRITISH PHOTOGRAPHIC LITERATURE. Scolar Press, 1984.

A publication of this nature is a service to scholarship. The author has produced further bibliographies.

There are several specialist publishers in the bibliographical field, including Bowker, Butterworth, Chadwyck-Healey, Clio Press, Gale, Gower, Greenwood, G. K. Hall, Harvester Press, Kraus, St Paul's Bibliographies, Scarecrow and H. W. Wilson. Several of these produce work in media additional to books.

There is no standard form for the style and content of selective bibliographies. They vary with the wishes of the compiler and the perceived needs of the user.

Annotation is almost obligatory in a selective bibliography, in that a reason is needed for the material which is included. A good introduction is also required, outlining criteria of inclusion and the scope of the subject. Where a very narrow, particularly a new, subject is dealt with then a simple list can be tolerated, on the grounds of 'anything is better than nothing'. For instance, the indication given by the entries in the British Library's *Online searching aids: a subject bibliography on front-ends, gateways etc.*, by E. N. Efthimiadis (1989) may delight the searcher; it is entirely uncritical, and indeed was itself compiled from information in computer databases.

The writing of annotations may cause problems to the newcomer to subject bibliography, in that he may be afraid to be too critical. In practice, it is good to remember the reader one has in mind and have confidence in a good knowledge of the literature. There are bibliographies which go even further than just annotation, where the details of the books are written into a narrative. A good example of this is H. Philip Bolton's *Dickens dramatized* (London: Mansell, 1987) which was a winner of the Besterman award for 1987, and calendars performances, with a bibliography of published texts and unpublished manuscripts.

Bio-bibliographies are rather similar, in that they run together details of books and the life of their subject, perhaps with publishing history. Such bibliographies are meant to be read, usually proceed chronologically through the subject's life, and are a great help to collectors.

Subject bibliographies – series

It is useful to the librarian and information officer when publishers produce series of bibliographies, and there are a number of these current at present. The librarian hopes to rely on the format and standard being maintained if he is to place a standing order for them. Amongst those at present running are: 'Guides to information sources for research and development' (London: Butterworth), whose titles used to begin *Use of* .... A recent volume is:

Wyatt, H. V. (ed.), INFORMATION SOURCES IN THE LIFE SCIENCES. 3rd ed. London: Butterworth, 1987.

This is a most readable bibliography, concentrating on the types of material in areas such as botany, ecology, biotechnology, and how they are used.

The 'World bibliographical series' (Santa Barbara, Ca., and Oxford: Clio Press) is a very fast-growing series, aiming to cover the countries of the world in a bibliography, giving sources on all aspects of the country's culture. Well over 100 volumes have appeared, and later editions are beginning to supplant the earlier ones.

The American publisher Meckler has begun an interesting series, its 'Bibliographies of British statesmen'. One early volume, *William Pitt the younger, 1759 – 1806*, by A. D. Harvey (1989) not only includes manuscripts as well as pamphlets and printed books, primary and secondary, but has some of the sharpest annotations to be seen in the bibliographical business!

Harvester Wheatsheaf publishes an interesting series of 'Annotated critical bibliographies', of which a recent example is:

Shaw, Marion, AN ANNOTATED CRITICAL BIBLIOGRAPHY OF ALFRED, LORD TENNYSON. (Hemel Hempstead, Herts.: Harvester Wheatsheaf, 1989).

It is useful to the librarian to learn that this is for the 'keen student', the 'teacher at school' and the 'postgraduate student'.

Mansell has a number of series, including the 'Keyguide' series, which includes topics such as animal and human rights and various subjects in the medical area, such as dentistry. A recently begun venture is 'Bibliographies of writings by American and British women to 1900'. The first volume, by Gwenn Davis, *Personal writings by women to 1900: a bibliography of American and British writers* appeared in 1989.

If volumes in a series are updated, this can be an added advantage. The 'Soho bibliographies', now published by Oxford University Press, try to add new material from time to time to their literary bibliographies. The compiler of several, B. J. Kirkpatrick, has produced second or further editions of most of her valuable works on figures such as Virginia Woolf and E. M. Forster.

It is not only the commercial publisher which creates a series. The Home Office for instance keeps a series going of 'Current library bibliographies and reading lists', based on stock in its information and library service. Topics include prisons and privatization, child abuse, recidivism.

SUBJECT BIBLIOGRAPHIES. Washington, DC: Government Publishing Office. Occasional.

Very wide-ranging series of several hundred titles, concentrating particularly on US government publishing.

Handbooks to the literature: bibliographical guides

To the special librarian or the librarian working in a new field, the bibliographical guide or handbook is of great interest and value. The bibliographer in these cases has attempted to grasp all the sources of information in a field and describe them so that readers may understand the structure of the literature and trace the main items within it. He may go further and outline the means whereby discourse takes place between the practitioners of a discipline. A good example is:

MacDonald, Barrie, BROADCASTING IN THE UK: A GUIDE TO INFORMATION SOURCES. London: Mansell Publishing, 1988.

Including such useful items as a chronology of broadcasting, and lists of organizations in the field with addresses, etc., this nevertheless manages to include many references to books, journals and official publications. Fully indexed.

The British Library Research and Development Department has very much encouraged this type of bibliography,[3] and by now we have some excellent examples of the type, such as the item edited by H. V. Wyatt mentioned earlier, where literature users and librarians may improve their knowledge of subject structures. Another is:

Auger, C. P., INFORMATION SOURCES IN GREY LITERATURE. 2nd ed. Bowker-Saur, 1989.

In addition to a general account of this material which can so easily escape the normal bibliographies, there are reviews of grey literature in various subjects. This book, originally titled *Use of reports literature*, is in the 'Guides to information sources' series.

SUBJECT BIBLIOGRAPHIES – COMPREHENSIVE

Comprehensiveness in bibliographies should mean that the compiler has aimed to include all aspects of the subject and be complete in tracing all relevant material. Examples of such care are rare, and Roberts[4] is ironical about bibliographers who make the attempt. In a small field it may be possible, such as the work of the indefatigable Eva Crane at the Bee Research Institute. Bibliographies of writers quite often aim to be comprehensive, in that their devotees are likely to want not just the word, but every word. Again in the historical field, there are some very thorough bibliographies indeed. One example is the set of volumes edited by John Burnett and others:

Burnett, J. and others, THE AUTOBIOGRAPHY OF THE WORKING CLASS: AN ANNOTATED CRITICAL BIBLIOGRAPHY. 3 vols. Harvester Wheatsheaf, 1984 – 9.

As may be expected, the main sequence, within two time periods, is in author order, but the indexes are complex and interesting – occupations, places, dates, etc. Whatever working-class autobiography can be found, published or manuscript, this research project wishes to include it. In some projects like this and the next, comprehensiveness is 'the name of the game'.

Shaw, Gareth and Tipper, Allison, BRITISH DIRECTORIES: A BIBLIO-GRAPHY AND GUIDE TO DIRECTORIES PUBLISHED IN ENGLAND AND WALES (1850 – 1950) AND SCOTLAND (1773 – 1950). Leicester: Leicester University Press, 1988.

This is based on a trawl of libraries throughout the country and in effect holdings are given. The thoroughness of the search makes the previous work by Jane Norton much less useful.

It would be hard too to imagine that much escape the net of:

Morton, S. Fiona, A BIBLIOGRAPHY OF ARNOLD J. TOYNBEE.
Oxford: Oxford University Press, 1980.

She not only had a previous journal listing to build on but also the cooperation of the philosopher's widow in catching further material. The contrast in method of compilation to the previous item is considerable but both are useful comprehensive bibliographies.

SPECIAL LIBRARY CATALOGUES

Special libraries are likely to have a better stock in their subjects than even the largest general libraries, public or academic. They try to make up losses, analyse in catalogues and indexes their stock of books and periodicals, and take 'grey literature' not available elsewhere and perhaps not even bibliographically listed. At best, special library catalogues are virtual bibliographies, current and retrospective, of their subjects and allied fields.

The **printed subject catalogue** or index, such as that done by the Royal Institute of British Architects (2 vols., 1937 – 8, reprinted 1972), is not now economically feasible for most libraries, thanks to the staff-intensiveness of editing such works, but a new life has been given to the form by the photographic reproduction of card catalogues, and by the making available of computerized cataloguing services on a wider basis. An example of the former is:

COURTAULD INSTITUTE OF ART PERIODICALS SUBJECT INDEX. London: Mindata

This important index to periodicals has been reproduced in microfiche, arranged by subject. The idea is excellent, the handwriting of the original cards unfortunately no better than yours or mine.

As an example of the computerized library catalogue:

SCIENCE REFERENCE LIBRARY (SRL) SCICAT (i.e. library catalogue).
London: British Library, microfiche, quarterly.

This is available as author/title and subject catalogues, separately. The classified catalogue has a subject index.

Whilst full library catalogues are hardly likely to be embarked upon, a section of the library may be worth concentrating on. An example is:

Lust, John, WESTERN BOOKS ON CHINA PUBLISHED UP TO 1850 IN THE LIBRARY OF THE SCHOOL OF ORIENTAL AND AFRICAN STUDIES, UNIVERSITY OF LONDON: A DESCRIPTIVE CATA-LOGUE. London: Bamboo Publishing, 1987.

LONDON BIBLIOGRAPHY OF THE SOCIAL SCIENCES. In traditional printed form 1931 – ; now via computer from Mansell Publishing. Vol. 23, the supplement covering 1988, appeared in 1989.

This classic bibliography is in effect a useful current bibliography of a wide range of literature taken by the important library of the London School of Economics.

Current accession lists from special libraries are very useful extensions of their catalogues, as in the case of the Victoria and Albert Museum and the Imperial War Museum libraries. The journal of an institution with a library is often the medium for library accessions lists as well as reviews. *Dr Williams's Library bulletin* is an example of a journal with varied contents, including classified lists of accessions in its field of religion, adding to printed catalogues which go back to 1841 – 85. Incidentally this is another library whose card catalogue has been published by G. K. Hall, in author, subject and chronological volumes, 12 in all (1968).

Guides to libraries

The tracing of catalogues of special libraries often means in effect the identification of relevant libraries and there are available many directories. Compiled on a variety of bases – geographical area, subject or type – these usually indicate the library's cataloguing system and publications. The standard British work is:

ASLIB DIRECTORY OF INFORMATION SOURCES IN THE UK. 5th ed. 2 vols. London: Aslib, 1982 – 4.

The subject indexes allow specialist sources to be found. Volume 1 includes science, commerce and technology; volume 2 social sciences, medicine and the humanities.

SUBJECT COLLECTIONS. 6th ed. 2 vols. New York: Bowker, 1985.

Covers 18,000 collections in North America. Access is by Library of Congress subject headings.

WORLD GUIDE TO LIBRARIES. 7th ed. Munich etc: K. G. Saur, 1986.

Another useful source (though without a subject index), complemented by *World guide to special libraries* (Munich: Saur, 1983). The works by R. B. Downs should not be forgotten:

AMERICAN LIBRARY RESOURCES. Chicago: American Library Association, 1951, with supplements 1962, 1972 and 1981.

BRITISH AND IRISH LIBRARY RESOURCES. 2nd ed. Chicago: American Library Association; London: Mansell, 1981.

These, and a similar work on Australian and New Zealand library resources, are particularly strong on where, through catalogues and descriptions, further details of the contents of the libraries can be found. All are indexed.

The Library Association regional guides to library resources began in 1958 but although some further editions were produced, as a series they were abandoned. Some areas have managed to continue the type, which listed libraries by area, with an indication of their contents and services, e.g.

DIRECTORY OF INFORMATION SOURCES IN WALES, edited by Dianne M. Hooper. Cardiff: Welsh Development Agency, 1989.

As for lists by subject, these have now become quite common:

Pearson, J. D., A GUIDE TO MANUSCRIPTS AND DOCUMENTS IN THE BRITISH ISLES, RELATING TO SOUTH AND SOUTH-EAST ASIA. Vol. 1, London. London: Mansell, 1989.

Viaux, Jacqueline, IFLA DIRECTORY OF ART LIBRARIES. New York, London: Garland Publishing, 1985.

Beyond actual library lists, general reference works such as *World of learning* (40th ed. Europa, 1990) can be used to find at least the organizations which may be expected to house a library. Longman is publishing specialized directories from its research centres database,[5] such as:

ELECTRONICS RESEARCH CENTRES: A WORLD DIRECTORY OF ORGANIZATIONS AND PROGRAMMES. London: Longman, 1986.

CURRENT BIBLIOGRAPHIES

Ideally, current bibliographies are needed to supplement their retrospective equivalents, but they are by no means as common. The current general bibliographies with a subject aspect must not be forgotten: *British national bibliography*, *Cumulative book index*, etc. Finding current bibliographies is not an easy task for the general librarian, and he may need to consult a specialist in the subject field. The types of current bibliography that one may hope to find are:

(a) a specific current bibliography of the subject, such as the *British catalogue of music*;
(b) a current subject index to periodicals, of which *British education index* is a good example;
(c) journals which review or report the contents of other periodicals. *Antiquaries' journal*, *Journal of transport history* are examples. *Mariner's mirror, the journal of the Society for Nautical Research* also does a bibliography of books and articles;
(d) library accessions lists, such as the Department of Education and Science's *Educational developments at home and abroad*, a classified monthly list;
(e) card schemes, such as the *Architectural periodicals index*, or the *International index to film periodicals*, from the Fédération International des Archives du Film;
(f) online computer schemes;

(g) current awareness bulletins, which, although they give information, are often based on a named printed source. The *Biotechnology newsletter*, from the British Library, is a useful (and free) example, appearing 2-monthly.

BIBLIOGRAPHICAL INDEXES

In this section are first noted a few special indexes which perform a similar function to bibliographies in directing the user further, but which in themselves give little information. Amongst them are some of the most useful reference library works in practice. E. Granger's *Index to poetry* (9th ed. New York: Columbia University Press, 1990); J. H. Ottemiller's *Index to plays in collections: an author and title index to plays appearing in collections (published between 1900 and 1985)* (7th ed. Metuchen, NJ: Scarecrow Press, 1988), are works of this kind which have achieved the status of classics. D. E. Cook and I. S. Monro, *Short story index 1900 – 1949* (New York: H. W. Wilson, 1953), with annual supplements, cumulating every four or five years since, is another.

Indexes to other material

Although **government publications** as reference material are covered in Chapter 18, a note on their subject bibliography is needed here. A librarian using government publications learns that there are departmental lists and general lists, which appear currently, from daily onwards, and that they cumulate. Most of the lists exclude out-of-print material and they are sometimes revised rather infrequently. Subject tracing of government publications can be done through the usual current and retrospective bibliographies, as far as these include them, but apart from HMSO itself, we do not have detailed retrospective listing of its publications. There are cumulations of the HMSO annual lists, but they are of little help from a specific subject point of view. An online database of HMSO lists from 1976 has been offered from 1989 on BLAISE-LINE and DIALOG, and a CD-ROM version is due. The subject angle is limited to subjects in titles, and their own subject headings.

Historically, an important addition to the bibliography is:

Cockton, Peter, SUBJECT CATALOGUE OF THE HOUSE OF COMMONS PARLIAMENTARY PAPERS, 1801 – 1900. 5 vols. Cambridge: Chadwyck-Healey, 1988.

This lists some 80,000 documents in 19 subject groups, and is a necessary adjunct to the same publisher's publication of the papers themselves.

Not all official publications are published by HMSO, and one very useful addition to their bibliographical tracing came in the 1980s with:

CATALOGUE OF BRITISH OFFICIAL PUBLICATIONS NOT PUBLISHED BY HMSO (COBOP). Cambridge: Chadwyck-Healey, 1982 – . Available online via DIALOG.

The organizations themselves are listed in Stephen Richard's *Directory of British official publications: a guide to sources* (2nd ed. London: Mansell, 1984). Government libraries are included in the British Library's *Guide to government department and other libraries* (28th ed. London: British Library, 1988). There is no guarantee that bibliographical information will be given from these libraries, cost-conscious as they must now be, but often it can be obtained there.

For older government publications, the academics P. and G. Ford provided valuable aid for subject tracing. Their works, mentioned on pages 442 – 3 are amongst those which all librarians should know and instinctively turn to at the right time.

SYSTEM FOR INFORMATION ON GREY LITERATURE IN EUROPE. London: British Library, 1984 – .

Usually known by its acronym, SIGLE is an important source in view of Britain's closer integration with the rest of Europe. It is available on Euronet-DIANE: BLAISE-INKA, as are many other databases.

Periodicals, dealt with mainly in Chapter 8, also have subject indexes to help the enquirer to articles on subjects contained therein. Indexes to individual journals vary greatly, from little more than author/title lists to really thorough works cumulated at decent intervals. General subject indexes to a range of periodicals developed late in the nineteenth century, a noted pioneer being William Frederick Poole in America, and the main development coming through the H. W. Wilson Co.[6]

British humanities index and *Current technology index* are two important British indexes published by Butterworth, formerly from the Library Association. They developed from the *Subject index to periodicals*, founded in 1913, and are essential tools for tracing material on subjects.

In practice a librarian will often work in the parallel channels of bibliographies for books, and subject indexes to periodical articles, to reveal materials for the reader.

There are also specialized indexes such as *British education index*, 1954 – , and the *Index Islamicus* (London: Mansell), the *International photography index* (Boston, Mass.: G. K. Hall, annual), which covers over 100 periodicals, *British archaeological abstracts* (London: Council for British Archaeology; Oxford: Oxford Microform Publications, two issues a year). This incidentally intends, within a defined area, to be comprehensive. A typical specialized venture now computerized is *Index Kewensis*, which began in 1895 (Oxford University Press). It is an enumeration of the general species of flowering plants, and the works in which they were first published. Supplements appear from time to time, such as the 16th, 1971 – 6 (1978). The botanical world is well organized in keeping an eye on its literary output, as is that of art. Speed is important in periodical publishing, and *Architectural periodicals index* (London: RIBA, 1972 – . Quarterly), is available in card, microform, magnetic tape or printed forms. Some databases are available on more than one network. The *Index to legal periodicals*, for instance, can be searched on Wilsonline, WESTLAW and LEXIS.

Citation indexes are a particular form of periodical index, in which publications which have been cited by writers, and those publications which cite them, are listed, the inference being that a much cited article has a special value. Abstracts and citation indexes are dealt with more fully in Chapter 8.

Theses may be found through the *Aslib index to theses 1950/1951* – (London: Aslib, 1953 –) and through *Dissertation abstracts international* (Ann Arbor, Mi.: University Microfilms, 1951 –). The former has rather more detailed indexing than it did at one time. The latter has a very thorough indexing system:

COMPREHENSIVE DISSERTATION INDEX (DI). University Microfilms International.

This lists 600,000 dissertations in (mainly) US colleges. The main set of 37 volumes covers 1861 – 1972, a further set of 38 volumes covers 1973 – 82, and there are annual volumes after this. Because of its bulk, the indexes are grouped by broad subject area, then there is detailed keyword indexing, as well as author indexing. There are now CD-ROM archival discs, with current discs updated every six months.

Festschriften, those collections of essays in honour of worthy scholars, so common in the history field, are partly tracked down through the *Essay and general literature index, 1900 – 1933*, etc. (New York: H. W. Wilson, 1934 –), where they are listed analytically under subject headings. Some specialist current bibliographies include them, such as the *International medieval bibliography* (Leeds: University of Leeds, 1967 – , two issues a year), and there are also specialist retrospective bibliographies for particular fields, such as J. P. Danton and J. F. Pulis, *Index to Festschriften in librarianship, 1967 – 1975* (Munich, etc.: Saur, 1979), which continues previous work. A further example is Barbara Tearle (ed.), *Index to legal essays . . . 1975 – 79* (London: Mansell, 1983), produced by the British and Irish Association of Law Librarians.

Microforms are listed by subject in:

SUBJECT GUIDE TO MICROFORMS IN PRINT. London: Mansell, annual.

GUIDE TO MICROFORMS IN PRINT: SUBJECT. Westport, Ct: Meckler, 1989.

CD-ROMs are now common enough to deserve their own listing, and *CD-ROMs in print: an international guide* has been produced by Meckler, from 1990, accessed by a variety of indexes, including broad subject groups. As CD-ROM includes many bibliographical works, such as *Art index*, *British Library catalogue*, *Deutsche Bibliographie*, *Ulrich's Plus*, Whitaker's *Bookbank*, *LISA*, it is a sphere to keep up with. Meckler produce the journal *CD-ROM librarian*, monthly, which includes reviews. The UK Online User Group (UKOLUG), has a CD-ROM User Forum.

CD-ROM DIRECTORY. 4th ed. for 1990. London: Task Force Pro Libra Publishing, 1989.
   Includes a subject index of products and databases.

CD-ROM INFORMATION PRODUCTS: AN EVALUATIVE GUIDE AND DIRECTORY. Aldershot: Gower, 1990.
   The second part is a directory of 500 CD-ROM products.

Series and the books in them, are listed in:

BOOKS IN SERIES. 4th ed. New York: Bowker, 1985.
   The six volumes cover series, authors and titles respectively, and the work is very comprehensive.

Baer, Eleanora A., TITLES IN SERIES: A HANDBOOK FOR LIBRARIANS AND STUDENTS. 3rd ed. 4 vols. Metuchen, NJ: Scarecrow Press, 1978.
   This is arranged by series title, with author and title index.

SEQUELS. 9th ed. London: Association of Assistant Librarians, 1989, and its companion volume covering junior sequels (Newcastle-under-Lyme: A.A.L., 1988) are useful works for devotees of sequels in fictional series.

Conference proceedings quite often need to be traced by subject, and *Index of conference proceedings received* (London: British Library) enables this to be done. It is published monthly and annually, and follows *Conference index 1964 – 1988* (London: British Library, 1989, on 48 microfiche, or Munich: Saur, 26 volumes). Arranged by keyword headings, this does have, and needs, additional subject entries for its 270,000 conferences. It is available in hard copy, on microfiche and online.

The *Fiction index* is an interesting bibliography which has appeared for many years now, giving the subjects of novels, for those readers who wish to follow a topic fictionally. The problems of preparing this have been covered by two of the editors.[7] Four volumes, published by the Association of Assistant Librarians as *Cumulated fiction index*, cover the period from 1945 to 1979. The *Short story index* also indexes its stories by subject.

Enser, A. G. S., FILMED BOOKS AND PLAYS. 1928 – 1986. London: Gower, 1987.

Another work which needs continuation from time to time. It aims to show which books and plays have been filmed, and from which source films have been made. It is a most useful work, without substitute.

Reviews of research are of great interest to others who intend to pursue a topic, or wish to check on results including publication details. British Library *Current research in Britain*, formerly *Research in British universities, polytechnics and colleges* is the major example in the UK. This is in four parts covering the physical sciences, biological sciences, social sciences and the humanities. By 1989 the fourth edition of most of these volumes had appeared. The material is also available online on Pergamon Infoline.

Some bodies, such as the Economic and Social Research Council, and the National Foundation for Educational Research in England and Wales, produce their own reviews of research. The former has its archive at Essex University, and an important guide is:

ECONOMIC AND SOCIAL RESEARCH COUNCIL DATA ARCHIVE CATALOGUE. 2 vols. Cambridge: Chadwyck-Healey, 1986.

In the librarian's own field, *CABLIS (Current affairs bulletin for librarians and information staff)*, monthly, published by the British Library, is useful, listing as it does additions to the BLISS library and the contents pages of journals etc. with an element of news less covered by Aslib's *Current awareness bulletin: a review of information management literature*, which concentrates rather on the literature.

Current-awareness services are not only carried out in special libraries by information units for the assistance of their staff, but some more general groups do the same. The British Library Document Supply Centre, for instance, runs its *Current awareness topics services*, and the *MEDLINE current awareness topics searches*, of which there are 19.

Indexes to illustrative materials are covered in Chapter 15. Two listings of material have their own names – discographies list recordings, and carto-bibliographies list maps.

TRACING BIBLIOGRAPHIES: BIBLIOGRAPHIES OF BIBLIOGRAPHIES

Bibliographies of bibliographies are quite rare and in practice seldom used. They are lists of books which at best will tell you what material might contain further material to have information to help you. They are a very indirect source, but when you want to know if there has been a bibliography of a subject, consult:

Besterman, T., WORLD BIBLIOGRAPHY OF BIBLIOGRAPHIES. 4th ed. 5 vols. Lausanne: Societas Bibliographica, 1965 – 6.

It is arranged by subject heading, and then chronologically by date of publication. The user is told how many items are included in each bibliography listed, and there are said to be 117,000 entries.

Toomey, Alice F. (ed.), A WORLD BIBLIOGRAPHY OF BIBLIO-GRAPHIES, 1964 – 74. 2 vols. New York: Bowker, 1977.

Supplements Besterman from Library of Congress sources.

Hill, T. H. Howard, BIBLIOGRAPHY OF BRITISH LITERARY BIB-LIOGRAPHIES. 5 vols. of a 7-vol. series. London: Oxford University Press, 1969 – 80.

The index of British literary bibliography, concerned with material on the bibliographical and textual examination of English manuscripts, books, printing and publishing.

Humphreys, A. L., A HANDBOOK TO COUNTY BIBLIOGRAPHY: A BIBLIOGRAPHY OF BIBLIOGRAPHIES RELATING TO THE COUNTIES AND TOWNS OF GREAT BRITAIN AND IRELAND. 1917. Reprinted London: Dawson.

Still a major source for local history, arranged by county with towns after the general material.

Eager, Alan, A GUIDE TO IRISH BIBLIOGRAPHICAL MATERIAL. 2nd ed. London: Library Association, 1980.

THE BIBLIOGRAPHIC INDEX 1937/1942 – . New York: H. W. Wilson Co, 1938 – .

This is the best current general bibliography of bibliographies, and should be consulted at an early stage of any serious bibliographical research. It will help to reveal 'hidden bibliographies', that is, those not easy to find in other books and periodicals. It is also available, like most Wilson indexes on their online service, Wilsonline, with a variety of charging arrangements based on whether hard-copy versions are also taken.

Aslib information has a useful function in listing recent bibliographies, such as those from the House of Commons; and on a wider front the *UNISIST bulletin*, which combined *UNISIST newsletter* and *Bibliography, documentation, terminology* (1960 – 78) lists bibliographies by country. *Library literature* has been published by H. W. Wilson since 1934 (coverage 1921 –) and is useful for its listing of bibliographies not likely to get into Besterman or the *Bibliographic index*. The *Arts libraries journal* has in each issue a 'bibliographic update', and in general the art library world is very active in this field. The *Library of Congress information bulletin* is another very useful source.

Libraries with good collections of bibliographies include the national libraries, the British Library Information Science Service (at Library Association HQ) and Aslib, but it is still true to say that there is no real public bibliographical centre in the UK. The British Library Document Supply Centre has the most impressive array in one place, and the Humanities and Social Sciences Division makes an effort to put on open shelves bibliographies which the public will need (recent developments just behind the scenes in the Round Reading Room have improved things considerably). The Bibliographical Society is not directly concerned with subject bibliography. *Library and information science abstracts (LISA)*, founded 1950 and now published by Butterworth, has perhaps become less 'bibliography-conscious', tying in with Library Association/BLISS, which says 'the collection of bibliographies (and of library catalogues) now held is not intended to be exploited for its subject content, but to illustrate the technique of compiling such works, and ranges over the history of their production'. The Library Association does, however, award the Besterman Medal for 'an outstanding bibliography or guide to the literature, first published in the UK during the preceding year'.[8]

ASSESSMENT OF BIBLIOGRAPHIES

A bibliography is successful if it gives the information you are looking for, or leads you quickly to it.[9] There are, as we have seen, many types of subject bibliography, and there is no ideal, for bibliography is a network with the mesh coarser than one would wish – complete retrospective and current listings by specific subject, with annotations. J. G. Barrow in his *Bibliography of bibliographies in religion* tells us that he did his work to find out what had already been done. Roberts[10] is still interesting on what ideal situation might exist, and the work of Paul Otlet, founder in 1895 of the International Institute of Bibliography, sought to encourage the ideal we have just mentioned, on an international scale. The ideal has not been forgotten, the concept of Universal Bibliographical Control (UBC), but unless the expansion we are engaged in is backed by resources to exploit it, one cannot be hopeful for UBC.[11]

There are gaps on the wide front and there are limitations at a practical level. We must be sure of what we are using when we consult a bibliography. We look for fitness for the purpose and are grateful when the arrangement and structure lead quickly to the information required. Annotation is a great help in assessing the value of what one finds. Assessment of material is a skill which comes with experience, and which the student should be encouraged to acquire.[12] I suspect that many bibliographers would echo G. H. Martin and Sylvia McIntyre in their *Bibliography of British and Irish municipal history* (Leicester: Leicester University Press, 1972): 'those who seek to compile bibliographies bring their cares upon themselves, and have a duty to conceal them, as best they can, from their readers', and Anne Grimshaw mentions her 'often flagging spirit'.[13] Compilers must remember that users require from the bibliographies they consult answers to very different questions, from the briefly specific to the very fully descriptive. Sequences in various orders – classified, by date, by sub-group, as well as by author – may be needed. Subject arrangement in grouped order, often hidden DC, is common, but a more specific subject index is still required, as is an author/title index. The importance of indexes cannot be over-emphasized.

A word on the limitations of subject bibliographies may be helpful to the student in assessing them:

1 **Coverage**. The printed bibliography has had to end somewhere, and the more selective the bibliography, the less permanent in value. Continuations and updatings are not as common as might be wished. Exemplary, however, is D. F. Keeling, *British library history: bibliography* (London: Library Association. 5 vols. published 1972, 1975, 1979, 1983, 1987).

2 Complementary **apparatus** may not be good – author and title indexes for instance. Even a brief subject list should have an author index, as subject bibliographies are also used as a short cut to identifying material.

3 **Location**. There is often no indication of where a rare item may be found. The *Guide to printed books and manuscripts relating to English and foreign heraldry and genealogy* (London: Mitchell and Hughes, 1892), by George Gatfield, still not superseded, is unhelpful, having no special indication of which items are

manuscript, but also no locations for any material, however rare. A bibliography, to the reader, is only a list; he then needs to see the material. George Ottley's *A bibliography of British railway history* (London: Allen and Unwin, 1965; reprint by HMSO, 1983; supplement, HMSO, 1988) is a good example of a bibliography where locations are given. Union catalogues by their very nature note the whereabouts of items and are found in the subject field. An example is *Art serials in Edinburgh libraries: a union list* (Edinburgh: National Library of Scotland, 1987).

4 **Errors**. Ghost entries and errors are quite often carried on from the past. The bibliographer should always indicate items not actually seen by him/her.

5 **Terminological changes**. This is a particular problem in the case of periodical subject indexes, and a conservative approach by the compiler is understandable where long-scale searches may be expected. Some would argue that this makes a good case for using a classified approach, with good indexes which can reflect changed terminology.

6 **Citation practice**. Methods of citing books and articles vary, though some help is available through standards.[14]

7 **Up-to-dateness**. To list current material in a comprehensive way is not easy, even in a special library, but some services do try to do this. The *Current technology index* and *Architectural periodicals index*, for instance, attempt very fast listing of up-to-date articles. This is easier to achieve in a centralized unit receiving the material, than in a cooperative scheme. A recent addition to the type is the *Applied social sciences index and abstracts* (ASSIA), 1987 – . Butterworth publishes this chain-indexed service in six issues per year, cumulated annually.

SUBJECT BIBLIOGRAPHY: THE FUTURE

We are in danger of being swamped by our own information, and news items reveal sometimes that those who most might be expected to keep up with information are relying upon hearsay and not 'scientifically' searching for the information as they might. This is where the librarian and information manager come in, so to speak, as the mediators between the mass of material and the next generation of workers. The librarian must know what sources of information on publications in the broadest sense are available, in print and other forms, including online. He or she may well be instrumental in setting up some computerized system on a subject or area basis, as noted below.

An excessive devotion to bibliographical sources is a form of mania, but an appreciation of their value at the right time is a mark of good librarianship. This knowledge can be encouraged during an educational course, and in early days as a professional, by informal instruction and use by a senior member of staff. It is also helpful if the librarian's interest and knowledge are encouraged by the preparation of subject lists, perhaps done hand-in-hand with stock revision. Personalized reader services may still be provided as well as the market-dominated ambitious schemes.

Whereas bibliographic listing of books in general arises from book production and preservation practices, subject bibliography has to be a more consciously directed occupation. The dedicated individual bibliographer still operates, but we do also now have the team:

THE MANUAL OF LAW LIBRARIANSHIP. 2nd ed. Aldershot: Gower, for British and Irish Association of Law Librarians, 1987.

This is a work edited by Elizabeth Moys from the combined experience of a large and very active group, whose latest work, *A bibliography of Commonwealth law reports*, edited by Wallace Breem and Sally Phillips, is published by Mansell in 1990.

NORTHERN BIBLIOGRAPHY, 1979 – .
Covers libraries in the Northern Regional Library system.

The Music Bibliography group has worked on computer language for music, and has been concerned with the content of the *British music bibliography*.

Methods also have changed, and it is clear that new forms and formats have evolved, microfiche, laser disc, computer-originated. Perhaps the first of these was microform, and microfiche has now become quite common. The *Bibliography of biography*, British

Library, covering biographical works from 1970 onwards, for instance, is mainly available in microfiche. The saving in space, and often in actual price of publication, in this form (though VAT may be chargeable) is considerable, but a disadvantage can be in the tying up of machines by assiduous readers if insufficient are provided.

It is of course in the computerized handling of bibliographical information that the greatest expansion has taken place. It cannot be said, however, that the computer has totally taken over, or that online bibliographies are sole masters of the field. No publisher of online material can afford not to make charges for the use of a database, and even small charges soon mount up, or are a barrier to the readers, though the saving of months of research on the part of the readers and the greater scope allowed are certainly potential plusses for them. In the present economic climate, libraries are not usually likely to bear the costs themselves. The other aspect of the computerized bibliography is that it may seem or be less easy to use. The librarian, and the reader, will need to learn search strategies. It is significant that the latest edition of D. Grogan's helpful textbook on reference work[15] quite naturally takes account of computerized sources in his examples. Nor of course need the computer lead to unaesthetic work – witness the *Isis bibliographies* or the *London bibliography of the social sciences*, both series from Mansell.[16]

The optical disc is at present being very actively encouraged in the bibliographical sphere, in the shape of the CD-ROM, as has been noted in details of publications throughout this chapter. Provided enough copies and enough machines (compatible computers plus CD-ROM players), the space-saving qualities, comparative cheapness (though again VAT is chargeable) and ability to search on many bases makes these most attractive, though the huge amount of material which can be displayed means that search techniques must be learned by the users, librarians or readers.

Interest in local history has recently given birth to some cooperative and computerized bibliographical services, giving great help in a field notoriously full of obscure ephemera. SCOTLOC, the Scottish Local Studies Information Database, as yet quite small, is one from the Scottish Library Association, with records compatible with MARC. *East Yorkshire bibliography* is online through the university computer network JANET, and is centred on Hull University from which members obtain printouts.

Whatever the changes still to come, the aim of subject bibliographers remains the same: to provide that link between the materials and the reader in need of those materials and the information they contain.

'Bibliography must have a purpose' says J. D. Cowley,[17] 'that purpose being to afford guidance in some branch of literature or record of knowledge and to tell us all there is to be known about it, how it came to be published and how it was intended to be used.' It is a high aim, and one which still leaves us much to do on the subject bibliography front. With the huge amount of material available, differentiation needs to be made, and the librarian very much has a function vis-à-vis the readers.

REFERENCES AND CITATIONS

1 Marco, Guy A., 'Subject bibliography in the 21st century', *Cataloging and classification quarterly*, **9** (1), 1988, 113 – 20.

2 Hill, F. J., 'Fortescue: the British Museum and British Library subject index', *British Library journal*, **12**, 1986, 58 – 63.

3 Taylor, P. J., *Information guides: a survey of subject guides to sources of information produced by library and information services in the UK*. London: British Library Research Department, report 5440, 1978.

4 Roberts, A. D., *Introduction to reference books*. 3rd ed. London: Library Association, 1956, 66 – 7.

5 Edwards, Ann, 'European research centres – indexing a new data base', *The indexer*, **13** (1), April 1982, 37 – 41.

6 H. W. Wilson Co., *A quarter century of cumulative bibliography: retrospect and prospect*. New York: H. W. Wilson Co., 1923.

7 Hicken, M. E., 'Compiling *Cumulative fiction index* 1975 – 1979', *The indexer*, **13** (2), October 1982, 88 – 9.

8 Winners are listed in the *Library Association yearbook*, annual, and discussed in the *Library Association record*, as awarded.

9 American Library Association. Reference Services Division. 'Criteria for evaluating a bibliography', *Research quarterly*, **11** (4), Summer 1971, 359 – 60.

10 Roberts, A. D., *op. cit.* Chapter 6.

11 Pomassl, G., 'Ten years: IFLA Committee on Bibliography 1966 – 1976', *IFLA journal*, **3** (4), 1977, 319 – 26.

12   Savage, E. A., *Manual of descriptive annotation for library catalogues*. London: Library Supply Co., 1906 is preferable to the shorter *First steps in annotation* by W. C. Berwick Sayers (Association of Assistant Librarians, 1955).

13   Grimshaw, Anne, *The horse: a bibliography of British books, 1851 – 1976*. London: Library Association, 1982.

14   Royal Society, *General notes on the preparation of scientific papers*. 3rd ed. London: Royal Society, 1974;
British Standards Institution, *Recommendations for bibliographic references*. BS 1629:1989;
Butcher, Judith, *Copy-editing*. 2nd ed. Cambridge: Cambridge University Press, 1981.

15   Grogan, Denis, *Grogan's case studies in reference work: vol. 3, Bibliographies of books*. London: Bingley, 1987.

16   Whitrow, Magda, 'The ISIS cumulative bibliography, 1913 – 65', *The indexer*, **13** (3), April 1983, 158 – 65;
Jones, S., 'Production of the *London bibliography of the social sciences* by computer', *Program*, **13** (3), 1976, 103 – 12.

17   Cowley, J. D., *Bibliographical description and cataloguing*. London: Grafton, 1939, 179.

SUGGESTIONS FOR FURTHER READING

Writing on bibliographies tends to concentrate on general and author bibliography, particularly on the historical aspects, rather than subject bibliography. Amongst books still worth reading are Collison, R. L., *Bibliographies, subject and national* (3rd ed. London: Crosby Lockwood, 1968). The first chapter of Roberts, N., *Use of social sciences literature* (London: Butterworth, 1977) is excellent. Mann, Thomas, *A guide to library research methods* (New York, Oxford: Oxford University Press, 1987) puts bibliographies into the reader's perspective. Needham, C. D. and Herman, E. (eds.), *The study of subject bibliography with special reference to the social sciences* (College Park, Maryland: University of Maryland School of Library and Information Services, 1970) is valuable for the educative approach, including sample bibliographies. The practical advice given in *Denis Grogan's case studies in reference work*, Vol. 3 (London: Bingley, 1987) is realistic and helpful. As for books on bibliographical practice, Krummel, D. W., *Bibliographies: their aims and methods* (London: Mansell, 1984) and Robinson, A. M. L., *Systematic bibliography* (4th ed. London: Bingley, 1979) are quite solid; a shorter but attractive work is Harner, James L., *On compiling an annotated bibliography* (New York: Modern Language Association of America, 1985).

14

Community Information

Allan Bunch

The inclusion of community information for the first time
in this third edition must be recognition that the concept
has entered into the mainstream of library practice, some
15 years after its introduction into this country. The term
'community information' derives from the United States where
it was used to describe the kind of services developed during the
1960s as part of the war against poverty and urban decay. Since
these services were neighbourhood-based and attempted to link
the enquirer with appropriate sources of help in the community,
they were called 'community-information services'. The first
community-information service in a public library, the Public
Information Center at Enoch Pratt Free Library in Baltimore,
was set up in 1970 after a study conducted by a team led by Joseph
C. Donohue of Maryland library school.[1]

It was Donohue who first attempted a definition of 'community
information' and it is still one of the best. He termed it as
information needed to cope with 'crises in the lives of individuals
and communities'.[2] Donohue expanded on this definition by
identifying two types of information provided by a community
information service:

1. survival information such as that related to health, housing, income, legal protection, economic opportunity, political rights etc.;
2. citizen action information, needed for effective participation as individual or as member of a group in the social, political, legal, economic process.[3]

Further experiments followed in other libraries in the United States and by the mid-70s reports of these began to filter through to Britain via the American professional press and as a result of a report by Ed Whalley, a Research Fellow of the Department of Library and Information Studies at Leeds Polytechnic, who visited several of these services in 1975.[4] By the end of the decade a number of libraries in Britain had set up services which, though differing from each other in some respects, could all be subsumed under the banner of 'community information'. These services showed greater diversity than their American counterparts where the emphasis was on the I & R (Information and Referral) file with enquiries received predominantly by telephone. In 1980 a British Library research project undertaken by the Department of Library and Information Studies at Leeds Polytechnic identified three models of community-information provision in this country, which they termed 'back up', 'direct service' and 'self-help'. A 'back-up' service was one in which librarians used their reference and bibliographical skills to produce directories, information packs, current-awareness bulletins, mainly for other professionals and voluntary organizations. A 'direct service' involved the librarian in the face-to-face transfer of information with the user by actively locating local sources of information and making local contacts. The 'self-help' approach involved the librarian in collecting, compiling and arranging material in a way that made it easier for the customer to use largely unaided.[5]

1980 also saw the publication of *Community information: what libraries can do*, the result of two years' deliberation by the Library Association Working Party on Community Information. The report defined community-information services as those which:

assist individuals and groups with daily problem-solving and with participation in the democratic process. The services concentrate on the needs of those who do not have ready access to other sources of assistance and on the most important problems that people have to face, problems to do with their homes, their jobs and their rights.[6]

The report also laid down practical guidelines for the development of community information in libraries and gave examples of good practice.

Today, most public-library authorities would admit to providing some kind of community-information service even if no more than a collection of material (booklets, pamphlets, leaflets, packs, etc.), usually arranged in broad categories and aimed at meeting the needs of those who experience problems in getting access to information on account of factors such as social position, economic status, ethnic origin, sex or health. At the other extreme, some authorities have set up teams of librarians to identify and supply their service points, other professionals and local organizations with community information. Several of these teams produce current-awareness lists or directories which have become a valuable national as well as useful local resource.

Before attempting to identify the major sources of community information there are a number of problems that this term presents both in itself and as a subject for inclusion in this book. Firstly, *Printed reference material* is FORM- not SUBJECT-oriented. Community information is not one form. It exists in a wide variety of forms, from single sheets of paper and irregular newsletters derived from local groups to online databases, multi-volume reference works and audiovisual material.

Secondly, community information is not a single subject but, as we have seen from the definitions above, it covers a range of subjects (or problem areas) and client needs. There is no agreed or official list of what these subjects should be, although a certain degree of consensus does exist from one library authority to another. For example, Cambridgeshire Libraries has identified 21 categories for inclusion in its self-help collections. These are: Benefits, Business (self-employed and small businesses mainly),

Careers, Community, Community relations, Consumer, Disability, Education, Employment, Environment, Family, Government, Health, Housing, Law, Money, Senior citizens, Transport, Unemployment, Women, Youth. Some libraries also include as separate categories: Equal opportunities, Gay rights, Trade union rights and Fuel (or Energy).

And thirdly, a lot of community-information material is ephemeral in format, costs very little and is often free. This means that it has a short life in terms of currency, is rarely recorded in national or book-trade bibliographies and thus is exceedingly difficult to track down. To record much of this material here would result in a long chapter with a very short life indeed. Consequently, priority has been given to those titles which, in gardening terms, have become 'hardy perennials'.

Community information exists at varying levels, from neighbourhood to national and international. Although this chapter concentrates mainly on national sources, it should not be taken as implying that local publications are of lesser value. In fact, it is surprising and pleasing how often local groups, responding to the needs of their community, produce excellent material which is transferable, useful and relevant in other parts of the country.

GENERAL SOURCES

Bibliographies and current awareness

There is no single bibliographical service which adequately covers community-information material. The *British national bibliography* provides a reasonable coverage of commercial publications and those of established organizations but is weak on the publications of smaller voluntary agencies and local groups. The time taken for items to be recorded in *BNB* is also a serious handicap to its usefulness, since up-to-dateness is a critical factor in community information. Leaflets, posters and broadsheets, audiovisual material, and items produced locally and deemed to be of purely local significance are simply not recorded in *BNB* as a matter of policy.

A few retrospective bibliographies have been published over

the years but these are now so out-of-date that they cannot be recommended with any degree of assurance.

For current material, there are a number of services which, if taken together, should give a reasonably comprehensive coverage of the field. As mentioned earlier, some library authorities have set up specialist teams or posts for community information and a number of these have begun to produce current-awareness bulletins for their localities. The longest running and most comprehensive is:

SUNDERLAND INFORMATION EXCHANGE. Community Librarians Team, Southwick Library, Beaumont Street, Southwick, Sunderland SR5 2JR. Tel. 0783 486362. Bi-monthly.

Provides details of new and updated leaflets and books; changes in legislation, benefit rates, addresses and contact points; periodical articles; new services; and forthcoming courses. Contains some information of relevance only to Sunderland and the North East. Available on subscription to other libraries.

A similar range is covered by the 'Community information' column in:

NEW LIBRARY WORLD. MCB University Press Ltd. Monthly.

Produced by the author of this chapter, the extent of the *NLW* column permits only a small selection of the current output of community-information materials to be covered. Also features new initiatives in the field of library-based community-information services and professional literature on the subject.

Leaflets

The vast number of leaflets that are available from statutory and non-statutory organizations present particular problems to librarians, both in identifying and obtaining them on a regular basis. Again, the task has been made easier through the initiative of a local community-information team, this time part of Camden Libraries.

FREE INFORMATION LEAFLET SUPPLIERS. Community Information Services, 100 Euston Road, London NW1 2AJ.

This directory originated as a re-ordering tool for use with Camden libraries' leaflet system and does not set out to be comprehensive, although the organizations listed will form the main part of leaflet collections in most libraries or voluntary groups. The main part of the directory is an alphabetical list of leaflet suppliers with a brief indication of the type of leaflets they produce, if a charge is made and whether a publications list or mailing service is available. If an organization produces material in ethnic minority languages, this is indicated below the entry. There is also a separate 'community-languages index' which lists suppliers of leaflets. The subject approach is catered for by a 'subject index' which brings together all organizations producing leaflets on particular subjects.

The list includes some addresses which are relevant only to the London or Camden area and care needs to be taken with organizations who distribute leaflets through a regional office because the addresses given are only those relevant to Camden. Despite this, the directory is usefully comprehensive, especially for those who do not have access to the *Extra copies of leaflets* list which comes as part of the National Association of Citizens Advice Bureaux Information Service (see below). The directory is updated every two years and is available for a small charge to other libraries and organizations.

Another useful list of leaflets in ethnic-minority languages is produced by Leicestershire Libraries and Information Service:

LEAFLETS IN LANGUAGES OTHER THAN ENGLISH. Information Centre, Bishop Street, Leicester LE1 6AA.

Lists national and local leaflets in languages by subject. New edition in preparation.

Information packs

NATIONAL ASSOCIATION OF CITIZENS' ADVICE BUREAUX INFORMATION SERVICE. NACAB, 115 – 123 Pentonville Road, London N1 9LZ.

This service consists of:

- a set of loose-leaf binders covering communication; travel, transport and holidays; immigration and nationality; administration of justice; education; employment; national and international regulations; family and personal matters; social security; health; housing, property and land; taxes and duties; consumer, trade and business; leisure activities. Each binder contains information sheets specially prepared by NACAB, plus leaflets produced by other agencies, all arranged by NACAB's own classification scheme;
- a set of basic reference books;
- a monthly pack containing:
  - new or updated information sheets produced by NACAB;
  - an Action List updating and amending material in the basic pack;
  - a copy of new and updated leaflets produced by other agencies;
  - a book list of new publications;
  - new editions of previously supplied reference books.

Two particularly useful items included with the service are an address list for obtaining *Extra copies of leaflets* and a list of additional *Reference books* which bureaux are recommended to buy if they have the money.

In addition to the above, subscribers also have access to the consultancy service offered by the central information department of NACAB.

In order to subscribe to this service, a library must first obtain the approval of their local CAB, the NACAB Area Office and NACAB Information Advisory Group. Approval is also reviewed every year when the subscription is due. There are several conditions laid down concerning the use of the NACAB Information Service; for example a subscriber must not claim to be a Citizens Advice Bureau or publicize that they subscribe to the service, and they may not reproduce any material prepared by NACAB.

The service costs several hundred pounds a year and could be afforded only by larger libraries. A considerable commitment in staff time is required to update the pack (about two days a month) but it is well worth the effort and expense for comprehensiveness, clarity of exposition, and up-to-dateness.

For those who do not have the space or the staff time to update the hard-copy pack, there is a **microfiche version** consisting of a single A4 binder holding more than 300 microfiche. These microfiche reproduce the contents of the 14 separate binders in the hard-copy version. Updating is simple as each month a new set of fiche is sent to replace the old one. It takes only about 10 minutes. There are some drawbacks to this version as a tool for current awareness since it is virtually impossible to identify which new or updated leaflets have been added to the pack during the month. This can be overcome by subscribing to NACAB's *Reading pack* which consists of the normal papers plus leaflets and booklist sent out each month to update the hard-copy pack. Another problem with the microfiche version is that it is less convenient to use when lengthy consultation is required. But these are minor cavils compared with the convenience of updating and storing. The microfiche version was developed by Royston CAB and enquiries about the service should be sent to Microfilm Information Project, North Lodge, 40 Kneesworth Street, Royston, Herts SG8 5AQ. The approval of local or area CAB is not required to receive this service.

For those who do not need the full pack in either hard copy or microfiche, NACAB produce:

BASIC INFORMATION PACK. London: NACAB. Monthly updates.

The pack consists of 2 × A4 ring binders containing information sheets and leaflets on benefits; housing; consumer; employment; legal aid, compensation and the courts; education; immigration; tax; health; and family and personal; an alphabetical index and a list of free leaflets and where to obtain them. Every month subscribers receive a small parcel of updates – instructions for keeping the information up-to-date – plus a current-awareness bulletin highlighting major changes or items of interest.

The pack is not aimed at experienced advice workers, rather those who want to extend the range of information and advice they can offer. A useful feature is the clearly flagged warnings in the text where an experienced adviser's help is usually needed to progress further. Although it is relatively easy to use and update, library staff would benefit from having training in its use and this can often be arranged in conjunction with the local CAB. Libraries do not need to get the approval of their local CAB to subscribe to this pack which is ideal for use in smaller branches and even mobiles.

The media

The importance of the media, particularly radio and television, as a source of community information should not be overlooked. Television and radio companies often produce useful free booklets in association with series they are running on particular problems or for special groups. The best way to find out about these programmes is to take out a subscription package to publications of the **Media team** at the Volunteer Centre UK (29 Lower King's Road, Berkhamsted, Herts HP4 2AB). Currently this includes its magazine *On air, off air* (published six times a year) and a copy of the *Directory of social programmes* (twice a year). However, from June 1990 changes are being introduced which, at the time of writing, had not been finalized.

Broadcasting support services (252 Western Avenue, London W3 6XJ) operate a library subscription service for Channel Four free and priced publications. Not all of these are on community-information subjects but it is a good way to ensure coverage of a wide range of useful material.

GOVERNMENT PUBLICATIONS

Official bodies in all their forms are a major source of community information but as there is a separate chapter in this book on Government publications, this section deals only with ephemeral material (leaflets, posters, etc.) rather than mainstream government publishing. A few items published by HMSO have been mentioned under the subject categories below where these were deemed essential.

Amongst individual departments there is no consistency in the way they list their publications or in the methods devised to enable the public and other outside bodies to obtain them. However, there have been some improvements over the last few years and there is a growing recognition by government departments that libraries are an important outlet for their publicity.

One of the best ways to keep in touch with the wide range of new and updated government leaflets is to subscribe to one of the information services available from the National Association of Citizens Advice Bureaux (see above). There is not scope within this chapter to list addresses from where government leaflets can be obtained. Instead, you are referred to the excellent list of *Free information leaflet suppliers* produced by Camden Libraries' Community Information Services (see above).

Another valuable source of information, not only about government leaflets but any changes or proposed changes in government legislation, is the press releases of individual departments. These can often be obtained free of charge from departments and some will even put you on a mailing list. But by far the best way for larger libraries to keep abreast of these is to take out a subscription to:

CENTRAL OFFICE OF INFORMATION PRESS RELEASE SERVICE. London: Central Office of Information. Daily.

Provides subscribers with a daily list of press releases from government departments and quangos plus provision of any press release on request. This service is also available online.

SUBJECT AREAS

Within the scope of this chapter, it has been possible to cover only some key sources of information within each subject area, with the emphasis on those organizations or publications which:

- provide a current-awareness service or book reviews of community-information materials within their subject area;
- are a source of regularly updated information on the subject;

333

- publish handbooks or guides which are generally considered essential for any community-information collection;
- provide a reasonably comprehensive coverage of the subject.

There are many other organizations producing worthwhile material that it has not been possible to mention. A key source of information about these is *The voluntary agencies directory* (see page 336) or some of the more specialized directories listed under individual subjects.

Often the best source of up-to-date information about new publications will be a periodical. Some of the most useful ones for current awareness and hard information have been covered under the subject headings below, but two titles that do not neatly fit into any one particular category are:

THE ADVISER. London: National Association of Citizens' Advice Bureaux/Shelter. Bi-monthly.

Covers social security, housing, money advice and employment from the viewpoint of advisers. A regular feature 'Abstracts' provides summaries of cases. There is also a review section of new publications.

THE RADICAL BOOKSELLER. Bi-monthly.

Carries news on alternative publishing and bookselling, plus a substantial list of 'radical' publications, including fiction and children's books, received by the London Labour Library. Coverage is mainly of political, trade union, and Third-World publications with little that might be termed reference material. The *Radical bookseller* publishes annually a supplement listing alternative bookshops which can also be bought separately.

CAREERS

There is so much material on careers that this section could not attempt to do justice to it. Space allows the mention of only two general titles which together should cover most of the basic information needed:

OCCUPATIONS. Careers & Occupational Information Centre. Annual.

A comprehensive reference book containing details of over 600 jobs and careers arranged by the Careers Library Classification Index (CLCI) with an alphabetic index.

THE JOB BOOK. Cambridge: Hobson Publishing. Annual.

A handbook of employment and training for school leavers produced by the Careers Research and Advisory Centre (CRAC).

For individual careers, the series published by Kogan Page can be recommended as informative, kept reasonably up-to-date, and good value for money.

CHILDREN AND YOUNG PEOPLE

The central agency providing information, advice and curriculum development materials for young people and all those who work with them is the **National Youth Bureau** (17 – 23 Albion Street, Leicester LE1 6GD). Its publications include information packages, regularly updated briefing sheets on current issues, free leaflets and priced publications. NYB's monthly magazine *Young people now* can be recommended not only for its lively articles on all aspects of youth work, but also for its book reviews, current awareness, news items and details of conferences and courses. The magazine has an occasional supplement called 'Ad-Lib' which features some of the material added to NYB's information collection.

The **Children's Legal Centre** (20 Compton Terrace, London N1 2UN) represents the interests of children and young people in matters of law and policy affecting them. It offers free advice and an information service by letter and telephone, publishes reports, handbooks, information sheets and leaflets. CLC's periodical *Childright* (10 issues per year) contains articles, news, changes in legislation and book reviews on issues affecting children's rights.

COMMUNITY

The major publisher on all aspects of running a voluntary organization, and of voluntary work generally, is the **National Council for Voluntary Organisations** (26 Bedford Square, London WC1B 3HU) which has an extensive range of publications, most of which are issued under the imprint of Bedford Square Press. An absolute essential for any community information collection is:

THE VOLUNTARY AGENCIES DIRECTORY. London: NCVO. Annual.

An alphabetical listing of some 2000 leading voluntary organizations, ranging from small, specialist self-help groups to long-established national charities. The directory also contains a list of useful addresses including professional and public advisory bodies concerned with voluntary action.

The following organizations are also valuable sources of information for and about the voluntary sector.

The **Volunteer Centre UK** (29 Lower King's Road, Berkhamsted, Herts HP4 2AB) produces a range of publications, including information sheets, resource packs, handbooks, training materials and bibliographies. Its periodical *Involve* (10 issues per year) combines features on policy, practice and politics of voluntary action with news on volunteering, book reviews and a current-awareness listing.

The **National Federation of Community Organisations** (8/9 Upper Street, London N1 0PQ) publish attractively produced practical handbooks for community organizations on topics such as community newspapers and how to start a community group and a series of over 60 information sheets on specific topics concerning community groups. Some of these have been translated into ethnic-minority languages.

An important aspect of the work of many voluntary organizations is identifying sources of funding. There are several reference books which can help, the most substantial being:

DIRECTORY OF GRANT-MAKING TRUSTS. Charities Aid Foundation. Annual.

An expensive but essential source of reference on the location, objects, policies and resources of grant-making bodies. Its main section is an alphabetical list of trusts, with separate geographical and subject indexes. Entries in the main sequence also note any publications issued by trusts and there is a general select bibliography.

Voluntary organizations also rely heavily on funding from government, at its various levels, and increasingly from the European Community. NCVO publishes two useful guides to these areas of funding:

GOVERNMENT GRANTS: A GUIDE FOR VOLUNTARY ORGAN-ISATIONS. London: Bedford Square Press. Annual.

Davison, A., GRANTS FROM EUROPE: HOW TO GET MONEY AND INFLUENCE POLICY. London: Bedford Square Press. Annual.

Funding from commercial organizations is of growing importance to voluntary work. There are several useful guides produced by the **Directory of Social Change** (Radius Works, Back Lane, London NW3) such as:

Norton, M., A GUIDE TO COMPANY GIVING. London: Directory of Social Change, 1988.

Norton, M., MAJOR COMPANIES AND THEIR CHARITABLE GIVING. London: Directory of Social Change, 1989.

The Directory also publish a number of other guides to grants and fundraising which can be thoroughly recommended.

The **London Voluntary Services Council** (68 Chalton Street, London NW1 1JR) produce two practical, clearly written and attractively designed guides to the law and management of voluntary organizations:

VOLUNTARY BUT NOT AMATEUR. 2nd ed. London: LVSC, 1988.

Adironack, S. M., JUST ABOUT MANAGING? London: LVSC, 1989.

A more up-market work on the management of voluntary organizations for libraries who can afford it is:

CRONER'S MANAGEMENT OF VOLUNTARY ORGANISATIONS. Croner Publications, 1989.
A comprehensive loose-leaf reference book covering everything from setting up an organization, through to finance, fund raising, personnel and marketing. The book is kept up-to-date by means of a quarterly amendment service.

Many voluntary organizations and community groups operate an information or advice service. The 'Bible' for setting up and running such services is:

Thornton, C., MANAGING TO ADVISE. London (13 Stockwell Road, London SW9 9AU): Federation of Independent Advice Centres, 1989.
Covers all the basic ingredients for running a successful advice service from conception to keeping records and resources for advice. Bibliographies are given at the end of sections and checklists underline points made in the text.

Bibliographies and current awareness

COMMUNITY CURRENTS. London: Community Developments Foundation. Bi-monthly.
A digest of 180 journals, books, newsletters, unpublished reports and databases for articles and news items that are specially relevant to community initiatives. Entries arranged under subject areas and then by subject headings. There is an index to subject headings and a list of periodicals regularly scanned. Mainly useful for background articles and books rather than reference material.
Community currents used to alternate with the Volunteer Centre's *Voluntary forum abstracts* but from June 1989 both organizations have collaborated in setting up an online database called:

VOLNET UK. Berkhamsted: Volunteer Centre.

Contains some 20,000 references to documents – books, newspaper and journal articles, reports, etc. – specifically relevant to the fields of volunteering and community development. New records are added at a rate of approximately 200 per week. References include an abstract summarizing the main points of the document. Available on annual subscription (rates dependent on type of organization) allowing unlimited access to the database. Future plans include addition of databases on current research, useful contacts, funding sources, training courses and projects.

SELECT BIBLIOGRAPHIES. Berkhamsted: Volunteer Centre.

An inexpensive series of bibliographies, each containing summaries of hundreds of books, journals and documents on subjects of interest to volunteers and volunteer projects. All bibliographies are regularly updated.

CONSUMER

The prominent organization in the field of consumer affairs is the well-known **Consumers Association**, publishers of the various *Which?* magazines and a range of books that are essential for any community-information collection. Some of these are covered under other subjects. Full details of all their publications appear in each issue of *Which?* magazine.

Directories and other reference books

CONSUMER CONGRESS DIRECTORY. Consumer Congress, c/o National Consumer Council. Annual.

A directory of organizations in the consumer movement giving contact address, telephone number and, in most cases, a named individual, together with a brief description of aims, objects, work and concerns.

FAIR DEAL. 2nd ed. London: HMSO, 1988.

A cheap, handy and attractive little guide to shoppers' rights and family budgeting prepared by the Office of Fair Trading.

Lists some of the major organizations, mainly trade associations, which have codes of practice.

A HANDBOOK OF CONSUMER LAW. 3rd ed. London: Hodder & Stoughton for Consumers' Association, 1988.

An invaluable handbook on the legal rights of consumers compiled by the National Federation of Consumer Groups. Contains appendices of useful addresses and further reading and an index.

DISABILITY

Information packages

DISABLED LIVING FOUNDATION INFORMATION SERVICE. 380 – 4 Harrow Road, London W9 2HU.

A very comprehensive information service that is essential for any library wanting both to make serious provision for disabled people and to disseminate information about disability. It comprises six mailings a year of loose-leaf information sheets which fit into special ring binders and are additional to or replace existing sheets. A 'General information' section gives details of courses, new groups, equipment, awards, new publications added to DLF's Reference Library, and amendments to DLF information lists.

A cheaper but less comprehensive alternative that covers much the same ground is the periodical:

RADAR BULLETIN. Royal Association for Disability and Rehabilitation. Monthly.

Gives details of new legislation, housing, holidays, entertainment, mobility aids and appliances, courses and conferences, and new publications. Each issue is indexed but does not cumulate.

The one indispensable reference book on the subject is:

DISABILITY RIGHTS HANDBOOK. Disability Alliance ERA. Annual.

This comprehensive guide goes into great detail as to what

benefits exist, how to apply for them and how to appeal if refused. It also explains other matters affecting people with disabilities including the various services available to them. The *Handbook* contains a directory of over 600 useful organizations in addition to articles about the rights of disabled people.

Disability rights bulletins (2 per year) update and expand on the *Handbook*. They are available individually or as a Rights Subscription comprising *Handbook* and *Bulletins*.

Directories and other reference books

Darnborough, Ann and Kinrade, Derek, DIRECTORY FOR DISABLED PEOPLE. 5th ed. Cambridge: Woodhead-Faulkner, 1989.

A mammoth reference book for disabled people, their carers and those who provide services, containing information and details of organizations and publications. Appendix lists publishers and stockists referred to in text.

EQUIPMENT FOR DISABLED PEOPLE. Mary Marlborough Lodge, Nuffield Orthopaedic Centre, Headington, Oxford OX3 7LD.

A series of 13 regularly updated booklets giving details of equipment available with addresses of suppliers and advice on choosing equipment. Most titles have a select bibliography. The one on 'Communication' is particularly useful to libraries as it covers reading aids and taped and large-print books.

Although not quite in the same league as the above, the following book is more client-oriented and 'user friendly':

Luba, J., THE DISABLED PERSON'S HANDBOOK. Sphere, 1989.

EDUCATION

An essential source of information about education is the **Department of Education and Science** itself, which produces a wide range of free leaflets and booklets which can be obtained from DES, Publications Despatch Centre, Government Buildings, Honeypot Lane, Stanmore, Middlesex HA7 1AY.

The main consumer organization in the field of education is the **Advisory Centre for Education** (18 Victoria Park Square, London E2 9PB) who publish a range of information sheets and handbooks aimed at parents and school governors. No community-information service would be complete without a subscription to *ACE bulletin* (bi-monthly) which contains features and information sheets as well as news of all ACE's work, case studies and recent publications. In addition the 'Digest' section gives a comprehensive review of the latest books, pamphlets, journals and HMI reports on education.

The other ACE publication that can be singled out is:

EDUCATION A-Z: WHERE TO LOOK THINGS UP. 5th ed. London: ACE, 1990.

An alphabetically-arranged reference book covering over 300 subject headings and listing nearly 1,000 organizations and relevant books and journals. The handbook is cross-referenced and indexed.

THE EDUCATIONAL GRANTS DIRECTORY. London: Directory of Social Change, 1988.

A comprehensive listing of national, local and parochial charities and commercial organizations which make funds available to meet educational needs. There is also background information on specific areas of educational need and sources of further information and advice.

SECOND CHANCES. Careers and Occupational Information Centre and National Institute of Adult Continuing Education. Annual.

Provides a wealth of information, advice and guidance on all aspects of education and training for adults.

ELDERLY PEOPLE

There are numerous organizations which represent the needs of elderly people but the one that is pre-eminent as a source of information is **Age Concern England** (Astral House, 1268 London Road, London SW16 4EJ). It publishes a wide range of material for elderly people and their carers, from information sheets to annual guides. No community-information collection should be without:

YOUR RIGHTS. Mitcham: Age Concern. Annual.
An excellent handy guide to state benefits available to older people, containing current information on income support, housing benefit and retirement pensions with advice on how to claim them.

Other aspects of financial management for elderly people are contained in:

Burke, J. and West, S., YOUR TAXES AND SAVINGS IN RETIRE-MENT. Mitcham: Age Concern. Annual.

At the time of writing the following book had not yet been published so it is recommended 'sight unseen', though, if up to Age Concern's usual standard, it should be useful:

BETTER HEALTH IN RETIREMENT: AN A-Z OF FITNESS. Mitcham: Age Concern, 1990.
A comprehensive source of information on health for elderly people, giving details of people and useful organizations from which advice and assistance can be sought.

Larger libraries wanting to make more comprehensive coverage of information for elderly people will need to subscribe to:

AGE CONCERN FACT SHEETS. Mitcham: Age Concern.
A set of 30 fact sheets, regularly updated, on various topics concerning elderly people, from help with heating to leisure education. Available individually or on subscription (including ring binder).

AGE CONCERN INFORMATION CIRCULAR. Mitcham: Age Concern. Monthly.
Reports developments of interest to people who work with and

for older people, including changes in legislation, reports, periodical articles, new publications, and courses and conferences. Annual index.

Darnborough, A. and Kinrade, D., DIRECTORY FOR OLDER PEOPLE: A HANDBOOK OF INFORMATION AND OPPORTUNITIES FOR THE OVER 55s. Cambridge: Woodhead-Faulkner, 1990.
   Comprehensive information for people approaching and those over retirement age. Lists helpful organizations and selected further reading.

Brown, R., GOOD RETIREMENT GUIDE. 3rd ed. London: Bloomsbury, 1989.
   A regularly updated mine of information on all aspects of retirement. Gives details of almost 800 organizations.

THE TIME OF YOUR LIFE: A HANDBOOK OF RETIREMENT. 6th ed. Help the Aged, 16 – 18 St. James's Walk, London EC1R 0BE, 1988.
   Less comprehensive than the above titles but substantially more attractive, readable and well laid out.

EMPLOYMENT

There is a substantial amount of free and priced literature written for workers and employers on aspects of employment law, job-seeking, coping with redundancy. Any community-information collection should have at least a reference set of free booklets and leaflets from the **Department of Employment, ACAS** (Advisory, Conciliation and Arbitration Service), and the **Training Agency**.
   There are several organizations which play an important role in providing information to workers and trade unionists.
   The **Labour Research Department** (78 Blackfriars Road, London SE1 8HF) publishes information on all aspects of employment for trade unionists. *Labour research* (monthly) covers news on the economy, major industries, social and political developments as well as topics of workplace interest. Regular features include book reviews, health and safety notes, statistics and major wage deals. The latter is covered more fully in *Bargaining*

report (bi-monthly) whereas statistics form a major part of LRD's *Fact service* (weekly). LRD also publishes a number of booklets of interest to trade unionists which are available either individually or on subscription (approx. 10 titles per year). Some are on political issues, others are useful reference guides. Two that can be singled out are:

THE LAW AT WORK. London: LRD, 1988.
A brief guide to employment law. New edition planned for 1990.

STATE BENEFITS. London: LRD. Annual.
A guide for trade unionists to all benefit rights.

The **Workers' Educational Association** (9 Upper Berkeley Street, London W1H 8BY) is mainly concerned with providing independent adult education for workers but some of its publications are a valuable source of information about employment issues. Particular mention can be made of:

GUIDE TO RECENTLY PUBLISHED MATERIAL IN INDUSTRIAL RELATIONS. London: WEA. Quarterly.
A checklist of books and pamphlets, journals and government publications.

STUDIES FOR TRADE UNIONISTS. London: WEA. Quarterly.
A series of pamphlets on major developments in industrial relations.

The **Low Pay Unit** (9 Upper Berkeley Street, London W1H 8BY) campaigns to improve the lot of low-paid workers. It produces leaflets and a bi-monthly periodical, *The new review*, which highlights interesting cases and developments in the law relating to low pay, gives in-depth analysis of rights issues and reviews new publications. *The new review* also contains an insert called *News brief from the Wages Rights Office* which provides up-to-date information on benefits for low-paid workers.

The **Trades Union Congress** (Congress House, Great Russell

Street, London WC1B 3LS) publishes a wide range of cheap booklets, pamphlets and a few free leaflets on various aspects of employment, the economy and trade unionism.

For an overall guide to employment law written in non-technical language and regularly up-dated, the best choice is:

Ward, C., GUIDE TO EMPLOYMENT LAW. London: *Daily mail*. Annual.

A quick-reference guide to employment laws and industrial tribunals for personnel managers, trade-union officials, employers and employees. Very clearly written and laid out, with short numbered paragraphs, marginal references to cases, a full contents list and an index.

Equal opportunities

The **Equal Opportunities Commission** (Overseas House, Quay Street, Manchester M3 3HN) has a range of free and priced literature on all aspects of equal opportunities, including employment. It is not possible to single out any particular item but write to them for a catalogue of publications.

An excellent summary of equal opportunities law and practice is provided by:

Shaw, J., EQUAL OPPORTUNITIES: THE WAY AHEAD. Institute of Personnel Management, 1989.

Health and safety at work

A good general guide for the layperson is:

Health and Safety Executive, ESSENTIALS OF HEALTH AND SAFETY AT WORK. London: HMSO, 1989.

Small businesses and self-employment

Boehm, K. and Lees-Spalding, J. (eds.), THE CAREERS BOOK. Papermac: 1989.

An A – Z guide to over 250 profiles of self-employment opportunities. Contains a list of useful addresses, a bibliography and a general index.

Barrow, C., THE NEW SMALL BUSINESS GUIDE: SOURCES OF INFORMATION FOR NEW AND SMALL BUSINESSES. 3rd ed. London: BBC Books, 1989.
A guide to over 2,000 organizations and publications that offer specific help to small businesses.

Golzen, G., WORKING FOR YOURSELF. London: Kogan Page. Annual.
Regularly updated, standard guide to setting up and running a small business. Appendices provide sources of further information, a select bibliography and a glossary of key business terms.

ENVIRONMENT

The current interest in 'green' issues should ensure the increasing importance of this category. The nearest to an overview of the subject is:

NEW GREEN PAGES: A DIRECTORY OF NATURAL PRODUCTS, SERVICES, RESOURCES AND IDEAS. Optima, 1990.
An impressive listing of books and information on environmental issues, alternative living, health and therapies, wholefoods and technology. Final section on 'Information' covers reference books, libraries, resource centres, advice centres, publishers, specialist bookshops, book clubs, directories, magazines and computer networks. There are also indexes of subjects and suppliers. To maintain its value, this book will need to be updated regularly.

Sources of funds for environmental projects are covered in:

Forrester, S., ENVIRONMENTAL GRANTS. London: Directory of Social Change, 1989.
A guide to grants from government, companies and charitable

trusts, including awards and competitions and organizations who provide information and help free or at a reduced cost.

FAMILY AND PERSONAL

There is no single source of information that will cover the range of topics to be found under this category but the following are some useful titles on some of the main areas.

Adoption and fostering

The **British Agencies for Adoption and Fostering** (11 Southwark Street, London SE1 1RQ) publish a range of booklets on aspects of adoption and fostering including:

ADOPTING A CHILD: A GUIDE FOR PEOPLE INTERESTED IN ADOPTION. 3rd ed. London: BAAF, 1986.
Gives background information on adoption including legal aspects and cost, and how to find an adoption agency. New edition scheduled (but not guaranteed) for 1990.

Death

WHAT TO DO WHEN SOMEONE DIES. London: Consumers' Association, 1986.
A practical guide to the decisions and arrangements that have to be made when someone dies, from getting a doctor's certificate to claiming the various state pensions and allowances. Needs updating but still useful.

WILLS AND PROBATE. London: Hodder & Stoughton for Consumers' Assocation, 1988.
A lay-person's guide to making a will, inheritance tax, administering someone else's estate and intestacy.

Lesbians and gays

DAVIDSON'S DIRECTORY 1989: A GUIDE TO LESBIAN AND GAY

ORGANISATIONS IN THE UNITED KINGDOM. D & I Publications, 1989.

Entries are arranged by broad areas e.g. south-west England, and then by subject – hotels, helplines, etc. – and then by county. Also lists national organizations under the categories of advice and support; professional groups; religious organizations; special interests; campaigning, counselling, caring.

One-parent families

The two main national organizations representing one-parent families are:

The **National Council for One-Parent Families** (255 Kentish Town Road, London NW5 2LX) which publishes statistics, policy documents, welfare and legal rights guides and a regularly updated loose-leaf *Information manual* covering an extensive range of topics of concern to single parents. Its quarterly newsletter *One-parent times* contains information on changes in the welfare and legal system affecting one-parent families and a books column. NCOPF operates a subscription scheme covering all its publications including *One-parent times*.

Gingerbread (35 Wellington Street, London WC2E 7BW) which publishes a number of booklets and leaflets on welfare benefits, family law, day-care schemes. Operates on Associate Membership scheme whereby subscribers receive a monthly mailing of every new leaflet/booklet and their monthly magazine, *Ginger*.

Parents

THE PARENTS' DIRECTORY. London: Bedford Square Press, 1989.

Details of help, advice and information available to parents from some 800 voluntary organizations.

Prisoners

Cooklin, S., FROM ARREST TO RELEASE. London: Bedford Square Press, 1989.

A practical guide, written in plain English, on how the courts work and what is involved in such processes as remand, bail and parole. A substantial part of the book is a chart setting out the arrangements for visiting prisons in England and Wales. There is a list of sources of further information and an index.

Separation and divorce

DIVORCE: LEGAL PROCEDURES AND FINANCIAL FACTS. London: Consumers' Association, 1989.

There are a number of lay-person's guides to divorce but this has the virtue of being the most up-to-date at the time of going to press and of CA's usual reliability. Covers mainly divorce in England and Wales with a short chapter on the differences in Scotland and Northern Ireland. There is a glossary and index.

FUEL

The basic text on rights to fuel supply is:

FUEL RIGHTS GUIDE. 7th ed. SHAC/WRUG, 189a Old Brompton Road, London SW5 0AR, 1989.

An essential book for any community-information collection for clients and advisers. Also covers financial help, overcharging and theft. Regularly updated.

GOVERNMENT

There is no one essential guide to aspects of government but the following are useful titles for a community-information collection:

Hutt, J., OPENING THE TOWN HALL DOOR: AN INTRODUCTION TO LOCAL GOVERNMENT. 2nd ed. London: Bedford Square Press, 1988.

A practical guide, aimed mainly at voluntary organizations, showing how local government works, what services are provided and how decisions are made. Gives advice on effective lobbying and discusses the complaints procedure.

Dubs, A., LOBBYING: AN INSIDER'S GUIDE TO THE PARLIA-
MENTARY PROCESS. Pluto Press, 1988.

A former MP provides a clear explanation of how local, national
and EEC government bodies work and how they can be influenced
in their decisions. Contains glossaries, lists of lobbying companies,
monitoring services and useful addresses, a bibliography and an
index.

HEALTH

The government department responsible for the National Health
Service and other health matters is the **Department of Health**.
It publishes free leaflets on the NHS and National Insurance which
should be in all community-information collections. The
promotion of health is the responsibility of the **Health Education
Authority** (Hamilton House, Mabledon Place, London WC1H
9TX) which has an extensive range of booklets, leaflets, posters,
periodicals and audiovisual materials available, many of which
are free. Bulk orders for free publications are dealt with by local
health education units. The HEA operates a subscription service
for a single copy of all new and updated publications, including
its publications list *What we publish.*

Self help

In addition to statutory health services, there are hundreds of self-
help groups providing information, advice and support to people
with particular ailments and disabilities. Most of them produce
publications aimed at sufferers and their families and carers. The
best source of information about these groups is:

Macdonald, F., THE HEALTH DIRECTORY, 1990 – 91. London: Bedford
Square Press, 1990.

Lists some 700 organizations ranging from established national
bodies to self-help groups dealing with particular disorders. It also
covers complementary medicine, organizations for ethnic minor-
ities and groups concerned with general well-being. Entries are
listed alphabetically and in a comprehensive index by subject area.

A little older but still of value for its advice on how to set up a basic collection of free or cheaply priced self-help literature is:

Knight, S. and Gann, R., THE SELF-HELP GUIDE: A DIRECTORY OF SELF-HELP ORGANISATIONS IN THE UNITED KINGDOM. London: Chapman & Hall, 1988.

Robert Gann has been associated with the pioneering Help for Health information service since it was established at Southampton General Hospital in 1979. The Help for Health database which was set up to support the enquiry service is available to other libraries on subscription under the name:

HELPBOX. Help for Health, Grant Building, Southampton General Hospital, Southampton SO3 4XY. Quarterly updates.

Microcomputer database consisting of three files: national voluntary organizations and self-help groups; self-help popular medical books published since 1980; and leaflets and other self-help 'grey literature'. Each file is indexed using the Help for Health thesaurus, derived from Medical Subject Headings (MeSH). The database has been set up using Cardbox Plus (Version 4) and runs on hard-disc microcomputers using PC-DOS and MS-DOS. Updating is by returnable floppy discs every three months and a read-only version of Cardbox is supplied with the initial package.

Indexes

Knight, S. (ed.), POPULAR MEDICAL INDEX. Mede Publishing, 77 Norton Road, Letchworth, Herts SG6 1AD. 3 issues per year plus cumulation.

An index to articles on medical subjects, written specifically for the lay-person, appearing in popular magazines. Arranged alphabetically by subject headings.

HOUSING

No community-information collection would be complete without a set of the free 'Housing booklets' series published by the Department of the Environment or several of the excellent guides produced by SHAC (189a Old Brompton Road, London SW5 0AR). This is the London arm of Shelter but their publications are of general relevance. Particular mention can be made of:

BUYING A HOME. 3rd ed. London: SHAC, 1990.

A step-by-step guide to house purchase written with the first-time buyer in mind, with simple examples as an aid to calculating costs.

RIGHTS GUIDE FOR HOME OWNERS. 9th ed. London: SHAC/CPAG, 1990.

Gives practical advice on negotiating with lenders, meeting repair bills, the problems associated with relationship breakdown and the welfare benefits home-owners may be entitled to. The 9th edition contains full details of the changeover from the rating system to the community charge in England and Wales as well as the position in Scotland.

THE HOUSING RIGHTS GUIDE. 3rd ed. London: SHAC, 1989.

Comprehensive and up-to-date guide for tenants and owners without specialist knowledge, giving clear explanation of the law and practical advice on how to tackle all major housing problems. Contains lists of useful publications and addresses and an index.

Shelter (88 Old Street, London EC1V 9HU), the national campaign for the homeless, also publishes some useful guides to buying a home with other people, housing finance, and mobile homes. Its periodical *Roof* (bi-monthly) includes feature articles on aspects of housing, plus regular housing advice notes, reports, news and book reviews.

BENEFITS. CHAR. Annual.

CHAR is the Housing Campaign for Single People and this regularly updated guide to income support and housing benefit explains in simple terms how the system works.

RENTING AND LETTING: THE LEGAL RIGHTS AND DUTIES OF LANDLORDS AND TENANTS. London: Hodder & Stoughton for Consumers' Association, 1989.

A guide to both private- and public-sector letting.

Particular mention should be made of the Sphere 'Rights guides' which are designed to explain the law in easy-to-read language for anyone without a legal background. The information is presented by question and answer and the books do not have an index, so they are more useful for clients than for reference. Several titles are on housing matters:

Arden, A., THE HOMELESS PERSON'S HANDBOOK. Sphere, 1988.

Pearce, L., THE MOBILE HOMES HANDBOOK. Sphere, 1989.

Luba, J., THE OWNER-OCCUPIER'S HANDBOOK. Sphere, 1990.

Arden, A., THE PRIVATE TENANT'S HANDBOOK. Rev. ed. Sphere, 1989.

Arden, A., THE PUBLIC TENANT'S HANDBOOK. Rev. ed. Sphere, 1989.

LAW

Many aspects of the law have been dealt with under other subjects so this category is usually taken to cover comprehensive layperson's guides to the law, legal aid, the courts and civil rights. Although its publications are aimed mainly at advisers, the **Legal Action Group** (242 Pentonville Road, London N1 9UN) produces some excellent and authoritative handbooks to such topics as emergency procedures, civil legal aid, police powers and police misconduct. Its periodical *LAG bulletin* (monthly) contains articles on aspects of the law, significant cases, book reviews and lists of books received.

Civil rights is very much the province of the **National Council for Civil Liberties** (21 Tabard Street, London SE1 4LA) which publishes a wide range of guides, fact sheets, and reports on particular aspects of rights.

There are a number of one-volume popular reference books

covering the law as it affects the citizen but it is difficult to recommend any particular title, other than the latest one published, as the law is changing daily. More useful are loose-leaf, regularly updated books, such as the various NACAB packs (see pages 329 – 332) or the slightly less user friendly:

CITIZENS' ADVICE NOTES SERVICE. London: National Council for Voluntary Organisations. 3 updates per year.

More familiarly known as *CANS*, this digest of social and industrial legislation in 22 sections is housed in two loose-leaf binders which allow insertion of the three supplements issued a year. Full references are given to original sources and there is a comprehensive index. From April 1990 it is possible to subscribe to sections singly. *CANS* is not as easy to use or to update as the publisher claims, nor, with only three supplements a year, can it be as up-to-date as the various NACAB packs.

MONEY

The 1980s have seen a considerable growth in Money Advice Centres and in debt counselling as part of other advice services, reflecting the problems of an increasing credit society. The charity **Money Management Council** (18 Doughty Street, London WC1N 2PL) was set up to promote education and better understanding of personal finance. It produces free fact sheets and reading lists on topics such as pensions, savings and investments, and credit.

There are innumerable books giving advice to those with money on what to do with it but rather less for those with money problems. Although it is rather old, the following book can still be recommended as much of the advice in it is timeless:

Andrews, A. and Houghton, P., HOW TO COPE WITH CREDIT AND DEAL WITH DEBT. Unwin Paperbacks, 1986.

Both authors were associated with the Birmingham Settlement which set up the first Money Advice centre. This book gives clear and helpful advice on what to do and how, and what to look out for, when borrowing money.

The Consumers' Association publish several reliable guides to aspects of personal finance of which space only permits a mention of:

GETTING THE BEST DEAL FOR YOUR MONEY. London: Consumers' Association, 1989.
Advice on borrowing, investing, saving and insurance, and the various services offered by banks and building societies.

WHICH? WAY TO SAVE AND INVEST. Rev. ed. London: Consumers' Association, 1989.
The basics of saving – where to get advice and who to complain to if things go wrong – and various areas of investment.

One of the best plain-English guides to pensions is:

Ward, S., THE ESSENTIAL GUIDE TO PENSIONS: A WORKER'S HANDBOOK. Pluto Press, 1988.
Shows how to tackle the small print of company pensions, rights and entitlements, how to negotiate for better terms, opting out and explains the role of investment managers, trustees, stockbrokers and merchant banks in administering pension funds.

The Housing Benefit Scheme introduced in 1989 and the Community Charge (or Poll Tax) introduced in Scotland in 1989 and England and Wales in 1990 are linked in an essential book:

Zebedee, J. and Ward, M., A GUIDE TO HOUSING BENEFIT AND COMMUNITY CHARGE BENEFIT. 3rd ed. London: SHAC/Institute of Housing, 1989.
Explains in full, with practical examples, who can claim housing or community charge benefit, the new rules for boarders, the new role of Rent Officers, how to calculate and maximize entitlement, how authorities should process claims, and how to appeal.

Zebedee, J. and Ward, M., GUIDE TO THE COMMUNITY CHARGE. London: SHAC/CPAG/Institute of Housing, 1990.

A clear explanation of all aspects of the Community Charge, with tables, practical examples and a full index.

RACE RELATIONS

There are a number of specialist agencies who are useful sources of information, such as the **Institute of Race Relations** (2 – 6 Leeke Street, Kings Cross Road, London WC1X 9HS), the **Joint Council for the Welfare of Immigrants** (115 Old Street, London EC1V 9JR), the **Minority Rights Group** (29 Craven Street, London WC2N 5NG), the **Commission for Racial Equality** (Elliott House, 10 – 12 Allington Street, London SW1E 5EH, and the **Runnymede Trust** (178 North Gower Street, London NW1 2NB). This latter organization has published a useful guide to resources on racial issues:

ANTI-RACIST RESOURCES: A GUIDE FOR ADULT AND CONTIN-UING EDUCATION. London: Runnymede Trust, 1988.
  Although the emphasis of this compilation is on adult education, it is generally of relevance as a guide to material about race and anti-racism. Covers bibliographies; books, pamphlets and articles; journals; bookshops; films and videos; posters and exhibitions; photographic agencies; museums and galleries; performers and theatre groups; translating and interpreting organizations; organizations and resource centres.

Grewal, H., THE RACE DISCRIMINATION HANDBOOK. Sphere, 1988.
  One of the Sphere 'Rights guides' written for anyone without a legal background.

WELFARE BENEFITS

In addition to at least a complete set of **Department of Social Security** leaflets and booklets, any community-information collection will require some books to explain in more detail how the social-security system works either in general or for particular groups. By far the most respected are those produced by the **Child Poverty Action Group** (1 – 5 Bath Street, London EC1V 9PY).

No collection of any size should be without the following two titles:

NATIONAL WELFARE BENEFITS HANDBOOK. London: CPAG. Annual.

Contains comprehensive information, with examples and case studies, about the social fund, family credit, housing benefit as well as the administrative and appeal procedures. Also covers health and education benefits and information on financial help for people with disabilities. Emphasis is on ease of access with cross-referencing and a full index.

RIGHTS GUIDE TO NON-MEANS-TESTED BENEFITS. London: CPAG. Annual.

Does much the same as the above for unemployment benefit, statutory sick pay, statutory maternity pay, provisions for industrial injuries and diseases, retirement and widowhood, and the administration and appeals procedure.

Both the above titles are regularly updated by means of CPAG's *Welfare rights bulletin* (bi-monthly) which provides coverage of new and significant Commissioners' decisions, as well as court judgements, changes in law and practice, news from welfare-rights workers and how to tackle common problem areas. Subscription includes an annual index. CPAG also publish a *Welfare rights bulletin index, 1982 – 1987*.

WOMEN

There are many organizations and campaign groups catering for women's interests, needs and rights but it is difficult to point to any as providing a current-awareness service or range of publications that represents the whole subject adequately. The following books have been singled out as being reasonably up-to-date and covering a substantial subject area:

A WOMAN'S PLACE: RELATIONSHIP BREAKDOWN AND YOUR RIGHTS. 2nd ed. London: SHAC, 1989.

Clear, simple-to-use guide designed to help women get the best deal for themselves and their children during and after separation.

Covers legal aid, violence, divorce and separation, maintenance, housing solutions, and money problems.

GOING IT ALONE: RELATIONSHIP BREAKDOWN AND YOUR RIGHTS. 2nd ed. London: SHAC, 1989.

Companion volume to *A woman's place* designed for unmarried women.

WOMEN'S HOUSING HANDBOOK. Resource Information Service, 5 Egmont House, 116 Shaftesbury Avenue, London W1V 7DJ, 1989.

Provides a wealth of detailed, practical information on housing options for women, their basic rights, and sources of information and advice (organizations, publications and helplines). There is also a separate London edition.

REFERENCES AND CITATIONS

1 Donohue, Joseph C., 'Planning for a community information center', *Library journal*, 15 October 1972, 3284.
2 Donohue, Joseph C., 'Community information services – a proposed definition', in Martin, S. K., *Community information politics: proceedings of 39th ASIS annual meeting.* Vol. 13. American Society for Information Science, 1976, fiche 8, frame E4.
3 Ibid. fiche 9, frame B12.
4 Whalley, E. D. and Davinson, D. E., *Developments in community information services in public libraries in the United States: a state of the art report and literature guide.* Leeds: Department of Librarianship, Leeds Polytechnic, 1976.
5 Watson, Joyce and others, *The management of community information services in the public libraries.* Leeds: Public Libraries Management Research Unit, School of Librarianship, Leeds Polytechnic, 1980, 65 – 6.
6 *Community information: what libraries can do: a consultative document.* London: Library Association, 1980, 12.

15

Audiovisual Materials

Anthony Hugh Thompson

THE VALUE OF AUDIOVISUAL MATERIALS

Printed materials are firmly established as the primary resources of librarianship and information science, and there is a coherent and well-developed infrastructure related to their acquisition and bibliographical control. This form of audiovisual material is dealt with in other chapters of this book. However, in the United Kingdom as in many other countries, our profession has not been wholehearted in its acceptance of the more recent audiovisuals (or as they are often disparagingly called, 'non-book materials') as resources. Often information professionals either pay lip-service to these materials or ignore them altogether. Sadly, this situation is almost invariably found in developing countries with low levels of print literacy, but whose populations are becoming increasingly aurally and visually literate through exposure to television, radio and audiocassettes. There are exceptions internationally to this situation, but information services which have achieved undoubted success in multimedia development go virtually unnoticed.

The development of photography, cinematography and sound-recording took place during the latter half of the nineteenth century, while video-recording is a comparative newcomer having been developed after the Second World War. Surely it must be obvious even to the most committed bibliophile that the vast range of information recorded by these technologies has value as an information-service resource? It should also be apparent that some of our users and probably nearly all the people who could but choose not to use our services, now prefer to obtain their information from these resources and not from the printed word. Research carried out in the United States by the Industrial Audiovisual Association in 1962 suggested that the book was the least effective means of communicating information! It was stated that people remember only 10% of what they read, while remembering 50% of what they saw and heard.[1] Obviously more research needs to be undertaken on this topic, but increasingly people's responses, especially those of younger people, would suggest that there is some validity to these statistics.

Can we any longer deny the power of audio, video and film to communicate information? These media satisfy the needs of many of those who see and hear, without their wanting to turn to printed or other resources to complement the information. Others may want further information and will investigate other resources. Is this not how it should be in a multimedia age?

Nor do the more recent audiovisual materials constitute a small and insignificant group of media related primarily to entertainment. In 1986, it was suggested that between 700,000 and 800,000 'non-book' items had been published over the preceding 20 years, compared to between 800,000 to 1 million monographs in the same period.[2] These cover a wide range of formats dealing with a similar range of subjects to those dealt with by books. A proportion of these 'non-book' items do relate to entertainment, but then so do a proportion of books published.

RECENT AUDIOVISUAL MATERIALS AS REFERENCE MATERIALS

Consider the momentous events of the past century – how much of your knowledge do you owe to print and how much to the visual/audio image? The horrors of the First and Second World Wars – trench warfare, concentration camps, reprisals, sea and air battles; the destruction of Challenger; the devastation by the recent San Francisco and Armenian earthquakes; Man's first landings and steps on the Moon; the breaking-down of the Berlin Wall and the movement to democracy in Eastern Europe; the recurrent famines in Ethiopia and other African countries? And where did your knowledge of other events – perhaps less momentous but equally important and fascinating – come from? The lifestyles of a multitude of birds, animals and insects never encountered in real life; the extermination of elephants and other animals for greed; art, paintings, music, sculpture, film, theatre, ballet, opera; the list is endless!

Virtually all people's perceptions of the world are created by the sounds they hear and the visual images they see. For most, their understanding of the world they live in is increased by audio and visual images on the cinema and television screen. For some, reading also enhances this understanding – but only approximately one-third of the population of the world is print literate in the true sense of the word, and even here the degree of literacy and the desire to learn from print varies enormously.

Yet for the most part, our profession still gives the impression that it believes that the only primary sources of information are print-based. Many information services stock these materials only, while in many others print-based materials still form by far the largest proportion of the stock.

But are all print-based resources **primary source materials**? For most people, the primary source material for a Shakespeare play would be a live performance – for Shakespeare wrote plays to be seen, not books to be read. Failing the holding of a troupe of actors, a library should have the second-best – and that now is a video-recording of the play, not the book of the play, which is now at best third-best! The definitive version of a Dylan Thomas story is a sound recording of Dylan himself reading it, not the book of the reading! The primary source of Kennedy's Cuba speech is the film of that speech, not the printed version, and the same can be said of the words of Hitler and many, many others. For these primary sources contain not only the words themselves, but much more information to help us understand better – the emotion, the accent, the histrionics, the actuality – or as close to it as we can get. Indeed, the moving images and sounds of most of the events covered in the last but two paragraphs form the **primary** source material for a study of those subjects.

Yet how many libraries and information services, other than those specialist organizations dedicated to specific formats or organizations, have adequate, let alone good collections of these records? And how many information services include the more recent audiovisual records *in their reference collections*? Our users must have access to primary source materials if they are to understand any subject properly – print-based resources alone cannot provide all the information and the experience necessary. Indeed our profession is failing in our stated duty if we fail to make such primary sources available.

Which sources would our users prefer? How much longer can we go on ignoring the needs and preferences of our actual and potential users, and our responsibilities to them? How much longer can we ignore the experience of those members of our profession who have become truly multimedia in their approach and to whom relevance rather than format is the selection criteria? Nowadays, any organization that does not fulfil its responsibilities has a short future indeed.

THE RANGE OF AUDIOVISUAL MATERIALS

What then are audiovisual materials? As with any other profession, we can become so involved in debating such topics that we fail to develop the necessary services in time. So for a definition, let us look outside the profession. Tom Hope, an American statistician, stated that 'audiovisual embraces all technologies, whether past, present or yet to be dreamed'.[3] He defined audiovisual as a concept of prepared programme communication and not just one medium. Any new system that enables information to be recorded is an audiovisual tool.

Another way of arriving at a definition is to split the word into its component parts. All forms of recorded information are audiovisual materials in that they are audio, visual or both. This includes print, because print is visual! Thus the main types of recorded audiovisual materials are books, newspapers, periodicals, maps, charts, posters; photographs, slides, filmstrips, overhead transparencies, cine-film, microforms; audio, video and computer tapes, cassettes, discs and other storage media; and real objects.

Both definitions give all forms of recorded information equality and overcome negative barriers created by format.

There are other forms of audiovisuals, but unless an effort to record them is made they remain transient. Television, the various forms of teletext, images on a computer screen and cinema are all transient images to the information professional. Increasingly some of them are becoming available in recorded form, but particularly in the case of cinema the copies may not be exactly the same as the original.

This chapter will concentrate on the more recent forms of audiovisual material in recorded form which are available for use in information services.

BARRIERS TO MULTIMEDIA DEVELOPMENT

One of the barriers to developing a multimedia information collection, where primary source material is held regardless of its format, is the lack of an infrastructure related to the acquisition and bibliographic control of the more recent audiovisuals. In some countries, such as the United States of America, where the national library has taken responsibility for books and all other major audiovisual formats, an infrastructure for all audiovisual formats has been developed. In the United Kingdom and other countries where the National Library has not fully accepted its responsibility to deal with the more recent audiovisual material, such an infrastructure has not had the opportunity to develop in anything other than a piecemeal and incomplete way.[4]

Another barrier to developing a multimedia collection is that of developing technology. While the book has had a long, distinguished lifetime as a container of knowledge, the same cannot be said of some of the more recently developed audiovisual materials which appear today and are gone tomorrow. But this is true of all technology today – change happens much more quickly than it did in the past and the information profession is no more immune to this than anybody else. Like everybody else, we have to learn to adapt; otherwise there will be even greater gaps in our preservation of the records of man's achievement than there already are. On the positive side, developments in audio-visual technology have lead to more effective and less expensive ways of communicating and storing information than the book.

Therefore an examination of the more recent audiovisual formats, their value and their likely future is pertinent, if we are to create balanced multimedia collections in appropriate formats. Only some of the audiovisual formats that currently exist are of value to library collections. Techniques for the storage and handling of these audiovisual materials are not dealt with in this chapter, but can be found elsewhere.[5]

MICROFORMS

These were originally designed to save space in that they occupy only about one-hundredth of the space of the original documents. Microforms consist of two main types, although there have been other formats which are now obsolete. Roll microfilm, in both 16mm and 35mm widths, carries a reduced image of print, illustrations or computer-generated information. Microfiche consists of sheets of film 15 × 10cm, each containing approximately 100 pages of information. Properly processed, microforms should have a lifetime of 150 years or more, but they are easily damaged in use.

They are used for a variety of purposes including the preservation of the information content of deteriorating formats such as books and newspapers; as a means of providing access to the information in rare documents without the users having to handle the document itself; for the publication of periodicals with limited circulation or in place of bound copies of back numbers; and for regularly updated documents such as library catalogues and periodicals holdings.

Reasonable costs of publication, the ease of in-house production and the ability of some computer peripherals to generate microforms cheaply, may extend the life of microforms for a while. They are likely to be replaced by recordable optical discs and CD-ROM in future, however.

AUDIO-RECORDINGS

Although normally associated with music, audio-recording techniques now permit virtually any sound to be commercially published or recorded by individuals. Audio-recordings are available in a variety of formats, only some of which are suitable for information-service use.

Audio-recordings encompass musical performances; the spoken word in many forms, including the readings of books, plays and poetry originally for the blind but found to be of great interest to others; radio broadcasts; and in-house-produced recordings such as oral histories.

Long-playing records, the original format used by many information services, are to all intents and purposes obsolete. Large collections of this audio format exist and are still being added to because many services and users have equipment to play them. However, it is a fragile and short-lived medium in library collections. Any information service initiating an audio-recordings collection now should consider only the compact disc (CD) and possibly audiocassette formats.

The CD is a development of the original optical analogue videodisc read by a laser. On the CD, information is recorded digitally giving a high quality of sound. Provided it is manufactured and handled properly, it should not deteriorate in use and should have a considerable lifetime. As such it is an ideal library medium.

The audiocassette is less effective than the CD, in that it is more susceptible to damage, although less so than the long-playing record. It is a popular format, easy to handle, and most libraries and users have suitable playback equipment.

Open-reel audiotapes are normally only used and found in information services where in-house production is part of the work of the organization. It is not a suitable general-purpose audio medium.

The future for some of these audio-recording media is unsure. The CD and the audiocassette can be expected to be available for the forseeable future. However, there is an increasing movement within the audiovisual industry to build equipment that will record and/or playback audio only as well as video-recordings, and to develop the range of CDs to include both audio and video material. It is logical, and beneficial to users, that these two areas of audiovisual media should combine in the future. For with the development of digital recording, both areas will use the same techniques and equipment.

OVERHEAD TRANSPARENCIES

The overhead transparency is widely used in education and training, replacing the blackboard and epidiascope over which it has many advantages. It can carry charts, diagrams, lecture outlines, pictures and other teaching and learning aids.

Overhead transparencies can be produced by a variety of means including freehand drawing, lettering, word-processing or photo-copying onto plastic sheets. Overhead transparencies can also be created by computer programs and projected directly onto a screen by means of a special projection unit connected directly to a computer and without the need for a plastic intermediary. Overhead transparencies are normally found in information services connected with education and training institutions. Paper copies of overhead transparencies are equally effective as library holdings and trainers and educators should be persuaded to deposit paper copies of their overhead transparencies, rather than the plastic copies, in the library. Overhead transparencies are a unique medium and are likely to remain so, as no other audiovisual format can do the same job more efficiently or economically.

SLIDES AND FILMSTRIPS

35mm photographic slide collections are to be found in a number of information services and are valuable in building up a visual collection economically. Such collections can be on any topic, but many relate to the arts.

If it can be photocopied there are almost certainly commer-cially published slides available. If not, it is not difficult for information professionals to create slides for library use them-selves. Slides are relatively fragile and need careful storage and handling. Colour slides, because of the nature of colour photographic film, have a comparatively limited lifetime which may be from 10 to 20 years in normal use.

Again, the future of the photographic slide may be limited – huge collections of visual images are now being published on optical videodiscs, and some of these are being produced and published by libraries. The current Japanese development of filmless cameras which record their images on magnetic discs and which can be viewed on a video screen, combined with the increasing costs of photographic colour film, will hasten the demise of this medium for all but professional or dedicated photographers.

Filmstrips, although still available, are both unsuitable for library collections and obsolete. Their only value now is as children's story material and as a cheap source of visual images. Their up-to-dateness needs to be carefully checked before purchase, however. Existing filmstrip collections should be carefully examined, out-of-date material discarded except for useful images, and the remainder cut up, mounted in slide mounts and incorporated into the slide collection.

CINEFILM

A similar situation exists in relation to cinefilm. Available in a variety of widths, the 16mm cinefilm format was the most suitable for information-service use. Although still available, commercially published cinefilms are so expensive that their purchase is unrealistic, except for information services dedicated to that medium. Much of the vast range of film material is now also available on videocassette, which is a far more robust and flexible format for use in an information service. The only suitable playback equipment for use in the study of cinefilm in an information-service situation is a film-editing table and these are also extremely expensive. The cheaper film projector permits only the continuous playback of film, not the detailed study of sequences, and contributes greatly to the rapid deterioration of the film itself. Increasingly cinefilm is being used only by professional film and television production companies, and even in the latter there is a gradual changeover to video-recording taking place.

VIDEO-RECORDINGS

As has been indicated, video-recordings now provide a much more flexible and a cheaper alternative to cinefilm for the information service. But in addition to the large number of cinema productions on video, an increasing range of original television productions and more specialized audiovisual programmes of value to information services are now being published in some video format.

Although video-recording was developed using open-reel tape, such tapes are now to be found only in professional television-production companies. As with audiotape-recording, the move has been towards the packaging of videotape into cassettes. In common with many other developing technologies, video-recording suffers from a lack of standardization, and rapid development. This can make life difficult for the information professional wishing to make use of video recordings. However, out of the welter of recent developments, some fairly stable areas can be discerned.

Three formats have gained the ascendency and it is with these formats that the information professional can proceed with some confidence. The first is the Sony U-matic videocassette format, used with considerable success by a number of libraries which developed some form of video service early on, when U-matic was the only reliable format available. Today, however, it provides a playback quality rather better than is required, the equipment is more expensive than information services need to pay, and the published programme range available in this format is strictly limited. So although still a valuable format for those committed to it, it is not a format that should be considered by information services developing video facilities now.

The best format available now, and likely to be so for the foreseeable future because of its extensive international take-up, is the VHS videocassette system. Constantly being improved, with equipment prices decreasing in real terms, this system is ideal for use in information services. Virtually every published programme is available in this format, and the equipment also allows the information service to undertake its own in-house off-air recording, copyright permitting. It can also be used for the in-house production of original material.

One outstanding multimedia library in the UK has adopted the recent Sony Video 8 format and, while the technology has proved to be entirely satisfactory, though still more expensive than VHS, there have been many problems over acquiring programmes in this format or obtaining permission to copy from another format to Video 8. Accordingly this format is not recommended at present, although if the range of programmes ever equals that of VHS, then it would be worth considering.

The third format worthy of consideration, and one in which there could be developments of immense value to information services, is that of the videodisc. These discs can carry audio recordings; visual materials – 54,000 slides can be recorded on one side of a 30cm (12in) videodisc; audiovisual moving-picture recordings; print; and computer programs and data. The videodisc is the only format so far developed that has the recording abilities of all the other audiovisual formats put together. The videodisc family comprises 30cm, 20cm, 12cm discs (including the compact disc, CD-ROM, CD-V and the proposed CD-I); and an 8cm disc used for audio-recordings only so far. To confuse the issue, Philips, the originators of the optical videodisc, now call the entire range 'compact discs'.

It is in this area that a new range of specialized audiovisual programmes of considerable value are being developed and published. Examples of these huge databanks of audiovisual information are the BBC's Domesday Discs, London University's discs on the Knee and on Dogs, and Cambridge University's disc on the Naga people. Some libraries, notably the Library of Congress, the Bibliothèque Publique d'Information (the Pompidou Centre) and the Mediathèque of the City of Science and Industry in Paris, are preparing and using a wide range of videodiscs, some of which will no doubt be available for purchase by other libraries. As this area develops, the videodisc and developments from it will make available to information services vast databanks that would previously have been impossible to publish by conventional means.

There is one further problem connected with both videocassettes, videodiscs and indeed broadcast television and that relates to the system by which the video signal is transmitted or recorded. Basically there are four systems used internationally. The United States, Japan and some other countries use the NTSC system, the United Kingdom, most of Europe and some other countries use the PAL system, while the French and some countries use the SECAM system. Some satellite transmissions use D-MAC. For an information service which wishes to acquire video-recordings produced only in the United Kingdom or from other countries using the PAL system, the purchase of a PAL VHS videocassette recorder or player, or a PAL videodisc player is perfectly satisfactory. However, if the information service wishes to purchase programmes, including the specialized audiovisual databanks mentioned above, from other countries, then it must purchase at least one multi-standard VHS recorder or player, or a multi-standard videodisc player, or both, *and* at least one multi-standard television receiver or monitor. Only when this equipment is purchased can the video-recordings from other countries be played back.

Increasingly the specialized programmes being produced on videodiscs require the interconnection of the player with a computer to enable the programme to be used interactively. Here the computer contains a program which responds to the instructions and answers of the user and controls the way in which the contents of the videodisc are accessed and used. It is in this convergence of videodisc technology and computer technology that the most exciting developments in information provision in the future will lie.

Another aspect of the convergence of these technologies lies in the use of CD-ROM, itself a development of the 12cm compact disc, in conjunction with a computer. The CD-ROM is presently capable of holding approximately the same quantity of information as would be found in a 20-volume encyclopaedia. Although at present CD-ROMs are being produced containing predominantly text-based information, they are capable of holding visual and audio information as well, and some recent CD-ROMs make use of this facility. Because of the enormous quantity of information found on these discs, they have to be accessed by the user through a computer using a suitable program to control the use of the disc. At present, CD-ROMs are usually produced in the 12cm format, but there is no reason why the 30 or 20cm discs could not be used for the same purpose, packing in even greater quantities of information from all audiovisual formats. It is possible that within a year or so there will be a multi-standard player on the market that will playback any size and type of videodisc. CD-ROM is dealt with in more detail in the next chapter.

REAL OBJECTS

Real objects, such as stuffed birds and crocodiles, model railway engines, skeletons, bricks and building materials, and a wide range of other objects, are usually found only in school resource centres, or libraries of organizations specializing in specific areas such as building or architecture. There is no bibliographic control of such materials.

COMPUTER PROGRAMS

Although libraries and information services initially used the computer to control many of their housekeeping systems, such as circulation and cataloguing, it is becoming increasingly common to provide computers for user use, either as word processors or with a wide range of computer programs. Computer technology is also bedevilled with problems of standardization and rapid developments in technology. It has an additional problem, for the information professional as well as for users, of incomprehensible instruction manuals both for equipment and, worse, for many programs. This makes it difficult to assist computer users to solve problems.

However, some fairly stable areas can be discerned here as well as in video technology. There is an increasing tendency amongst some equipment manufacturers and program producers to produce compatible equipment and programs. An example of this is the IBM PC-compatible range of computers which will usually run the same computer programs. It would be logical for information services to have computer equipment within such a 'standardized' range. Unfortunately, even within this range of compatible computers some lack of standardization is created by new developments, for example in increased disc storage capacities. This can mean that some older computers will not read the same-sized discs containing data created on a more modern compatible computer, for example. This is a problem that information professionals with large collections of computer software must be aware of when selecting new equipment; otherwise the software already held could quickly become obsolete.

PRINT-BASED MATERIALS

Finally, in a book about printed reference materials, is it not relevant to examine their value and their future? Certainly books are still seen by many as primary sources in libraries and information services. In some cases they are just that and their value cannot be denied. But this chapter suggests firstly that this may not be true for all printed materials. For it has been shown that there are primary source materials in other formats that information services must take. Secondly, this chapter indicates that change in the immediate future is inevitable – indeed it is already happening. Already a number of traditional book-based reference materials are now being published in one or other of the more recent audiovisual formats described in this chapter. Some established encyclopaedias and dictionaries are now being published as CD-ROM. Some trade directories and timetables are now being published as CD-ROM or computer databases. A number of major bibliographies are also changing their publication format. Other reference materials will follow suit where and when necessary. And ultimately the book format will find its appropriate place in a range of primary information sources available to our users.

THE INEVITABILITY OF CHANGE

But should these changes, over which we have little or no control, cause us to worry? After any initial teething problems are sorted out, could the new form of publication not be an improvement on the old? Could not encyclopaedias published on videodisc give us far more valuable information than the traditional book-based encyclopaedia? If we look up 'Mahler' in a book-based encyclopaedia, we can only read about him and perhaps see a photograph. If we look up 'Mahler' in a videodisc encyclopaedia we can not only read about him, see many relevant photographs of him and his environment, but also hear some examples of his music, see an historic sequence of film of him conducting a concert, and hear his voice. It could also be published and updated much more regularly than the paper version, as well as taking up far less space. Using a computer, it could also be far quicker and easier to access the information than ever before. With a computerized world airways timetable we could not only find out the time of flights as we can now, but also book our ticket, reserve our seat on the aeroplane, specify what type of meal we want, book a taxi and hotel at the other end of our journey, pay by credit card *and* know that the information we are accessing is right up-to-date.

So change will bring many advantages. And librarians who have converted from card catalogues to computerized catalogues with online terminals have survived, and learned new professional skills in the process. Could it be that developing multimedia audiovisual collections could be the most exciting development for us and especially our users?

ARRANGEMENT OF MULTIMEDIA COLLECTIONS

Having begun to develop multimedia collections, how can they best be brought to the attention of the user? Total separation of the more recent audiovisual materials from the book and earlier formats is both illogical and retrograde in the light of the success of subject arrangement. What we should not do is to treat the more recent audiovisuals as something different, create separate departments to deal with them and place them under the control of an 'audiovisual librarian' or its equivalent. Unfortunately, many libraries who do adopt this method of dealing with the more recent materials go one stage further and 'hide' the audiovisual department in the basement or some other inaccessible area of the service, ensuring that few users will be aware of its existence and guaranteeing minimal usage of these materials.

Equally the total integration of all audiovisual materials including books into one sequence, while it may solve some problems of user awareness in some smaller information services, is a practical impossibility in a large information service. Such services will already have had to create several sequences of book materials, for a variety of reasons including economy of space, subject departmentalization, etc. It would be unrealistic to think that one could take a step backwards when adding additional formats to the collection.

The best solution is one of partial integration, shelving the various materials on the same subjects in separate sequences but as close to each other as possible and always in the same area. The necessary playback equipment should be on open display in the same area, and preferably switched on and working during opening hours. Videocassettes filed in the same sequence as books look like books; videocassettes shelved separately but next to the books on the same subject look like videocassettes and as such self-advertise their presence in the collection. Working equipment also advertises the presence of the new media in the information service. Thus it ensures that all staff are aware of and responsible for all materials, and this ensures that the user receives the best possible multimedia service.

THE BIBLIOGRAPHY OF THE MORE RECENT AUDIOVISUAL MATERIALS

Despite the considerable numbers of the more recent audiovisual materials that have been published over the years, Antony Croghan showed in a recent article that disproportionally small numbers of these items have found their way into some information services. He rightly dismissed the old excuse for small or non-existent collections of the new media – 'you can't find out about the media!' with the response 'you can if you look hard enough!'[6] And he stated that there is an urgent 'need for the central archival collection – the British Library – to take the provision of NBM much more seriously than it does'.

And this is the crux of the matter. How hard should it be to find out about the publication of the more recent audiovisual materials? Logically, in a country with well-organized national bibliographies for print materials it should not be any harder to search for the more recent audiovisual materials than it is for print. Surely our concern is with information, not the format in which it is produced?

Yet it is often harder to find details of the more recent audiovisual materials than it is to find details of print-based documents. And although the situation is slowly improving, information professionals still have to conduct lengthy searches over a wide range of potential sources. With some materials, such as film and sound-recordings, searching for some items can be comparatively easy. For some audiovisual formats, searching is hard; and for some, extremely difficult. And the major cause of these problems is the lack of legal deposit and a central archive of all information materials, regardless of their format. And the implications of this situation for future generations of information professionals, users and researchers are appalling.

CURRENT AND RETROSPECTIVE BIBLIOGRAPHY

In compiling the following list of current and retrospective bibliographies I must acknowledge the assistance of Chris Baggs, Lecturer in the Department of Information and Library Studies of the University of Wales, Aberystwyth.

Multi-format bibliographies

The ideal for information professionals would be one source to which they could refer for all audiovisual materials, regardless of format. One way forward could be a development of the *British National Bibliography* to include all information materials in one classified sequence. But even in the United States, where the National Union Catalog published by the Library of Congress includes the more recent audiovisual materials, these are published in a separate section of the catalogue. Such a division may be helpful for an information professional specifically looking for particular formats, but it does perpetuate the barrier of format and encourage some to think only of one format, or only of one format first, that of print.

Although the *British National Bibliography* has never achieved this ideal, it did experiment in 1979 with the publication of a separate national catalogue of audiovisual materials. The tragedy is that, despite the success of the catalogue, the experiment was suspended in 1983. However, the work done was of considerable value, and although nothing was added to it for five years, 1989 saw the addition of a considerable number of new items. Therefore this catalogue is valuable, both as a retrospective and current bibliography, though by no means complete.

BRITISH CATALOGUE OF AUDIOVISUAL MATERIALS. 1st ed. London: British Library, 1979. First supplement, 1980. Second supplement, 1983.

This began as an experimental catalogue based on the more recent audiovisual materials processed by the British Library/Inner London Education Authority Learning Materials Recording Study.

It attempted to produce a comprehensive bibliography of the whole range of the more recent audiovisual materials of interest to education in the widest sense. Its arrangement was similar to that of the *British national bibliography*. It included most types of audiovisual materials including some printed documents such as portfolios, posters and wallcharts. However, it excluded most 16mm film and videocassettes, as these were already covered by the *British national film catalogue*, and music, which was covered by commercial catalogues such as those published by the *Gramophone*.

The experiment was undertaken 'with some caution' by the British Library to explore the problems associated with the publication of such a catalogue and before adopting a general responsibility for the bibliography of audiovisual materials of all kinds. The British Library indicated that if they could overcome the problems, it would be inappropriate to confine the catalogue to educational materials only. However, after the second supplement the publication of the catalogue ceased.

As well as being published in paper form, the catalogue and

supplements can be accessed online via BLAISE-LINE as AVMARC. Although no new entries were added between 1982 and 1988, a considerable number of new entries based on new items received by ILEA were added to this database in 1989.

BRITISH UNIVERSITIES FILM AND VIDEO COUNCIL CATA-LOGUE. London: BUVFC, 1983 – . Annual.

The 1989 volume of this catalogue contains information on some 6,700 videocassettes, videodiscs, films, tape-slide programmes, slide sets, sound tapes and computer software. It is arranged by UDC. It also contains an alphabetical list of distributors.

The catalogue is compiled from the HELPIS online database available through the BLAISE-LINE service. The database is updated monthly and is therefore more up-to-date than the *Catalogue.*

A useful catalogue allied to the *BUFVC catalogue* is the BUFVC's *Distributors index*, an annotated subject guide to companies and institutions who distribute programmes for education and training.

NATIONAL UNION CATALOG. AUDIOVISUAL MATERIALS. Washington, DC: Library of Congress, 1983 – .

The Library of Congress *National union catalog* consists of four parts: NUC books; NUC US books; NUC audiovisuals; and NUC cartographic materials. Published on microfiche, the *NUC audiovisual materials* covers films, filmstrips, overhead transparencies, slides, videograms and kits published in the United States and Canada, that have educational or instructional value. Each part consists of a Register, arranged in numerical order, and accessed via name, title, subject and series indexes. The 1989 indexes cover all items published in the Register from 1983 onwards.

Other sources include the catalogues of the Educational Foundation for Visual Aids, now very dated, and the catalogues of the many commercial and institutional audiovisual material producers and distributors.

Film and videogram bibliographies

BRITISH NATIONAL FILM AND VIDEO CATALOGUE. London: British Film Institute, 1984 – . Quarterly.

Published quarterly, with annual cumulations, this well-established bibliography gives details of all films and videocassettes that may be screened to non-theatrical, that is non-fee-paying audiences, in the United Kingdom. It covers non-fiction, short fiction and full-length feature films and videograms, including a small but growing number of interactive videodiscs. By 1988, the *BNFVC* included some 63,000 films and videocassettes.

Arranged by UDC, there is an additional alphabetical listing of fiction films and videocassettes with brief annotations. It is well indexed with subject, title and production (sponsors, production companies, distributors, technicians, artists and others associated) indexes.

The catalogue began in 1963 as the *British national film catalogue.*

Two other useful catalogues from the British Film Institute include the *National film archive catalogue*, an irregular publication which covers the holdings of the National Film Archive from all over the world. It is arranged by country and then by date of publication. There are title and subject indexes. The *National film archive catalogue of viewing copies* is an irregular publication compiled from the Archive's computerized database.

GIFFORD, Denis, THE BRITISH FILM CATALOGUE: A REFERENCE GUIDE. 2nd ed. Newton Abbott: David and Charles, 1986.

This claims to be the first complete catalogue of every British film produced for public entertainment since the invention of cinematography.

Other sources include:
- Film and video distribution-library catalogues such as those of the Guild Organisation; BBC Enterprises; CFL Vision, formerly the Central Office of Information Central Film Library.
- Catalogues of specific collections such as the Scottish Central

Film Library; the Higher Education and Video Library administered by BUFVC; the Imperial War Museum.

Specialist subject guides are being produced by both the British Film Institute and the British Universities Film and Video Council.

There are a number of guides to video materials only, such as the *Video source book UK*; *Penguin video source book*; *Good video guide*; and numerous periodicals which list and annotate new videograms.

Audio recordings

THE GRAMOPHONE CATALOGUES. London: General Gramophone Publications, 1951 – .

There are several catalogues published by *The Gramophone* at varying intervals. These list music and other audio-recordings in all formats that are available at the time of publication of the catalogue: *Classical catalogue* (four times a year); *Compact disc digital audio catalogue* (four times a year); *Popular music catalogue* (four times a year); *Spoken word and miscellaneous catalogue* (annual).

LIBRARY OF CONGRESS CATALOG: MUSIC, BOOKS ON MUSIC AND SOUND RECORDINGS. Washington, DC: Library of Congress: 1973 – . Semi-annual.

This is a comprehensive catalogue of American music materials, unique in terms of its coverage.

Other sources include record company catalogues; the BBC Music Library catalogue; *Early music discography*, compiled by Trevor Croucher; *The world encyclopaedia of recorded sound*, by F. F. Clough and G. J. Cuming; and the *Penguin stereo record and cassette guide* which includes a star rating for performance.

There is as yet no published catalogue of the holdings of the **National Sound Archive**, now part of the British Library. However it is expected that the joint project between the National Sound Archive and the Mechanical Copyright Protection Society to produce a highly detailed computer database from both their holdings and records will become available in 1990. The catalogue will be published on CD-ROM, and there will also be a limited availability online computer database for some users.

Still visuals

This is a more difficult area in which to obtain information as there is no centralized source for this material, nor are there any up-to-date published bibliographies.

BIBLIOGRAPHY OF MUSIC AND ART GALLERY PUBLICATIONS AND AUDIOVISUAL AIDS IN GREAT BRITAIN AND NORTHERN IRELAND, 1979/80. 2nd ed. Cambridge: Chadwyck Healey, 1980.

Wall, J., DIRECTORY OF BRITISH PHOTOGRAPHIC COLLEC-TIONS. London: Heinemann, 1977.

Other sources include the catalogues of individual art galleries, museums, and slide producers – such as the Slide Centre.

Microforms

MICROPUBLISHERS TRADE LIST ANNUAL. Westport, Ct: Meckler Publishing: 1985 – . Annual.
  Published on microfiche, this is a collection of catalogues of the various publishers of microforms.

GUIDE TO MICROFORMS IN PRINT. Westport, Ct: Meckler Publishing: 1983 – .
  In two sections, author/title and subject, with a cumulative annual listing of microform titles.

MICROFORM REVIEW
  A periodical which includes reviews of recent publications in microform.

Computer software

MICROCOMPUTER SOFTWARE AND HARDWARE GUIDE. Online on DIALOG, file 278.

Other sources include:
- Periodicals such as *Library software review*, *Personal computer world* and other computer journals;
- Directories such as *Directory of microcomputer software for librarians* and *PC yearbook*.
- Information from the National Computing Centre.

REFERENCES AND CITATIONS

1 Patterson, O. (ed.), *Special tools for communication*. USA: Industrial Audiovisual Association, 1962. Quoted in Rigg, Robinson P., *Audiovisual aids and techniques*. London: Hamish Hamilton, 1969.
2 Croghan, Antony, 'Non-book media in general collections', *Audiovisual librarian*, **12** (3), August 1986.
3 Hope, Tom, Comment in *Audiovisual*, September 1984, 19.
4 Croghan, Antony, 'Half of one per cent: the British Library and non-book media', *Audiovisual librarian*, **12** (2), May 1986;
  Thompson, Anthony Hugh, 'Knowledge or format?', *Audiovisual librarian*, **12** (4), November 1986.
5 Thompson, Anthony Hugh, *Storage, handling and preservation of audiovisual materials*. Holland: Nederlands Bibliotheek En Lektuur Centrum, 1983. (IFLA AV in action, no. 3).
6 Croghan, Antony, 'Non-book media in general collections', *Audiovisual librarian*, **12** (3), August 1986.

16

Electronic Publishing

John Gurnsey

E lectronic publishing is a generic term, coined in the late 1970s and used to cover an increasingly diverse and disparate range of technologies in which the ultimate objective is the dissemination of information in electronic form. As with other essentially new terms, 'electronic publishing' suffers from being somewhat randomly and inconsistently used. Thus in the past it has been used to cover, not just the dissemination of information of electronic form, but also the use of electronic means to generate a conventional printed product. This, with hindsight, is not electronic publishing, though it does serve to demonstrate how integrated and confused this whole area is becoming, as publishing generally moves inevitably into the electronic arena.

If further definitions are necessary, electronic publishing may be defined as:

- the use of computers and telecommunications systems to distribute data electronically;
- the use of various storage media to allow the distribution of data on demand.[1]

This is simple enough to be attractive, although it is covering a steadily increasing range of products, encompassing online, videotex, teletext – including the new subscription services, subset technologies – whether via magnetic or optical means, audiotex, video, software-based products and still more.

The very diversity of products now available in electronic form, points to one of the weaknesses of a term like electronic publishing. By seeking a generic definition, a range of very different services, often having virtually nothing in common save their link with an electronic format or delivery mechanism has been brought together. If this needs emphasis, it can surely be seen in comparing audiotex – which in its more serious applications uses a multi-frequency (MF) telephone to deliver stock exchange price data – and video. These technologies could not really be more different, nor could the markets they serve be more remote. This fact emphasizes, if nothing else, a belief that we are moving on to the next stage of electronic information-handling, one where products can exist in their own right with no need to seek spurious linkages with other sectors of the information industry.

A more mature approach to electronic information now permeates the professional information sector. Gone, hopefully for ever, are the days when abstract journals and bibliographic online services were regarded as largely separate, one spawning its own host of user groups, the other a host of near-Luddites unable or unwilling to use a terminal. Now, electronic information is near what it was always destined to be, one of a range of tools in the professional armoury, but not a universal panacea or a development likely to see the end of either libraries or dedicated information units.

Although revenues for video products and penetration levels for teletext make it questionable, most now regard online technology as electronic publishing's most mature product sector. Certainly in the professional – as distinct from domestic – market, online now has a long history of established use. More importantly, since its inception in the early 1970s, online has been steadily evolving. This applies both to the technology itself and to the market it is serving. It is this evolution, far more than revenues or penetration levels, that makes online a mature market sector.

The history of online is well documented. It began, both in Europe and the US, with the switch in the late 1960s of a number of major abstract journals to computer-assisted photocomposition.

While the key objective of this switch may have been to streamline production systems faced with major problems from the growth in STM (science, technology and medicine) literature, a spin-off was the creation of a machine-readable tape which facilitated the generation of online services. What followed, certainly in the UK, was a brief period of confusion, in which batch services and even tentative – though arguably illegal – trial online services were tested. Then, in 1972, Lockheed'a DIALOG and SDC's ORBIT systems became available, and online was truly launched in Europe.

The early emphasis of online in the bibliographic area was both inevitable and unfortunate. It was inevitable because this was the sector which had the information available in machine-readable form. It was unfortunate because it tied the initial use of the technology far too closely to the library and intermediary sector, a market which sadly always seems to lack the revenues to exploit any new technical initiative. In this context, we must also recognize that, certainly in the early stages, most database producers were unsure about the long-term potential of online. Embarrassed by this new source of income, and unsure how it would affect their core hard-copy services, most adopted a low-key approach to selling online, something which certainly hampered its development well through into the 1980s.

But if the bibliographic sector was unsure of the potential of online, this was far from the case with more dynamic areas. By the late 1970s, numeric databases and data files began to make their appearance, products which were unashamedly designed for use by end-users not librarians. No revenue-constricted library market was sought here, and suddenly the potential of online as a major information-dissemination medium became apparent. Changes in storage technologies and more importantly cost ratios in the early 1980s, also had a significant affect on online development. They made it possible – and practical – to hold very large volumes of data online; the era of full-text delivery had now arrived.

Although they were the markets which saw the first use of online, the 1970s and 1980s saw the steady erosion in revenue terms, of both the bibliographic and the STM sectors of the online market. That this erosion is still continuing is graphically shown in Table 1, LINK's figures suggesting that the STM area will decline from around 8% of the pan-European online market in 1988 to some 5.5% by 1994.

Table 1   West Europe online market by product sector: 1988 to 1994. US $ million

Product	1988	1989	1990	1991	1992	1993	1994
Securities	765	880	1000	1260	1490	1745	2025
FOREX	550	685	845	1000	1225	1475	1775
Commodities	70	80	90	120	145	170	205
Econometric	80	90	100	105	110	135	135
Comp/product	17	19	26	27	37	45	54
Fund corp	150	170	197	235	272	318	375
Comp credit	90	110	122	142	175	205	245
Pers credit	55	62	82	94	120	145	180
Marketing	68	90	122	167	242	341	454
STM	165	180	205	225	245	275	295
Miscellaneous	45	51	55	62	69	75	85
Total	2055	2417	2844	3432	4120	4929	5828

Source: LINK Resources 1989.[2]

It is not so much the failure of the STM market, and its close link with the intermediary area, which causes this change. Far more is it the strong growth of online use elsewhere, particularly in the financial sector. In LINK's figures, more than 65% of the 1988 revenues shown occur on real-time products (those covering securities, foreign exchange and commodity information). This is a strange, idiosyncratic market which owes its growth entirely to the very close link between information and its end-use, in this case financial dealing, a link and benefit the wider online area has never been able to demonstrate.

This is also an area where we need to be careful about definitions. Although undoubtedly online, real-time services are not strictly speaking a database technology. Thus, products like Reuters Monitor or Equities 2000 are mainly concerned with listing price changes, not in holding definitive historic data online.

They may – and indeed do – as part of the total package also provide access to historic price information, but their *raison d'être* is the ability to support market activity by providing access to current information.

Real-time services are highly specialist and it is hardly surprising that this sector has developed both its own peculiar form of fulfilment and its own range of providers. Thus, companies like Reuters, Telerate, Quotron, Datastream, Telekurs and others are almost entirely tied to the real-time or financial-information sector; they have traditionally relatively little contact with wider online areas. Only more recently, with a widening of the demand for online information by financial analysts, together with companies like Data Star and PFDS (Pergamon Financial Data Services) looking for more lucrative markets, are we beginning to see any cross-contact between the financial area and other online sectors. This could prove an important trend both for database producers and hosts as the 1990s progress.

Whatever else, it is clear that the real-time area offers some of the most advanced online technology currently available. This is an area which has historically developed its services in a page-based video format, typified by Reuters' Monitor, but has more recently moved on to a number of both adapted video/digital services – using a range of highly sophisticated video switches – and true digital services delivered in page-based and record form. Add to this the wide range of display, graphics and software-based technologies linked to this sector, and it is clearly well in advance of anything seen in other online areas.

Perhaps the most advanced online technologies of all are seen in the link between PC technology and record-based real-time digital feeds. These systems, which include ADP's MarketPulse, Pont's PC Quote, Wang's Shark and the Telekurs' INDES service, all make use of high-speed, record-based digital feeds to provide a high degree of functionality. Not only do they provide fast access to current prices, they also allow a degree of manipulation in real-time of the data the user is receiving. This is typically achieved by using a wide range of graphics, display and windowing techniques, which make it possible for users to design virtually the display of their choice.

The rise of the numeric database, and particularly the real-time area, has fundamentally affected the type of fulfilment seen in the online sector. Thus, where the early days saw a comfortable division between database providers and hosts, the financial area now sees a higher level of integration. Here database providers are also their own hosts and network operators, a fact which if nothing else serves to emphasize yet again the high revenues involved in this section of the market.

But it is not just revenues which have increased in the online area. The number of files available has increased out of all proportion and their cover now impinges on every facet of human activity. If this needs emphasis, the Cuadra *Directory of online databases*[3] – a work which is increasingly becoming the definitive global source – now lists some 4,200 databases, together with over 1,700 producers and 570 (host) service suppliers. More importantly, it is now issued four times a year, and is itself available in online form, acknowledging, if nothing else, the very dynamic nature of the modern database industry.

Listing online services has become a cottage industry in its own right and a large number of **directories** are now available. Not surprisingly, many of these originate in the US, emphasizing that country's strong early take-up of the technology. In this context, we must recognize that online from the start has never achieved a common level of use even in more developed Western countries. In the LINK figures shown in Table 1, some 52% of the total European revenues come from the UK, a fact which emphasizes its role as the region's time-zone investment market as well as the relatively strong take-up of online in more general areas. More surprising perhaps are the figures for France (14%) and West Germany (10%), markets where – amongst other things – language difficulties have always impinged on growth in the online area. Here only now, with changes in relative costs and the growing importance of financial files, is growth in online use beginning to reach the levels taken as the norm in North America.

Cuadra apart, the main US-originated database listings are the American Library Association's *Computer-readable databases*[4] and Gale's *Encyclopaedia of information services.*[5] Although undoubtedly US-biased in content, both of these listings are international in nature. They also cover slightly different areas, the ALA's work being concerned purely with databanks and databases, the Gale directory having a far wider remit and including information providers, access services, support services (bureau consultants, etc.) as well as information services directed at the information industry itself.

A comparison of these three directories makes for an interesting exercise. Where Cuadra has followed the obvious format, a straight alphabetic listing of the databases it contains, both the Gale work and the ALA directory have adopted a more sophisticated – though arguably less effective – approach. Thus the Gale directory is arranged essentially in geographic form, an approach which tends to expose still further its heavy US bias. Conversely, the ALA listing, edited by Martha Williams, uses a rather cumbersome subject approach, perhaps again emphasizing the US professions' preoccupation with subject headings. Perhaps this accounts in part for why it is the Cuadra directory which is becoming increasingly recognized and cited as the definitive source.

Online information, whether bibliographic, numeric or full-text, is becoming increasingly international in outlook. Despite this, most countries seem to feel the need to have directories which cover their own national listings, and the UK is no exception. *Brit-Line*[6] is a 400-page directory covering databases available in the UK. Again arranged by subject, it covers 375 databases produced in the UK, and while a useful support tool cannot hope to stand in place of a definitive source like Cuadra.

More valid, and I suspect more useful, are **subject listings** of databases. Among those produced in the UK are a number of Aslib publications covering among other areas law, medicine, management and marketing.[7] The Aslib lists are simple, effective tools, having the added advantage of being produced with the strong involvement of the Aslib Groups. This makes them very practically oriented works not merely concerned with including the maximum number of files. They supplement the main Aslib *UK online search services*[8] directory, which is scheduled to go into its fourth edition in early 1990.

Also relevant in the UK is the Fosters' *Online business sourcebook.*[9]

This aims to cover both bibliographic and numeric files, but is a rather inconsistent listing in which it is all too easy to find significant omissions. Another very useful source is the *Clover comparative cost chart for online files* which shows the range of costs of databases from different hosts.[10]

As well as the simple database listings, online technology has spawned a significant literature of its own. Among one of the more persevering sources is Aslib's *Going online*.[11] This reached its eighth edition in 1989 and it is still a useful source for inexperienced searchers looking to enter the bibliographic arena. While this is no place for a comprehensive review, other similar works which deserve mention are Armstrong and Large's *Manual of online search strategies*[12] and Stack's *Online searching made easy*.[13] Both are useful reference tools.

Online primers, which is what these tools really represent, are not the remit only of commercial publishers. A good deal of useful information is provided by the database producers and online hosts themselves. Thus, the *Pocket guide to DIALOG*[14] and the subject-based online guides produced by Data Star[15] both make an important contribution and are good examples of works which are produced by each of the leading hosts. The fact that the Data Star guides are designed to support two 'teach yourself' floppy discs serves to show just how far online hosts have now gone to ensure the effective use of their services. These form an important part of the online literature and are no less welcome because they are invariably low cost or even free.

Even more comprehensive are the **manuals** which support the individual hosts or database products. These, like the *CAB abstracts manual*,[16] can run to more than one volume and are designed to assist in solving even the most abstruse or complex enquiry. Not as low cost as the primers mentioned earlier, manuals typically come as part of a subscription or attendance at a training course. They nonetheless make an important contribution to our overall understanding of online technology.

Past experience has tended to concentrate heavily on the numbers of databases produced. Happily, as we come to a more mature market sector, we now see a greater concentration on **evaluation**. This applies even at the individual level, and works like Nicholas and Ehrbach's *Online information sources for business and current affairs: an evaluation of Textline, Nexis, Profile and DIALOG*[17] could become a feature of a future market concerned with the quality of information and not just with its delivery.

Evaluation of individual databases is also becoming important because, even in the full-text and bibliographic areas, the typical end-user is changing; where the early online market was dominated by librarians, this is no longer the case. Many modern databases are designed specifically with the end-user in mind and indeed make sense only if they are used by the individual initiating the enquiry. Similarly, even in the bibliographic area – the last bastion of the librarian – companies like DIALOG and Data Star report that far more end-users are attending their training courses. For those concerned with marketing databases and host services, such trends are, or should be, important. If they recognize this, then they could do worse than consider David Nicholas' book *Online information retrieval systems: use by end-users of online information systems: an analysis*[18] which tries to put the whole issue in context.

Any examination of the documentation surrounding the online industry shows a series of peaks and fads, periods when some issues took on crucial significance followed by times when they were virtually ignored. Just such a stop-go approach was seen with the problem of **downloading**. This came to the fore as a major issue in the early 1980s, fuelled largely by the hosts' concern at the increased use of intelligent terminals and PCs. By the mid-1980s, this issue was spawning a literature all of its own,[19] and had caused most, if not all, hosts to reassess their charging practices.

In fact, downloading is not the contentious issue it was first thought to be. True, it raises problems for bibliographic services but, as we have seen, these form a relatively small part of the total online industry. Elsewhere, downloading may actually be desirable for both the host and the database provider, ensuring that the end-user is far more locked-in to their services. In this respect, it is not accidental that Jordans – the UK company-database provider – runs courses in downloading. It links closely with their wider activities, which include FAME (financial analysis made easy), a data-manipulation software package designed to run on a PC. Clearly, outside the bibliographic arena, downloading is not a negative issue, many files being designed and sold specifically with downloaded use in mind.

Far from threatening revenues, downloading here actually makes possible the sale of an enhanced range of services. Thus, while the financial sector is undoubtedly highly successful, by the late 1980s most major service providers were beginning to recognize that they were too closely, and exclusively, tied to the dealing function. While this was fine to an extent, and certainly guaranteed their base revenues, it also meant a link with a very volatile and uncertain market. It is also a fact that, while unquestionably advanced and sophisticated, information products aimed at the dealing area have limited scope for enhancement. Once the vendors have addressed the twin issues of speed and content – both of which are reaching their optimum – then there is little scope to extend or develop the services.

The arrival of record-based digital feeds, plus the increased use of PC systems in the financial sector, have opened up a whole range of new product options for financial information vendors. Many of these concentrate on what has been loosely termed the '**value-added**' area. This ill-defined term covers a whole range of services including textual products, which give a high degree of interpretation and analysis, and software-based services where the vendor also supplies programs to interact with data which has been downloaded. At their ultimate, value-added services extend into full trading products, where the dealer does not just obtain information online but actually completes the transaction in electronic mode.

Value-added services are relatively new but look certain to be a major development and growth area in the 1990s. In some cases they come from established providers like Reuters, in others new and dynamic vendors like Bloomberg and First Call. In the financial sector, the increasing role of value-added products is changing the key providers. With such services being concerned not just with information, but with its use and interpretation, we are seeing a growing role for financial institutions – like banks and brokers – to operate as information vendors. With the authority and standing of their creators often being a key issue in the value-added market, this is a trend which can be expected to continue, though whether such organizations will prefer to work direct, or via one of the established commercial providers, remains to be seen.

The growing significance of value-added services raises important charging issues. So far these have not really been addressed, such services often being costed more on the basis of market development than their true value to the customer. One problem is that there has never been a truly systematic approach to charging for online services generally, a deficiency that applies equally to the bibliographic and financial sectors. If one thing looks likely in the 1990s, it is that the growing role of value-added products will push charging, not just prices, to the forefront. If this happens it will be long overdue.

One development inevitably linked to the value-added area is the potential of meaningful subset products delivered in machine-readable form. This has been forced into the limelight by the arrival of **CD-ROM** but it would be wrong to assume that it is only this that has caused the interest. As early as the late 1970s, BIOSIS with its BITS service attempted to launch a subset product on floppy disc. That this largely failed was not because of any deficiency in the product, although it was clearly constrained in what it could offer. It was simply because the market at that time lacked a standardized installed base at which BIOSIS could target the service, i.e. it was ahead of its time.

What CD-ROM offers, apart from vastly enhanced storage capacity, is a wide and standardized base of equipment at which vendors can target their services. This is unquestionably an important development, though it is not the watershed change some might think from reading the professional literature. While CD-ROM and other emerging optical media undoubtedly have potential, to talk about this technology displacing online is not merely premature, it is also highly irresponsible.

In this context, we must recognize that CD-ROM is not a technology likely only to interact with what we regard as the conventional information area. Although some applications will undoubtedly be directed at products currently online, where CD-ROM can offer the publisher a degree of control not obvious in online applications, still more will fall elsewhere. In 1988, LINK in the UK attempted to isolate those areas where CD-ROM was likely to have an early impact in Europe. Some of their results are shown in Table 2. They suggest that while database publishing, the key area where CD-ROM interacts with online, will be important, it will be quickly displaced by applications in other areas. Among these will be corporate publishing and technical documentation – applications undersold in the LINK report, and certainly the areas where CD-ROM could be expected to gain some of its most important early markets. In terms of online, LINK concluded that, for the foreseeable future, CD-ROM and online were likely to be complementary technologies. It is hard to disagree with this.

Table 2   Western Europe. CD-ROM drives by application area, 1987 – 1992. Units

	1987	*1988*	*1989*	*1990*	*1991*	*1992*
Database publishing	400	600	900	1500	2300	3000
Reference/value-added	200	1800	3600	9000	15700	27000
Technical documents	20	350	1200	3900	11500	18000
CIP/Ed and training	-	200	600	1500	3000	4500
Total	620	2950	6300	15900	32500	52500

Source: LINK Resources 1988. [20]

Whatever its real potential in the conventional information area, Europe has not been slow to develop a range of CD-ROM published products, many of them directed unashamedly at the library market. By 1989, the TFPL (Task Force Pro Libra) directory[21] listed some 400 services, while the parallel Meckler directory[22] gave details of over 200. It seems the arrival of CD-ROM has given a spur to the directory industry. With another offering from Learned Information[23] this area is particularly well served, though whether a market exists for all these services only time will tell.

If the CD-ROM area seems over-supplied with reference works, the same cannot be said of the **video** sector. Whilst some technical listings covering equipment and companies exist here,[24] there is still a need for a definitive listing of exactly what is available on video. Although it is easy to dismiss much that appears on video as purely entertainment, this is surely not a reason to ignore the need for a definitive source. It is also a fact that, from its strong installed base, video is ideally placed to move on to more serious applications. This, if nothing else, will stress the need for far greater control in this area. It is not enough to leave it to the present rather *laissez-faire* approach, where listing new issues is left to a number of sources none of which would claim to be either comprehensive or definitive.

The cause of the problem of assigning some form of control to the video area is not hard to find. This is a multi-million pound market which has emerged from nothing in little more than ten years. Given that bibliographic control in the printed area took years – and legal deposit – to achieve, it is hardly surprising that such a dynamic market should struggle. The fact that it is also a global market, and one characterized by a large number of small – and often rather erratic or idiosyncratic – suppliers, does not alter the need for some major initiative. Despite this, little seems to happen and most of the national bibliographies, who at least understand the problem, show little interest. Perhaps they lack the political remit, finance or will to tackle this area. If so, it means the situation will continue as it is, with little happening and the continuing risk that material will be lost or genuine researchers unable to find individual items in the mass available.

What has been said of the video area applies equally to **packaged software**, in some ways an even more pressing problem. While some attempts, typically in the education or games areas, have been made to list software, these are certainly the exception rather than the rule. In business, commercial and other more serious software applications, there is a total absence of any definitive listing. Again, it makes it difficult for users to judge objectively what is available and places them firmly in the hands of their retailer. Even if such retailers are honest – and many are – this is not a satisfactory situation, because even they can advise only on what they *know* to be available.

Video and software are technologies whose very success presents problems. In the case of **videotex**, it is the slow build-up of the technology which is causing difficulties. Thus, in the UK, while the Prestel service was launched in the mid-1970s, its slow growth has now brought a reassessment of the long-term potential of the technology. The UK experience with videotex, which now sees virtually zero growth in the public area, but strong growth in private systems, has its parallels elsewhere in Europe. Only in France, where the government has given financial and philosophical support, has the technology enjoyed strong growth. This variation and uneven pattern of take-up is clearly seen in Table 3.

Table 3   Videotex penetration in Western Europe. Dates various – early to mid-1989

Country	System	Standard	Terminals	IPs
France	Teletel	Antiope	4,500,000	10,000
Sweden	Videotex	CEPT	30,000	150
UK	Prestel	Prestel	90,000	1,300
W Germany	Bildschirmtext	CEPT	130,000	3,000
Netherlands	Viditel	CEPT	30,000	1,000
Switzerland	Videotex	CEPT	10,000	300
Austria	Bildschirmtext	CEPT	9,000	750
Finland	Telset	various	5,000	40
Luxembourg	Videotex	CEPT	200	n/a
Norway	Teledata	CEPT	1,500	100
Denmark	Teledata	CEPT	2,000	85
Belgium	Videotex	CEPT	3,000	30
Ireland	Cognotec	several	1,000	n/a
Italy	Videotel	CEPT	10,000	250
Spain	Ibertex	CEPT	300	n/a
Greece	trial	n/a	n/a	n/a
Portugal	trial	n/a	n/a	n/a
Hungary	trial	n/a	n/a	n/a

Source: LINK Europe 1989.[25]

The slow growth in the Prestel public service has had a major influence on the UK Videotex Industry Association (VIA), this sector's major trade representative. Where once this was very much concerned with the public service, its membership is now primarily network and hardware providers and companies active in the private viewdata area. Thus, where VIA once issued the major industry directory[26] – still a useful work – most of its activity is now concentrated on hardware and standardization issues. VIA has indicated it is unlikely to reissue further editions of its *Videotex directory*, a decision which seems to leave a gap in the UK market.

If the UK now lacks a major videotex directory, some information can be gleaned from *The Prestel start-up directory*.[27] This gives brief details of services and information providers active on Prestel but must suffer to some extent from being a source tied to the carrier. Thus, it would be unrealistic to expect objective or critical advice from the Prestel booklet, though it does serve an important function, not least in helping new Prestel users get started.

Elsewhere the main emphasis seems to be on private viewdata systems. In this area, and related to library use, LASER has done sterling work in the UK for a number of years. This currently includes one of the few directories of the private viewdata area,[28] a disc-based listing which includes 45 entries. LASER has no intention of formally publishing its directory at present, although it is available on request, a small charge being made for the print-out service.

While Prestel has struggled, the private viewdata sector appears to have gone from strength to strength in the UK. Functioning far more as an easy-to-use communications, rather than a publishing, medium, this area has a number of major and highly successful applications. This trend can be expected to continue despite the fact that private viewdata systems now face increased competition from a range of other technologies.

By now, public teletext must also be deemed a successful electronic dissemination application in the UK. By mid-1989, some 5.5 million teletext decoders were in use in the country, with the vendors Ceefax and Oracle both seeking to extend the general, news, sport and weather information via which their services gained their initial use. In both cases, the provision of regular financial price data is one way the services have moved forward, applications which bring them directly into competition, for users if not revenues, with the financial database providers.

Quite why teletext should have been such an immediate success in the UK is not clear. It owes some of its growth to its low cost and ease of use, still more to the television rental industry's willingness to make low-cost decoders available. Whatever the cause, IBA's Oracle is now the world's first public teletext service supported totally from advertising revenue, a point from which the industry should move on strongly in the 1990s.

Subscription teletext, the private spin-off from the public networks, also shows every sign of developing quickly. Already Datacast (BBC) and Air Call (IBA) have demonstrated a significant range of applications and still more can be expected. Although this technology has its information-based services, with products like the International Stock Exchange's Market Eye and (in France) SDIB's Chronoval, it is in the point-to-multipoint communications area where it is likely to make its major impact. Here, it has been demonstrated to be both highly successful and cost-effective. In all applications it could be a technology to watch as the 1990s progress.

This chapter has wandered through the electronic publishing field, indicating some of the works of particular interest and use, as an appraisal of the working documents in the database and market-research areas. Whilst the works listed may not be the only ones available, they do at least have the benefit of being tried and tested.

REFERENCES AND CITATIONS

1   Gurnsey, J. and Henderson, H., *Electronic publishing trends in the United States, Europe and Japan*. Commission of the European Communities Electronic Document Delivery VII. Oxford: Learned Information, 1984.

2   LINK Resources, *The European electronic information industry, 1988 – 1992*. 2 vols. London: LINK Resources, 1989.

3   Cuadra, C., *Directory of online databases*. Vol. 11, Part 1. Amsterdam: Elsevier, 1989.

4   Williams, M. F., *Computer-readable databases, Vol.1: Business, law, humanities, social sciences; Vol. 2: Science, technology, medicine*. Chicago/Amsterdam: American Library Association/Elsevier, 1985.

5   Lewis, A. and Marcaccio, K., *Encyclopaedia of information services, Vol.1: US listings; Vol. 2: International listings; Vol. 3: Indexes*. 7th ed. Detroit: Gale, 1987.

6 *Brit-Line: directory of British databases.* London: McGraw-Hill, 1989.

7 Aslib, *Online guides.* London: Aslib, various dates. Include: law databases; patents and trademarks; company and business databases; medical databases; management and marketing; online bibliographic databases.

8 Aslib, *UK online search services.* 4th ed. London: Aslib, 1990.

9 Foster, P. and Foster, A., *Online business sourcebook.* Cleveland: Headland Press, 1989.

10 *Clover comparative cost chart for online files.* Biggleswade, Beds: Clover Publications. Quarterly.

11 Aslib, *Going online.* 8th ed. London: Aslib, 1989.

12 Armstrong, C. J. and Large, J. A., *Manual of online search strategies.* Aldershot: Gower, 1988.

13 Stack, H., *Online searching made easy.* Richmond, Yorks: PJB, 1988.

14 DIALOG, *Pocket guide to DIALOG.* Palo Alto, Ca: DIALOG, 1988.

15 DataStar, *Business information: teach yourself guide for the DataStar online service.* London: DataStar, undated;
DataStar, *Biomedical information: teach yourself guide for the DataStar online service.* London: DataStar, undated.

16 Commonwealth Agricultural Bureau, *CAB abstracts: online manual.* 2 vols. Wallingford: CAB, 1988.

17 Nicholas, D. and Erhbach, G., *Online information sources for business and current affairs: an evaluation of Textline, Nexis, Profile and DIALOG.* London: Mansell, 1989.

18 Nicholas, D., *Online information retrieval systems: use by end-users of online information systems: an analysis.* (BLR&D Report 5929.) London: Mansell, 1988.

19 Jameson, A., *Downloading and uploading in online information retrieval.* Bradford: MCB, 1987;
Foulkes, J., *Downloading bibliographic records: proceedings of a one-day seminar sponsored by the MARC users group.* Aldershot: Gower, 1986.

20 LINK Resources, *Market opportunities for CD-ROM in Europe, 1987 – 1992: a multi-client study.* London: LINK, 1988.

21 Task Force Pro Libra, *CD-ROM directory.* 4th ed. London: TFPL, 1990.

22 *CD-ROMs in print, 1988 – 89.* Westport, Ct. and London: Meckler, 1989.

23 Learned Information, *Database guide.* Oxford: Learned Information, Spring 1990.

24 *Professional video.* Croydon: Link House Publications, 1987 – 8.

25 See note 2 above.

26 Videotex Industry Association Ltd., *UK videotex directory.* London: VIA, 1984.

27 Prestel, *The Prestel start-up directory.* London: Dialcom UK, 1989.

28 London and South East Region (LASER), *Directory of local government private viewdata systems.* London: LASER (disc based produced on demand).

17

Indexes

K. G. B. Bakewell

THE IMPORTANCE OF THE INDEX

Asked on BBC Radio's 'Any Questions' in May 1968 what he would bring into force if he were Prime Minister, Bernard Levin said that he would make it compulsory for publishers of works on non-fiction to supply them with an index.[1] Anybody who has read some of Mr Levin's book reviews knows how much importance this distinguished reviewer attaches to the index. In 1976 he requested the restoration of the death penalty for publishers and authors who produce works without indexes and threatened to come back after his death and 'haunt those criminals who, through cunning, luck, a defect in the law or an abrupt flight from justice, have managed to evade the fate they deserve'.[2]

More recently Bernard Levin has severely criticized Oxford University Press for an appalling index to an important reference work, Ian Ker's biography of John Henry Newman.[3] His comments on the skills of indexing and the value of using a registered indexer to compile indexes provoked some critical responses from people who should have known better. One of these, Nicholas Albery, stated that Bernard Levin wrote 'a load of tosh', that indexing required no real skill and that he (Albery) had produced an index of 1,200 entries to the *Encyclopaedia of social inventions* (published by the Institute for Social Inventions in

400

December 1989) between 4 am and 5 am one morning with the aid of a computer.[4] In fact this 'index' simply contains entries under inventors (surnames only), names of corporate bodies and titles of inventions. An invention entitled 'Bringing hobbies into the school curriculum', therefore, has an entry under 'Bringing' but nothing under 'hobbies', 'curriculum', 'schools' or 'national curriculum'. A suggestion for an 'alternate heads' scheme for the Civil Service, given the title 'Two Sir Humphreys' (because of the comedy series *Yes, Minister* and *Yes, Prime Minister*) has an entry under 'Two' but not under 'Civil service' or 'alternate heads' (or even 'Sir Humphrey' or 'Humphrey, Sir'). The value of what might have been a useful reference book is thus diminished by a totally inadequate index which the compiler thinks is good. One is reminded of J. Payne Collier's attempt in the nineteenth century to demonstrate the simplicity of cataloguing to Panizzi, then Principal Keeper of Printed Books at the British Museum Library, by cataloguing 25 books from his own collection. Panizzi retorted that the entries contained every error it was possible to make in cataloguing!

A very distinguished librarian once startled this writer by suggesting that the only books used in any depth by librarians are quick-reference books, which in the main (he said) are self-indexing. This is nonsense. How much less effective such 'quick-reference' works as *Whitaker's almanac*, *The world of learning*, *Directory of British associations* and *The statesman's yearbook* would be without indexes. In any case, there is much more to reference service than the use of quick-reference material.

Another very distinguished librarian, Lionel McColvin, has explained how he accepted the advice of somebody who had told him not to provide an index for *The public library system of Great Britain*, the famous 'McColvin report', because, if he did, everybody would look up what he had said about 'them' and nobody would read the report right through.[5] He later learned that another librarian had passed the published report to one of his staff, saying 'I suppose I'll have to read it but for heaven's sake make an index to it. Fancy charging five bob for the damned thing – and no index.' (Younger readers should perhaps be told that 'five bob' means 25 pence – the exorbitant price charged by the Library Association for a reference book in 1942!)

It is important for reference librarians to know something about indexes and indexing. Not only do they need to make use of indexes in order to exploit reference material effectively, but they must also be able to judge the quality of the index when selecting reference material and they may have to compile indexes to library publications such as bibliographies and contributions to local studies. They will also need to maintain their own internal indexes to local organizations and activities, previously answered 'awkward' enquiries, etc. and for community information input to Prestel or a private viewdata system.

DEFINITIONS AND PURPOSES OF INDEXES

Hans Wellisch has written, in a survey of the history, meanings and usage of the word 'index':

> If you are asked at a wine and cheese party ... what your profession or hobby is, and you answer proudly, 'I am an indexer', you may, depending on the background of your inquirer, be assumed to be a mathematician, a physicist concerned with optics, an anthropologist, a palaeontologist, a geologist, an economist, a mechanical engineer, a forestry expert or a computer scientist; or possibly even a printer, a designer of playing cards, an employee of a motor vehicle licensing agency; or, of course, a person who tries to make the contents of books and journals retrievable by listing names and subjects in a predictable order, with an indication of their physical place in the source.[6]

Henry B. Wheatley, often described as 'the father of indexing', has defined an index as 'an indicator or pointer out of the position of the required information.'[7] This, and the final sentence of the quotation from Wellisch, certainly indicates the *main* purpose of an index – to facilitate the speedy location of specific items of information – but there are others, as McColvin has pointed out.[8] The index arranges material in a different way from the main text, bringing together scattered references to a topic. A *good* index indicates what is *not* in the item and is, therefore, a valuable aid to selection. It can also limit wear and tear on a book because the reader will not have to flip through the whole text each time a piece of information is sought.

In his message welcoming the formation of the Society of Indexers, the late Harold Macmillan (afterwards first Earl of Stockton) mentioned yet another value of an index: authors are frequently indebted to indexers for pointing out errors, discrepancies or repetitions that had otherwise escaped detection in the proofs.[9]

An index does not *have* to be arranged alphabetically, though it often is. Sometimes a classified or numerical index is called for; for instance, *Examples illustrating AACR 2*[10] has an index arranged by rule number and a secretary in an industrial organization where this writer was once librarian decided to arrange her correspondence files by the Universal Decimal Classification because she was so impressed by its use in the library.

WHAT AN INDEX IS NOT

Concordances are frequently quoted as examples of indexes, and certainly such works fulfil a very useful function in enabling users to locate words in the Bible, Shakespeare, etc. However, a modern subject index is emphatically *not* a concordance. There is no point in indexing **words** unless there is something significant in the document about the word indexed; and a good index will index **concepts**, whether or not the word representing those concepts is used in the text. Kathleen Binns has explained how, under pressure from a publisher, she was guilty of turning an index into a concordance by indexing words simply because they were mentioned in the text.[11] She rightly calls such entries, which bulk the index and irritate the reader, 'non-entries'. Stephen Leacock has written an amusing piece about such 'non-entries':[12] there might be several entries under 'Napoleon' in the index leading to such sentences as 'wore his hair like Napoleon', 'in the days of Napoleon', 'as fat as Napoleon', 'not so fat as Napoleon', etc.

Nor is an index a contents table – though Valerie Alderson has pointed out that 'indexes' to children's reference books may be little more than chapter headings which should have appeared on the contents page.[13] And an index of meaningless titles, such as that to the *Encyclopaedia of social inventions*, cannot be termed an adequate subject index.

STANDARDS FOR INDEXING

The British Standard on indexing is now in its third edition.[14] It defines the function, types and features of indexes and gives advice on content and general organization, arrangement of entries in indexes and presentation of indexers. It was published following deliberations by a committee containing representatives of ten organizations: Aslib (the Association for Information Management), the Association of British Directory Publishers, the British Library (Humanities and Social Sciences), British Telecom, Her Majesty's Stationery Office, INSPEC, the Library Association, Oxford University Press, the Society of Indexers and the Standing Conference of National and University Libraries. The fact that representatives of these bodies were prepared to devote a great deal of their time to the preparation of this standard contradicts the suggestion by Nicholas Albery, the Marquess of Anglesey and others, in reply to Bernard Levin's article referred to earlier,[15] that indexing requires little or no skill. It is also interesting that it should be Oxford University Press which was the object of Levin's condemnation, since their representative (now no longer employed by OUP) made many invaluable contributions to the standard.

The revised British Standard was warmly welcomed by the international indexing community. It will form the basis of the International Organisation for Standardisation's revised standard on indexing currently (January 1990) in its final stages of preparation.

WHAT SHOULD BE INDEXED?

Clearly most non-fiction reference books need an index, but what of fiction books? None can deny the reference value of the four known indexes to Sir Walter Scott's Waverley novels,[16] the compilation of one of which has been described by Philip Bradley.[17] Hilary Spurling's index to a more modern classic, Anthony Powell's *A dance to the music of time*,[18] is a valuable reference tool, and there are indexes to other novels.

Newspapers are used extensively in reference libraries as sources of contemporary information. Some national newspapers publish their indexes and many libraries maintain their own indexes of local newspapers. Some of these have been published.

Many periodicals are covered by the indexing and abstracting services described in Chapter 8, but every serious periodical should also publish its own index. Too often this does not happen, or a periodical may publish an index and require its subscribers to request copies rather than receiving it automatically as should be their right; sometimes an additional charge is made for the index. Often an 'index' to a periodical contains little more than entries under authors and titles of articles.

Reference librarians may well wish to compile their own indexes to other sources of information, such as reports (all too often published without an index), letters and illustrations.

With regard to the content of indexes to individual documents, clause 5.1.1 of the British Standard[19] states that indexes should normally cover all matter in the document including, for example, introductory matter, notes, addenda, illustrations and appendices except when a special purpose is defined for a particular index. Exclusions should be brought to the user's attention in a note.

CUMULATIVE INDEXES

The following definition of a cumulative index was given in the 1964 British Standard on indexing but dropped from the 1976 and 1988 revisions:

> Where a book is published in several volumes, each with its own index, or where a periodical is provided with an index each year or part of a year, and these separate indexes are combined to form an index to the whole series, the product is called a cumulative index.[20]

An excellent example of a cumulative index which will be well known to all librarians is that compiled by Laurie J. Taylor for volume 2 of his compilation *A librarian's handbook* (London: Library Association, 1980), which was awarded the Wheatley Medal for an outstanding index in 1980. It indexes the 1,072 pages of volume 2 and the unsuperseded pages of volume 1 of the handbook, published in 1977.

The compilation of cumulative indexes to newspapers and periodicals presents special problems because of changes in terminology and the use of different terms by different contributors. This is recognized in the 1988 revision of the British Standard on indexing, clause 5.5.3 of which makes various suggestions for overcoming the problem. Appendix A of the standard gives recommendations for keywords which may be assigned to such documents as reports and periodical articles and which may act as an aid to manual cumulative indexing.

Doreen Blake and Ruth Bowden have explained some of the problems of compiling the centenary index to the *Journal of anatomy* (1866 – 1966), published by Cambridge University Press for the Anatomical Society, for which they were awarded the 1968 Wheatley Medal.[21] It was impossible to use the individual indexes because they lacked uniformity, were incomplete and were sometimes inaccurate. Terminology presented a special problem because there was no nationally agreed anatomical nomenclature until 1895 and since then there have been five!

THE LONG INDEX

Some indexes to be used by the reference librarian are likely to be very long, and E. S. De Beer has pointed out that the longer an index is, the more difficult it is likely to be to use: 'No one imagines that a large index will be all easy going; long entries cannot yield all their secrets at a glance; consultants must do some work.'[22] Part of the art of indexing is to reduce as much as possible the difficulty of using the index, and here such matters as a clear introduction and layout can help. De Beer's 600-page index to *The diary of John Evelyn* (Oxford: Clarendon Press, 1955) has a ten-page introduction, which is too long, but in it the user of the index is given some very important information. For example:

1   Abbreviations used in the index are explained.

2   Arrangement of subheadings is not always alphabetical; sometimes it is chronological and sometimes the more important references are placed first.

3   All clerics, apart from Popes, are entered under surname with cross-references from benefices.

4   Peers are indexed under their family names with cross-references from their titles.

5   Words and phrases are indexed in a single alphabet headed *Words and phrases*.

6   There are special notes on the entries for members of Evelyn's family.

7   There is a synopsis of subject headings.

De Beer's index to Evelyn's diaries influenced the compilers of another monumental index, that to *The diary of Samuel Pepys* (London: Bell & Hyman, 1983; Vol. 11 of *The diary*). Robert C. Latham and his wife Rosalind tried to capture the flavour of the diary in this index and to make the index acceptable to the amateur as well as to the historian.[23] Inevitably, there are some very long entries – 31 sections, for example, under *Charles II* and several pages under *Parliament*. Asterisks are used to minimize the use of words: under *Meals*, * indicates that Pepys gives the menu; under *Taverns*, * indicates that Pepys ate a meal there; under *Books*, * indicates that Pepys read a book and ** that he comments on it. There was never much doubt that this outstanding index, the culmination of four and a half years' work, would win the Wheatley Medal; in his review of it in *The Observer*, 27 February 1983, Bernard Levin wrote: 'I have tried every kind of trick question I could think of on this astonishing guide to the *Diary* and have not been able to catch it out in a single *lacuna*.'

HOW TO RECOGNIZE A GOOD INDEX

This is the title of a useful paper by Geoffrey Hamilton, a former chairman of the Wheatley Medal Selection Committee.[24]

The index may need to be prefaced by a clear and concise **introductory note**, explaining the indexing decisions made such as omissions, unusual features, abbreviations and any peculiarities about the arrangement.

Obviously the index must be **accurate** and must cover all significant items in the text. It should normally be **comprehensive**, though certain limitations on comprehensiveness may be allowable if clearly explained. John L. Thornton has pointed out that many indexes to medical books are unsatisfactory because they are not sufficiently comprehensive:[25] frequently they ignore plates, diagrams and tables, which often contain information not readily accessible via the text and are sometimes located several pages away from the text to which they refer; bibliographies should be indexed, as should appendices; introductions can be lengthy and informative and should be considered for indexing.

The index should have enough **subheadings** to avoid strings of undifferentiated location references – one of Bernard Levin's objections to the OUP index to Ian Ker's biography of John Henry Newman.

Accuracy applies to the **arrangement**, whether alphabetical, numerical or some other order, as well as to the location references. If alphabetical arrangement is used, 'word-by-word' or 'letter-by-letter' must be chosen and adhered to rigidly; the two systems can result in quite different sequences, as seen in the following brief examples:

word by word	*letter by letter*
Arab World	Arabian . . .
Arabian . . .	Arab World
Bank of England	*Banker, The*
Banker, The	banking
banking	Bank of England

The British Standard on indexing favours word-by-word arrangement, as do the companion British Standard on alphabetical arrangement[26] and the *BLAISE filing rules.*[27]

There should be enough **cross-references** to connect related items in the index:

abstracting services *see also* indexing services
dictionaries *see also* encyclopaedias

In the case of synonyms and alternative forms of name it is often quicker, as well as being more helpful to the user of the index, to make additional entries rather than '*see*' references:

client needs   57
user needs   57
LASER   251
London and South Eastern Library Region   251

'See' references should, however, be used if there are a large number of subheadings:

LASER
   Prestel umbrella scheme   242
   transport scheme   249 – 51
   VISCOUNT project   243 – 7
London and South Eastern Library Region *see* LASER

The **layout** of the index is important. The following example shows that 'set out' subheadings are clearer than 'run on' subheadings, although the latter may occupy a little less space than the former:

set out	*run on*
company information	company information
banking 153	banking 153; BLDSC
BLDSC policy 62	policy 62; fee-based
fee-based information	information services
services 185 – 9	185 – 9; loose-leaf
loose-leaf services 26 – 7	services 26 – 7; methods
methods of presenting	of presenting 24, 25;
24, 25	online services 38,
online services 38, 222 – 9	222 – 9; sources 156 – 68;
sources 156 – 68	trade literature 27,
trade literature 27, 259	259

When sub-subheadings need to be used, there is really no alternative to 'set out'. The following example is taken from *Anglo-American cataloguing rules* (2nd ed. 1988 revision):

Parts of work
  definition, App. D.
  description
    computer files, specific material designation, 9.5B1
    music, specific material designation, 5.5B1 – 5.5B3
    printed monographs, 2.5B18
  uniform titles, 25.6
    explanatory references, 26.4D2
    liturgical works, 25.23
    musical works, 25.32
    sacred scriptures, 25.18
    "see" references, 26.4B2, 26.4B3

A 'run-on' version of this would be very confusing:

Parts of work
  definition, App. D.; description: computer files, specific
  material designation, 9.5B1; music, specific material
  designation, 5.5B1 – 5.5B3; printed monographs,
  2.5B18; uniform titles, 25.6: explanatory references,
  26.4D2; liturgical works, 25.23; musical works, 25.32;
  sacred scriptures, 25.18; "see" references, 26.4B2,
  26.4B3

THE COMPUTER AND INDEXING

The use of the computer to produce indexes to periodicals is commonplace, two well-known examples being *Current technology index* and the PRECIS subject index to *British national bibliography*. More recently, programs have been developed for the production of book indexes, including MACREX,[28] COMDEX,[29] and CINDEX.[30] It is now possible for a *proper* subject index to be produced with the help of a computer and not simply an index of names and titles! Priscilla Oakeshott's report on the impact of new technology on the publication chain[31] contained only one rather unfortunate reference to indexing: she suggested that the new technology would soon replace 'not merely manual skills but some which are more demanding, although largely routine, such as indexing.' There is rather more to indexing than Ms Oakeshott imagines, as she might have discovered had she attempted to provide an index to her report.

COULD INDEXES REPLACE LIBRARY CATALOGUES?

Pauline Atherton (now Pauline Cochrane) and her associates at Syracuse University have shown, with their Subject Access Project,[32] that book indexes could be very significant for retrieval generally if more use were made of them. They compared retrieval via keywords taken from contents tables and indexes with retrieval via MARC records and the results indicated that retrieval via BOOKS (the keyword database) was quicker and more effective than retrieval via MARC. Among the benefits claimed for BOOKS were:

1 greater access to books with relevant information;
2 greater precision;
3 less costly online searching;
4 the ability to answer some queries which would not be possible using 'today's catalogue information'.

The important point was made, however, that some effort needs to be made to improve the contents pages and indexes in books to make this kind of retrieval truly effective.

A great deal of information could be retrieved via book indexes which is not apparent from the title or main subject. Ronald Blythe's *Akenfeld: portrait of an English village* (Harmondsworth: Penguin Books, 1972) would probably be classified as social history but this hides the fact that the book contains much useful information about Suffolk schools, industrial and agricultural life in the first 40 years of the twentieth century. Similarly, *Speak for England*, Melvyn Bragg's 500-page essay on England, 1900 – 75, based on interviews with inhabitants of Wigton, Cumberland (London: Secker & Warburg, 1976) includes material on family life, factory life, farming, schools and the church among many other subjects.

Alas, neither of the two books mentioned above has an index, and an article on the Subject Access Project[33] indicated that this is not unusual. The following analysis showed that books examined for the project frequently did not have indexes:

books examined	2087
number with index	1147
percentage with index	55%

INDEXING SOCIETIES

In 1957 a retired civil servant, G. Norman Knight, wrote various letters to the press inviting people interested in the formation of a society of indexers to communicate with him. Knight had been a self-tutored freelance indexer for 30 years but had never met any other indexers and was keen to remove the 'intense feeling of solitude' in which the freelance indexer had to work. Sixty people responded to Knight's invitation to attend a meeting at the National Book League's premises in London on 30 March 1957 – including one gentleman (Dr William Heckscher) who had flown from Utrecht in the Netherlands – and the Society of Indexers was formally constituted. The objectives of the Society were and are to safeguard and improve indexing standards and to secure some measure of uniformity in technique; to promote the professional interests of indexers; and to act as an advisory body on qualifications and remuneration. The first edition of the British Standard on indexing was produced largely on the initiative of the Society.

One of the Society's outstanding achievements has been the regular publication, since March 1958, of a twice-yearly journal, *The indexer*. Successive issues of this have included scholarly and practical articles on all aspects of indexing and a regular feature on extracts from book reviews which referred to the index in laudatory or derogatory terms or to the absence of an index.

The Society has encouraged the use of the new technology for the production of indexes and its newsletter, *Microindexer*, regularly contains much useful and practical advice on the use of microcomputers and indexing packages.

Several conferences have been held in various parts of Britain (and one in Yugoslavia) since the first National Conference on Indexing in March 1976 (the proceedings of which were published in *The indexer*, **10** (2), October 1976) and the first International Conference on Indexing, which was organized in 1978 to celebrate the Society's 21st anniversary and attended by more than 100 people from 16 countries. One of the speakers at the 1978 conference was the same William Heckscher who had flown from Utrecht to attend the inaugural meeting in 1957, but this time he came from the United States! The Society's ailing founder (and then President), Norman Knight, was able to attend the Conference Dinner and to give his greetings only one month before his death. The proceedings of the conference were published in *The indexer*, **11** (2), October 1978.

The Society has published five monographs in a series of Open Learning Units[34] and more are in progress.

The American Society of Indexers was formed in 1968 and became formally affiliated to the Society in 1971; the already strong links between the two Societies were strengthened further when the President of the British Society attended the American Society's 21st Annual Meeting in 1989. The Society is now also affiliated to the Australian Society of Indexers (formed in 1976) and the Indexing and Abstracting Society of Canada/Société canadiènne pour l'analyse de documents (formed in 1977), and *The indexer* is the official journal of all four societies. The parent Society is now an organization in liaison with the Library Association.

AWARDS FOR INDEXERS

In 1960 the Library Association instituted the **Wheatley Medal**, so called in honour of Henry B. Wheatley (1838 – 1917). It was originally an annual award to the compiler of the most outstanding index published in Britain during the preceding year, but in 1968 the conditions of the award were modified following a joint meeting of the Society of Indexers and the Library Association Cataloguing and Indexing Group. One of the changes was that indexes published during the preceding *three* years would be eligible for the award, because it was recognized that an index can be judged only by its performance over a reasonable period.

The winner is chosen by a panel consisting of three nominees of the Library Association and three nominees of the Society of Indexers. It says much for the high standards expected for the Medal – and perhaps something for the quality of indexes – that no award was made for the first two years or for six other years. The following are the winners to date:

1960   No award
1961   No award
1962   Michael Maclagan   for the index to Michael Maclagan *'Clemency' Canning* (Macmillan)

1963   J. M. Dickie   J. M. Dickie *How to catch trout* (W. & R. Chambers)

1964   Guy Parsloe   Guy Parsloe *Wardens' accounts of the Worshipful Company of the Founders of the City of London 1497 – 1681* (University of London, Athlone Press)

1965   Alison M. Quinn   Richard Hakluyt *The principall navigations, voiages and discoveries of the English nation* (Cambridge University Press/Hakluyt Society and Peabody Museum of Salem)

1966   No award
1967   G. Norman Knight   Randolph S. Churchill *Winston S. Churchill, Vol. 2: Young statesman 1901 – 1919* (Heinemann)

1968   Doreen Blake and   *Cumulative index to Journal of*
       Ruth Bowden   *Anatomy 1866 – 1966* (Cambridge University Press/Anatomical Society)

1969   James C. Thornton   M. House and G. Storey (eds.) *The letters of Charles Dickens, Vol. 2: 1840 – 41* (Clarendon Press)

1970   E. L. C. Mullins   E. L. C. Mullins *A guide to the historical & archaeological publications of societies in England and Wales 1901 – 1933* (University of London, Athlone Press)

1971 No award
1972 No award
1973 K. Boodson

K. Boodson *Non-ferrous metals: a bibliographical guide* (Macdonald Technical & Scientific)
and

L. M. Harrod

H. M. Colvin (ed.) *History of the King's works, Vol. 6: 1782 – 1851* (HMSO)

1974 C. C. Banwell

Encyclopaedia of forms & precedents. 4th ed. 24 vols. (Butterworths)

1975 Margaret D. Anderson

Judith Butcher *Copy-editing: the Cambridge handbook* (Cambridge University Press)

1976 John A. Vickers

G. R. Cragg (ed.) *The works of John Wesley. Vol. 11: The appeals to men of reason and religion and certain related open letters* (Oxford University Press)

1977 T. Rowland Powel

Archaeologia Cambrensis, 1901–1960 (Cardiff: Cambrian Archaeological Association)

1978 No award
1979 K. G. B. Bakewell

Anglo-American cataloguing rules. 2nd ed. (Library Association)
and

Annette Surrey

D. G. James (ed.) *Circulation of the blood* (Pitman Medical)

1980 Laurie J. Taylor

L. J. Taylor (comp.) *A librarian's handbook*, Vol. 2 (Library Association)

1981 J. Edwin Holmstrom

Analytical index to the publications of the Institution of Civil Engineers, January 1975 – 79 (Institution of Civil Engineers)

1982 Peter W. M. Blayney

Peter W. M. Blayney *The texts of King Lear and their origins, Vol. 1:*

		Nicholas Okes and the first quarto (Cambridge University Press)
1983	A. R. Hewitt	*The laws of Trinidad and Tobago.* Rev. ed. (Government of Trinidad and Tobago) and
	Robert Latham	Robert Latham and William Matthews (eds.) *The diary of Samuel Pepys: a new and complete transcript*, Vols. 1 – 11, 1970 – 83 (Bell and Hyman)
1984	No award	
1985	John Gibson	Sir John Walton *Brain's diseases of the nervous system*. 9th ed. (Oxford University Press)
1986	No award	
1987	Neil R. Fisk	D. H. Allport and N. J. Friskney *A short history of Wilson's School*. 3rd ed. (Wilson's School Charitable Trust)
1988	Bobby Burke	Lord Hailsham of St Marylebone (ed.) *Halsbury's laws of England* (Butterworths)

The Society of Indexers established an occasional award for outstanding services to indexing in 1977 and designated it the **Carey Award** in memory of the Society's first President, Gordon V. Carey (1886 – 1969). So far there have been five recipients of this award, which takes the form of an appropriately worded and beautifully decorated citation: G. Norman Knight in 1977, L. Montague Harrod in 1982, Margaret D. Anderson in 1983, William S. Heckscher in 1987 and John Ainsworth Gordon in 1989.

In 1979 the **H. W. Wilson Company Index Award** was inaugurated for excellence in indexing of an English-language monograph or other non-serial publication published in the United States during the previous calendar year. The Award, which consists of a cash prize for the indexer and a citation for the publisher, is presented by the American Society of Indexers on behalf of the well-known index publishers. The recipients so far have been:

1978	Hans. H. Wellisch	for the index to Hans H. Wellisch *The conversion of scripts, its nature, history and utilization* (Wiley)
1979	Linda I. Solow	David Epstein *Beyond Orpheus: studies in musical structure* (MIT Press)
1980	Delight Ansley	Carl Sagan *Cosmos* (Random House)
1981	Catherine Fix	Donald Resnick and Gen Niwayama *Diagnosis of bone and joint disorders* (W. B. Saunders Company)
1982	No award	
1983	Mary Fields and the indexing staff of Information Services	*Index and directory of the US industry standards* (Information Handling Services)
1984	Sydney Wolfe Cohen	Christopher Cerf and Victor Navasky *The experts speak* (Pantheon Books)
1985	Marjorie Hyslop	*Metals handbook*. Desk ed. (American Society for Metals)
1986	No award	
1987	Jeanne Moody	*Raptor management techniques manual* (Institute of Wildlife Research)
1988	Philip James	J. Willis Hurst (ed.) *Medicine for the practicing physician*. 2nd ed. (Butterworths)

The **Australian Society of Indexers** presented its first Medal, intended to promote standards of excellence in indexing in Australia, in 1988. The recipient was Elmar Zalums for his index to *A history of Australia*, Vol. 6, by C. M. H. Clark (Melbourne University Press, 1987). The 1989 medal was awarded to Alan Walker for the index to the *Penguin new literary history of Australia*, edited by Laurie Hergenhan (Penguin, 1988).

REFERENCES AND CITATIONS

1   *The indexer*, **6** (2), 1968, 73.
2   Levin, Bernard, 'A haunting, I promise, for those who refuse to tell who's who and what's what', *The Times*, 17 December 1976; reprinted in *The indexer*, **10** (3), 1977, 139 – 41.
3   Levin, Bernard, 'Don't come to me for a reference', *The Times*, 10 November 1989.
4   *The Times*, 15 November 1989.
5   McColvin, L. R., 'The purpose of indexing', *The indexer*, **1** (2), 1958, 31 – 5.
6   Wellisch, Hans H., '"Index": the word, its history, meanings and usage', *The indexer*, **13** (3), 1983, 147 – 51.
7   Wheatley, Henry B., *What is an index?* London: Index Societey, 1878, 7.
8   See note 5 above.
9   *The indexer*, **1** (1), 1958, 3.
10   Hunter, Eric J., *Examples illustrating AACR 2 1988 revision*. London: Library Association, 1989.
11   *The indexer*, **9** (1), 1974, 2.
12   Leacock, Stephen, 'The perfect index: there is no index, and why', in Leacock, Stephen, *My remarkable uncle and other sketches*. London: Bodley Head, 1942, 212 – 15;
Leacock, Stephen, *The Leacock roundabout*. Garden City, NY: Dodd, Mead & Co., 1946, 420 – 2;
Stevens, Norman (ed.), *Library humor*. Metuchen, NJ: Scarecrow Press, 1971, 419 – 22.
13   Alderson, Valerie, 'Towards a scholarly A to Z', *The Times educational supplement*, 19 March 1976, 22.
14   *British Standard recommendations for preparing indexes to books, periodicals and other documents*. Rev. ed. London: British Standards Institution, 1988. (BS 3700:1988).
15   See note 3 above.
16   Cornish, S. W., *The Waverley manual: a handbook of the chief characters in the Waverley novels*. Edinburgh: Black, 1871;
Rogers, M., *The Waverley dictionary*. Chicago: S. C. Grigg & Co., 1879;
Husband, M. F. A., *Dictionary of characters in the Waverley novels*. London: Routledge, 1910;
Bradley, Philip, *An index to the Waverley novels*. Metuchen, NJ: Scarecrow Press, 1975.
17   Bradley, Philip, 'A long fiction index', *The indexer*, **8** (3), 1973, 153 – 7.
18   Spurling, Hilary, *Handbook to Anthony Powell's Music of time*. London: Heinemann, 1977.
19   See note 14 above.
20   *Recommendations for the preparation of indexes*. London: British Standards Institution, 1964. (BS 3700:1964).

21 Blake, Doreen and Bowden, Ruth, 'The *Journal of Anatomy*: index to the first hundred years, 1866 – 1966', *The indexer*, **6** (2), 1968, 48 – 51.

22 De Beer, E. S., 'The larger index', *Journal of documentation*, **12** (1), 1956, 1 – 14.

23 Latham, Robert C. and Latham, Rosalind, 'Indexing Pepys' diary', *The indexer*, **12** (1), 1980, 34 – 5.

24 Hamilton, Geoffrey, 'How to recognize a good index', *The indexer*, **10** (2), 1976, 49 – 53.

25 *The indexer*, **9** (1), 1974, 8 – 9.

26 *British Standard recommendations for alphabetical arrangement and the filing order of numbers and symbols*. Rev. ed. London: British Standards Institution, 1985. (BS 1749:1985).

27 British Library Filing Rules Committee, *BLAISE filing rules*. London: British Library, 1980.

28 MACREX, available from Macrex Indexing Services, 38 Rochester Road, London NW1 9JJ (071 – 267 3793) or Bayside Indexing Service, 265 Arlington Avenue, Kensington, CA 94707, USA (415-524-4195).

29 COMDEX, a pioneer program developed by Dr A. C. Purton but now superseded by MACREX and CINDEX.

30 CINDEX, available from Indexing Research, The Sanderson Centre, Lees Lane, Gosport, Hampshire PO12 3UL (0705-511113) or Indexing Research, P.O. Box 27687, River Station, Rochester, NY 14627-7687, USA (716-461-5530).

31 Oakeshott, Priscilla, *The impact of new technology on the publication chain*. London: British Library, 1983.

32 *Books are for use: final report of the Subject Access Project to the Council on Library Resources*. Syracuse, New York: Syracuse University, School of Information Studies, 1978. (Pauline Atherton, director).

33 Gratch, Bonnie and others, 'Characteristics of book indexes for subject retrieval in the humanities and social sciences', *The indexer*, **11** (1), 1978, 14 – 23.

34 Booth, Pat F., *Documents, authors, users, indexers*. London: Society of Indexers, 1988. (Training in indexing, Unit 1);
Booth, Pat F. and Piggott, Mary, *Choice and form of entries*. London: Society of Indexers, 1988. (Training in indexing, Unit 2);
Bakewell, K. G. B., *Information sources and reference tools*. London: Society of Indexers, 1988. (Training in indexing, Unit 3);
Booth, Pat F., *Arrangement and presentation of indexes*. London: Society of Indexers, 1988. (Training in indexing, Unit 4);
Booth, Pat F. and Wallis, Elizabeth, *The business of indexing*. London: Society of Indexers, 1989. (Training in indexing, Unit 5).

SUGGESTIONS FOR FURTHER READING

The definitive book on indexing, by Hans W. Wellisch, is likely to be published during 1990. Meanwhile the following can be recommended:

Anderson, M. D., *Book indexing*. Cambridge: Cambridge University Press, 1971 (Cambridge authors' and printers' guides).
A most useful pamphlet, full of excellent advice. Replaces the equally useful *Making an index* by G. V. Carey (Cambridge University Press, 1965), now out of print but worth reading if you can find it in a library.
British Standard recommendations for preparing indexes to books, periodicals and other documents. Rev. ed. London: British Standards Institution, 1988. (BS 3700: 1988).
The British indexer's 'bible', which is also forming the basis of the revised international standard on indexing. Includes sections on the function of an index, types and features of indexes, content and general organization of indexes, arrangement of entries in indexes and presentation of indexes. Has an exemplary index, compiled by Janet Shuter.
Collison, Robert L., *Indexes and indexing: guide to the indexing of books and collections of books, periodicals, music, recordings, films and other material, with a reference section and suggestions for further reading*. 4th ed. London: Benn, 1972.
Was for many years the standard work on indexing. Now overtaken to some extent by the computer and the revised British Standard, but still contains many useful hints.
Hunnisett, R. F., *Indexing for editors*. London: British Records Association, 1972.
A very useful, if now rather dated, guide with good chapters on terminology, places, persons, subjects, filing and presentation.
Knight, G. Norman, *Indexing, the art of: a guide to the indexing of books and periodicals*. London: Allen & Unwin, 1979.
The founder of the Society of Indexers' final contribution to indexing. Inevitably somewhat dated now, but it remains a first-class comprehensive guide and has an exemplary index compiled by the author and Anthony Raven. The short foreword by the Rt Hon Harold Macmillan (later first Earl of Stockton) is also well worth reading.

The Society of Indexers' 'Training in indexing' manuals (see reference 34 above) are open-learning units, each one of which comprises self-study test and a self-administered test. Each unit conforms to BS 3700:1988. Tuition and formal testing leading to the status of Accredited Indexer are available at extra cost to members of the Society of Indexers. The units are available from Mrs S. Mitchell-Cameron, 16 Coleridge Close, Hitchin, Herts SG4 0QX. Further units are in preparation including *Computer-assisted indexing* and *Indexing of images*.

Indexes

The issues of *The indexer* contain many helpful articles. As part of the celebrations of the Society of Indexers' 21st anniversary, some articles from earlier volumes of *The indexer* were published as:

Harrod, Leonard Montague (ed.), *Indexers on indexing*. New York & London: Bowker, 1978.

Finally you should try to look at some good indexes. Those which have won the Wheatley Medal and the H. W. Wilson Award are obviously worth examining.

18

Government Publications

Valerie Nurcombe

Mention 'Government Publications' in Britain and most librarians and others immediately assume *British* Official Publications. Few have any extensive knowledge of the great body of official publications generated by every country during the daily work of the executive and administrative bureaucracy. The depth of the coverage of British official publications in this chapter reflects the orientation of this book. The pattern of publishing in most countries is similar, reflecting the machinery of government. It is virtually impossible to understand most countries' official publications without an up-to-date working knowledge of, or good current reference guide to, the structure of their administrative machinery.

Official publishing in most countries usually follows one of two models:

1   a central publishing agency is responsible for the majority of official publishing, particularly in relation to the legislative assembly. It controls and documents its output, thus reflecting the activities of the government.

2   laws, papers and proceedings of the administrative and executive bodies, including any representative assembly, are recorded in an 'official journal' publication. This is usually published regularly and frequently. Relevant information must

be sought in order of occurrence through any indexes which may exist. Any other documents are published by the department responsible. The departments are left to organize their own publishing activities and may or may not keep adequate bibliographic records.

Whichever model is encountered the trends in the 1980s have been towards an increasing number of publications in conjunction with increased emphasis on economy. Thus cost recovery has meant that more publications are priced which were formerly available freely. Pricing encourages marketing. Marketing requires listing or cataloguing. Hence there is an increase in the individual catalogues and lists available. The degree of detail and comprehensiveness of the content may be variable. However bibliographic control of official publications has rarely been a strong point in any country and although the British complain about their problems many countries look towards the British model as one of the ideals, envying the level of information available on the existence of official publications.

In Britain since the Second World War there has been a growth in major collections of official publications with the increased demand outside the immediate vicinity of Whitehall and Westminster. This was partly because of the large-scale development of universities and polytechnics but also because there was no national repository scheme such as in the United States. In Britain official publications are subject to copyright deposit, thus ensuring that there are major collections in the British Library, the National Libraries of Scotland and Wales, at Trinity College, Dublin, and the Universities of Oxford and Cambridge. The depository system in the United States ensures that all States have at least one major collection of official publications receiving deposit copies of most publications. This encourages the development of specialist librarians to service and exploit them. Other countries have a greater or lesser degree of depository regulation.

British collections of official publications from other countries include those mentioned above, the libraries of the larger universities and polytechnics and the larger public libraries. Many academic institutions with courses relating to particular countries will have good official publications collections in those areas, e.g. the various University of London Institutes. Alternatively some embassies will have a limited current collection and know the whereabouts of resources. The most useful guides are mentioned below.

In terms of official publications no collection or listing can ever be regarded as comprehensive. Most give brief warnings that they contain reference to as many publications as have been brought to the attention of the listing body, or deposited with the library. In the days of swift photocopying and laser-printers producing word-processed documents quickly and easily in sufficient copies for a level of distribution which would constitute publication, many 'publishers' do not realize that their department is publishing at all and do not comply with deposit requirements. This is due either to the cost of the number of copies required, or to ignorance, or to a desire to ensure that only a few select eyes see the item. This lack of deposit, even with the local libraries and information units within government departments and related bodies, frequently contributes to other factors which make official publications difficult to identify or locate.

No government's publications reveal all the information about its activities which the public may wish to have. Unpublished information of historical interest is made public, selectively, under the 30-year rule, by the deposit of documents at the Public Record Office. But whether the information released is new or old, the provisions of the Official Secrets Acts must be observed. It should be remembered on both sides of the Atlantic that much unpublished official information has not been withheld because it is 'classified' but only because it was not regarded as worth publishing. Such information is probably obtainable, in some form or other, on request to the appropriate department.

BRITISH GOVERNMENT PUBLICATIONS

The term 'British government publications' is not synonymous with 'HMSO publications'. Today, so many documents are published directly by British government departments and institutions that only about 20% of official publications are actually published, or even stocked, by Her Majesty's Stationery Office.

It should be pointed out that the Patent Office and the Ordnance Survey are massive publishers in their own right. Nor are the following available from HMSO although some HMSO bookshops stock them for counter sales: Geological Survey maps, Admiralty charts, British Standards Institution and BBC publications. This causes no difficulty. The demarcation is clear-cut and easily recognized.

Every government department, institution, advisory board and nationalized industry acts, to some extent, as its own publisher. Many departments publish both through HMSO and independently according to the type and market of the publication concerned. The sheer number and the potential value of non-HMSO official publications have caused such concern that steps have been taken to list them and improve their availability.

Official publishers

(a) **HMSO**

HMSO is vitally important because HMSO alone has the authority to publish on behalf of Parliament. As the guardian of Crown Copyright and Parliamentary Copyright HMSO may negotiate with commercial publishers to reprint Parliamentary publications, but their initial publication remains its own privilege and responsibility.

The singular importance of HMSO publications coupled with their large number are reasons enough for studying them. In 1989 about 8,600 titles were published of which around 5,400 were Parliamentary, statutory and regulatory, and nearly 3,000 agency items were stocked.

The scope and importance of HMSO's publications may be appreciated by visiting one of the HMSO Bookshops where the display of HMSO and agency publications is more elaborate than in a library. Secondly try browsing through HMSO's *Monthly catalogue*. Thirdly, for the most resolute, try spending a few hours with either Butcher, Pemberton (see bibliography) or the other guides.

Guides to government publications, where they exist, are usually unofficial.

Rodgers, Frank, A GUIDE TO BRITISH GOVERNMENT PUBLIC-
ATIONS. New York: H. W. Wilson, 1980.

Rodgers explains, with considerable administrative and
bibliographical detail, the present pattern of our government
publications. Unless there are radical changes in the machinery
of government, this guide may not require revision for a while
as it abstracts major publications with a résumé of the context
and notes on publishing practice.

There is a very useful set of three articles also from the USA.

Smith, Barbara E., BRITISH OFFICIAL PUBLICATIONS: 1. Scope and
substance, *Government publications review*, **4** (3), 1977, 201 – 7; 2. Publication
and distribution, *Government publications review*, **5** (1), 1978, 1 – 12; 3.
Accessibility and use, *Government publications review*, **6** (1), 1979, 11 – 18.

Governments themselves rarely explain their publications. As
agents for the legislature and the government departments, the
central government publishers, such as HMSO, feel it is not their
responsibility.

The coverage of HMSO publications by the *British national
bibliography*, although not arbitrary, is selective. For economic
reasons it cannot be otherwise. Many libraries therefore acquire
HMSO's official lists and catalogues. The most important are
the *Daily list*, the *Monthly catalogue*, the *Annual catalogue*, and the
Sectional lists.

In the *Daily list* the main divisions are 'Parliamentary
Publications' and 'Non-Parliamentary Publications', called the
'Classified List' in the *Monthly catalogue* and *Annual catalogue*,
bringing together Parliamentary and Non-Parliamentary reports
of each department, e.g. Command Papers are entered under
'Command papers' in the Parliamentary section and again under
the name of the relevant department in the Non-Parliamentary
section. The *Daily list* is available on Prestel and publications may
be ordered directly.

The production of the *Monthly catalogue* and the *Annual catalogue*
is now computerized and publication is usually within six weeks
of the end of the month. The annual volume usually appears
within three months. HMSO's full database has been on BLAISE

since 1989, DIALOG from Spring 1990, and is also on CD-ROM (see below).

The *Sectional lists* detail HMSO publications (and selected international organizations' publications for which HMSO is the British agent) currently in print. Most lists are departmental, e.g. Employment, Transport, Home Office. They are listed in the monthly and annual catalogues. HMSO has published a quarterly comprehensive catalogue *HMSO in print* on microfiche since 1987.

HMSO also publishes lists, primarily for its own use, of which the most useful is the weekly *At press*. There is no list of forthcoming Parliamentary Publications, as these are usually printed and published at short notice. In a rather casual way ministers sometimes announce that a White Paper, or the report of some investigating committee, is due to be published 'shortly', 'next week' or whatever. Other items are published to coincide with speeches or debates, e.g. the text of the budget speech each March.

HMSO's sales service

The average bookseller is little concerned with HMSO publications, but in most of the larger cities of the UK one bookseller has been appointed as official agent for HMSO. In London, Birmingham, Bristol, Manchester, Edinburgh and Belfast HMSO has its own 'HMSO Bookshops' selling HMSO publications and supplementing the postal service of the Publications Centre in London.

For an advance annual subscription a library can obtain all HMSO's major publications automatically as published. This 'Selected Subscription Service' (SSS) may seem rather expensive, but it saves time and labour in ordering. It is possible to subscribe to Parliamentary or Non-Parliamentary publications or Statutory Instruments separately. Thus a subscribing library may have only a partial collection of documents relating to a particular topic. The diversification of publishing media means that some are now excluded from the SSS: agency publications, electronic and microfiche publications, Customs Tariff, forms and posters, House of Commons *Votes & proceedings* and House of Lords *Minutes of proceedings*, periodicals on subscription, *Hansard*, *London gazette*,

Services regulations, manuals, licences and amendments (including Department of Trade and Industry ones relating to Civil Aviation), separately published maps and charts, art reproductions, Defence specifications, Statutes in Force, nationalized industry reports not published by HMSO, all reprints, Northern Ireland publications with ISBN prefix 0 337. These can be obtained on Standing Order or subscription services.

A useful background to HMSO's services is found in the bicentennial book:

Barty-King, Hugh, HER MAJESTY'S STATIONERY OFFICE: THE STORY OF THE FIRST 200 YEARS 1786 – 1986. London: HMSO, 1986.

(b) Non-HMSO publications

Since World War II, there has been a massive growth in the number of non-HMSO official publications. In addition to the many published directly by government departments, there are many others published by the nationalized industries and the extraordinary number of Councils, Committees and Boards in the public sector which are in some way linked with the central government, e.g. the British Council, the Milk Marketing Board.

HMSO includes only those which it publishes in its lists and catalogues. Thus the publications of some departments and agencies are listed both by HMSO and elsewhere. The libraries of many departments and sections such as Trade and Industry, Education, Property Services Agency (privatized April 1990) and Health and Safety Executive have published their own lists of publications not published by HMSO but most are willing to admit that they know they do not see everything published.

With the cooperation of most of the departments, agencies and institutions acting partly, or entirely, as their own publishers (with the obvious exceptions of the Patent Office and the Ordnance Survey), Chadwyck-Healey began in 1980 to publish a comprehensive list of non-HMSO publications, and also to provide microfiche copies of most of those items listed in:

CATALOGUE OF BRITISH OFFICIAL PUBLICATIONS NOT PUBLISHED BY HMSO. Cambridge: Chadwyck-Healey, 1980 to date.

Bimonthly, annual cumulations and Keyword index.

Now firmly established as the equivalent listing to HMSO's lists, Chadwyck-Healey cover as many of the official departments and bodies issuing publications as possible. Each issue lists all publications sent to them during that period, not necessarily those issued during that period. For example, if a Division joins the list of contributors at a certain date it will often deposit its back file of publications at one time and these will appear over several issues although they may date back to the 1970s, the previous year and so on. There is good subject indexing and a detailed directory of addresses and contacts. Alternatively subscriptions are available for subject and complete collections of the documents listed on microfiche. The few publications not available for reasons of confidentiality are clearly marked in the listings. This is also available as a database.

Of vital importance in locating sources of these publications is:

Richard, Stephen DIRECTORY OF BRITISH OFFICIAL PUBLIC-ATIONS: A GUIDE TO SOURCES. 2nd ed. London: Mansell Publishing, 1984 (3rd ed. in preparation).

This shows how wide is the scope of non-HMSO publications, in subject and form. It includes a surprising number of serials, including some very useful ones distributed free, e.g. *British Library news*, monthly. Particularly important are the reports and papers not issued by HMSO. There are also advisory booklets on subjects as various as education, food and nutrition, construction research and the prevention of accidents. Most major departments are covered and many smaller advisory and research bodies, some of which do not use HMSO at all.

CATALOGUE OF UNITED KINGDOM OFFICIAL PUBLICATIONS (UKOP). London: HMSO/Chadwyck-Healey. Quarterly.

For the first time there is now the possibility of tracing British official publications in one stage. UKOP represents the complete set of HMSO's catalogues and of the Chadwyck-Healey catalogues since 1980. Launched in September 1989 it is a cooperative venture between HMSO and Chadwyck-Healey, producing on one CD-ROM, the joint listing known as UKOP, updated quarterly and available from either publisher.

Machinery of government

The government's interests, which are linked with its responsibilities, and the vast amount of expert knowledge and experience it can draw upon to minister them, produce a remarkable range of publications, varied both in form and subject.

Government publications cannot be divorced from the departments, etc. which produce them. The machinery of government is not constant. Serials and series change their names and departments; reports that were Parliamentary may become Non-Parliamentary; publications which were HMSO may become non-HMSO. Catalogues announce or list publications but do little to explain them.

Departmental changes have been frequent over the past 40 years. Since 1970, HMSO has noted them briefly in its catalogues. Otherwise it is essential to consult either a regular list such as the *Civil Service yearbook* or Vacher's quarterly *Parliamentary companion*. For example, the Ministry of Transport was absorbed into a new super-ministry called the Department of the Environment, but later emerged as the present Department of Transport. More recently the Department of Health and Social Services has split into two: Department of Health and Department of Social Security.

To help with understanding the working of the government in relation to its publishing, scan Butcher or even Pemberton (the working of Parliament changes little) and the texts by Englefield mentioned below. The House of Commons Information Office issues a series of leaflets on the working of Parliament which are updated when major changes occur.

Useful in tracing these patterns of organization in all countries are the Chadwyck-Healey microfiche *Government organisation manuals, 1900 – 1980* available by region and country. 526 microfiche relate to Britain.

Parliamentary publications

A point which soon becomes evident when one uses HMSO's lists and catalogues is that British government publications have an official classification, unrelated to subjects, based on their administrative history. There are Parliamentary Publications and Non-Parliamentary Publications. Parliamentary Publications are directly related to the activities of Parliament. The more important types of Parliamentary Publications are all either series or serials and all are HMSO publications.

PARLIAMENT

HOUSE OF LORDS PUBLICATIONS	HOUSE OF COMMONS PUBLICATIONS
Minutes	*Votes and proceedings*
Journal	*Journal*

Official reports of the Parliamentary debates (Hansard)

Papers and bills	*Bills*
	Papers
	Weekly information bulletin

PAPERS PRESENTED TO PARLIAMENT BY COMMAND

Command papers

ACTS AND MEASURES

Public general acts
Local and personal acts
Measures of the General Synod of the Church of England

In the above table, all the major series and serials which make up the Parliamentary Publications are listed separately. But to explain them, it is more convenient to divide them into two groups:

(a) House of Commons, House of Lords including papers, Journals and Hansard
(b) Bills, Acts and measures

(a) *House of Commons, House of Lords*
Votes and proceedings (Commons) and *Minutes* (Lords) equate with the agendas and minutes of most committees elsewhere. They are published daily, mainly for members of the two Houses.

The *Journals* of the two Houses are the official and permanent annual record of their proceedings. As their main use outside Westminster is for historical research, they are seldom found except in academic libraries.

The *Official reports of the parliamentary debates*, commonly known as *Hansard* (in honour of their first publisher), are a complete and reliable record of what is said in Parliament. They are far more informative than the parliamentary reports in the press. There are two series, one for each House. Both are published daily while Parliament is in session. Later they are cumulated into bound volumes which incorporate any corrections deemed necessary. There are weekly, volume and sessional indexes.

The section of the Commons *Hansard* devoted to its daily ritual called 'Question Time' is worth remembering, as it includes useful information, some of it statistical. A good deal of trouble and expense is devoted to providing answers to Members' questions. Note that *Hansard* includes written as well as oral answers, and that the numerical column numbering is in two sequences, proceedings and questions. It can be unnerving to discover that column 239 reverts to 63 and some time later, perhaps after column 98 column 240 may follow.

Hansard does not, however, include the reports of the several Standing Committees of the House of Commons. These are the important committees which consider the details of Bills. The reports of their debates are published separately by HMSO, listed in the catalogue under *House of Commons Parliamentary debates*.

The demand by historians for back runs of *Hansard* and the *Journals* has led to the publication of complete sets of them in microform (see below). There is neither a *Journal*, nor a *Hansard*, for the meetings of the Cabinet and its Committees.

The HOUSE OF COMMONS PAPERS are a numerous and important series, including returns printed by direction of the House; reports and accounts required under the provisions of certain Acts; the Minutes of Proceedings of Standing Committees; and the reports of the Select Committees of the House.

The number of **Select Committees** has increased over the past decade. They now include Committees on Expenditure, Employment, Energy, European Community Documents, Science and Technology. Designed to strengthen the influence of Parliament over the executive, the Select Committees have no powers, except to report, and they are often denied the information they need to do that effectively. Increasingly, however, their reports are given publicity by the media. Check with Vacher's *Parliamentary companion* (quarterly) for current Select Committees in any session.

The HOUSE OF LORDS PAPERS form one series, are fewer and of less importance.

Both *House of Commons papers* and *House of Lords papers* are numbered serially within the parliamentary session. Formerly the numbering was by regnal years but this was dropped during the 1970s after a period of dual numbering.

A **Command Paper** is presented to Parliament by a minister, by command of the sovereign. It may be a treaty, a statement of government policy or a report. If the latter, it could be a serial report, or the *ad hoc* report of a Royal Commission or departmental committee.

Many Treaties and exchanges of notes emanate from the Foreign Office as Command Papers, but reports of investigating commissions and committees are often headline news. Such reports of Commissions, Committees, Working Parties and Tribunals are commonly referred to by the names of the respective chairmen. For example, the Department of Trade *Report of the Committee to consider the law on copyright and designs* (Cmnd 6732, 1977) is known as 'The Whitford Report', after Mr Justice Whitford, the chairman of the Committee. In addition occasional reports from individuals are known by the names of their authors. A quick way of identifying such reports is to refer to the various series of indexes:

Richard, Stephen, BRITISH GOVERNMENT PUBLICATIONS: AN INDEX TO CHAIRMEN OF COMMITTEES AND COMMISSIONS OF INQUIRY. London: Library Association. Vol. I: 1800 – 99, 1982; Vol. II: 1900 – 40, 1974; reprinted 1982; Vol. III: 1941 – 78, 1982; Vol. IV: 1979 – 82, 1984.

INDEX TO CHAIRMEN OF COMMITTEES. COMMITTEE REPORTS PUBLISHED BY HMSO INDEXED BY CHAIRMAN. London: HMSO, 1983 – 7. Quarterly with annual cumulations.

Although the reports of Royal Commissions are always published as Command Papers, the evidence submitted to them appears among the Non-Parliamentary Publications. For peculiar administrative reasons, the reports of departmental committees may be published either in the Command Papers series, or as Non-Parliamentary Publications.

Command Papers are numbered in series of indefinite length, one series being distinguished from another by a prefix taken from the letters of the word Command. The present Cm series, which is the sixth, began towards the end of the 1986 – 7 session. Abbreviations have been:

	1 – 4222	1833 – 69	Cmd.	1 – 9889	1919 – 56
C.	1 – 9550	1870 – 99	Cmnd.	1 – 9927	1956 – 85/6
Cd.	1 – 9239	1900 – 18	Cm.	1 – –	1986/7 –

The *House of Commons weekly information bulletin* (London: HMSO, 1978 –) is compiled in the House of Commons Library and provides information on the progress of new legislation and the composition of Commons' committees. It also lists the latest White Papers and Green Papers. From 1978 – 81 there was also a *House of Lords weekly information bulletin*.

(b) *Bills, Acts and measures*
A Bill is a draft of a proposed Act of Parliament. It may be Public, Local, or Personal. Local Bills, which are numerous, are promoted by local authorities, nationalized industries and other corporate bodies. Often they are concerned with transport matters, e.g. the *Merseyside Metropolitan Railway Bill*, which became the *Merseyside*

Metropolitan Railway Act 1975.

Public Bills are published by HMSO. Local and Personal Bills, now rare, are published by their promoters. A Public Bill, if it is not thrown out, is likely to be reprinted several times, with amendments, on its way through Parliament.

A Public Bill which has passed both Houses and received the Royal Assent becomes a Public General Act (sometimes called a Statute). Public General Acts are first published separately and then in annual bound volumes called *Public General Acts and Measures*, as they include the Measures passed by the General Synod of the Church of England. (Up to 1971, 'Measures' meant the 'Measures of the National Assembly of the Church of England'.)

HMSO publishes an annual *Index to the Statutes covering legislation in force on 31st December 1987* (1989) annual *Chronological table of the Statutes* indicating which are in force. In 1972 the Statutory Publications Office inaugurated a loose-leaf edition of current Public General Acts called *Statutes in force*. For this edition, the Acts are reprinted, in their latest amended form, as booklets, which are filed in loose-leaf binders in subject groups, e.g. Agriculture, Road Traffic. *Statutes in force* and the bound volumes of the *Public General Acts* are compiled by the Statutory Publications Office. Local and Personal Acts, unlike the original Bill, are also published by HMSO, but not in collected volumes. Many of the above volumes are listed by HMSO as Non-Parliamentary publications.

Up to 1962, Acts of Parliament were cited by the years of the sovereign's reign covered by the relevant parliamentary session, but since 1963 the numbering has been within the calendar year, e.g. the *New Towns Act 1975* c 42. (c., sometimes written as ch., meaning 'chapter' within the Statute Book, the bound volumes).

PARLIAMENTARY ONLINE INFORMATION SYSTEM (POLIS). House of Commons Library's Indexing Unit.

Some libraries must have up-to-date information on parliamentary activities. Obvious examples are the two parliamentary libraries, the libraries of the national newspapers and broadcasting organizations. Since October 1980 the House of Commons Library's Indexing Unit has operated a

Parliamentary On-Line Information System (POLIS). Although it was created primarily for the benefit of the members and staffs of the two Houses of Parliament, POLIS is also available to external users on a subscription basis.

POLIS includes subject-indexed references to the parliamentary debates; parliamentary questions and answers; the debates of the House of Commons Standing Committees; the Papers and Bills of both Houses; the Command Papers series; references to EC legislative material, UK and foreign official publications; the book catalogue of the House of Commons Library. Like most computerized information sources, POLIS is a database, not a databank, i.e. it provides bibliographical references to published sources of information – in this case to Parliamentary Publications.

Full details of POLIS may be obtained from the Computer and Technical Services Section, House of Commons Library, London SW1A 0AA or from Meridian Systems Management Ltd, 18 Elmfield Road, Bromley, Kent BR1 1LR.

Non-parliamentary publications

This term was first used by HMSO in 1923. Previously, these documents had been referred to either as 'Official Publications' or as 'Stationery Office Publications'.

Non-Parliamentary Publications may be published by HMSO and are listed in their catalogue and in Chadwyck-Healey's according to the departments, institutions, boards, etc. from which they emanate.

Non-Parliamentary Publications may be conveniently reviewed in four groups, as follows:

(a) Statutory Instruments, which, like the Statutes, are primary sources of the law;
(b) the reports of those investigating committees which are *not* published as Command Papers;
(c) most of the numerous statistical series;
(d) a miscellany of advisory and information publications by experts (not all of them in the government's employ) on many

aspects of science, technology, medicine, education and the fine arts.

(a) *Statutory Instruments*

Statutory Instruments are the most obtrusive part of that complicated body of legal source literature called subordinate legislation. A Statutory Instrument is made by a minister under the authority of the specific Act of Parliament, to which it is a vital, although sometimes only a temporary, appendage. SIs, like Acts, can be of national or local application. The latter may not be published by HMSO.

SIs deal with aspects of legislation too detailed to be incorporated in Acts. As they can be amended, or revoked, at short notice, SIs can be applied to emergencies more conveniently than can Acts. A typical example: SI 1989 No. 1212 *The Copyright (Librarians and Archivists) (Copying of Copyright Material) Regulations 1989*, made by the Secretary of State, Department of Trade and Industry, in accordance with the sections 37(1), (2) and (4) and 38 to 43 of the *Copyright, Designs and Patents Act 1988*, c. 48.

SIs are first published separately and listed in HMSO's *Daily list*. They are later collected into the monthly and annual *List of statutory instruments*. This used to exclude local instruments, and some which have been revoked during the year in which they were promulgated, or which are listed as 'unpublished'. They are *not* listed in the HMSO monthly and annual catalogues. The appropriate Department usually keeps copies and the relevant local authorities are sent copies.

(b) *Reports*

Since World War I, a number of reports of departmental investigative committees and working parties which formerly would have been issued as Command Papers, have been issued as departmental Non-Parliamentary Publications. To research workers, whose happy hunting ground is the bound volumes of the Sessional Papers, the alienation of some reports from the Command Papers series is a nuisance. Over the past 50 years, most of the famous reports on educational matters have been Non-Parliamentary.

Not all reports on matters of public interest are government reports. *The structure and reform of direct taxation* (the Meade Report) was published by Allen and Unwin for the Institute of Fiscal Studies in 1978.

(c) *Statistical publications*

Government departments are assiduous in the collection of statistics. The government itself needs them, and has both the authority and the resources to compile them. In the publicity brochures distributed by the Central Statistical Office, there are references to 'the Government Statistical Service', a term not to be found in HMSO's catalogues. This refers to the Central Statistical Office itself and the statistics divisions of all the major government departments, including the Office of Population Censuses and Surveys, which is responsible, among other things, for the decennial census in England and Wales; and the Business Statistics Office, formerly of the Department of Industry but transferred to the Central Statistical Office in 1989, which compiles an extensive series of *Business monitors* (monthly and quarterly), providing statistics of production within a wide range of industries.

The Central Statistical Office (CSO) collects statistics from all the statistical divisions of the departments, and digests them in convenient form for general use. It also draws the attention of commerce, industry and the general public to the existence and value of government statistics, through exhibitions, press announcements and the widespread distribution of free pamphlets.

The CSO's principal HMSO publications are the *Monthly digest of statistics, Annual abstract of statistics*, *Social trends* (annual), *Regional trends* (annual) and *Economic trends* (monthly). There is also *Population trends* (monthly) from OPCS.

The major source of information on the government's statistical series, of which there are many, is the detailed CSO *Guide to official statistics* (6th ed. London: HMSO, 1990), but the more important are listed in a free pamphlet, revised annually, called *Government statistics: a brief guide to sources* and obtainable from Central Statistical Office, Information Services Division, Cabinet Office, Great George Street, London SW1P 3AL. This is particularly valuable as it not only lists publications but departments with telephone numbers and extensions for statistical enquiries.

Worthy of note is the Chadwyck-Healey microfiche set of *British government publications containing statistics, 1801 – 1977* available in 17 subject sets.

(d) *Miscellaneous*

In a short space it is impossible to do justice to the variety of HMSO publications which fall under this heading. They include important reference works, such as *Britain: an official handbook* (note the HMSO publications cited in the bibliography) and *Commonwealth yearbook*, and periodicals such as *Employment gazette* and the *London gazette*, the medium for official notices. Many of the figures formerly available in *British business* (originally HMSO but latterly published commercially) are now available either in Central Statistical Office Press Notices (subscriptions are available from the Information Division) or in the commercial Association of British Chambers of Commerce serial *Business briefing*, using information from the Department of Trade and Industry.

A random sample of subjects dealt with by HMSO Non-Parliamentary Publications in any year gives some support to HMSO's claim that its publications deal with almost every subject under the sun: industrial air pollution, information technology, adult literacy, safety in nuclear power stations, early musical instruments as works of art, and the history of Kew Gardens, for example.

A **White Paper** is a statement of government policy. It may indicate the broad lines of particular future legislation. It may or may not have a white cover. A **Green Paper** is a statement of proposed action by the government which is published for discussion. HMSO annually (but not always) provides the document with a green cover and usually adds (Green Paper) to the catalogue entry. Confusingly, some consultative documents (Green Papers) are non-HMSO publications and the Department may publish only a few duplicated and stapled sheets. A good example of a Green Paper, published by HMSO, is the Department of Trade *Reform of the law relating to copyright, design and performers' protection: a consultative document* (Cmnd 8302, 1981), a follow-up to the Whitford Report on copyright (also a Command Paper).

Relevant official departmental publications are now cited in the many online databases, particularly those from government departments such as HSELINE, DHSSDATA, BRIX, the input from Transport and Road Research Laboratory to IRRD, the input from Property Services Agency to ICONDA and so on.

Standing Committee on Official Publications

The Standing Committee on Official Publications (SCOOP), a Sub-Committee of the Information Services Group of the Library Association, was formed in 1971 to provide helpful liaison between HMSO and its major customers. The Committee has worked towards improvements in HMSO's services including some changes in its catalogue and sales services. SCOOP reports on official publishing developments regularly in *Refer*, the journal of the Information Services Group, which has also published the proceedings of SCOOP seminars. These reflect the latest information on official publishing, particularly examining departmental publications and changes.

Retrospective bibliographies and reprints

The demand for these has risen steeply since World War II, partly because many people have cultivated a taste for historical research, more specifically because there is now boundless interest in the political, social, and economic life of the nineteenth century.

HMSO keeps some publications in print and maintains stocks of others in demand. HMSO will supply photocopies of out-of-print Parliamentary Publications and Statutory Instruments through the British Library Document Supply Centre.

Research libraries which need complete or extensive runs of Parliamentary Publications have access to reprint and microtext series, thanks to the diligence of scholars, the initiative of reprint publishers, and the cooperation of HMSO. Access to government publications was not the only problem; their bibliographical control was imperfect and confusing.

Some research libraries have sets (original or microtexts) of the House of Commons Sessional Papers. At the beginning of the nineteenth century, a Speaker of the House of Commons devised a scheme for binding the Bills, Papers and Command Papers published each session in four classes:

Bills
Reports from Committees
Reports from Commissioners
Accounts and Papers.

Within each class arrangement was alphabetically by subject. This system survives, but has been modified since 1969 – 70 to two classes:

Bills, Reports, Accounts
Papers.

There is no obligation to use this system with its own contents lists and indexes. Many libraries arrange Parliamentary Papers numerically within their respective series.

The House of Commons Sessional Papers have their own indexes, including decennial cumulations, and an excellent half-century cumulation:

House of Commons, GENERAL INDEX TO THE BILLS, REPORTS AND PAPERS PRINTED BY ORDER OF THE HOUSE OF COMMONS AND TO THE REPORTS AND PAPERS PRESENTED BY COMMAND, 1900 TO 1948-1949. London: HMSO, 1960.

The Readex Microprint Corporation, New York, has reissued, by its unique method of microreproduction called Microprint, almost complete sets of the *Journals, Hansard* and the *House of Commons Sessional Papers.*

The former Irish University Press published between 1967 and 1972, in about 1,000 volumes, handsomely bound in half leather, facsimile reprints of many important nineteenth-century government reports, selected with the help of Professor and Mrs P. G. Ford. For full details of this series see the classified *Catalogue of British Parliamentary Papers in the Irish University Press 1000 volume series and area studies series 1801 – 1900*, Dublin. Irish Academic Press, 1977. This includes an abstract of every Paper in the series.

HOUSE OF COMMONS SESSIONAL PAPERS OF THE EIGHTEENTH CENTURY, compiled and edited by Sheila Lambert. 147 vols. Wilmington, Delaware: Scholarly Resources, 1975 – 6.

This includes all eighteenth-century Bills and Papers known to be extant, reproduced in facsimile. Volume I includes a long introduction by the editor and a list of the Papers for 1715 – 60. Volume II lists Papers for 1761 – 1800.

Chadwyck-Healey's microfilm editions include:

REPORTS FROM COMMITTEES OF THE HOUSE OF COMMONS 1715 – 1801 PRINTED BUT NOT INSERTED IN THE JOURNALS OF THE HOUSE, with a *General index.*

HOUSE OF COMMONS PARLIAMENTARY PAPERS, 1801 – 1900, Edited by P. Cockburn. In 46,196 microfiche with a *Subject catalogue* separately and a *Guide* due to be published shortly.

During the 1980s they have published microfiche sets of *Hansard,* House of Commons *Journal,* House of Lords Parliamentary papers and a monthly COM index to Commons papers from 1989/90. The list expands.

There are too many shorter catalogues and indexes to list here. Most can be found with the good Parliamentary papers collections. Most important are the Ford indexes and breviates which list parliamentary papers from 1833 to 1983. These well-known bibliographies, compiled by Professor P. G. Ford, Mrs G. Ford, and their associates at Southampton University, are systematically arranged under subjects, and well indexed. The bibliographies called breviates include abstracts of the reports listed. The selection was based upon the known needs of students.

Ford, P. and Ford, G., A GUIDE TO PARLIAMENTARY PAPERS: WHAT THEY ARE, HOW TO FIND THEM, HOW TO USE THEM. 3rd ed. Shannon: Irish University Press, 1972.

HMSO sale catalogues are also reprinted.

ANNUAL CATALOGUES OF BRITISH GOVERNMENT PUBLIC-
ATIONS 1894 – 1970. 7 vols. Cambridge: Chadwyck-Healey, 1974 – 5.

This microfiche reprint includes the quinquennial indexes to
them from 1936 to 1970.

The United States Historical Documents Institute has published
a complete microfiche collection of HMSO publications which
is accompanied by *Cumulative index to the annual catalogues of Her
Majesty's Stationery Office publications 1922 – 1972*, compiled by Ruth
Matteson Blackmore. 2 volumes. Washington, DC: Carrollton
Press, 1976. HMSO have made a microfiche which continues this.

NORTHERN IRELAND

From 1921 to 1972, the province of Northern Ireland had its own
Parliament, commonly referred to as Stormont. During that
period there was a pattern of Parliamentary and Non-Parliamentary Publications for Northern Ireland similar to that for the
United Kingdom, although the number of publications was, of
course, very much smaller. But in 1972 the Northern Ireland
Parliament was abolished. Since then the province has had direct
rule from Westminster except for the duration of the elected
Assembly 1982 – 8. Its function was monitorial and consultative.

The official publications emanating from Northern Ireland have
always been published and distributed by HMSO Belfast, which
issued monthly and annual lists until 1987. The main HMSO
lists and catalogues now include them separately.

The retrospective bibliography of the Parliamentary
Publications of Northern Ireland is on similar lines to the Ford
breviates:

Maltby, Arthur, THE GOVERNMENT OF NORTHERN IRELAND
1922 – 1972: A CATALOGUE AND BREVIATE OF PARLIAMENTARY
PAPERS. Dublin: Irish University Press, 1974.

Maltby, Arthur and Jean, IRELAND IN THE NINETEENTH CENTURY:
A BREVIATE OF OFFICIAL PUBLICATIONS. London: Pergamon, 1979.

CROWN COPYRIGHT

The enacting of the *Copyright designs and patents act 1988* has created a new category of 'Parliamentary copyright'. This includes Bills (but not Acts), *Hansard, Votes and proceedings*, Lords *Minutes* and House *Papers*. It does not cover statutory rules, orders and instruments. It also includes Parliamentary material not published by HMSO. Crown copyright exists in non-Parliamentary publications, whether published or not, including all maps and charts, MOD and Ordnance Survey. HMSO have been asked to administer Parliamentary Copyright in those titles which they publish. All librarians should be aware of HMSO's advisory letter on copying from any of these publications. If in doubt consult the Crown Copyright office at HMSO in Norwich.

Of particular note is the wide permission to copy Statutory Instruments three months after publication and Acts six months afterwards. But care should be exercised in the non-commercial use of such copies. Commercial arrangements must be made specifically with HMSO. Librarians should also be aware of the Statutory Instrument *1989/1212 Copyright (Librarians and Archivists) (Copying of Copyright Material) Regulations 1989.*

UNITED STATES GOVERNMENT PUBLICATIONS

In terms of variety, number of titles and sales, HMSO claims to be the largest publisher in the British Commonwealth. By the same token, the Office of the Superintendent of Documents (SUDOCS), Washington, DC, can claim to be the largest publisher in the world. The printing of Congressional and departmental documents is the special responsibility of the Government Printing Office (GPO). In 1895, the Office of Superintendent of Documents was created, within the GPO, to handle efficiently their cataloguing, sale and distribution.

James Bennett Childs has called the USA 'the classical land for government publications'. The production of government publications in the USA is enormous. This provides a great challenge for American librarians which they cannot ignore, owing to the elaborate depository system for federal documents.

The Federal Depository Library System is administered by SUDOCS, and through it, nearly 1,200 American libraries receive free copies of publications, excluding those intended specifically for official use. The depository system was strengthened, in the 1960s, by the establishment of a small number of regional depository libraries, which are obliged to receive and retain one copy of all the publications nominated for deposit. The other depository libraries are allowed to select the classes of publications they require. The increased volume of microfiche and CD-ROM publications in the 1980s reflects the space problems now being encountered by these libraries.

Interest in US government publications in Britain is concentrated in comparatively few libraries, among them the British Library Official Publications and Social Sciences, London; the British Library of Political and Economic Science, London School of Economics; and the libraries of the provincial universities which support related research. The acquisition of US government publications by British libraries is a perennial source of difficulty. HMSO ceased to be the British agent some years ago but Alan Armstrong Ltd have a Washington office which specializes in obtaining GPO publications and online ordering through DIALOG facilitates purchase.

Official catalogues of US government publications

The major source of information on US government publications is:

Superintendent of Documents, MONTHLY CATALOG OF UNITED STATES GOVERNMENT PUBLICATIONS. Washington, DC: Government Printing Office, (GPO) January 1985 to date. (The title has changed several times since 1895.)

Although a substantial publication, this does not list all federal publications. Like the HMSO catalogues, it has block exclusions, notably patent specifications and maps, but some items are excluded only because there are many non-GPO documents which have not been reported to SUDOCS.

Since July 1976, the production of the *Monthly catalog* has been computerized, and compiled according to the Anglo-American code. It is arranged under the names of federal departments and independent agencies alphabetically. Each issue is indexed in four separate sequences: author, title, subject and series/report, which cumulate half-yearly and annually. Index references are to the serial entry numbers, not to the pages of the *Catalog*. It is also available on DIALOG. There is an annual *Serials supplement*.

Publications reference file (PRF) catalogues all in-print items and is available in microfiche. The six yearly cumulations give access to out-of-print publications. DIALOG also includes an order service.

Various subject bibliographies of US government publications are available from SUDOCS on request.

Among the unofficial, selective sources of information on new US government publications are 'Views and over-views on/of US Documents' in *Government publications review*. Many reports and similar types of publications are included by National Technical Information Service (NTIS) in their abstract services and online databases which includes an order service through DIALOG and is available on CD-ROM. Most publications can be obtained in Britain online or through Alan Armstrong Ltd.

The major reference works on US government publications are listed in the *Guide to reference books*, 10th ed. by Eugene P. Sheehy, Chicago: American Library Association, 1986, which also includes a comprehensive list of retrospective bibliographies of US government publications.

The range of US government publications

US government publications have a comparable structure to that of British government publications, but this is not readily apparent in the arrangement of the *Monthly catalog*. The writers on US government publications define their basic structure in various ways. Most simply it consists of:

a)   Congressional Publications
b)   Publications of the Presidency
c)   Departmental and Agency Publications

d) Publications of the Judiciary.

The first is comparable to British Parliamentary Publications, and the third to British Non-Parliamentary Publications. There have been many indexes to and reprints or microfiche editions of each series mainly by companies such as Congressional Information Service Inc., Carrollton Press, United States Historical Documents Institute Inc. These are best located in one of the guides. Morehead presents the titles in lists according to the type of document.

a) *Congressional publications*
The daily *Congressional record* includes a remarkable body of miscellaneous material and the edited reports of the debates of the Senate and the House of Representatives. It is indexed fortnightly.

The *Journals* of the Senate and the House are published at the end of each session.

'Papers' are published in four series, *Senate reports, House reports, Senate documents, House documents* collectively known as 'The serial set'. Each is designated by the session and by number.

Congressional committee *Hearings* is the transcripts of testimony given to various types of Congressional Committee.

Congressional *Bills* and *Laws* are otherwise known as *Statutes*. Many Bills are introduced to Congress; few become Laws. Those that do are first published separately ('slip laws'), and later in sessional volumes called *Statutes at large*. As in the UK, there are public laws and private laws, and in addition there is secondary legislation, i.e. Presidential proclamations and executive orders.

Congressional reference works include the *Official Congressional directory*.

The Congressional Information Service publishes a number of lists including an *Index to publications of the United States Congress*, **1** (1), 1970 – . This is monthly with a quarterly cumulated index and annual volume. There are detailed subject and document number indexes. It is available online on DIALOG, who are putting many of their databases onto CD-ROM.

b) *Publications of the Presidency*

Orders, proclamations and other Presidential documents emanate from the White House Office, the Executive Office of the President, and other sources. This is not a clear-cut group but a large one. The Office of the Federal Register has since 1965 published a *Weekly compilation of presidential documents* which is distributed by GPO. It also publishes a number of other series both currently and retrospectively covering presidential papers. All aspects of the State Department are part of the Presidency including the budgetary process.

The *Federal register* on DIALOG is a full-text database of US federal agency regulations, proposed rules, legal notices, meeting and hearing notices including compliance requirements.

c) *Departmental and agency publications*

The range of publications issued by the 12 departments (Agriculture; Commerce; Defense; Health; Education and Welfare; Housing and Urban Development; Interior; Justice; Labor; Transportation; the Treasury; the Department of State) and the numerous agencies defy summary.

The departmental publications include periodicals, reference works, subject series and a wealth of statistics. The frequent changes in the machinery of government in the USA are reflected in the official *United States Government manual*, published annually.

d) *Publications of the judiciary*

This group, normally of interest only to law librarians, includes the publications of the Supreme Court and other federal courts. Their reports and notations are well covered in guides to legal resources. Much is available online through LEXIS. LEXIS also covers the legislation of the USA.

OTHER COUNTRIES

As interest in Europe increases so does the interest in official publications of European countries in particular. In Europe, although some countries follow the British model, many have an Official Gazette covering all legislation, debates, papers and so on. This is the model for the European Commission *Official journal*. As it is impossible to discuss the publications of other countries in this brief space this is best done using:

Johansson, Eve (ed.), OFFICIAL PUBLICATIONS OF WESTERN EUROPE. Vol. 1: Denmark, Finland, France, Ireland, Italy, Luxembourg, Netherlands, Spain and Turkey; Vol. 2: Austria, Belgium, Federal Republic of Germany, Greece, Norway, Portugal, Sweden, Switzerland and United Kingdom. London: Mansell, 1984, 1988.

Each country is covered in a similar pattern and written by a specialist from that country or with long experience in their publications. The pattern of government is outlined with an indication of the publications ensuing and a section on bibliographic control.

SUGGESTIONS FOR FURTHER READING

Government publications in general
Cherns, J. J., *Official publishing: an overview: an international survey and review of the role, organisation and principles of official publishing*. Oxford and New York: Pergamon, 1979.

For recent developments in government publishing at large, and informed articles on all aspects of government publications, see the file of: *Government publications review*. New York and Oxford: Pergamon Press, 1974 to date. Bi-monthly. The emphasis is on American official publications, but there are useful articles on British and other countries' official publications.

British government publications
Butcher, David, *Official publications in Britain*. London: Bingley, 1983. (2nd ed. due out in 1990).
This introductory textbook is concise and up to date.
Pemberton, John E., *British official publications*. 2nd ed. Oxford: Pergamon Press, 1973.
In need of revision, this textbook remains useful for its thorough coverage of Parliamentary publications.

There is a considerable literature on British Parliamentary procedure:
Taylor, Eric, *The House of Commons at work*. 9th ed. London: Macmillan 1979.
Walkland, S. A. and Ryle, M., *The Commons today*. 2nd ed. London: Fontana, 1981.

In particular the Deputy Librarian of the House of Commons Library has published a number of texts which clarify the relationship between publications, Parliamentary procedures and Whitehall.

Englefield, D. J. T., *Parliament and information: the Westminster scene*. London: Library Association, 1981.

Englefield, D. J. T., *Whitehall and Westminster: government informs Parliament: the changing scene*. Harlow: Longman, 1985.

Government publications of the USA

Downey, James A., *US Federal official publications: the international dimension*. Oxford and New York: Pergamon, 1978.

Morehead, Joe, *Introduction to United States public documents*. 3rd ed. Littleton, Col.: Libraries Unlimited, 1983.

Government publications of other countries

Although government publications exist the world around, not many countries have authoritative manuals on their official publications. This is being remedied slowly.

Bishop, Olga, *Canadian official publications*. Oxford and New York: Pergamon, 1981.

Coxon, Howard, *Australian official publications*. Oxford and New York: Pergamon, 1980.

Fry, Bernard M. and Hernon, Peter, *Government publications: key papers*. Oxford and New York: Pergamon, 1981.

Kuroki, Tsutomu, *An introduction to Japanese government publications*. Oxford and New York: Pergamon, 1981.

Maltby, Arthur and McKenna, Brian, *Irish official publications: a guide to Republic of Ireland papers*. Oxford and New York: Pergamon, 1980.

Pemberton, John E., *The bibliographic control of official publications*. Oxford and New York: Pergamon, 1982.

Westfall, Gloria, *Bibliography of official statistical yearbooks and bulletins*. Cambridge: Chadwyck-Healey, 1986.

Westfall, Gloria, *French official publications*. Oxford and New York: Pergamon, 1980.

Zink, Steven D. (series ed.), *Government documents bibliographies*. Cambridge: Chadwyck-Healey, ongoing with the first two being general and the next two relating to the USA.

19

Statistical Sources

Angela M. Allott

S tatistics have become newsworthy. They are no longer considered to be 'just figures'. Nationally in the UK, television nightly shows statistics being used as political ammunition, hurled across the House of Commons in heated exchanges. An important Select Committee has issued critical comments on official UK economic statistics.[1] The Pickford review[2] and the Department of Trade and Industry (DTI) report[3] have resulted in major changes in the administration, collection and dissemination of UK official statistics.[4] The Central Statistical Office (CSO) has assumed a more directive role in the Government Statistical Service (GSS) and the post-Rayner decade has now been critically assessed for its effects on the government statistics.[5] Internationally, though statistics are one of the bases of world policy decisions, the non-reliability of previous official statistics has been admitted openly in the post-Glasnost era. The integrity of statistics as economic indicators has been critically examined.[6] Everyone has been made aware of statistics, both their importance and their fallibility.

But statistics are of value, importance and use to all sections of the community; they provide a basis for analysis, development and evaluation of every facet of life. They are produced, collected, collated and processed on behalf of both official and non-official organizations and groups. The results are stored in several formats, electronic, microform and printed publications. Availability varies: a percentage of statistics is restricted to closed user groups, made accessible on a need-to-know basis, provided free on request or charged for pro rata from the originating source.

THE STATISTICS COLLECTION

Reference librarians must provide access to statistical publications relevant to the special needs of both the subject areas in which they are working, and to their users' general requirements, in appropriate formats. Apart from acquiring the publications concerned with statistics they should keep in mind the statistical aspects of all subjects. For special and government libraries, the statistics collection is an integral part of their essential information service.

Professional librarians need to know what statistics exist, where to buy, borrow or consult them; how to access them in whatever format, and how to use them on behalf of their clients. Some familiarity with the main international, national, regional and local statistical series is desirable and a knowledge of subject compilations on a selective basis is helpful. An awareness of the leading statistical collections and centres of excellence in the UK and major industrial countries is also an advantage.

Within a given library, the statistics collection is used by the staff on behalf of the user, through the information enquiry service, and by individuals. The latter, when they consult statistical tables and publications in the subjects of their concern, rely on the professional expertise of the librarian for the selection, organization and bibliographical management of the collection. The problems and challenges involved in keeping the collection current, valid and vital are major financial and intellectual burdens on the librarian. Librarians must also be able to advise and liaise with other sections of their organization on the availability of statistics.

Serving all these needs and requirements, when resources are limited and statistical services are ever changing, requires three responses from the librarian: first, to know what statistical series exist, who issues them, and their availability; second, to select and acquire the publications of most use to existing and potential client groups, and to form these into an organized, coherent and accessible collection; and third, through both staff training and user education to obtain maximum benefit from this essential but expensive special resource. It is better to have a smaller collection which is well used, fully understood, up-to-date and actively serviced, plus an expertise in IT retrieval, than a larger collection of ill-defined parameters, varying degrees of currency and largely unfamiliar to staff and user alike. There must also be a management commitment to providing a good statistics collection and an intelligent statistical information service.

GUIDES TO STATISTICS: GENERAL

Books about statistics abound. Only an indication of some typical examples is listed below. They fall in the main into two types: those answering the question 'Who issues what?' and those answering the question 'What has been issued on a given subject and by whom?' The first group lists and describes the statistical publications issued by governments, organizations, societies, etc. covering all subjects and areas at every level. The second group are publications arranged on a topic or subject basis.

As in all information work, the guides and bibliographies cannot lead the librarian and statistics user to all possible sources of statistics, but they can indicate the most likely, the most useful. In turn, these lead to more detailed sources. Librarians have to choose within their budget restrictions.

Statistical data are liable to change and even the most conscientious guide or bibliography can be correct only for the day it is produced. Users and librarians must be aware of the constant changes taking place in all statistical series. Whilst vigilance and observation of footnotes, amendments, altered bases, changed priorities, deleted tables in the statistics themselves, etc. are important, so too is checking for discontinued or new titles, changed publication programmes, new formats, altered access, improved availability conditions, etc.

INTERNATIONATIONAL STATISTICS:
GENERAL GUIDES

Guides to international statistics show a similar pattern as those for other categories of statistics but they are on a grander scale. They range from introductory pamphlets to scholarly monographs, from reference works to bibliographical serials.

The United Nations is the major influence on international statistics but with increasing importance being given to regional groups, e.g. the European Communities statistical office. The 1968 UN Economic and Social Council resolution urged the then Secretary-General to take steps 'to ensure the development of an integrated and co-ordinated statistical progrramme'. To achieve this, international standards for statistics are needed, and they are listed in UN *Directory of international standards for statistics*[7] (including a bibliography of method). The UN *Directory of international statistics*, volume 1[8] is comprehensive for UN publications and also covers other main international statistics issuing bodies. Its excellent technical listing of databanks of economic and social statistics has been overtaken by IT developments since 1981. The second volume is still 'in preparation' but it promises to deal with the organization of the statistical office of the UN and other international bodies, plus information on concepts, definitions and classifications, and standards for statistical use worldwide. The complexity of the international coordination of official statistics is succinctly described by Clarke.[9] Useful system charts are given.

UNDOC[10] includes the full range of statistical titles. It has subject and UN document-reference number indexes. UN statistical publications have an identifying abbreviation as part of their reference number. *UNDOC* indicates the status of each document – priced, unpriced or restricted item. The *United Nations publications catalogue*[11] is free from all UN sales offices. UN agencies, e.g. United Nations Educational, Scientific and Cultural Organisation (UNESCO), Food and Agriculture Organisation (FAO), International Labour Office (ILO), have their own bibliographical arrangements for publications. Each agency issues free lists of current titles publicly available.

The *Index to international statistics (IIS)*[12] issued by the

Congressional Information Service, covers UN statistical publications, and those of the European Communities (EC), Organisation for Economic Co-operation and Development (OECD), Organisation of American States (OAS) and 30 other intergovernmental organizations. Statistical publications, monographs, annuals, serials or periodicals are listed. Subject and title indexes are given. *IIS* is issued in hard copy with a microfiche back-up service available of documents indexed. UK agents for *IIS* are Thompson, Henry Ltd, Sunningdale, Berkshire. *IIS* is available on CD-ROM.

Brief introductory guides to international statistics include: Library Association/Royal Statistical Society, *Recommended basic sources: international* (the result of cooperation of the Committee of Librarians and Statisticians);[13] Harvey's *Sources of statistics*,[14] Burrington's *How to find out about statistics* (London: Pergamon, 1972) (the last two are dated, but still helpful, compact and straightforward).

British Overseas Trade Board's Export Market Information Centre (EMIC), formerly DTI's SMIL (Statistics and Market Intelligence Library), is the foremost publicly available collection of international statistics. The EMIC enquiry service is an important part of official assistance to exporters. Fellow-librarians will find EMIC is always helpful too. EMIC issues a free, annual leaflet *National statistical offices of the world*[15] which lists countries A – Z, and has an appendix of international statistics issuing bodies.

The Chadwyck-Healey *Bibliography of official statistics yearbooks and bulletins* is comprehensive.[16]

SISCIS: subject index to sources of comparative international statistics[17] is a unique reference tool. It is now a little dated but its subject-arranged index is still a good starting-point to the international publications (official and non-official) which contain the statistics. Its checklist of key international statistical titles is comprehensive. A new edition, not necessarily as a printed publication, would be very welcome to all statistics librarians.

Wasserman's *Statistics sources*[18] has long established its usefulness. It concentrates mainly on North American sources (USA and Canadian) but it does contain some international publications.

INTERNATIONAL STATISTICS: ECONOMIC, GEOGRAPHICAL, POLITICAL AND TRADE GROUPINGS – GUIDES

Whereas international statistical publications reflect a global view, the world is also divided into spheres of influence, with groups of nations based on economic, geographical, political and trade interests. Each of these categories is further subdivided or cross-divided by other points of reference, e.g. North/South, developing/developed nations, socialist nations etc. (This last named group, for example, in Europe, is in a state of bewilderingly rapid change, with cross-cultural, cross-political movements which promise (or threaten, depending on one's viewpoint) a destabilizing realignment of resources and political affiliations – circumstances which will greatly affect the collection, retrieval, dissemination and interpretation of statistics.) The many different groupings are reflected in the various established compilations and publications mentioned below.

Joan Harvey, the doyenne of editors of statistics guides, has continued to bring out her series of continent-based publications.[19] These deal with Africa, America, Asia, Australasia and Europe, the statistical sources and resources for all the countries of the area. They are impressive reference books and, because they have a common approach and plan, once one title has been used, the others in the series are the more easily accessed for information. They are well-organized bibliographically, and well-produced by CBD. For each group (e.g. European Communities) and each country (e.g. France) she gives details of their central statistical office and other important organizations that collect and publish statistics; the principal libraries where statistical collections may be consulted; the information services and libraries in other countries where these publications can be consulted; the principal bibliographies of statistics; and the major statistical publications arranged in standard categories i.e. general production, agriculture, etc. All the volumes have indexes for titles and subject.

The Organisation for Economic Cooperation and Development (OECD) issues a free *Catalogue of publications.*[20]

European Communities statistics are well documented. Details of the current publications available are given in *Eurostat catalogue*.[21] *Eurostat news*[22] has news items and comments and a supplement listing titles currently available. Ramsay's *Eurostat index*[23] is a helpful compilation. A pamphlet, in a series produced by the UK Association of European Documentation Centre libraries, on *European Communities statistics* is also published.[24] The EDCs all stock the majority of EC statistical material. Many of the bibliographical guides to the EC have chapters on EC statistics, e.g. Jeffries' *Guide to the official publications of the European Communities*,[25] or Thomson's *Documentation of the European Communities*.[26]

NATIONAL STATISTICS: GUIDES

In every country the government has to have an involvement with statistics and the United Kingdom is a typical example. In common with all developed countries the UK has a comprehensive Government Statistical Service (GSS). In 1989, the GSS was restructured in answer to both government criticism[27] and the growing disenchantment of statistics users with the collection, availability and integrity of national figures.[28] Previously the GSS was provided for the government mainly by decentralized specialist staff employed in the statistics divisions of individual departments,[29] such as DE (Department of Employment) and the statistics made available through the CSO via CSO/HMSO publications. From 31 July 1989, the reorganized CSO became a separate government department responsible to the Treasury (not the Cabinet Office as formerly) and it took over direct responsibility for the government's macro-economic statistics. CSO is now responsible for the Business Statistics Office (BSO), for BSO's statistical series (formerly DTI), for the overseas trade figures, and for the Retail Prices Index (RPI) (formerly Department of Employment).[30] CSO will continue to deal also with international liaison matters (UN, EC); with GSS policy and management; and with methodological research, survey control and classification. CSO is destined to be an Executive Agency.

UK government ministries increasingly publish statistics independently as departmental publications, not as HMSO or CSO items.

Earlier changes in the organization of official statistics were the direct result of 1980 Rayner reform recommendations being put into practice.[31] The White Paper (Cmnd 8236)[32] brought in many cost-cutting exercises. From the foundation of GSS in 1941 (itself an outcome of developments in the Bank of England's Statistics Office),[33] through its expansion in the 1960s, 1970s, the role, activities and policies of GSS have been under various pressures. Adverse post-Rayner reactions by statisticians, statistics users, librarians, academics, politicians and economists have been well documented.[34]

The statistics published by the GSS and by government departments, together with those produced by their predecessors in earlier ministries, form a complex resource. They appear in many formats – hard copy, microform, IT-based modes of dissemination. The guides and bibliographies which are the keys to tracing them are also complex. They cover both current and historical statistics.

NATIONAL STATISTICS: GENERAL GUIDES

The United Kingdom, United States of America and other foreign publications listed below illustrate the main types of general guides:

Central Statistical Office. *Guide to official statistics*[35] is authoritative and well-produced. The latest edition has 16 detailed chapters, 100 sections and 600 subsections. It contains information on government and important non-official statistics for the United Kingdom. Its first edition in 1976 won a Besterman Medal as an outstanding bibliography. Post-Rayner, the *Guide* is slimline and indicates more negatives – 'ceased' titles, privatized series and altered frequencies – than formerly. Nevertheless, it is an essential information tool.

Government statistics: a brief guide to sources[36] is an annual, free pamphlet giving the major titles and series. It is an invaluable starting-point, a model of compact presentation of information. By its helpful footnotes, it alerts librarians to the specific addresses from which it is necessary to obtain certain Scottish, Welsh and Northern Irish (and less frequently, English) non-HMSO titles, thereby introducing them to the radical idea that all is not centralized through HMSO or CSO. Its contact-points list encourages positive information-seeking habits and makes available expertise to the ordinary enquirer.

United Kingdom statistical sources: a selection guide for libraries[37] is a highly select list of titles chosen to help the non-expert librarian to be aware of significant series. The LA/RSS union list of statistical serials in British libraries[38] is now of only historical interest, its details eroded by time and Rayner.

The *Reviews of United Kingdom statistical sources (RUKSS)*[39] series has issued 25 volumes (43 subjects), between 1974 and 1988. All are subject-based bibliographical treatments except for vol. 5, *General sources of statistics*.[40] RUKSS was preceded by the pioneering *Sources and nature of the statistics of the United Kingdom*.[41] The future of the *RUKSS* was the subject of Economic and Social Research Council (ESRC)-funded research by Elizabeth Chapman.[42] Amongst its 22 recommendations were suggestions that a successor series be started, a CD-ROM version be made available, and a new title be chosen.

Statistical news,[43] like its counterparts in other countries, is an updating, current-awareness journal published by CSO. It has news items, details of new, altered, changed or deleted statistical series or titles plus specialist articles.[44]

In the USA, amongst the many guides to statistics, the *American statistics index*[45] covers official government publications whereas *Statistical reference index*[46] concerns itself with non-official titles. *Statistics Canada*[47] is an example of the free catalogues of current titles available from the national statistics-issuing bodies.

EMIC has a comprehensive and excellent collection of international statistical serials and publications.[48]

Language is important in relation to statistics. Although the statistics themselves, i.e. the actual number in the series and tables, are generally thought to be universally understood, there are associated language problems when using foreign statistical publications. Footnotes, warnings, exceptions, definitions, etc. may not be understood fully. In many statistical publications, English or French subtitles enable greater understanding, e.g. *Statistical abstract of Sweden*.[49] The Swedish *Journal of official statistics*[50] (formerly *Statistical review*) is issued in English as well as Swedish.

Certain other publications are translated *en bloc* into English, e.g. the *Statistical yearbook of the Netherlands*.[51] For countries with more than one official language, e.g. Canada, Switzerland, etc., their publications are issued in parallel versions. For international statistics an agreed selection of languages is built in to their publishing programme. The UN efforts towards standardization of statistics nomenclature, classification and presentation should diminish some of the difficulties when adopted by the individual national statistics bodies.

REGIONAL STATISTICS: GUIDES AND SOURCES

The terms 'regional' and 'local' when applied to statistics may be interpreted in several ways. 'Regional' may refer to areas as large as Europe, e.g. European Communities (EC), or to the regions, states and towns of a particular country.[52] The former have been mentioned above.

In the UK, 'regional' is applied by Government to the eight standard regions plus Scotland, Wales and Northern Ireland. There are specific statistical annuals and serials for Scotland, Wales and Northern Ireland but there is no separate general statistical title for England. It is not always clear from the title of a publication if its coverage is total for the UK or Great Britain (GB), or for England, Scotland and Wales excluding Northern Ireland, or for England and Wales together, or, even, for England alone so care must be taken.

Information on the general sources of regional statistics is given in CSO's *Guide to official statistics*[53] with more specialized sources in CSO's *Regional trends*.[54] CSO's *Regional accounts*[55] has not been updated. The *Scottish abstract of statistics*[56] has its list of sources, and the *Scottish economic bulletin*[57] has both statistical tables and authoritative articles. The *Northern Ireland annual abstract of statistics*[58] has been issued since 1982. There are guides to Northern Irish statistical sources.[59]

LOCAL STATISTICS: GUIDES AND SOURCES

There is no totally comprehensive guide to all available local statistics. Improved information concerning local areas and local communities depends on the proper appreciation and exploitation of local data.

The Office of Population Censuses and Surveys (OPCS) *Census reports* are major sources of local statistics. Great Britain censuses have been held every ten years 1801 – 1981. OPCS have issued *Guides*[60] to the census reports.

After 100 years, the original census records are made available to the public. They become an essential historical resource for the locality and in microform are often available in local-studies departments of the public libraries. OPCS keeps the public well informed on all aspects of the publications programme of the census through OPCS *Monitor*,[61] *Population trends*[62] and the OPCS Census 1981 *User guide catalogue.*[63]

The census results are available on magnetic tapes for computer access, on microfilm or microfiche, as well as in hard copy. The Economic and Social Research Council (ESRC) Data Archive Unit, University of Essex, is the major depository for census records, current and retrospective. Its *ESRC Data archive bulletin*[64] reports on all aspects of census material including small-area statistics (SAS) – a vital tool for local-authority decision-making. Local authorities may promote the use of census results within their organizations, e.g. Sheffield City Council.[65]

The Chartered Institute of Public Finance and Accountancy (CIPFA) *Local government trends*,[66] CIPFA *Local government comparative statistics,*[67] CIPFA *Commonity indicators*[68] all contain notes, definitions and sources of statistics, etc. as well as statistical tables.

Local authorities have now a need to show greater local account-ability and have a statutory duty to produce reports and financial statements on their activities. The metropolitan counties, disbanded in 1986, were in the forefront of publicizing their activities and introduced many useful statistics.[69] The statistical publications from the 500-plus local authorities in the UK are varied. Some are general, some specific; others are single-subject reports, or more in the nature of regional surveys.[70]

The need for local economic growth and the responsibility of local authorities and local industries to go forward in partnership to ensure the continued development of the area have resulted in the establishment of local economic-development units (under various names) which research, collect and publish useful local data.[71]

No single information service covers all local authority or localarea statistics in the UK. The significant information-providers are the Planning Exchange; the Centre for Local Economic Strategies; Capital Planning Information; and the London Residuary Body.[72] Mort's summary of local statistics sources, the Warwick Business Information Service's publication on the counties and regions of the UK, and Owen's *Mind your local business* are all aids to tracing the scattered and bibliographically hard to find local statistical information publications and sources.[73]

Local authority publications have been investigated and promoted in the last few years and the proceedings of recent seminars will yield details of their statistical publications.[74]

SUBJECT-BASED GUIDES AND BIBLIOGRAPHIES

As the same statistics have relevance in many subject areas, there is much cross-classification, e.g. population statistics are of importance to national and local government, to education, to marketing, to industry and business, etc. The intellectual levels of subject-based guides vary from introductory pamphlets to specialist monographs. Treatments vary from total or partial, to historical or current. The frequency and manner of source publications also differ. Some appear as Press Notices (PNs) (increasingly electronically produced) from ministries, government departments and agencies; others as monthly, quarterly, occasional or annual supplements to statistical series, with explanatory notes and details of latest changes; as one-off expensive volumes; in specialist articles; or as series volumes in ongoing bibliographies.

An indication of the wide range of subject-based guides is given in the reference.[75]

NON-OFFICIAL STATISTICAL PUBLICATIONS AND SOURCES

The awareness of the importance of non-official statistics has been growing in recent years in the United Kingdom. The problems of their identification, availability, bibliographical control and dissemination have also been noticed. In the continuing aftermath of the White Paper on the GSS,[76] the cut-back effects of the Rayner report on each of the Govenment departments and the restructured responsibilities of the Central Statistical office,[77] non-official statistics have an increasingly important role for both statistics users and librarians. There is no 'official' definition of non-official statistics *per se* but possibly 'figures collected and issued on a regular basis but not published by central government', might suffice.

Pioneering research by Siddall led to an important 'first'. With Mort, she produced *Sources of unofficial UK statistics*.[78] Now the partial references to non-official statistics in the *CSO's guide to official statistics*,[79] are supplemented, amplified and consolidated by this bibliographical source. Non-official statistics are still difficult to trace in general bibliographies, such as *British national bibliography*,[80] where they do not automatically appear, but *British reports, translations and theses* (BRTT)[81] published by the British Library does manage to include a significant number. As for identifying the holdings of non-official statistics within British libraries, this is a task yet to be addressed. The non-official statistics which appear in periodicals are often found listed in Birmingham Public Library's *Statistics and market research* as well as in the excellent Warwick University Business Information Service publication *Market and statistics news*.[82] The latter contains specialist articles on non-official statistics, e.g. on European Trade Associations' statistics.[83] In this article the many different patterns of dissemination for associations in the Federal Republic of Germany illustrate the non-uniformity of access to the non-official statistics of private organizations, *viz.* restricted to members; non-circulation/non-publication; through statistical yearbooks and annual reports with statistical sections; through journals including statistics.

Non-official statistics are collected and disseminated by a wide range of organizations: Chambers of Commerce, research and trade associations, trades unions, national and local societies, local and regional authorities, banks, firms, market researchers, etc. Though they have many plus factors – more up-to-date, more focused than official figures – they also have some minus attributes. Non-official statistics do not have as much authority as official ones; they need to be taken with caution. The special pressures, circumstances, biases, under which they are collected, the prejudices and limitations of their parent bodies, etc., should be borne in mind. They are often the unique source of data and they complement and supplement official statistics.

Additional useful titles include Mort's *European directory of non-official statistical sources*,[84] Brittin and Mort *Euro high-tech*.[85] Some guides to statistics collected by building societies, property dealers, trade associations, banks, etc. are noted in reference 86.

HISTORICAL STATISTICS: PUBLICATIONS AND SOURCES

Generally, the titles mentioned so far have referred to current statistics and the importance of being 'up to date' has been stressed. But all today's figures stand on the foundation of earlier statistics and the latter put the former in perspective.

Historical statistics and the commentaries on them have a unique pattern of publication at every level – national, international and subject-based. The discipline of historical statistics has a wide range, with specialist guides and bibliographies.[87]

The inherent interest in historical statistics is in the attempt to make meaningful comparisons to further the understanding of the past (whether for social, economic, financial, demographic or political reasons) and to illuminate the present. 'How did we get here?' is a question which may be helped by reliable historical data. This is a difficult aspect of statistical analysis and it involves, in addition to a careful application of statistical techniques, an understanding of the varying economic, political, social, geographical and 'technical' circumstances of the collection of the original data. The lack of availability of known statistics; the loss of comparability through problems of definition; variable quality; boundary changes; industrial classification alterations; variations in the original purposes for which the statistics were collected; deliberate falsification or suppression of data – all of these affect the reliability of historical statistics and confuse their interpreters. Note Mitchell's cautionary comment: 'All one can do is to be careful and keep a firm rein on credulity without going to the extreme of stultifying total scepticism' and his enlightening comments in *International historical statistics: Africa and Asia.*[88] Even more than for current statistics, it is imperative to read and heed the numerous caveats, footnotes, special references, etc. when consulting historical statistics.

To answer the common everday UK enquiries (e.g. the price of bread, petrol; the internal purchasing power of the pound; the level of wages 50 or 100 years ago compared with today) by quoting a mere statistic, index number or quantity of money converted to modern decimal currency, can in itself be a little misleading, unless the social context is understood. The 'instant answer' compilation can be useful, e.g. Priestley's *The 'what it cost the day before yesterday' book – from 1850 to the present day*[89] but the more academic titles are needed to sustain an argument or understand the historical relevance. The enquirer should not be left with a misleading impression. The 'How long would it take to earn enough to buy X or Y product?' approach may be a more creative and more easily understandable way of conveying certain historical facts.

Since 1945, retrospective surveys, economic and social science projects treat historical statistics in ever-more sophisticated ways. For future historians and economists, the improved current statistics now being collected – the mirror of society at the end of the twentieth century – will provide fuller data, always assuming the physical life of modern records, the printed publications, magnetic films, discs, microforms, etc. is as long and as enduring as they are now presumed to be. The loss of conservation quality in paper records of the nineteenth and twentieth centuries is a salutary reminder of the frailty of a 'permanent' record. Destructive viruses in computers threaten electronic records' permanence.

Some titles, to show the range of international, national and subject historical statistics, are given under reference 90. Increasingly international organizations, government departments and other producers of official statistics, will provide 'historical' (i.e. retrospective extensions of certain current statistics), at a charge, to the individual user.[91]

'ALTERNATIVE' STATISTICS: THE RADICAL RESPONSE

The vast majority of statistics used and quoted, with or without acknowledgement, with or without modification, are those issued by official bodies, governments, etc. Whilst the naive approach to statistics takes all figures at their face value, increasingly the data are being used and interpreted according to the user's economic, social, political and racial viewpoint.[92] The critique of 'official data' has gone beyond criticism; it questions their methodology, their veracity, and is distrustful of their ostensible purpose. These changes affect libraries and librarians in their information-giving role. As the questioning grows stronger, libraries (especially public libraries) must include these alternative views of statistics in their stock just as they do for the wider range of books and periodicals. The campaigners for a 'greener' world, for the greater accountability of industrial concerns for the health, safety and environment of the population at large, re-interpret existing data or collect, store and disseminate alternative statistics in support of their views. Recently, controversy has existed concerning statistics relating to eggs and salmonella; radiation hazards from nuclear-reprocessing plants; AIDS; employment/unemployment/poverty levels; the numbers of persons with disabilities; the costs of and spending on the National Health Service, etc. No industry, no sector of life appears to escape this radical response – 'we are all radicals now'.

Social audit is concerned mainly with the social, environmental and safety accountability of pharmaceutical companies. The Radical Statistics Group, with its sub-interest groups, issues publications.[93] Shelter, the housing pressure group, has leaflets on housing facts and figures.[94] Academics research, write articles and bring out volumes on social and health matters etc.[95] Committees of the House of Commons struggle with the non-reliability of official statistics on sensitive topics.[96]

A similar pattern of investigation, publication and discussion occurs wherever statistics are a vital component in the understanding of the current situation. Statistics have lost their aura of official authoritativeness. They can be questioned, packaged, manipulated, analysed, modified and suppressed, etc. just as other media, the printed word, television and film. The Freedom of Information movement applies to statistics too. Data can mislead as well as inform, obfuscate as well as clarify. The validity tests for statistics will not shake the belief that 'Lies, damn lies and statistics' is still a true statement.[97]

CLASSIFICATION SCHEMES FOR STATISTICS: INTERNATIONAL AND NATIONAL

The classification schemes and codes for statistics of economic activity, industry and trade assist in the meaningful analysis and interpretation of the data collected. Abbreviations abound – ISIC, SITC,[98] HS, BTN, CCCN, CN,[99] NIMEXE, NIPRO, NACE,[100] SIC,[101] CPC,[102] etc. The necessity to consult the latest editions plus explanatory notes, guidance manuals, updating supplements or official notices is paramount. De-coding the codes is difficult. Establishing exact correlations and correspondences between the different schemes or between current and superseded editions of the same codes is an interesting task. The EC Sabine system of databanks covers 200 classifications and their interconnections.

Internationally the United Nations is the major influence on the classification of economic and industrial statistics. At the 25th session of UN Statistical Commission, February 1989, approval was given to the final drafts of *International standard industrial classification of all economic activity* (ISIC Revision 3)[103] and to the provisional (CPC) *Central product classification.*[104] The Statistical Commission requested the Secretary General to help and encourage greater uniformity and standardization in this eclectic area of classification, *viz.* (i) to prepare and publish ISIC Revision

3, with indexes and correlation tables between ISIC Revision 3, the Harmonized Commodity Description and Coding System (HS), the Standard International Trade Classification (SITC) Revision 3 and the provisional CPC; (ii) to prepare the publication of a provisional CPC, with explanatory notes, for the services part of the classification; and (iii) to publish and circulate ISIC Revision 3 and CPC.[105] The UN Statistical Office will provide national statistical offices with guidance, technical cooperation and supplementary documentation. ISIC covers economic activity, SITC trade, and CPC (provisional) products at international statistics level.

At the regional, or groupings of countries, level, the 1980s have seen much activity in the upgrading, revision and extension of use of classifications. The Customs Cooperation Council (CCC) based in Brussels, produced its *Harmonized system nomenclature* (HS), the successor to the earlier *Brussels tariff nomenclature* (BTN) and the *CCC nomenclature* (CCCN).[106] The HS was used as the basis for the European Communities' own *Combined nomenclature* (CN)[107] which, for goods, meets the requirements of both the EC's Common Customs Tariff and of its EC external trade statistics. Both HS and CN issue *Explanatory notes* and the two publications should be seen as complementary. From January 1988, CN was introduced both for duty purposes and for import and export statistics.

NIMEXE, the nomenclature used for EC external trade and for trade between EC member states, was in force until 1988 when it was superseded by CN. NACE is the classification scheme of the European Communities for its economic activities. NIPRO is the EC common nomenclature of industrial products.[108]

Nationally, each country has its own classification codes for economic activity, trade and tariffs. In the UK, the *Standard industrial classification* (SIC) (80)[109] has been in use since 1983. Whilst SIC (80) follows ISIC in general terms, it is closer to NACE. For UK trade with other countries, as summarized in the *Overseas trade statistics of the United Kingdom*,[110] SITC (R3) has been used since January 1988. *Guide to the classification for overseas trade statistics* and the *Guide to the classification for overseas trade statistics: correlation tables*[111] explain the system.

The *UK integrated tariff of the United Kingdom*[112] has full correlation of the pre-1988 and post-1988 nomenclatures for duty purposes. For information, a sample line of the commodity code is like this:

Digits	1 2 3 4 5 6	7 8	9	10 11	1 2 3 4
	HS Code	EC Duty and statistics	National sub-division	TARIC	Additional code if required

Note: 6-digit HS code is used worldwide, 9-digit code is for all EC exports and all intra-Community imports; 11-digit TARIC (*Tarif intègre communautaire*) is used for imports to the EC from non-EC countries; the additional 1 2 3 4 digits are available if needed.

An efficiency scrutiny of HM Customs and Excise's administration and interpretation of the Integrated Tariff recommended certain management changes. From September 1989, the tariff enquiry service will be from Classification Liaison Officers (CLO's) at local centres throughout the UK.

BUILDING THE COLLECTION: CHOOSING AND USING

Having established the existence of statistical publications through using the guides and bibliographies, the next stage is to choose appropriate titles, according to the needs of a particular library, so as to form a viable statistics collection.

The proven needs of individual statistics users, and the demands for statistical data via the library's information service, will influence the choice of titles and their most useful format. Choosing may be slightly easier in a special, research, or subject-based library, than in a 'general' reference one where the focus is harder to establish. The size and coverage of the statistics collection must equate to the purpose, level and philosophy of the parent organization. In cost-conscious times, a frequently used, well-organized collection of carefully chosen 'core' statistics will be more efficient and cost-effective, and more acceptable managerially, than an extensive one which proves to be too expensive to maintain in an up-to-date condition.

The same raw data are used by many agencies to produce different statistical tables and they appear and reappear in many guises. There is much duplication of information between statistical series. Every title, at every level, selected for stock, should be assessed as to whether its quota of 'extra' information justifies the initial purchase price, the cost of processing/ cataloguing and the continuing cost of storage.

Choices have to be made, too, concerning complete standing orders or intermittent ones for regular statistical publications, bearing in mind the burden of having a high proportion of resources mortgaged in advance.

A further facet of choice is that of format: whether to buy the statistical information as printed publications, microfilms, microfiche, computer tapes, CD-ROMs or floppy disc – or to access them online or via Viewdata. There is much duplication of information and choosing the appropriate mix of formats is a difficult task, cost having to be balanced against accessibility. There is no single 'correct' mix of annuals, serials, subjects and formats in a statistics collection. Each library must establish its own unique combination of resources for its needs and clientele.

OFFICIAL INTERNATIONAL AND NATIONAL STATISTICS: CHOOSING AND USING – FORMATS AND TITLES

The cost of providing, collecting, processing, storing and disseminating statistics is very high. The greatest fixed costs are involved in the first four tasks; the last has an element of choice. International, regional and national statistics are the product of cooperation between a myriad of interdependent statistics providing and collecting bodies at all levels. Increasingly, the official statistical offices, and their governments, are conscious of the heavy costs involved in economic, social, industrial and demographic statistics collection and dissemination programmes.

Typically, in the post-Rayner,[113] post-Pickford,[114] post-Armstrong[115] UK situation, fewer and less frequent industry surveys are being undertaken, and privatization of statistical series occurs. The *Business monitor* series,[116] now a CSO responsibility, has been curtailed; *British business*,[117] the outlet for many statistical series, has ceased; *Business bulletins*[118] have been introduced as a cheaper alternative dissemination title; *Business briefings*,[119] a Chamber of Commerce publication has lessened statistical content. Such diminutions in national statistics may well, in turn, affect the quantity, quality, reliability and availability of regional (e.g. EC) and international (UN, OECD) statistical series.

The mode of publications and range of formats reflect this cost-conscious approach to statistics dissemination. Decisions on public v. private publication; on parallel provision of hard copy, and/or microfiche/microfilm, and/or computer-based access, etc., depend more on commercial rather than on need-to-know or public-availability considerations. The comparative costs of different formats and storage factors influence decisions about acquisition as against access only via IT. North American libraries, USA and Canada, have already felt the loss of access through privatization. CASIM, for example, privatized its *Small business statistics* and Canadian librarians are still having difficulty in establishing current availability status, access and coverage of this series.[120]

ONLINE DATABASES: STATISTICS: SOURCES

In the *Directory of international sources of business information*,[121] Ball lists details of over 600 databases of possible interest to those needing economic, financial, social or industrial information. This list cross checks with the relevant hard-copy statistical publications.

American statistics index (ASI)[122] is online and covers US Federal statistical publications. Each national statistical office indicates services which are available online. For international statistics, UN *Directory of international statistics*[123] has an inventory of economic and social statistics databases. Clinch's recent *Business statistics*[124] covers international, European Community and UK statistical sources with special attention to computer databases of time series.

Headland Press – a pre-eminent force in business information awareness publications – has a monthly newsletter, *Online business information*[125] which covers electronic business databases of all types – online, floppy disc, CD-ROM and video disc. It assesses and tests the products and services noted. Foster's *Online business source book*[126] has an inventory of numerical and statistical databases. For trends and developments, articles in *Business information review*[127] are essential reading. For other subjects too, access to statistics is increasingly via IT but the number of publications devoted to identifying new databases, new formats, etc. are not so numerous as for business-information awareness.

Official statistical offices issue updating press notices (e.g. '*Economic trends annual supplement* is now on disc as well as tape' CSO.PN 23.3.1989). General online directories contain information on the availability of statistics online.[128] CD-ROM is a growing trend too for statistics dissemination.

Ulrich's international periodicals directory[129] identifies the online availability of titles listed.

The major hosts for databases concerned with statistics including DIALOG, WEFA, GSi-ECO, DRI, Reuters/IP Sharp[130] etc. are described in the sources mentioned above. All issue updating newsletters.

MICROFORM: MICROFICHE STATISTICAL PUBLICATIONS

Microfiche are space-savers as well as money-savers and most libraries have microfiche reader/printers as a matter of course. Other organizations tend to forego microforms in favour of electronic access – unless the microfiche and reader/printer are provided as a complete package. Some hard-copy statistical publications include the tables on microfiche as a cost-cutting exercise. Though many statistical serials are issued in microfiche format, they are increasingly rivalled by magnetic tapes, diskettes/floppy discs, direct access online or CD-ROMs as alternatives to the printed version. The existence of microfiche editions is noted in most statistical source compilations. Chadwyck-Healey's catalogue of *Official statistical serials on microfiche*[131] lists select British official publications containing statistics from 1801 – 1977, including the *Annual abstract*, 1928 – 77. *Guide to microforms in print* is comprehensive.[132] At international level, UN *Commodity, trade statistics*;[133] OECD Series B. *Trade by country* and Series C. *Trade by commodity*[134] are issued on microfiche. In the UK, OPCS *Census 1981: economic activity: counties*,[135] DHSS *Mortality tables*[136] are examples of publications which include microfiche in the printed publication.

VIEWDATA STATISTICS

Prestel, the UK viewdata service, has certain statistics included in its resources. The nature of viewdata limits the amount of information on each frame. It is an easy and useful source of up-to-date popular economic statistics. There are drawbacks, e.g. no built-in authority check for Prestel information providers; no single directory listing by which the same data are identified as appearing in different information services (so that cost, accuracy, currency comparisons can be made); there is no regular form of updating. Prestel columns in the professional library press are useful.

A Prestel set, well placed in a library, can however introduce new groups of users to the idea of 'instant information', to statistical and financial data presented pleasantly and easily. It may well lead to more sophisticated computer-based access.

TITLES

For the most used UK titles, *Government statistics: a brief guide to sources* is an invaluable, annual publication.[137] For more detail, check the *Guide to official statistics*.[138] In every discipline, the depth and number of statistical publications is truly daunting. For those responsible for specialist statistical collections, detailed knowledge of all aspects of relevant data is essential. For the general-reference librarian, awareness of major titles plus an ability to identify and locate the specialist series (whether in hard copy, microfiche or through electronic sources) is an important skill. Many titles have already been noted, but the following short list is intended to illustrate further the breadth and variety of publications available, whether international or national.

International

UN publications range from the major titles, UN *Statistical yearbook* (updated by UN *Monthly bulletin of statistics*) to the introductory *World statistics in brief*; the UN *World economic survey* and UNIDO's *Industry and development: global report* cover economic trends and the industrial economy.[139]

Specialist UN organizations have regular series,[140] e.g. FAO *The state of food and agriculture*; UNESCO *Compendium of statistics on illiteracy*; irregular titles,[141] e.g. *World comparison of purchasing power and real product, 1980*; and expert monographs e.g. *Guidelines on statistics of tangible assets.*

OECD economic statistics for the 25 leading countries include the general *Main economic indicators, Labour force statistics, National accounts*;[142] the specialist *Energy statistics*, and *Review of fisheries in OECD countries etc.* Where necessary, OECD issues *Methodological supplements.* OECD *Economic surveys* are issued annually for each member country.[143] European Communities EUROSTAT publications are issued in nine themes (colour-coded for easy identification); general statistics e.g. *Basic statistics of the Community* (midnight blue); foreign trade, *External trade statistical year book* (red) etc.), and in six series e.g. yearbooks, short-term trends, accounts, studies, methods and rapid reports. Where necessary, EUROSTAT issue explanatory supplements.[144]

Non-official international statistics, e.g. *Non-ferrous metal data, World steel in figures, World air transport statistics, World motor vehicle data*.[145]

International statistics, such as those of the UN, are generally issued in the major world languages, English, French, Russian, Chinese. The European Communities recognize nine official languages but not all titles are in all languages.

National

The official and non-official national statistics series and publications of the UK are typical of those issued by most countries of the world. All have general statistical yearbooks plus specialized annuals and serials. The quantity of foreign titles purchased for a statistics collection will depend on library funds and users' needs. With 1992 and the completion of the Single Market, perhaps more EC and other European national statistical titles will be found on UK library shelves. Unlike their UK counterparts, which are only in English, many foreign national publications have headings, contents, notes etc. in several languages,[146] or are issued in complete English-language versions.[147]

UK general statistical publications include *Annual abstract of statistics, Monthly digest of statistics, United Kingdom in figures, Key data;*[148] more detailed information is in *Social trends, Economic trends.*[149] UK and GB specialist titles are numerous. Even the *Brief guide*[150] lists well over 100 basic publications (in addition to those which deal with Scotland, Wales and Northern Ireland separately), e.g. *UK balance of payments, Energy trends, Agricultural statistics, Transport statistics: Great Britain, Education statistics for the UK, Employment gazette.*[151]

Scottish titles of interest include *Scottish abstract of statistics, Scottish statistics fact card, Scottish economic bulletin, Agriculture in Scotland.*[152]

Welsh statistical publications are wide-ranging, e.g. *Digest of Welsh statistics, Welsh social trends, Welsh economic trends, Welsh agricultural statistics.*[153]

Northern Ireland statistics are generally available from Belfast, e.g. *Northern Ireland annual abstract of statistics, Statistical review of Northern Ireland agriculture.*[154]

Non-official national statistics are important and, post-Rayner, they are often the main source of data, e.g. *Waterborne freight in the UK, Betting and gaming bulletin, University statistics, Port statistics.*[155]

BUILDING THE COLLECTION: MAINTAINING THE STOCK

Once the statistics collection has been established, it must be maintained. This involves the selection of new titles, assessment of existing serials; monitoring of developments (through planned current awareness of publications relating to statistics and their continuing availability); training of all staff and users; and the physical organization of the stock – its classification, cataloguing, binding and allocation. Lastly, there is the awareness of, and use of, the major national statistical collections.

Monitoring developments involves checking for alterations, deletions, additions, amendments to individual tables within the statistical series as well as responding to changes of title, format, frequency, availability, price, publisher, of the publications themselves. *Statistical news*[156] (UK) and its foreign counterparts from official statistical offices are essential reading for the professional librarian. The more general journals, e.g. *Employment gazette*,[157] *Economic trends*,[158] etc., all have significant information in their subject fields. The statistical journals, e.g. *Monthly digest of statistics*,[159] and their explanatory notes and methodologies, indicate the changes to individual tables. Major changes affecting statistical series must be noted and statistics users alerted to discrepancies of interpretation, comparability, historical files, differences of criteria for inclusion/exclusion, index weightings, etc. All these efforts to keep up-to-date have only one objective – the better and more intelligent use of the statistics collection.

For the statistics users, the librarian must ensure that, for example, statistical publications within the collection clearly indicate changes in relationship to earlier or later series, to alternative sources, to the cessation of their availability, to format changes or to when the format has changed or the publisher is different.[160] Occasionally, the title of a publication is kept, but the policy for its contents has changed.

The pace of change in statistical publications has accelerated in the 1980s. Privatization or de-officializing of statistics is an added complication. The development in the UK of non-HMSO departmental statistical publications is a continuing trend. Non-official statistics are difficult to monitor or control. Many titles which were formerly free are now priced.

At a practical level there are physical problems as well as textual ones when changes occur. Where formerly they were separate publications, tables are issued now as part of a series, as e.g. *Statistical bulletins*,[161] so it is necessary to decide whether to bind or shelve these as a continuation of the original titles, or to treat them as part of a serial, with annotations as to previous format. Many library systems are organized to treat books and serials differently for storage purposes, and for cataloguing or classification. By some means, the variations and changes must be recorded, so that statistics users may easily find historical and current series.

Increasingly, statistics are available in non-book format, and librarians have to familiarize themselves with the ever-changing pattern by attending relevant conferences, seminars and courses to update their professional expertise.

TRAINING: RESEARCH AND DEVELOPMENT

In-house training relating to statistics for all reference-library staff is essential to increase appreciation of the range of resources and to improve the service to users. At professional level, there is long-standing cooperation through the Committee of Librarians and Statisticians (Royal Statistical Society/Library Association).

Statistics users' groups hold informative seminars and conferences. The Statistics Users' Council, formed in 1970, provides a forum for discussion. Its annual conference is subject-based. Intrastat (International Trade Statistics Users' Group) began in 1988. The Transport Statistics Users' Group, a joint group of the Statistics Users' Council and the Chartered Institute of Transport, has been active since 1985; it issues a newsletter, and a looseleaf *Directory*. [162]

Warwick University, Business Information Service organizes seminars on selected statistical topics, e.g. UK non-official statistics, October 1989. They have also launched an updating service, *UK market facts*. [163]

The European Communities are reassessing the provision of statistical information. DOSES (development of statistical expert systems) is part of its R & D effort for statistics. In 1989, the EC statistics information programme 1989 – 92 was agreed (COM(88)696). An EC seminar in April 1989 was on the European statistical information system after 1992.

SPECIALIST STATISTICAL COLLECTIONS

At local level, the cooperative schemes (LADSIRLAC, HATRICS, SINTO, etc.) foster interest in resources in the area. Library and Information Plans (LIPs) are being established in many localities, and they will take into account local sectoral resources such as statistics collections when developing their strategies for cooperation and exploitation of all the area's information services.

Nationally, the UK is fortunate to have many well-organized collections. Apart from the major copyright libraries, there are collections more easily available to the general public. The Office of Population Censuses and Surveys has an important reference library in St Catherine's House, Kingsway, London.

The Export Market Information Centre in London is part of the government's services to exports. Its collection of international and national trade and marketing statistics is the most extensive in the UK, and highly experienced government librarians provide an efficient information service.

At Warwick University, the major statistics collection has developed research and consultancy facilities as well as the training sessions mentioned earlier.

STATISTICS AS AN INFORMATION RESOURCE: COMMENTS AND CONCLUSIONS

The statistics collection in a library becomes a living information resource only when actively developed, carefully maintained and effectively exploited by both the professional and non-professional information staff on behalf of the users. Its continued usefulness is in direct relation to the standard of trained professional care bestowed on it and to the level of resources allocated to it. As the importance of the statistical aspects of subjects becomes more appreciated by all sections of the community, the quality of service from the library's statistical collection should at least keep pace with that interest or, by anticipation, be ahead of its development.

The continuing changes in content and presentation of traditional statistical publications, and the variations in their compilation and dissemination, are factors to be taken into account by the librarian responsible for the administration and organization of a statistics collection. At every level – international, national, official, non-official – and for every subject, statistics are acknowledged as major information tools.

Electronic access to statistical data is now in many varied modes: online, CD-ROM, tapes, discs. Such choices bring unparalleled resources into a library. The next decade will see the changeover from hard-copy publication to electronic provision accelerate. The 'visible' statistics collection may well diminish on the shelf. Whatever the final circumstances, reference librarians and information staff will endeavour to provide the most informed, efficient and effective service to the user.

REFERENCES AND CITATIONS

1   House of Commons. Treasury and Civil Service Committee. *Official economic statistics: minutes of evidence.* London: HMSO, 1988. (Session 1988 – 9 HC 181).

2   Pickford, S. and others, *Government economic statistics: a scrutiny report.* London: HMSO, 1989.

3   Department of Trade and Industry, *Review of DTI business surveys*, by Alan Armstrong and others. London: DTI, 1989.

4   'The new Central Statistical Office', *Statistical news*, 86, August 1989, 9, 47.

5   Mayes, D. G., *Statistics by and for government: recent changes in official statistics.* London: National Economic Development Office, 1984. (Discussion paper 9);
    Thomas, R., 'A critique of the government statistical service', *Public administration*, 62, Summer 1984, 224 – 9;
    Hoinville, G. and Smith, T. M. F., 'The Rayner review of government statistical services', *Journal of the Royal Statistical Society* [A], **145** (2), 1982, 195 – 207;
    Boreham, Sir J., 'Integrity in the government statistical service', *Statistical news*, **68**, February 1985, 19 – 20;
    Allan, Alastair J., *The myth of government information.* London: Library Association Publishing Ltd, 1990.

6   Illarionov, A. N., 'Where are we?: ['Gde my nakhad-imsya?'], EKO, **12**, 1988, 46;
    Treml, V. G., 'Perestroyka and Soviet statistics', *Soviet economy*, **4** (1), 1988, 65 – 94;
    Simonyan, R. [Comments on the lack of transparency of Soviet economic statistics], *Izvestiya*, 13 October 1988, 2;

Knanin, G., 'Economic growth: an alternative estimation': ['Ekono-micheskii rost: alternativnaya otsenka'], *Kommunist*, **65**, November 1988, 83;

Aganbegyan, A., 'The Soviet economy – a view into the future': ['Sovetskaya ekonomika – vzglyad v buduschchee'], *Ekonomika*, 1988; 'Perestroyka: recent developments in re-structuring the Soviet economy', *West-Ost journal*, **6**, 1987, 33.

(The references above were given in *Economic survey of Europe in 1988 – 1989*. New York: UN, Economic Commission for Europe, 1989. 120 – 2.)

7   United Nations, *Directory of international standards for statistics*. New York: UN, 1960.

8   United Nations, *Directory of international statistics*, vol. 1. New York: UN, 1982.

9   Clarke, George, 'International coordination of official statistics: United Nations – OECD – Eurostat', *Statistical news*, **83**, November 1988, 12 – 19.

10   United Nations, *UNDOC: current index*. New York: UN. Monthly with cumulations.

11   United Nations, *United Nations publications: a reference catalogue*. New York: UN. Annual.

12   Library of Congress, *Index to international statistics*. Washington: Congressional Information Service. Monthly with annual cumulation.

13   Library Association and Royal Statistical Society, *Recommended basic statistical sources: international*. London: LA, 1975.

14   Harvey, Joan M., *Sources of statistics*. 2nd ed. London: Bingley, 1971.

15   Export Market Information Centre, *National statistical offices of the world*. London: EMIC. Annual.

16   *Bibliography of official statistical yearbooks and bulletins*. London: Chadwyck-Healey, 1986.

17   Pieper, F. C. (ed.), *SISCIS: subject index to sources of comparative international statistics*. Beckenham: CBD Research Ltd, 1978.

18   Wasserman, P. (ed.), *Statistics sources: a subject guide to data on industrial, business, social, educational, financial and other topics for the United States and internationally*. 2 vols. 12th ed. Detroit, Michigan: Gale, 1988. Available online.

19   Harvey, Joan M., *Statistics Africa: sources of social economic and market research*. 2nd ed.; *Statistics America: sources of social, economic and market research*. 2nd ed.; *Statistics Asia and Australasia: sources for market research*; *Statistics Europe: sources for social economic and market research*. 5th ed. Beckenham: CBD Research Ltd. 1978, 1980, 1974, 1987.

20   Organisation for Economic Cooperation and Development (OECD), *Catalogue of publications*. Paris: OECD. Biennial. Available in French and English.

21   European Communities, *Eurostat catalogue: publications and electronic services*.

Luxembourg: Office for Official Publications of the EC, 1989.

European Communities, *Eurostat vade-mecum: guide to the Statistical Office of the European Communities*. Luxembourg: Office for Official Publications of the EC, 1989;

22 *Eurostat news*. Luxembourg: Office of Official Publications of the European Communities. Quarterly. (Articles, etc. e.g. Clarke, George, 'Organisation and structure of a European Community statistics system', *Eurostat news*, **3 – 4**, 1988, 4 – 7.)

23 Ramsay, Anne (ed.), *Eurostat index: a detailed keyword subject index to the statistical series published by the statistical office of the European Communities*. 4th ed. Stamford: Capital Planning Information, 1989.

24 Ramsay, Anne (ed.), *European Communities statistics*. 4th ed. Newcastle upon Tyne: Association of European Documentation Centre Libraries, 1987. (EDC European Communities Information).

25 Jeffries, John, *Guide to the official publications of the European Communities*. London: Mansell, 1981.

26 Thomson, Ian, *Documentation of the European Communities*. London: Mansell, 1989.

27 See note 1 above.

28 The new Central Statistical Office [text of written statement by the Prime Minister in reply to a Parliamentary question by Terence Higgins, 5 April 1989], *Statistical news*, **85**, 1989, 4 – 5;

'The new Central Statistical Office' [organization chart], *Statistical news*, **86**, August 1989, 9;

'Reorganisation of DTI statistical services', *Statistical news*, **86**, August 1989, 48;

Norton, Roger, 'Statistics: less of a burden and better', *British business*, 14 July 1989, 16 – 17; *ditto*, 21 July 1989, 3. (This refers to changes brought about by the Armstrong review of DTI's statistical responsibilities); See also note 3 above.

Social Science Forum, *Official statistics: a statement of principle for their collection and use*. London: SSF, 1989;

'Department of Employment figures show Government official unemployment count last year overstated by 40,000 the number out of work as defined by internationally agreed guidelines', *Financial Times*, 5 August 1989, 5;

'CSO's current account balance of payments figures continue to be plagued by "black holes" caused by errors and omissions', *F. T.* 16 June 1989, 8;

'Bad statistics worse than none', *F. T.* 14 September 1987, 15;

'CSO produces heavily qualified g.d.p. figures due to serious under-recording of national expenditure measure', *F. T.* 20 December 1988, 8b;

'Chemical Industries Association slams DTI statistics policy', *Chemistry and industry*, 17 April 1989, 237.

29 Deuchars, Fiona, 'Statistics of trade and industry: a bi-centennial review',

Statistical news, **74**, August 1986. (Historical developments in DTI); Harvey, Neil and Stibbard, Peter, 'The headquarters divisions of the Department of Trade and Industry: [statistical divisions]', *Statistical news*, **75**, November 1986, 5 – 13.

30 See note 4 above.

31 Rayner, Sir D., *Review of Government Statistical Services: report to the Prime Minister*. London: Cabinet Office, 1980.

32 Lord President of the Council, *Government Statistical Services*. London: HMSO, 1981. Cmnd 8236.

33 'Sir Humphrey Mynors: [obituary]', *Daily Telegraph*, 27 May 1989, 15. 'He applied himself to transform [the Bank's] statistics office into an exhaustive record of monetary statistics, a forerunner of the Central Statistical Office'.

34 See note 5 above.

35 Central Statistical Office, *Guide to official statistics*. 6th ed. London: HMSO, 1990.

36 Central Statistical Office, *Government statistics: a brief guide to sources*. London: HMSO. Annual.

37 McShane, P., *United Kingdom statistical sources: a selection guide for libraries*. 4th ed. London: Library Association, 1985.

38 Library Association and Royal Statistical Society, *Union list of statistical serials in British libraries*. London: Library Association, 1972.

39 Maunder, W. F. and others (eds.), *Reviews of United Kingdom statistical sources (RUKSS)*, vols. 1 – 5. London: Heinemann, 1974 – 6; vols. 6 – 22. London: Pergamon Press, 1978 – 87; vols. 23 – 5. London: Chapman and Hall, 1988.

40 Lock, G. F., *General sources of statistics*. London: Heinemann for the Royal Statistical Society and the Social Science Research Council, 1976. (*RUKSS* vol. 5).

41 Kendall, Maurice George (ed.), *Sources and nature of the statistics of the United Kingdom*. 2 vols. London: Oliver and Boyd, 1952 – 7.

42 Chapman, Elizabeth A., *Report to the Economic and Social Research Council on reviews of United Kingdom statistical sources*. London: ESRC, 1988.

43 *Statistical news*. London: HMSO for CSO. Quarterly.

44 Wilde, Maurice and others, 'Statistics in the Ministry of Defence', *Statistical news*, **77**, May 1987. Series on different Government Departments;
Rice, Philip, 'World crude oil prices – the statistical problems', *Statistics news*, **74**, August 1986;
Alexander, John, 'The Statistics Users Conference on financial statistics', *Statistical news*, **72**, February 1986;
Fessey, Martin, 'Bridging the gap: the work of Committee and Librarians and Statisticians', *Statistical news*, **79**, November 1987, 8 – 9.

45 *American statistics index: a comprehensive guide and index to the statistical publications of the US Government*. Washington: Congressional Information Service.

Annual, with monthly supplements. Available online.

46 *Statistical reference index to current American statistical publications from sources other than the US Government.* Washington: Congressional Information Service. Monthly with cumulations.

47 *Statistics Canada: catalogue.* Ottawa: Information Department, Canada. Annual.

48 Export Market Information Centre (EMIC), 20 Victoria Street, London SW1H 0NF. 071 – 215 5444/5445.

49 *Statistisk årsbok: statistical abstract of Sweden.* Stockholm: Statistika Centralbyrån. Annual.

50 *Journal of official statistics* 1985 – in English. Stockholm: Statistika Centralbyrån. (Continuation of *Statistical review* 1963 – 84).

51 *Statistical yearbook of the Netherlands.* Amsterdam: Netherlands Central Bureau of Statistics. 1969/70 – . (In English).

52 Balachandran, M. (ed.), *Regional statistics: a guide to information sources.* Detroit, Mich.: Gale Research Co., 1980.

53 See note 35 above.

54 Central Statistical Office, *Regional trends.* London: HMSO. Annual.

55 Central Statistical Office, *Regional accounts.* London: HMSO, 1978. (Studies in Official Statistics no. 31).

56 Scottish Office, *Scottish abstract of statistics.* Edinburgh: HMSO. Annual.

57 *Scottish economic bulletin.* Edinburgh: HMSO. Twice per year.

58 Northern Ireland Office, *Northern Ireland annual abstract of statistics.* Belfast: HMSO. 1982 – .
Previously: *Digest of statistics, Northern Ireland.* Belfast: HMSO, 1954 – 81.

59 Policy Planning and Research Unit, *A guide to Northern Ireland statistics.* Belfast: PPRU. (Occasional paper 16);
Collett, R. J., *Northern Ireland statistics: a guide to principal sources.* Belfast: Queen's University, 1979;
Park, A. T., 'Northern Ireland government statistics', *Statistical news,* **2**, August 1968.

60 Office of Population Censuses and Surveys, *Census 1801 – 1966 Great Britain: a guide to census reports.* London: HMSO, 1977;
Office of Population Censuses and Surveys, *Census reports of Great Britain 1801 – 1931.* London: HMSO, 1951. (Guides to official sources, no. 2).

61 Office of Population Censuses and Surveys, *OPCS Census 1981, Monitor series.* London: OPCS, v.d.

62 *Population trends.* London: HMSO. Quarterly.

63 Office of Population Censuses and Surveys, *OPCS Census 1981, user guide catalogue.* London: OPCS.

64 Economic and Social Research Council, *ESRC data archive bulletin.* Colchester: Essex University. 3 per year.

65 Sheffield City Council, Central Policy Unit, *Sheffield Census report 1981: nos. 1 – 21.* Sheffield: SCC CPU, v.d.

66 Chartered Institute of Public Finance and Accountancy, *Local government*

trends. London: CIPFA. Annual.

67 Chartered Institute of Public Finance and Accountancy, *Local government comparative statistics*. London: CIPFA. Annual. Also available on disc.

68 Chartered Institute of Public Finance and Accountancy, *Community indicators*. London: CIPFA. Annual.

69 Greater London Council, *Annual abstract of Greater London statistics*. London: GLC. Ceased;
South Yorkshire County Council, *South Yorkshire statistics*. Barnsley: SYCC. Ceased;
Greater Manchester County Council, *Greater Manchester – facts, figures and finance*. Manchester: GMCC. Ceased;
Some aspects of GMCC are continued by Manchester Research and Information Planning Unit.

70 *Humberside facts and figures*. Beverley: Humberside County Council. Annual;
Shetlands in statistics. Lerwick: Shetland Island Council. Annual;
Annual population forecasts for Oxfordshire. Oxford: Oxfordshire County Council. Annual;
Outlook for the oil and gas industries. Aberdeen: Grampian Regional Council, 1988.

71 Sheffield City Council, *Unemployment statistics*. Department of Employment and Economic Development. Monthly.

72 Planning Exchange, *Planning information digest and economic development digest*. PE. Monthly.
PE has an online service PLANEX;
Centre for Local Economic Strategies, *Local economic news*. CLES. Monthly.
CLES has a database of local economic information on disc;
Capital Planning Information, *Urbandoc news*. Stamford: CPI. Monthly.
CPI collects local government publications for the British Library; these are included in *BRTT* (see note 81 below) and into SIGLE database of 'grey' literature;
London Residuary Body, *Urban abstracts*. London: LRB. Monthly.
LRB is responsible for databases ACCOMPLINE and URBALINE.

73 Mort, David, 'How to find UK local statistics', *Business information review*, 5 (1), July 1988, 3 – 10;
Business Information Service, *The counties and regions of the UK: economic, industrial and social trends in local authority areas*. 2nd ed. Aldershot: Gower Press for University of Warwick Business Information Service, 1988;
Owen, Tim, *Mind your local business*. 2nd ed. Newbury: Eurofi, 1988.

74 Nurcombe, Valeria J. (ed.), *Access to local authority official publications: proceedings of a seminar, London, 14 March 1985*. London: Library Association, RSIS, 1985.

75 **International**:
UN op. cit., note 8; Vol. 1 section III is in subject order; Pieper, op.

cit., note 17: the whole work is analysed by subject; Ramsay, op. cit., note 23: EC subjects;

National:

US Bureau of the Census, *Statistical abstract of the United States*. Washington: Bureau of the Census. Annual. 'A guide to sources of statistics' appears regularly as an appendix – all subjects;

Central Statistical Office, *Monthly digest of statistics*: supplement: definitions and explanatory notes. CSO. Annual.

Covers all sources used in *Monthly digest of statistics*: all subjects;

Library Association, op. cit., note 13;

Central Statistical Office, op. cit., note 35: covers all subjects, both official statistics and significant, complementary non-official statistics sources. *Statistical news*, op. cit., note 43: articles, news, updates etc: good index.

Subject:

RUKKS (see note 39): each volume has one, two or three topics: exhaustive subject-based treatment of sources of statistics.

'Key European market information sources', in *European marketing data and statistics*. 24th ed. London: *Euromonitor*, 1988, 31 – 62;

Bell, D. and Greenhorn, A. (eds.), *A guide to Financial Times statistics*. 3rd ed. London: F. T., 1989.

An excellent guide to a specific source;

'William Farr 1807 – 1883: his contribution to present day vital and health statistics', *Population trends*, **31**, Spring 1983, 5 – 7.

Excellent background articles;

Alderson, Michael, *International mortality statistics*. London: Macmillan, 1981. (Macmillan reference books).

Specialized bibliography covering mortality of the twentieth century for European and other selected countries;

'Retail prices index Advisory Committee appointed', *Dept of Employment Press Notice*, 17 October 1988 no. 223/88. (A reconvened Committee considered 'longer term recommendations' (re RPI) made in Cmnd 9848, July 1986);

Department of Employment, *A short guide to the Retail Prices Index: a non-technical description of the method of measuring the rate of change in prices faced by consumers in the United Kingdom*. London: DE, 1987.

A regularly revised 'easy reading' guide;

'Retail prices index: updating the weights', *Employment gazette*, April 1989, 197 – 200;

Central Statistical Office, *Internal purchasing power of the pound*. London: CSO. Press Notice. Monthly;

Department of Employment, *Treatment of the community charge in the retail prices index*. London: HMSO, 1989. (Cm 644);

'The Average Earnings Index', *Employment gazette*. November 1989, 606 – 12.

A new statistical series for the AEI has been introduced; reweighting the

index, rebasing it to 1988 = 100. It brings up-to-date information on the AEI, which has been published since 1963;
Pepper, Michael, 'The development of statistics in the Welsh Office', *Statistical news*, **84**, February 1989, 5 – 8.
The eighteenth in a series of articles on the structure and functions of the Government Statistical Service;
Mayes, David G., 'The National Economic Development Office: a quarter of a century of statistics', *Statistical news*, **85**, May 1989, 6 – 9.
NEDO's role and the work of NEDO Statistics Group, is explained; the development of links between the sources of official statistics, the Government Statistical Service and users in the private sector has been a feature of the group's activities;
Market and statistical news: a monthly review of business information. Warwick University Business Information Service. Monthly;
Statistics and market research: a guide to current periodical articles. Birmingham Public Libraries. Monthly.

76   See note 31 above.
77   See note 2 above.
78   Mort, David and Leona Siddall, *Sources of unofficial UK statistics*. 2nd ed. Aldershot: Gower, 1989.
     Based on Siddall's research project *Survey of non-official statistics and their role in business information*, Warwick Statistics Service, 1983.
79   See note 35 above.
80   *British national bibliography*. BL. Weekly with cumulations: hard copy, microfiche, CD-ROM.
81   *British reports, translations and theses (BRTT)*. BL. Monthly. Cumulated microfiche index.
82   For both these, see note 75 above.
83   Walker, Clare (ed.), 'European trade associations statistics', *Market and statistics news*, March 1983, 10 – 16.
84   Mort, David, *European directory of non-official statistical sources*. London: Euromonitor Publications, 1988.
85   Brittin, Margaret and Mort, David, *Euro high-tech: survey of non-official statistical sources in the field of high technology products and services in the member states*. Stamford: Capital Planning Information, 1987.
86   Building Societies Association, *A compendium of building society statistics*. 7th ed. London: BSA, 1988.
     Covers 1955 – 86; amplifies, supplements data in the *Annual report of Building Societies Commission*. London: HMSO. Annual;
     Ramsay, Anthony, *Property development and management into the nineties: a guide to sources of information*. London: BL, 1988;
     Scarrett, Douglas, *Sources of property market information*. Aldershot: Gower Publishing Co., 1988.
     Earlier editions 1984, 1986, 1987, issued by Leicester Polytechnic Press. See also note 31;

Phylaktis, Kate, *Finance: financial data of banks and other institutions*. Oxford: Pergamon Press for RSS/ESRC, 1987.

Reviews of United Kingdom Statistical Sources, vol. xxi;

Birds Eye, *Frozen foods: a review of the market in 1986*. London: Birds Eye, 1987;

Pannell Kerr Forster Associates, *Outlook – London trends, 1989*. London: PKFA, 1989;

Metalworking production: the sixth survey of machine tools and production equipment in Britain. London: Morgan Grampian, 1988;

Bone, Roger, *Security equipment: a growth market for British industry: a study for the National Economic Development Office*. London: EDU International, 1989;

Hynard, J. M., 'Trade Association statistics', *Market and statistics news*, July 1985, 16 – 21.

Paper presented at British Library Seminar on non-official statistics in London, 28 February 1985: first published in *Statistical news*, **69**, May 1985.

87 Maunder, W. F. (ed.), *Bibliography of index numbers: an international team project*. London: Athlone Press for the International Statistical Institute, 1970;

'International bibliography of historical demography', *Annales de demographie historique*. International Statistical Institute. Annual.

88 Mitchell, B. R., *International historical statistics: Africa and Asia*. London: Macmillan, 1982.

89 Priestley, H. E., *The 'what it cost the day before yesterday' book – from 1850 to the present day*. Emsworth: K. Mason, 1979.

90 **International:**

United Nations, *Demographic yearbook: historical tables*. New York: UN, 1981;

Organisation for Economic Cooperation and Development, *Main economic indicators: historical statistics, 1960 – 1979*. Paris. OECD, 1980;

Organisation for Economic Cooperation and Development, *Consumer price indices: sources and methods and historical statistics: special issue*. Paris: OECD, 1980;

Mitchell, B. R., *European historical statistics, 1750 – 1975*. 2nd ed. London: Macmillan, 1980;

Anderson, M. (comp.), *International mortality statistics, 1901 – 1975*. London: Macmillan, 1981.

National:

Mitchell, B. R. and Deane, P., *Abstract of British historical statistics*. Cambridge: Cambridge University Press, 1962. (Department of Applied Economics, Cambridge University monograph no. 17);

Mitchell, B. R. and Jones, H. G., *Second abstract of British historical statistics*. Cambridge: Cambridge University Press, 1971. (Department of Applied Economics, Cambridge University monograph no. 18);

London and Cambridge Economic Survey, *The British economy: key statistics 1900 – 1970*. London: *The Times* for the London and Cambridge Economic

Survey, 1973;

US Bureau of the Census, *Historical statistics of the United States: colonial times to 1970*. Washington: Bureau of the Census, 1976;

Finlayson, J., *Historical statistics of Australia: a select list of sources*. Canberra: Australian National University, 1970;

Urquhart, M. C. and Buckley, K. A. H. (eds.), *Historical statistics of Canada*. London: Macmillan, 1965;

Department of Employment, *British labour statistics: historical abstract, 1886 – 1968*. London: HMSO, 1971 (o/p, microfiche edition available);

Lee, C. H., *British regional employment statistics, 1841 – 1971*. Cambridge: Cambridge University Press, 1979;

Munby, Denys, *Inland transport statistics of Great Britain, 1900 – 1970, Vol. 1: Railways, public road transport, London transport*. Oxford: Oxford University Press, 1978;

Chapman, Agatha L. and Knight, Rose, *Wages and salaries in the United Kingdom, 1920 – 1938*. Cambridge: Cambridge University Press, 1953. (Studies in the national income and expenditure of the United Kingdom, no. 5);

Business Statistics Office, *Historical record of the Census of Production, 1907 – 1970*. London: HMSO, 1979;

'Employment statistics', *Employment gazette*, November 1989. (Historical supplement no. 2). London: HMSO, 1989.
The latest of a series of articles, supplements etc. covering historical statistics of employment;

Department of Education and Science, *Student numbers in higher education – Great Britain, 1975 to 1987*. London: DES, 1989. (*DES statistical bulletin*, no. 4/89);

Lomax, K. S., 'Production and productivity movements in the UK since 1900', *Journal of the Royal Statistical Society Series A*, **122**, 1955, 185 – 220;

Stafford, J., 'Development of industrial statistics', *Statistical news*, **5**, May 1969, 1 – 8.

91   Central Statistical Office, *CSO databank*. London: CSO.
Macro-economic time series data on magnetic tape and high-density floppy disc. Available online through host bureaux. For the charges for CSO databank, contact 071 – 270 6386.

92   Open University, *Statistics in society*. Milton Keynes: OU, 1983.

93   Radical Statistics Group, *The unofficial guide to official health statistics*. London: RSG, 1981;

Radical Statistics Group, *The nuclear numbers game: understanding the statistics behind the bomb*. London: RSG, 1982;

Radical Statistics Group, *A better start in life? Why perinatal statistics vary in different parts of the country*. London: RSG, 1980;

Radical Statistics Health Group, 'Profits in tomorrow's health care', *Science for the people*, 1989, 15 – 16.

94   Shelter, *Housing facts and figures*. London: Shelter, 1980.

95   Townsend, Peter, *Poverty in the United Kingdom: a survey of household resources and standards of living*. London: Penguin, 1979;
     Irvine, J. and others, *Demystifying social statistics*. London: Pluto Press, 1979;
     Harvey, I. M., 'Meningitis: can we trust the statistics?' *Health trends*, **21**, 1989, 73 – 6.

96   House of Commons. Home Affairs Committee, *Ethnic and racial questions in the Census*. London: HMSO, 1983;
     Moser, Sir Claus, 'Statistics about immigrants: objectives, methods and problems', *Social trends*, **3**, 1972, 20 – 30;
     Runnymede Trust and Radical Statistics Race Group, *Britain's black population*. London: Heinemann, 1980.
     Chapter 7. 'The politics of statistics';
     Commission for Racial Equality, *Ethnic minorities in Britain: the statistical background*. London: CRE, 1980.

97   Cook, Thomas and Campbell, Donald T., *Quasi experimentation – design and analysis issues for field settings*. Chicago: Rand McNally, 1979.
     Four validity tests for statistics in educational research: statistical conclusion; internal validity; external validity; and construct validity.

98   United Nations, *International standard industrial classification of all economic activities* [ISIC] [Rev. 3]. New York: UN, 1989;
     United Nations, *Standard international trade classification. Revision 3* [SITC] [R3]. New York: UN, 1987;
     United Nations, *Commodity indexes for standard international trade classification. Revision 3*. New York: UN, 1981. 2 vols.

99   Customs Cooperation Council, *Harmonized commodity description and coding system* [*HS*]. Brussels: CCC, 1988;
     Customs Cooperation Council, *Harmonized commodity description and coding system and explanatory notes*. Brussels: CCC, 1989. 2 loose-leaf vols.
     Index to both publications;
     Customs Cooperation Council, *Brussels tariff nomenclature* [BTN]. 5th ed. Brussels: CCC, 1976;
     Customs Cooperation Council, *Correlation tables between HS and the 1978 version of CCCN*. Brussels: CCC, 1989;
     Customs Cooperation Council, *CCC nomenclature* [CCCN]. Brussels: CCC, 1978.

100 European Communities, 'Regulation 2658 1987 introducing Combined Nomenclature and TARIC', *Official journal L256*. 7 September 1987.
     Legal basis for CN;
     European Communities, *Nomenclature of goods for external trade statistics of the Community and statistics of trade between member states (NIMEXE)*. Luxembourg: EC. Annual.
     Superseded by the Combined Nomenclature;
     European Communities, *General industrial classification of economic activities within the European Communities*. [*NACE*]. Luxembourg: EC, 1970;

European Communities, *Common nomenclature of industrial products* [*NIPRO*]. Luxembourg: EC, 1975.

101 Central Statistical Office, *Standard industrial classification revised 1980* [SIC] [80]. London: HMSO, 1979;
Central Statistical Office, *Indexes to the standard industrial classification, revised 1980*. London: HMSO, 1981;
Central Statistical Office, *Standard industrial classification, revised 1980; reconciliation with standard industrial classification, 1968*. London: HMSO, 1980.

102 United Nations, *Central Product Classification* [CPC]: *provisional*. New York: UN, 1990[?] [in preparation].

103 See note 98 above.

104 See note 102 above.

105 'Economic classifications': [the revision of the International Standard Industrial Classification of all Economic Activities [ISIC] and the new Central Product Classification [CPC]], *Statistical news*, **85**, May 1989, 38.

106 See note 99 above.

107 See note 100 above.
European Communities, *Explanatory notes to the combined nomenclature of the European Communities*. Luxembourg: EC, 1989.

108 For all three, see note 99 above.

109 See note 101 above.

110 *Overseas trade statistics of the United Kingdom*. Central Statistical Office, HMSO.
Monthly (with annual cumulation in the December issue). Business monitor MM20 and MA20.

111 Department of Trade and Industry, *Guide to the classification for overseas trade statistics*. London: DTI/Business Statistics Office. Annual. Business monitor MA 21;
Department of Trade and Industry, *Guide to the classification for overseas trade statistics: correlation tables*. London: HMSO, 1988.

112 HM Customs and Excise, *The integrated tariff of the United Kingdom*. London: HMSO, 1990. 4 vols. in 3 loose-leaf binders.

113 See note 5 above.

114 See note 2 above.

115 See note 3 above.

116 *Business monitor* series. CSO/Business Statistics Office. Various titles; various series. Tel. no. 0633 812873 for details. (Formerly DTI publications).

117 *British business*. Weekly, DTI, ceased September 1989 (formerly *Trade and industry*, previously *Board of Trade journal*).

118 *Business bulletins*. CSO, Business Statistics Office, 1990 – .

119 *Business briefings*. Association of British Chambers of Commerce. Weekly. 1989 – .
Issues supplements on selected topics, e.g. *Companies Bill*.

120 Private communication.
121 Ball, Sarah, *Directory of international sources of business information*. London: Pitman, 1989; *European directory of marketing information sources*. London: Euromonitor, 1987.
122 See note 45 above.
123 See note 16 above.
124 Clinch, Peter, *Business statistics: how to find them, how to present them*. Preston: Lancashire Polytechnic, 1989.
[Business Research Guide no. 5] .
125 *Online business information: the monthly newsletter analysing electronic business databases – online, floppy disc, CD-ROM and videodisc*. Headland Press. Monthly.
e.g. Update: Tradstat enhancements: Taiwan, Norway and Sweden now included, *Online business information*, July 1989, 137.
126 Foster, Allen, *Online business sourcebook*. Headland, Cleveland: Headland Press. 2 issues per year.
127 *Business information review*. Headland Press, July 1984 – .
e.g. Foster, Allen, 'Online numeric databases: four years later', *Business information review*, 5 (3), 1989, 3 – 12.
128 *Directory of on-line databases*. New York: Cuadra/Elsevier. Annual. 2 main vols. 2 supplements.
Mentions CD-ROM availability as well as online.
129 *Ulrich's International periodicals directory*. New York: R. R. Bowker. Annual. Also available online.
130 DIALOG, CRONOS, GSi – ECO, DRI, Reuter/IP Sharp.
See also note 126 above.
131 *Official statistical serials on microfiche: catalogue*. Cambridge: Chadwyck-Healey, 1982.
132 *Guide to microforms in print*: author, title [incorporating *International microforms in print*]. Westport, Ct: Meckler. Annual.
Popularly known as 'Microforms in print'; companion volume in subject order.
133 United Nations, *Commodity trade statistics*. UN. Quarterly, annually. Microfiche ed.
134 Organisation for Economic Cooperation and Development, *Series B. Trade by country; Series C. Trade by commodity*. Paris: OECD. Annual. Microfiche ed.
135 Office of Population Censuses and Surveys, *Census 1981: economic activity: counties*. London: OPCS, 1984.
Microfiche eds.
136 Department of Health and Social Security, *Mortality tables 1987*. London: DHSS, 1988. Tables on microfiche included with printed copy.
137 See note 36 above.
138 See note 35 above.

139 **International**:
United Nations, *Statistical yearbook*. New York: UN. Annual. (Updated by UN. Monthly bulletin of statistics);
United Nations, *World statistics in brief*. New York: UN. Annual;
United Nations, *World economic survey*. New York: UN. Annual.
United Nations. Industrial Development Organisation, *Industry and development: global report*. Vienna: UNIDO. Annual.

140 Food and Agriculture Organisation, *The state of food and agriculture*. Rome: UN. FAO. Annual;
United Nations Educational, Scientific and Cultural Organisation, *Compendium of statistics on illiteracy*. Paris: UNESCO. Annual.

141 United Nations, *World comparison of purchasing power and real product 1980*. New York: UN/EUROSTAT, 1986;
United Nations, *Guidelines on statistics of tangible assets*. New York: UN, 1979.

142 Organisation for Economic Cooperation and Development, *Main economic indicators*. Paris: OECD. Monthly;
Organisation for Economic Cooperation and Development, *Labour force statistics*. Paris: OECD. Monthly;
Organisation for Economic Cooperation and Development, *National accounts*. Paris: OECD. Monthly.

143 Organisation for Economic Cooperation and Development, *Energy statistics*. Paris: OECD. Annual;
Organisation of Economic Cooperation and Development, *Financial statistics: methodological supplement*. Paris: OECD;
Organisation of Economic Cooperation and Development, *Review of fisheries in OECD countries*. Paris: OECD. Annual;
Organisation for Economic Cooperation and Development, *Economic surveys*. Paris: OECD. Annual.
Issued for each country member of OECD.

144 European Communities, *Basic statistics of the Community*. Luxembourg: Eurostat. Annual;
European Communities, *External trade statistical year book*. Luxembourg: Eurostat. Annual;
European Communities, *External trade statistics: user's guide*. Luxembourg: Eurostat, 1987;
See also note 130 above: CRONOS database; COMEXT external trade databank.

145 **Non-official international**:
America Bureau of Metal Statistics, *Non-ferrous metal data*. Secaucus, NJ: ABMS. Annual;
International Iron and Steel Institute, *World steel in figures*. Brussels: IISI. Annual;
International Air Transport Association, *World air transport statistics*. Geneva: IATA. Annual;

Motor Vehicle Manufacturers Association of the US, *World motor vehicle data*. Detroit, Michigan: MVMA. Annual.

146 See note 50 above.

147 See notes 49 and 51 above.

148 **National general**:
Central Statistical Office, *Annual abstract of statistics*. London: CSO/HMSO. Annual;
Monthly digest of statistics. HMSO. Monthly;
See also note 75 above;
Central Statistical Office, *United Kingdom in figures*. London: CSO. Annual (free);
Central Statistical Office, *Key data*. London: CSO. Annual.

149 Central Statistical Office, *Social trends*. London: HMSO. Annual;
See also note 54 above;
Economic trends. HMSO. Monthly plus annual supplement.

150 **National specialist**:
See note 36 above.

151 Central Statistical Office, *UK balance of payments (CSO Pink Book)*. London: CSO. Annual;
Department of Energy, *Energy trends*. Dept. of Energy. Monthly;
Ministry of Agriculture, Fisheries and Food, *Agricultural statistics: United Kingdom*. London: HMSO. Annual;
Department of Transport, *Transport statistics: Great Britain*. London: HMSO. Annual;
Department of Education and Science, *Education statistics for the UK*. London: HMSO. Annual;
Employment gazette. Department of Employment. Monthly.

152 See notes 56 and 57 above.
Scottish statistics fact card. Edinburgh: Scottish Office. Annual (free);
Scottish Office, *Agriculture in Scotland*. Edinburgh: Scottish Office. Annual.

153 Welsh Office, *Digest of Welsh statistics*. Cardiff: Welsh Office. Annual;
Welsh Office, *Welsh social trends*. Cardiff: Welsh Office. Annual;
Welsh Office, *Welsh economic trends*. Cardiff: Welsh Office. Annual. (Plus supplement);
Welsh Office, *Welsh agricultural statistics*. Cardiff: Welsh Office. Annual.

154 See note 58 above.
Statistical review of Northern Ireland agriculture. Belfast: Dundonald House. Annual.

155 *Waterborne freight in the UK*. Chester: Maritime and Distributions Systems. Annual;
Betting and gaming bulletin [revenue statistics]. Esher: Business and Trade Statistics Limited. Monthly;
Universities Statistical Record, *University statistics*. Cheltenham: USR. Annual. 3 vols.;
British Ports Federation, *Port statistics*. London: BPF. Annual.

156 See note 43 above.
157 See note 152 above.
158 See note 150 above.
159 See note 75 above.
160 Home Office, *Offences relating to motor vehicles, England and Wales*. London: Home Office. Annual. (*Home Office statistical bulletin*, various numbers); Department of Employment, *Time rates of wages and hours of work*. London: DE. Annual (loose-leaf format).
161 See note 16 above.
162 Transport Statistics Users' Group, *Directory of sources and contacts in transport statistics and sources of information*. Ramsbottom, Lancs: TSUG, 1987. (Loose-leaf; kept up to date by reissues).
163 University of Warwick, Business Information Service, *UK market facts*. Coventry: Business Information Service, 1989.
A subscription service.

20

Official Publications of International Organizations

Elizabeth Anker

Iwnternational organizations, their aims and achievements, are now a prominent feature of the world community. So too, are the publications of a number of these bodies. In the past, however, international official publications have represented a somewhat grey area. There was little desire to write bibliographical works on the subject. Indeed, the whole concept of international official publishing seemed of little consequence, other than to the organizations themselves. What has happened to change this situation?

Without too much difficulty we can trace the evolution of the most significant global organization – the United Nations. We know also that the United Nations Charter of 1945 has made the prevention of war and the continued vigilance of peaceful negotiations in matters of conflict, the top priorities of the organization. But, important though the aim towards peace may be, there is still much more to be achieved globally if the prospects of international society are to be enhanced in the twenty-first century.

Although currently the emphasis seems to centre on the developments in Europe, international perspectives are important too. Outside the European Community, the implications of the Single European Act are being debated. There is speculation that 1992 stands to have an effect on trade almost worldwide. Major issues of the environment, such as the prevention of ozone depletion, generate much high-level discussion around the world. Already it is becoming apparent that the Montreal Protocol on substances that deplete the ozone layer may need amendment. Also, an International Panel on Climate Change has been established, and there is mention of a World Climate Conference late in 1990.

Current developments clarify the issue, that in support of the many aims to be achieved globally, there has been, in the last two decades, an unprecedented increase in the amount of international official publishing. The developments taking place now generate much concern, and this is reflected in the growing need of modern society to make regular reference to the wealth of important facts to be found in the publications of international official bodies. It is the responsibility of librarians, as providers of information, not only to be acutely aware of these needs, but also to aid the efficient use of such an important source of reference material. As a contribution towards this responsibility, this chapter aims to survey ten major international organizations although, of course, many lesser bodies exist and are included in the current edition of the *Yearbook of international organizations*.[1]

The chapter will begin at the root of international official organizations (i.e. treaties); a few general comments on bibliographical control will follow with a detailed examination of the services provided for international official publications by Her Majesty's Stationery Office. The organizations will then be introduced by a brief description of their individual aims; an evaluation of selected publications known to be appropriate for reference purposes will follow. It must be borne in mind, however, that there are many more official sources to explore and that those mentioned should be regarded as an introduction to other existing works. Principles of acquisition and library provision will be included where appropriate. Hopefully, the choice of materials will not only stimulate further interest, but will also provide some guidance in problem areas.

TREATIES

The *Vienna convention of the law of treaties* gave consideration to 'the fundamental role of treaties in the history of international relations.' Article 5 of the same treaty relates to 'treaties constituting international organizations and treaties adopted within an international organization.' These thoughts are reiterated in the preamble to the *Convention on the law of treaties between states and international organizations or between international organizations.* Much more evidence can be found to show the importance of treaties to the foundation and development of international organizations. Indeed a number of enquirers find that they need to consult treaties as a primary part of their research into international organizations. This need has shown that there is often some measure of doubt concerning the location of these legal instruments, therefore some guidance on sources might serve a useful purpose. Confusion can arise because the word 'treaty' does not always feature in the title or because insufficient detail is known, e.g. there has been more than one 'Vienna Convention'. In this case one needs to be sure of either the full title or some other unique feature by which to identify the document, i.e. correct date of publication, command number, or treaty series number.

There is often more than one source of location for treaties, e.g. the Treaty of Rome has appeared in a number of texts, and currently the Single European Act can be found in at least five sources:

European Communities, OFFICIAL JOURNAL. LEGISLATION. Vol. 30 L. 169. 29 June 1987.

This would be the most appropriate version to cite for legal purposes.

European Communities, Commission, BULLETIN: SUPPLEMENT 2. 1986. Luxembourg: Office for Official Publications. 1986. ISBN 92 825 5965 3

European Communities, Council, SINGLE EUROPEAN ACT AND FINAL ACT. Luxembourg: Office for Official Publications. 1986. ISBN 92 824 0328 9

European Communities [1986] 12. Cmnd.9758. London: HMSO. 1986. ISBN 0 10 1975805

International legal materials. Vol. 25. 1986, 503 – 42. Washington, DC: American Society of International Law. ISSN 0020 7829.

Useful reference sources

Bowman, M. J. and Harris, D. J., MULTILATERAL TREATIES. Index and current status. London: Butterworths, 1984. ISBN 0 406 25277 7

This compact reference tool has been compiled at the University of Nottingham Treaty Centre. In addition to the adequate references to treaty locations there are also comprehensive notes. The main volume is updated by cumulative supplements of which there have so far been seven – the latest issued at the time of writing is updated to 1 January 1990. [The cumulative supplements from issue 4 onwards are published by the University of Nottingham Treaty Centre and it is possible to place a standing order with the Centre to receive later supplements as they become available.]

European Communites, TREATIES ESTABLISHING THE EUROPEAN COMMUNITIES AND DOCUMENTS CONCERNING ACCESSIONS TO THE EUROPEAN COMMUNITIES. 2 vols. Luxembourg: Office for Official Publications, 1988. ISBN 92 77 19294 1

United Nations, MULTILATERAL TREATIES DEPOSITED WITH THE SECRETARY-GENERAL. Status as at December 1988. New York: UN, 1989 (ST/LEG/SER.E/7) (UN pub. Sales No. E.89. V6) ISBN 921 133319 9

This index facilitates the use of the United Nations Treaty Series.

BIBLIOGRAPHICAL CONTROL

The fundamental use of international official publications is to serve the purposes of the organizations for whom they are produced. Therefore, it has perhaps seemed unreasonable that librarians should expect the organizations to regularly produce guides and indexes to these materials for the benefit of libraries and the general public. There is now, however, a greater acknowledgement that this area of publishing produces valuable sources of informative material for research and other purposes. Indeed it is now a category of material that is exploited by persons from many disciplines. It is, therefore, increasingly important that there is more commitment by official publishers to provide not only better access to their published works, but adequate tools of bibliographical control too. Although positive developments may not be too evident, discussion on problems of bibliographical control and distribution of international official publications does take place.[2]

There is insufficient scope in this chapter for detailed comparisons of bibliographical standards. However, a useful overview of the problems and possible solutions is provided in the following works:

Hajnal, Peter I. (ed.), INTERNATIONAL INFORMATION: documents, publications and information systems of international government organizations. Englewood, Colorado: Libraries Unlimited Inc., 1988. ISBN 0 87287 501 6

Peter Hajnal, who contributes four of the ten chapters of this work, is a prominent writer and researcher in the field of international documentation. His discussion in this volume is complemented by a team of experts including Robert W. Schaaf, who was awarded the American Library Association's 1987 James Bennett Childs Award for his contribution to documents librarianship. The team discuss the organic relationship that exists between the organizations and the material that is issued by them. There are also sections relating specifically to bibliographical control.

Well-structured writing and a clear format make it a very readable work of reference.

Jacque, Sylvie, BIBLIOGRAPHIC CONTROL OF INTERGOVERNMENTAL PUBLICATIONS: user survey. *International cataloguing*, **15**, January/March 1986, 10 – 12.

A useful article issued in relation to a research project sponsored by the International Federation of Library Associations and Institutions.

Pemberton, John E. (ed.), THE BIBLIOGRAPHICAL CONTROL OF OFFICIAL PUBLICATIONS. Oxford: Pergamon Press, 1982. (Guides to Official Publications, Vol. 11). ISBN 0 08 127419 6

This work provides a number of informative examples of classification and organization of official publications. Chapter 11 explains the detail and the thinking behind the scheme which John Pemberton was instrumental in setting up at Warwick University. Operational for over 20 years, the ease of accessibility to the use of official publications that the scheme provides, has been much appreciated by many users.

Schaaf, Robert W., INFORMATION POLICIES OF INTERNATIONAL ORGANIZATIONS. *Government publications review*, **17** (1), January/February 1990, 49 – 61.

This article examines the ways that information is received from international organizations for use in libraries.

HER MAJESTY'S STATIONERY OFFICE (HMSO)

It seems logical at this point to describe the supply and the bibliographical services provided by the British official publisher.

HMSO provides an agency service for 12 international organizations. The publications provided by this service are available directly from HMSO and this facility is available to individual subscribers and smaller libraries, as well as to larger academic institutions.

Full bibliographical details of the international official publications supplied by HMSO's agency service are printed in the agency section of the *HMSO daily list* (published on weekdays except for Bank Holidays). This list is available on subscription from HMSO, either on a daily or a weekly basis. [The weekly subscription is just over half of the price of that quoted for lists that are posted daily.]

HMSO agency titles are also listed on the Prestel database on the date they are placed on sale. Details are available for one week. Access can be made via Prestel (lead frame 50040).

A monthly cumulation of *HMSO daily lists* is issued as *HMSO monthly catalogue*. In addition to a listing of the agency publications for sale during the month, there is a section on periodicals and subscription rates which includes serial publications of international organizations with details of issue (i.e. monthly, 10 issues, etc.).

Mail order enquiries concerning agency publications should be directed to: PC13C, HMSO Books, PO Box 276, London SW8 5DT. The telephone number is 071-873 8409; the telex number is 29713; and the Fax number is Gp3 071-873 8463.

There is also an annual cumulation of agency titles issued under the title *HMSO agency catalogue* for the year. The latest edition of the catalogue at the time of writing was published in May 1990 and contains all items placed on sale during 1989. An ISBN index is also included in the catalogue.

In addition to the printed catalogue services, HMSO, in partnership with Chadwyck-Healey, now produces a combined catalgoue of UK official publications and publications of international organizations. This new enterprise, known as the *Catalogue of United Kingdom official publications (UKOP)* (the title is slightly misleading), is produced on CD-ROM. The coverage of international organizations on CD-ROM is similar to that of the HMSO agency service, and the current volume of records is from 1980 to date.

Suitable hardware needs to be acquired before CD-ROM can be operational (a descriptive leaflet which includes technical details is available free from either HMSO or Chadwyck-Healey). Demonstration diskettes may be obtained from the Bibliographics Manager, HMSO Books, PO Box 276, London SW8 5DT. The current cost of UKOP is £816.50 (including VAT) for four quarterly issues per year. Once acquired, CD-ROM technology does not incur additional operational costs such as online or telecommunications expenditure.

Generally, access to materials via CD-ROM is 'user friendly' – UKOP is no exception. Being designed for use by both the professional and the uninitiated IT user, UKOP can be operated in either 'expert' mode or locked into 'novice' mode. The facility of a categories menu enables the user to choose a particular section of the file in which to search.

Perhaps the greatest advantage for the librarian or the researcher is the less time-consuming and the more flexible method of searching which CD-ROM offers. It is also an easily up-datable medium.

HMSO also provides a bibliographic database available on DIALOG and on BLAISE-LINE. These databases also include the records of the international official publications which HMSO supply through their agency service. The volume of records on these databases is from 1976 up to the date of the latest HMSO monthly catalogue. These services are obviously useful as a means of updating information that is supplied on the UKOP CD-ROM disc, between the quarterly issues. Further details on DIALOG and BLAISE-LINE may be obtained from the Bibliographic Manager, HMSO Books, 51 Nine Elms Lane, London SW18 5DR, or, alternatively, from the information services of the database hosts.

EUROPEAN COMMUNITIES

The organization now known as the European Community, has evolved from the signing of two well-known treaties. The Treaty of Paris, signed in 1951, established the European Coal and Steel Community (ECSC); the Treaty of Rome, signed in 1957, established the European Economic Community (EEC) and the European Atomic Energy Community (EURATOM). The joining together of these three separate communities comprising the countries of Belgium, France, the Federal Republic of Germany, Italy, Luxembourg and the Netherlands, formed the original organization. Membership of the Community now comprises 12 member states – Denmark, Ireland and the United Kingdom joined in 1973; Greece joined in 1981; Portugal and Spain joined in 1986. An important aim of the Treaty of Rome was 'to promote throughout the Community an harmonious development of economic activities'.[3] This aim is now embodied in Article 130A of the Single European and Final Act which amends and complements the former Treaties.[4]

Community institutions

It is not possible to assimilate the institutions of the Community with those of the British government. Nevertheless, it is useful to be aware of the basic EC institutional framework, if one is to appreciate the various categories of documentation that exist and the kind of information that such documents may contain. A recent work that provides this information is:

Thomson, Ian, THE DOCUMENTATION OF THE EUROPEAN COMMUNITIES: a guide. London: Mansell, 1989. ISBN 0 7201 2022
The bibliographical services provided by the Commission are covered in detail in Chapter 3. There is comprehensive coverage of the institutions of the Commission, and especially useful are the sections on documentation and further information in Chapters 2, 6 and 8 – 12.

In view of the detail provided in Ian Thomson's book, it will suffice here to list briefly the institutions, their membership and functions, followed by a selection of useful publications relating to each institution.

1   The Commission at present consists of 17 members – two from each large state (e.g. United Kingdom) and one from each of the smaller states (e.g. Belgium). One of the main duties of the Commissioners, which must be performed impartially, is the founding and drafting of legislation. Other duties include the preparation of the budget and ensuring that the conditions of the Treaties are observed. The Commission is divided into 23 Directorates-General (e.g. DG.I – External relations).

Publications:
The Official Journal of the European Communities (OJ) is an important primary source of the Community's activities. The OJ 'C' series includes draft proposals for legislation.
Commission Documents (COM DOCS) are another important primary source. They often provide an informative background to legislative proposals in the form of explanatory memoranda.

A classified index to COM DOCS is issued monthly by the Office for Official Publications of the European Communities (OOPEC). A list is also issued weekly in the House of Commons *Weekly information bulletin*. London: HMSO. ISBN 0 10 863190 7 ISSN 0261 9229

The *Bulletin of the European Communities* (issued 11 times per year) with *Supplements*, provides a very useful and regular record of EC activities and developments. This is also a good source of reference for OJ citations.

The Commission's general report on the activities of the European Communities[5] is described as 'the most compact and comprehensive source book on the history of European integration.' Published annually, this report is also supplemented by reports on:

a) *The agricultural situation*[6]
b) *Social developments*[7]
c) *Competition policy*[8]

There are also a number of specialist serials issued by the Commission. Two useful examples are:

i) *European documentation*. This series provides in-depth coverage of the main Community policies as well as other informative material (e.g. the internal market; Community law). The booklets, issued at least five times per year are available free on a regular order from Brussels; individual copies may be obtained from the European Communities Press and Information Office, 8 Storey's Gate, London SW1P 3AT.

ii) *Social Europe*. This has been produced since 1983. It is issued three times per year with a number of specialist supplements. *Social Europe* 1/90 is particularly significant as it is the first issue of a new arrangement of content and format. Part one is now going to cover a particular topic (Issue 1/90 covers the Social Charter in relation to 1992). Part two, entitled 'Facts and documents', will cover the main Community initiatives since the previous issue. Community texts will also be included, (reproduced from the OJ). This should be a useful service for those who need access to topical issues on social affairs.

To complete this overview of the publications of the European Commission there is European Communities. Commission. *Directory of the Commission of the European Communities*. This includes up-to-date information on each of the Directorates-General. (It has been issued as a separate publication since 1976 – prior to this date it was issued as a supplement to the *Bulletin of the European Communities*).

2   The Council of Ministers is the decision-making body of the Community. Each member state is represented by one Council Minister. The meetings of the Council are attended by Ministers whose departmental experience is appropriate to the agenda, (i.e. Ministers for education will attend when educational matters are to be discussed). The Council is served by an administrative body known as the Committee of Permanent Representatives (COREPER).

Publications:
European Communities, Council, *Guide to the Council of the European Communities*. (Published half-yearly).

European Communities, Council, *Review of the Council's work*. (Published yearly).

3   The European Parliament, now comprising 518 Members (MEPs), has been elected by universal suffrage since June 1979. The MEPs are elected every five years. The larger member states are represented by 81 MEPs (e.g. United Kingdom). The European Parliament acts basically in an 'advisory and supervisory'[9] capacity: it is not, therefore, a law-making institution.

Publications:
European Parliament. Debates of the European Parliament. (Since 1967 these debates have been issued as an Annex to the *Official journal*, available as paper copies or microfiche).

European Parliament. Directorate-General for Research. *Forging ahead: European Parliament 1952 – 88*. 3rd ed. 1989. ISBN 92 823 0154 0

European Parliament. Directorate-General for Research. *Fact sheets on the*

European Parliament and the activities of the European Communities. 4th ed. 1989. ISBN 92 823 0163 4

European Parliament. *List of members of the Bureau, Parliament, political groups, committees and interparliamentary delegations*, 11-6-1990.

European Parliament. *Bibliography 1987 – 1989.*

There are also a number of free documents issued by the Information Office of the European Parliament. These are:

a) *Press release* – provides a summary of the agenda before the beginning of a session.
b) *The briefing* – published in advance of a session it provides a summary of the reports for debate.
c) *EP news* – covers major events of each session.
d) *The week* – a more detailed summary of events; issued about two weeks after each session.

Wood, A. (ed.), TIMES GUIDE TO THE EUROPEAN PARLIAMENT. Times Books Ltd, 1989. ISBN 0 7230 0336 X

This contains a wealth of information, including election statistics, in a single volume.

More detail of the European Parliament can be found in Chapter 9 of Ian Thomson's book.

4   The Court of Justice consists of 13 judges and 6 advocates. It undertakes various legal duties including the settlement of disputes, administrative court rules and tribunal hearings. A typical survey of the activities of the Court can be found in European Communities: Court of Justice, *Synopsis of the work of the Court of Justice of the European Communities in . . . and record of formal sittings in . . . 1987.*

A useful general source of information is European Communities: Commission, *The Court of Justice of the European Communities* (European documentation 5/86). This booklet also explains the importance of the Court of Justice to the process of European integration.

A summary of judgments, etc. is recorded weekly in European Communities: Court of Justice, *Proceedings of the Court of Justice of the European Communities.* (Available direct from the Court of Justice of the European Communities, Service interieur, L-2925 Luxembourg).

5   The Court of Auditors, *The Treaty of Brussels of 22.7.75 Article 1* (ratified 1.7.77), was instrumental in creating the Court of Auditors. The Court comprising 12 members, is concerned with the expenditure and revenue matters of the Community. It is also particularly vigilant in matters relating to the Common Agricultural Policy.

Publications:

European Communities, *Court of Auditors of the European Communities 1988.*

This booklet provides an introduction to the Court of Auditors and explains how it works.

An annual report of the Court of Auditors is published in the *Official journal.*[10]

6   The Economic and Social Committee comprises 189 members who are appointed for four years. The members are representatives of employers, trade unions and many other groups of society. Although a purely consultative body, it makes a significant contribution to discussions on major draft proposals of the Commission.

Publications:

European Communities, Economic and Social Committee, *Opinions.* (Available on microfiche).

European Communites, Economic and Social Committee, *Annual report.*

A booklet describing the work of the Economic and Social Committee and a catalogue of publications are both free from the Offices of the Commission.

The provision of information

The European Community must be regarded now (1990) as the most significant international organization – economically, politically and socially. So many developments are already taking place in these areas. Indeed 1992 should be regarded as the culmination of the changes, not the beginning, as widely advertised.

Developments are taking place in the provision of EC information too. The Commission now recognizes the important role of librarians. A *Plan of action for libraries in the EC*, includes proposals on machine-readable catalogues; European interlending systems and automated systems; and professional library skills. These proposals are now embodied in a working document of the Commission (COM (89) 234). This COMDOC is available from the Office for Official Publications of the European Communities ISBN 92 77 49631 2 (OOPEC Cat. No. CB-89-190-EN-C.) Information on these developments is also included in the *Library Association record*[11] and in:

Cunningham, George, EUROLIS: A REPORT ON LIBRARY AND INFORMATION SERVICES ACTIVITY IN THE EUROPEAN COMMUNITY AND THE COUNCIL OF EUROPE. London: Library Association, 1988.

This report includes a description of the involvement of European consultative and decision-making processes.

As part of the positive moves to ensure that there is an improvement in the dissemination of EC information, the Commission has been especially active in the setting up of Euro-Info Centres throughout the Community for use by business people in particular. The use of European Documentation Centres, located in a number of academic institutions, is expanding. These Centres may, at the moment, be used by anyone with a need for EC information. Discussions are now taking place, with a view to providing 'information relay schemes'. There is already in existence a regional 'relay scheme' in Newcastle-upon-Tyne, known as 'Sign-Post Europe'.

Another helpful information service now provided by the Commission, is the Citizen's European Advisory Service. This scheme provides the general public with information on matters relating to the internal market.

As the impact of the internal market becomes more of a reality, librarians are expected to answer an increasing number of

European-related enquiries. Because of this increase in demand, librarians cannot afford to treat EC publications with indifference. Enquiries for this material are now received from various sectors of society from the general public who need to be sure of basic information regarding the Single European Act. Information provision to the business sectors has increased significantly as a consequence of the wealth of material being produced on 1992. Businesses not only need to know the facts, they also need them quickly in order to plan ahead. Librarians can find themselves involved as a consequence of their association with academic-related business schools, etc.

The legal profession now find that they require the expertise of professional librarians to access European documentation. In the academic world too, where a brisk demand for European official material already exists, any developments relating to the Jean Monnet Project aimed at extending European studies in academic institutions, may generate even more demand for EC material.

Satisfying the increasing demands for EC documentation involves the use of a wide range of sources. Many libraries have only a limited range of these sources. So where does one start to find out about this valuable source of reference material?

Overview of current awareness sources and reference books

An introductory book which provides a useful section on sources of information:

Budd, Stanley A. and Jones, A., THE EUROPEAN COMMUNITY: A GUIDE TO THE MAZE. 3rd ed. Repr. London: Kogan Page, 1990.

(N.B. Reference books of this kind provide useful information, but specific details always need to be checked with primary sources if possible – *British business* has now been replaced by *Business briefing*. There are now 23 Directorates-General of the European Commission, not 22).

A current awareness guide that aims to provide valuable sources of European and related materials to suit many needs is:

Thomson, I. (ed.), EUROPEAN ACCESS. Cambridge: Chadwyck-Healey Ltd, 1989. Bi-monthly. ISSN 0264 7362. (This publication has been issued since 1980, enquiries for issues 1980 – 8 can be made to the Editor. Tel: 0222 874262).

Reference materials relating to 1992:

Inglis, A. and Hoskyns, C., THE EUROPE 1992 DIRECTORY: A RESEARCH AND INFORMATION GUIDE. 2nd ed. Completely revised by ITC and Coventry Polytechnic. London: HMSO, 1990. ISBN 0 11 7014915

This directory is already highly recommended by many, including the British Library and the European Commission. It should be an invaluable aid to any librarian or information provider who needs to have 1992 sources readily available in one volume. (A disc-based text and update is possible for this public-ation – details from: ITCU, 189 Freston Road, London W10 6TH).

Owen, R. and Dines, M., TIMES GUIDE TO 1992: BRITAIN AND EUROPE WITHOUT FRONTIERS – A COMPREHENSIVE HANDBOOK. London: Times Books, 1989. ISBN 0 7230 0316 5

This work should be useful for the chapters on trans-frontier mergers and 1992 and world trade, as these seem to be current topics for research.

European Communities, Commission, RESEARCH ON THE COST OF NON-EUROPE. 16 vols.

Written by a team of experts under the guidance of Paolo Cecchnini these research reports provide guidance on the subject of the internal market. A number of industries and services are covered (e.g. Vol. 8: Business services; Vol. 15: Pharmaceutical industry). Volume 1 provides Basic studies and Executive summaries.

CRONER'S EUROPE (a loose-leaf service with monthly updates). London: Croner Publications Ltd. (Tel. 081-547 3333)

This service provides a balance of current reports from Brussels with more in-depth analysis of developments and their practical implications for business.

A useful statistical reference work:

European Communities, Commission, PANORAMA OF EC INDUSTRY 1990. ISBN 92 825 9924 8   ISBN 92 830 0171 0
  Business enquiries often require both report and statistical material. The statistical data can be difficult to compile when a number of different countries are involved. Many sources may be needed. This work presents in one volume a comprehensive range of statistical data. As with 'Europe in figures' and the Eurostat supplement to 'Europe in figures', there is a comparison of Community figures with those of the USA and Japan. The 1990 edition of this work includes details of the 70 largest industrial groups in the EC and a macroeconomic outlook. (This item can be obtained directly from Alan Armstrong Ltd, 2 Arkwright Road, Reading, Berks RG2 0SQ. Tel: 0734 751855).

The British Library Document Supply Centre also provides services for access to EC and other official material. Further information can be obtained by contacting: Customer Services, The British Library Document Supply Centre, Boston Spa, Wetherby, West Yorkshire LS23 7BQ. Tel: 0937 346080.

Current awareness and reference sources are also provided by a number of databases. These include:

CELEX – covers European Community Law
INFO 92 – covers the development of the internal market
SCAD – provides bibliographical references
CELEX and SCAD are available online or on tape. Further information is available from OOPEC, Sales-Databank Section, L-2985 Luxembourg. Tel: 499 28 2564 (Mr Mortimer). Access to CELEX and SCAD is available via some European Documentation Centres.

ECLAS is also a bibliographical database and is created by the Central Library of the European Communities. In addition to EC material, it also includes publications and documents of UN, OECD and ILO. Further information can be obtained from: EUROBASES, Rue de la Loi, 100 B-1049 Brussels. Tel: 23500.01.

A comprehensive reference work on acronyms, etc.:

Ramsay, A., EUROJARGON. 2nd ed. London: Capital Planning Information, 1989. ISBN 0 906011 57 4

UNITED NATIONS

The fundamental aim of the United Nations is to promote international peace and security. But other factors are also important and are therefore part of the ultimate aim. These include a basis of respect for human rights and the need for cooperation in both economic and social affairs.

The major governing body is the General Assembly comprising all member states (currently 159). In addition to the General Assembly there are three Councils: the Security Council, the Economic and Social Council and the Trusteeship Council. The principal judicial body of the UN is the International Court of Justice consisting of 15 judges. The Secretariat is the administrative body of the UN.

Each session, the General Assembly and the three Councils produce the accounts of their proceedings, resolutions and reports (including annual reports). The International Court of Justice also produces reports in addition to judgments, advisory opinions and orders.

The principal reference work of the UN is:

United Nations, Department of Public Information (ed.), YEARBOOK OF THE UNITED NATIONS. Vol. 39. New York: UN, 1985. E.88.I.1. ISBN 0 7923 0503 5

Beginning with a report of the Secretary-General on the work of the United Nations for the year, this extensive reference annual includes various activities involving a multitude of issues. Part 2 covers the intergovernmental organizations related to the United Nations and appendices. An historical introduction to the UN can be found in Volume 1 which covers the year 1946/7. The yearbook of the UN is not available as an agency publication from HMSO. It can be obtained either from Kluwer Academic Publishers, Falcon House, Queen Square, Lancaster LA1 1RN,

Tel: 0524 68765, or as a standing order item from the UN or a local distributor. Back issues are available in microfiche.

United Nations material falls basically into four groups.

1 Official records: the accounts of proceedings and the published documents of the official bodies of the UN. Official records are given a document symbol (e.g. GA.OR) = General Assembly. *Official Records.*

2 Working documents: agendas, draft resolutions, etc. in mimeographed form. A useful tool for identifying official documents is:

United Nations, UNITED NATIONS DOCUMENT SERIES SYMBOLS 1976 – 1984. E.851.21. ISBN 92 1 199281 8

3 Periodicals: there are many titles which can be classified as UN serials. Apart from the statistical items, one of the most popular and perhaps one of the most widely consulted serials is: *UN chronicle* (published quarterly). This gives coverage to each session of the Security Council and the General Assembly and reports on a wide range of activities of the entire UN system. A descriptive listing and keyword index of approximately 1,800 serials is available in:

United Nations, DIRECTORY OF UNITED NATIONS SERIAL PUBLICATIONS. New York: UN, 1988. GV.E.84.0.5. ISBN 92 9048 295 8

4 Sales publications: these are publications which are not included in any of the other three groups. Items in this group are issued in a more commercial format. Two examples of sales items are:

United Nations, Department of Public Information, BASIC FACTS ABOUT THE UNITED NATIONS. New York: UN, 1988. E.88.I.3. ISBN 92 1 100299 9

This provides a general introduction to the role and functions of the UN and its related agencies.

United Nations, Department of Public Information, ON COMMON GROUND. (VHS video). New York: UN, 1987. E.87.I.9

This features a visual tour showing great moments and great leaders with a cultural and organizational background of the UN.

A standing order service is available for categories of publications and these may be subscribed to singly or with one or more of the other categories. The subjects covered by this service are:

I	General information and references
II	Economics
III	Affiliated bodies
IV	Social questions
V	International law
VII	Political and Security Council affairs
VIII	Transport and communications
IX	Disarmament and atomic energy
X	International administration
XI	Narcotic drugs
XIII	Demography
XIV	Human rights
XV	UNITAR
XVI	Public finance and fiscal questions
XVII	International statistics

Standing orders for official records may also be added to these categories.

Indexes and guides

The United Nations Bibliographic Information System (UNBIS) is the name given to the online bibliographic and factual information systems developed by the Dag Hammarskjold Library. The operation of this system provides comprehensive bibliographical control of United Nations publications. The system also provides a wide range of information and reference services relating to the many activities of the UN.

The United Nations Documents Index (UNDOC) is a product

of UNBIS. UNDOC gives a comprehensive coverage of United Nations documentation including full bibliographic description and subject, author and title indexes. This service also produces a checklist of UN documents received at headquarters (isued 10 times per year). The production of the cumulative edition of UNDOC has proved to be unmanageable, therefore all cumulative volumes of UNDOC: CURRENT INDEX are now issued in microfiche form. Since 1987 UNDOC has been produced at quarterly intervals.

UNBIS Dag Hammarskjold Library, United Nations, New York, NY 10017, USA, is the address for obtaining information concerning the availability of UNDOC current index database tapes, and also the UNBIS Thesaurus for which there is now a 2nd ed. published.

The following guides are available free on request:

a) *Introductory catalogue of United Nations publications*: provides an overview of UN documentation.
b) *Standing order service*: describes the service in detail.
c) *United Nations publications in print*: a complete listing, issued annually, of available sales publications.
d) *Microfiche price list*: states availability.

A reference work on acronyms:

United Nations, Department of Public Information, ACRONYMS AND ABBREVIATIONS COVERING THE U.N. SYSTEM AND OTHER INTERNATIONAL ORGANIZATIONS. New York: UN, 1981. ISBN 92 4 002021 9

Within the United Nations system of organizations there are a number of specialized agencies. For the purpose of this chapter five of these have been chosen.

FOOD AND AGRICULTURE ORGANIZATION (FAO)

The Food and Agriculture Organization, established in 1945, aims to raise the levels of nutrition and living standards of the populations of the member states; to improve the efficiency of the production and distribution of all food and agricultural products; to improve the conditions of rural populations and by contributing to a growing world economy thus ensuring humanity's freedom from hunger.

The head of the Food and Agriculture Organization is the Conference and the Council is the governing body. There is also a consultative framework made up of a number of Commissions and subsidiary groups.

As the fundamental aims of the FAO are related to food, agriculture and the world economy, the publications of this organization are of necessity based upon these and related subjects.

Various series of studies and technical papers are issued throughout the year, each of them has some relevance to the basic aims. Agriculture is represented by FAO research and technology paper 4: *Sustainable agricultural production: implications for international agricultural research*. Rome: FAO, 1989. ISBN 92 5 102773 0.

A general statistical overview is provided by:

FAO YEARBOOK: TRADE. Vol. 42. 1988. Rome: FAO, 1990. ISSN 0071 7126. ISBN 92 5 002901 2

Bibliographical access can be achieved by consulting *FAO books in print* or *FAO documentation: current bibliography*. For those requiring historical bibliographical detail, the catalogue of FAO publications is a useful reference tool.

The IT resources of FAO are probably the most advanced of all the UN agencies. The database of the International Information System for Agricultural Sciences and Technology (known as AGRIS) contains the details of AGRINDEX which is also accessible in DIALOG File 203.

The United Nations Bookshops, both in New York and Geneva, carry a full range of 'Specialized agency' material. The appropriate address for FAO is: Food and Agricultural Organization of the United Nations, Via delle Terme di Caracalla, 00100 Rome, Italy.

INTERNATIONAL LABOUR ORGANIZATION (ILO)

The International Labour Organization is the longest established organization of the UN system. The constitution of the ILO was included in the League of Nations Peace Settlement, 1919. During the period of 1945 and 1946, the constitution was amended, and subsequently the ILO became a 'special agency' of the UN.

The ILO is mainly concerned with the creation of programmes which will not only help to secure full employment, but help to promote higher living standards. Further to these aims is the ILO's commitment towards establishing job satisfaction and training as well as fair play and working conditions.

The principal organ of the ILO structure is the International Labour Conference. The International Labour Office, headed by a Director-General, is also part of the ILO. This body serves as secretariat to the ILO and provides publishing facilities for the organization.

Being a long established organization, the ILO has developed an extensive publishing programme. *Minutes* of the ILO Governing Body contain the Official records. Laws and regulations are recorded in the *Legislative series*, 1920 – 89 and in *Labour law documents*: treaties and legislation on labour and social security from 1990 – (ISSN 1014 – 7071). This series contains a section of legislative references (including EEC directives) which have been indexed in Laborlex. The *Official bulletin. Series A* contains information concerning the activities of the ILO, texts adopted by the International Labour Conference and other official material (issued three times per year). *Social and labour bulletin*, a quarterly publication, reflecting tripartite response to social legislation and policy developments, etc. (ISSN 0377 5380). *International labour documentation*, an abstracting bulletin, is produced from the LABORDOC database. Cumulative editions: 1965 – 77 and 1978 – 84 are available on COMfiche.

A very useful statistical reference work has recently been published:

ILO. YEARBOOK OF LABOUR STATISTICS: Retrospective edition on population censuses, 1945 – 89.

This provides an overview of population censuses since 1945 using data collected from 184 countries, areas and territories.

Researchers requiring a comprehensive historical record of the ILO, will probably be interested in the microfilm editions of the Reports and Record of proceedings of the ILO Conferences from 1919 – produced by World Microfilms Publications, London.

INTERNATIONAL MONETARY FUND (IMF)

The International Monetary Fund, established in 1945, aims to promote international monetary cooperation and to stabilize international currencies. It also seeks to aid the balanced development of world trade and provides funds to assist member states in temporary financial difficulties.

The IMF is headed by a Board of Governors representing all member states. The official business of the IMF is recorded in the *Summary of proceedings* of the annual meeting of the Board of Governors held during September of each year. This report has been produced since 1946. An annual report is also issued containing sections on the world economy and 'The Fund' [in the year of the report], and appendices. The appendices to the Annual Report contain various financial statements and articles. Especially useful is the list of publications issued for the year, e.g. in the Annual Report for 1988/9 the list of publications appears on pp. 82 – 3.

The IMF produces a number of other informative publications. These include a series of occasional papers and a number of surveys on world economic issues. A recent useful occasional paper is:

Kelly, Margaret, ISSUES AND DEVELOPMENT IN INTERNATIONAL TRADE POLICY. IMF, 1988. ISBN 1 55 1775037

This paper includes a five-page bibliography and is available from HMSO as an agency publication.

Another useful publication is the *IMF survey*, published since August 1972. It contains a digest of news concerning the 'Fund' presented as sections on selected topics, national economies and fund activities (in varying order). It is produced 23 times per year (on alternate Mondays). An index to this serial and the supplements is produced annually.

UNITED NATIONS EDUCATIONAL, SCIENTIFIC AND CULTURAL ORGANIZATION (UNESCO)

UNESCO, formally constituted in November 1946, aims to contribute towards peace and security by encouraging nations to work together in the areas of education and science, culture and communication in order that advances may be made in justice, the rule of law, human rights and fundamental freedoms.

The three major bodies of UNESCO are the General Conference, consisting of representatives of all member states, the Executive Board and the Secretariat.

It is the role of the General Conference to formulate policies and to decide which areas of work will be given priority. Decisions also have to be made by the Conference concerning programmes passed to it by the Executive Board. These activities are financed from the budgetary resources of member states with additional help from such bodies as the UN Development Programme (UNDP).

In the mid-1980s there was dissatisfaction concerning the politicized image of UNESCO. There were also failures in administration and inadequate planning procedures.[12] This situation resulted in the withdrawal of Britain, the United States and Singapore. Many British organizations have been able to maintain some contact with UNESCO despite Britain's withdrawal. The Library Association participated in the British Observership at the Intergovernmental Council Meeting of the General Information Programme of November 1988.

The official publications of UNESCO comprise Records of the General Conference whose Ordinary sessions are held every two years. The Records are multilingual: Arabic/Chinese/English/French/Russian/Spanish

Vol. 1: Resolutions;
Vol. 2: Reports;
Vol. 3: Proceedings.

UNESCO also issues a report of the Director-General on the activities of the Organization. This report complies with Article VI.3.6. of the Constitution and is made available to member states and the Executive Board.

UNESCO has published a guide to common formats for bibliographic information entitled *CCF: the Common Communication Format*. The purpose of this document is to provide detailed and structured means for recording mandatory and optional elements in computer readable bibliographic records for exchange purposes between two or more computer based systems. The CCF document is available on request from:

UNESCO
Section for the Promotion of Methods, Norms and Standards
General Information Programme
7 Place de Fontenoy
F-75700 PARIS

Some useful bibliographical aids are:

UNESCO. BIBLIOGRAPHY OF PUBLICATIONS ISSUED BY UNESCO OR UNDER ITS AUSPICES. THE FIRST TWENTY-FIVE YEARS: 1946 – 1971. France: UNESCO Press, 1973. ISBN 92 3 001037 5 (Multilingual).

UNESCO. UNESCO LIST OF DOCUMENTS AND PUBLICATIONS 1977 – 1980. 2 vols. France: UNESCO Press, 1984. ISBN 92 3 102179 2 (Trilingual).

UNESCO. UNESCO LIST OF DOCUMENTS AND PUBLICATIONS 1981 – 1983. 2 vols. France: UNESCO Press, 1985. ISBN 92 3 002330 (Trilingual).

UNESCO. UNESCO LIST OF DOCUMENTS AND PUBLICATIONS, 1984 – 1986. 2 vols. France: UNESCO Press, 1989. ISBN 92 3 002602 6

UNESCO PUBLICATIONS CATALOGUE. Issued annually. In addition to the main text this booklet contains a list of sales agents, an alphabetical index and price list (in French francs only).

WORLD HEALTH ORGANIZATION (WHO)

The World Health Organization was established in 1948. The main aim of WHO is to achieve the highest possible level of health for all peoples. Indeed the main programme of the Organization is the 'Global strategy for health for all by the year 2000'.

The main body of WHO is the World Health Assembly, a policy-making body comprising delegates chosen for their technical health expertise, from all member states. There are also six regional offices throughout the world. Each office has its own programme which is appropriate to the needs of the countries it serves. The WHO Regional Office for Europe produces an Annual Report of the Director General entitled *Work of WHO in the European region.*

A useful bibliographical tool covering the publications of the European region is:

WHO. Regional Office for Europe. CATALOGUE OF PUBLICATIONS 1972 – 1989 INCLUSIVE.

Publications relating to public health in Europe include:

No. 28: FOOD SAFETY SERVICES. 2nd ed. 1988. ISBN 92 890 1164 5

A list of unpublished documents covering Europe is available free from:
WHO Regional Office for Europe
Scherfigsvej 8
DK-1200 Copenhagen
Denmark

There is an introductory booklet entitled *WHO: what it is: what it does*, 1988. ISBN 92 4 154227 6. (This is available from HMSO).

GENERAL AGREEMENT ON TARIFFS AND TRADE (GATT)

The General Agreement on Tariffs and Trade was established

in 1948. It is a multilateral treaty currently supported by 96 governments. The contracting parties to the GATT represent the major authority during each session.

The major official publication of the GATT is: *Basic instruments and selected documents (BISD) series*. ISSN 0072 0623. This series is a record of the important decisions, resolutions, recommendations and reports adopted by the Contracting Parties. Currently available in this series are the following:

Volume II – covers the period 1948 – 52
Volume IV – contains the text of GATT as currently in force. (This volume supersedes the previous Vols. I and III)

Supplements are available from First – Thirty-fifth.

Other useful and informative publications are: *GATT activities (the year): an annual review of the work of the GATT*. ISSN 0072 615X; *GATT focus*. ISSN 0256 0119 (a free newsletter issued about ten times per year); *GATT, what it is, what it does* (a free brochure); *GATT publications* (a catalogue of currently available items). GATT publications for sale may be obtained from HMSO or directly from:

GATT Secretariat
Centre William Rappard
Rue de Lausanne 154
CH-1211 Geneva 21
Switzerland. Tel: (022) 739 52 08; Telex: 412 324 GATT CH;
Telefax: (022) 731 42 06

ORGANIZATION FOR ECONOMIC COOPERATION AND DEVELOPMENT (OECD)

The Organization for Economic Cooperation and Development, established on 30 September 1961, succeeded the Organization for European Economic Cooperation (OEEC). OECD endeavours to promote development and economic and social welfare throughout the OECD area.

The OECD is headed by the Council comprising representatives from each of the member countries. The Council, which meets about once a week under the chairmanship of the secretary-general, is assisted by an Executive Committee.

Although OECD maintains a prolific output of published material, its documentation is not included, and therefore is not generally available.

Useful publications that are available: OECD. *Activities of OECD in [the year]*. Report by the Secretary-General (free from OECD); *News from OECD* (free from OECD); OECD. *Economic surveys* (annual for each country); *OECD economic outlook. Historical statistics 1960 – 1988*. ISBN 92 64 03372 6; *OECD observer* (bi-monthly), ISSN 0029 7054. This contains informative articles and a useful listing of new OECD publications.

The *OECD catalogue of publications* is available free and is a very useful bibliographical tool. It also contains some general background information relating to OECD.

COUNCIL OF EUROPE (CE)

The Statute of the Council of Europe was signed on 5th May, 1949, by the ten founding member states: Belgium, Denmark, France, Ireland, Luxembourg, the Netherlands, Norway, Sweden and the United Kingdom. Having celebrated its 40th anniversary in 1989, this organization now comprises 23 members. The common aims which these countries have are: 'to work for greater European unity; to uphold the principles of parliamentary democracy and human rights; to improve living conditions and promote human values'.[13]

The work of the Council is channelled through two main organs – the Committee of Ministers and the Parliamentary Assembly. These are served by an international secretariat, headed by the secretary-general, who is elected for a five-year period.

Useful publications that are available: *Council of Europe: a guide*. Strasbourg: Council of Europe (Directorate of Press and Information) 1986. (Available free on request); Council of Europe, *Report on the activities of the Council of Europe* (the year); Council of Europe. *Publications*, (the year). ISSN 0252 0524.

LIBRARY PROVISION FOR OFFICIAL PUBLICATIONS

The collection needs suitable treatment (i.e. the best acquisition policy and classification scheme) accordant with budgetary limits, type of user, size of collection, availability of space and staff time.

It is not enough to acquire as many official publications as an individual budget will allow. Quantity is not always an important factor. A smaller collection that is well chosen and well kept can be a greater asset than a collection that is larger and inefficiently run.

Prospective users need to be aware of the location and arrangement of the material. Accessibility can be improved if the material is shelved in one area. A display of the more significant recent acquisitions can provide a good current awareness service, and one which any hard-pressed user might be grateful for. But, whereas a display of material can be regarded as optional, the provision of adequate shelf signs is essential; especially if the collection is arranged within a larger area of social science materials.

A hand-out, explaining the scope of the collection and the principles of arrangement, is a useful tool. Alternatively, if there are automated facilities available, a 'help screen' on the main library terminals will serve a useful purpose.

Catalogues, indexes and any other bibliographical aids should be easily accessible, and their use fully explained. If there are online facilities or CD-ROM, these should also be available near to the collection.

There will inevitably be some limitations to the service that can be provided, but reasonable access to the collection should be a priority.

REFERENCES AND CITATIONS

1   Union of International Associations (Brussels), *Yearbook of international organizations* 1989/90. Vol. 1: *Organization descriptions and index*. 26th ed. edited by Romuald Covalescu. Munich: Saur, 1989. ISSN 0084 3814. ISBN 598 22201 7.

2   *International symposium on the documentation of the United Nations and other intergovernmental organizations*, Geneva 1972; Unesco, *International congress*

on national bibliographies, Paris, 12 – 15 September 1977; *Second world symposium on international documentation*, Brussels 1980; *International Federation of Library Associations and Institutions research into IGO bibliographic tools and survey of IGO depository libraries*, 1988.

3 *Treaty setting up the European Economic Community Rome*, 25 March 1957. Article 2. London: HMSO 1967.

4 European Communities, Council, *Single European Act and Final Act*, 1986. Article 130 A. Luxembourg: OOPEC, 1986. ISBN 92 824 0328 9.

5 European Communities, *General report.* Luxembourg: Office for Official Publications.

6 European Communities, *Report on the agricultural situation in the Community.* Luxembourg: Office for Official Publications.

7 European Communities, *Report on social developments*. Luxembourg: Office for Official Publications.

8 European Communities, *Report on competition policy*. Luxembourg: Office for Official Publications.

9 *Treaties establishing the European Communities, 1987.* Vol. 1: Articles 140, 143 and 206b. Luxembourg: Office for Official Publications, 1987. ISBN 92 77 19225 9.

10 European Communities, *Official journal C series*. C.312 Vol. 32 12/12/89, *Annual report concerning the financial year 1988*. ISSN 0378 6986.

11 *Library Association record*. Vol. 90, No. 9. 15 September 1988, 489.

12 G. B. *House of Commons Foreign Affairs Committee Session 1989 – 90. First report* (HC.255 – I) p.v. London: HMSO, 1990. ISBN 0 10 283590 X.

13 Statute of the Council of Europe 1949 Article 1 in *Council of Europe. The Parliamentary Assembly: procedure and practice*. Strasbourg: Council of Europe, 1983.

SUGGESTIONS FOR FURTHER READING

Birchfield, M. E. and Coolman, J., *The complete reference guide to UN sales publications 1946 – 1978*. 2 vols. New York: UN, 1982. ISBN 0 89111 011 9.

Dimitrov, Theodore (gen. ed.), *International documents for the 80's: their role and use*. (2nd World Symposium on International Documentation, Brussels 1980). New York: Unifo, 1982. ISBN 0 89111 015 1; *World bibliography of international documentation*. 2 vols. New York: Unifo, 1981. ISBN 0 89111 001 1.

Europe (known as Agence Europe) despatched daily (except Sunday). Current awareness paper. Agence Internationale d'Information pour le Presse, 10 Bd Saint Lazare, B-1210 Brussels, Belgium.

European report (2 issues per week (except Aug.)). European Information Service, 46 Avenue Albert-Elizabeth, B-1200 Brussels, Belgium.

G. B. House of Lords. Select Committee on the European Communities [reports on various subjects (e.g. Social Charter) each parliamentary session].

Hajnal, Peter I., *Guide to UNESCO*. Dobbs Ferry, New York: Oceana, 1983; *Guide to the United Nations Organization, documentation and publishing for students, researchers, librarians*. Dobbs Ferry, New York: Oceana, 1978.

Hanson, T., *A survey of European Communities databases*. In *Aslib proceedings*, **42** (6), June 1990, 171 – 88. ISBN 0001 253X.

Hinds, Thomas S., 'The United Nations as a publisher', in *Government publications review*, **12** (July/Aug.), 1985, 297 – 303. ISSN 0277 9390.

Hopkins, Michael (ed.), *European Communities information: its use and users*. London: Mansell, 1985. ISBN 0 7201 17011; *Policy formation in the European Communities: a bibliographical guide to the Community documentation 1958 – 1978*. London: Mansell, 1981. ISBN 0 7201 1597 3.

International legal materials. Washington, DC: American Society of International Law. Bi-monthly. ISSN 0020 7829.

International organization. Cambridge, Mass.: MIT Press. Quarterly. ISSN 0020 8183.

Johansson, Eve (ed.), *Official publications of Western Europe*. 2 vols. London: Mansell, 1984 – 8. ISBN 0 7201 1623 6 (vol. 1); ISBN 0 7201 1662 7 (vol. 2).

Journal of Common Market studies. Oxford: Blackwell. 4 times per year. ISSN 0021 9886. (Special issue Vol. 28 No. 4 contains annual review of the activities of the European Community in 1989).

Lodge, J. (ed.), *The European Community: bibliographical excursions*. London: Pinter, 1983. ISBN 0 86187 2444 (hb).

Schiavone, Guiseppe, *International organizations: a dictionary and directory*. London: Macmillan. 2nd ed. 1986.

United Nations, *Everyone's United Nations*. New York: UN, 1985. 10th ed. ISBN 92 100273 7.

Index

Tony Oulton
Shelagh Fisher

This index has been compiled on the principle of direct entry to cited works and subjects. It contains entries under authors, organizations, titles, countries and subjects. Entry under the first author only is used for works with more than two authors. Title entries have been omitted for works cited in bibliographies (except those without a significant author) and for some works with non-distinctive titles which can easily be traced by subject or country. Country entries have been provided where the country is a significant access point except for Britain, because of the nature of the majority of the material. Entries have been provided for the home countries. British government departments are entered directly under their name.

The index has been compiled according to the 1988 British Standard for preparing indexes (BS 3700:1988) with some amendments intended to simplify searching, e.g. omission of definite and indefinite articles. Word by word alphabetization is used for the filing order except that encyclopaedia and encyclopedia are interfiled.

A page reference followed by a 'b' indicates a reference to an entry in a bibliography. Where a bibliography is arranged in numeric order the 'b' is followed by the sequence number of the item.